MAX-PLANCK-GESELLSCHAFT

Universität Augsburg University

TECHNISCHE UNIVERSITÄT MÜNCHEN

THE GEORGE WASHINGTON UNIVERSITY WASHINGTON, DC

MIPLC Studies

Volume 40

Vincent Angwenyi

Merger Regulation in Eastern and Southern Africa

The Need for Effective Implementation

Nomos

MIPLC Munich Intellectual Property Law Center

Augsburg München Washington DC

This publication was supported by the Max Planck Society.

MAX-PLANCK-GESELLSCHAFT

The Deutsche Nationalbibliothek lists this publication in the Deutsche Nationalbibliografie; detailed bibliographic data are available on the Internet at http://dnb.d-nb.de

a.t.: München, Ludwig-Maximilians-Univ., Diss., 2021

ISBN 978-3-8487-8311-3 (Print)
978-3-7489-2701-3 (ePDF)

British Library Cataloguing-in-Publication Data
A catalogue record for this book is available from the British Library.

ISBN 978-3-8487-8311-3 (Print)
978-3-7489-2701-3 (ePDF)

Library of Congress Cataloging-in-Publication Data
Angwenyi, Vincent
Merger Regulation in Eastern and Southern Africa
The Need for Effective Implementation
Vincent Angwenyi
368 pp.
Includes bibliographic references.

ISBN 978-3-8487-8311-3 (Print)
978-3-7489-2701-3 (ePDF)

1st Edition 2021

Published by
Nomos Verlagsgesellschaft mbH & Co. KG
Waldseestraße 3–5 | 76530 Baden-Baden
www.nomos.de

Production of the printed version:
Nomos Verlagsgesellschaft mbH & Co. KG
Waldseestraße 3–5 | 76530 Baden-Baden

ISBN 978-3-8487-8311-3 (Print)
ISBN 978-3-7489-2701-3 (ePDF)
DOI https://doi.org/10.5771/9783748927013

Onlineversion
Nomos eLibrary

Acknowledgements

This book is based on a thesis that was submitted to obtain a doctorate degree in law at the Ludwig-Maximilians-Universität München. A number of legal updates have since been made to this book. The publication of this book was financed in part by the Max Planck Society.

I would like to first and foremost extend my sincere gratitude to Prof. Dr. Josef Drexl for not only giving me the opportunity to pursue this project, but for also trusting in my ability to deliver on it. Despite his packed schedule, he remained available to give detailed guidance and support throughout my doctoral studies. I would also like to specially thank Dr. Mor Bakhoum whose wise words and encouragement gave me the motivation to pursue my doctoral studies. His friendship, mentorship and supervision truly made this journey a fulfilling one.

My doctoral studies would not have been possible without the generous financial assistance from, as well as the world-class academic facilities provided by the Max Planck Society, for which I remain deeply grateful. Through the various poster sessions and PhD conferences organized by the Max Planck Society I was able to present my research to a wider scientific community both within and beyond the Society. The academic ecosystem fostered by the Max Planck Society was not only invaluable in helping me to improve and add on to the quality of my research, but also instrumental in allowing me to explore various perspectives that added value to my dissertation. The academic community at the Max Planck Society continues to play a critical role in my professional development even beyond my doctoral studies.

I am also deeply indebted to the Munich Intellectual Property Law Center (MIPLC) for availing a very conducive environment for me to carry out my research. It was an honour to have had the chance to work as a tutor and to give back to the MIPLC family whose support was a crucial cornerstone in my doctoral journey. I cherish the professional and personal friendships that I forged at the Max Planck Society and the MIPLC.

Last but far from least I would like to sincerely thank my family for the unending encouragement, especially at those times when I was unsure whether I would see through this journey.

Table of Contents

Abbreviations

ABA	American Bar Association
ACF	African Competition Forum
AFDB	African Development Bank
CFI	Court of First Instance
COMESA	Common Market for Eastern and Southern Africa
DOJ	Department of Justice
ESA	Eastern and Southern Africa
EU	European Union
FDI	Foreign Direct Investment
FTAIA	Foreign Trade Antitrust Amendment Act
FTC	Federal Trade Commission
GATS	General Agreement on Trade in Services
GATT	General Agreement on Tariffs and Trade
GDP	Gross Domestic Product
GWB	Gesetz gegen Wettbewerbsbeschränkungen
HHI	Herfindahl-Hirschman Index
IBA	International Bar Association
ICN	International Competition Network
ICPAC	International Competition Policy Advisory Committee
ICT	Information and Communications Technology
IGE	Intergovernmental Group of Experts on Competition Law and Policy
ILC	International law commission
ITO	International Trade Organisation
MNC	Multinational Corporation
OECD	Organisation for Economic Co-operation and Development
REC	Regional Economic Community
SA	South Africa
SIEC	Significant Impediment to Effective Competition
SLC	Substantial Lessening of Competition
SSA	Sub-Saharan Africa

TFEU	Treaty on the Functioning of the European Union
UK	United Kingdom
UN	United Nations
UNCTAD	United Nations Conference on Trade and Development
US	United States
USD	United States Dollar
WGTCP	Working Group on the Interaction between Trade and Competition Policy
WTO	World Trade Organisation

1 Introduction

1.1 Sub-Saharan Africa Competition Policy in Perspective

Competition policy has over the years established a very wide footprint with some of its most nascent adopters being Sub-Saharan African (SSA) jurisdictions. However, the socio-economic and political characteristics of the SSA jurisdictions call for a different approach to competition policy. A consideration of Competition Policy in the SSA context invariably draws one's mind to three major themes: development, small market economies and regional integration.

This is against a backdrop of several other socio-economic and political factors that led to the adoption of competition policies in SSA. At the national level, SSA consists of small, highly concentrated economies at different levels of economic development. These clusters of small economies are often composed of regional economic champions such as Kenya, South Africa and Nigeria. One of the main similarities shared by a majority of the SSA countries is their colonial history, which played an integral part in shaping the socio-economic and political climate and policies that led to the adoption of competition law by these countries.

At the regional level, there are several regional integration blocks including the Common Market for Eastern and Southern Africa (COMESA), Southern African Development Community (SADC) and the East African Community (EAC) consisting of overlapping memberships in some instances.

Internationally, the globalization of economies has reshaped the global legal regulatory landscape, forcing nations to rethink some of the traditional notions of territoriality and consequentially fostering a greater convergence of legal norms.[1]

The reduction (and in some instances elimination)[2] of barriers to international trade has been accompanied in many countries by the adoption

1 Bertrand Crettez, Bruno Deffains and Olivier Musy, 'On Legal Cooperation and the Dynamics of Legal Convergence' (2010) (Economix Working Paper 17), 2 <http://ideas.repec.org/p/drm/wpaper/2010-17.html> accessed 16 September 2019.

2 For instance in the case of Regional Economic Communities where trade tariffs between the member states are eliminated.

of competition laws to prevent private frontiers from being erected that hinder the efficiency of their markets and which would consequently make their national markets less attractive.[3]

The integral role of competition law as one of the components of this legal convergence trend is evident from its inclusion in the post-war period of the 1940s in the Havana Charter[4] for the formation of an International Trade Organization (ITO).[5] Though it was subsequently excluded from the 1947 General Agreement on Tariffs and Trade (GATT), its role in international trade has continued to gain increasing importance in the years since then.[6]

Outside of the World Trade Organization (WTO) context, one of the main avenues through which co-ordination of international competition law measures and co-operation is being achieved is the International Competition Network (ICN). The main attraction of the ICN is the fact that proposals, recommendations or measures arising from its activities are not binding on any countries. This coupled with the voluntary participation creates a forum through which a continuous and consistent effort towards international competition law regulation can be realized.[7]

From the perspective of transnational business, a main goal of competition law convergence is to cut down on transaction costs, that result from the hurdles faced in seeking to comply with the merger regulation provisions of the various and diverse national legal systems.[8] Multinational corporations (MNCs) play a central role as a driving force behind economic globalization.[9] The process of global restructuring through mergers and

---

3 Eleanor M. Fox, 'Toward World Antitrust and Market Access' (1997) 91 Am. J. Int'l L.1, 1.

4 Havana Charter for an International Trade Organization (U.N. E/Conf. 2/78 (1948) reprinted in UN. Doc. ICITO/1/4 (1948) (Havana Charter).

5 Clifford A. Jones, 'Toward Global Competition Policy?; The Expanding Dialogue on Multilateralism' (2000) 23 World Competition, Issue 2, 95-100; see also David J. Gerber, Global Competition: *Law, Markets and Globalization* (Oxford University Press 2009) cap 2.

6 Ibid Jones (2000).

7 Mariana Bode and Oliver Budzinski, 'Competing Ways Towards International Antitrust: The WTO versus the ICN' (2005) New Developments in Antitrust (Nova No 3), 13-15.

8 Dani Rodrik, 'Globalization and growth - looking in the wrong places' (2004) 26(4) Journal of Policy Modelling, 513-517.

9 Shangquan Gao, 'Economic Globalization: Trends, Risks and Risk Prevention' ST/ESA/2000/CDP/1, 2 <http://www.un.org/en/development/desa/policy/cdp/cdp_background_papers/bp2000_1.pdf> accessed 22 August 2019.

acquisitions by which MNCs aim at accessing new markets and increasing efficiency should be facilitated by efficient and effective merger regulation systems.

A discussion on global competition law is not possible without looking into the United States (US) and the European Union (EU) which are the leading jurisdictions in terms of development, application and enforcement of competition law.[10] The EU-US cooperation mechanism on merger control plays a central role in any debate on international cooperation and convergence.[11]

Some of the dominant themes surrounding the adoption of competition law in SSA include the promotion of regional integration, economic development, incentivizing Foreign Direct Investment (FDI), or at times from recommendations of international institutions or as part of bilateral or multilateral trade agreement packages.[12]

Adoption of competition laws is seen as a catalyst for economic development in SSA unlike in the developed jurisdictions where it is predominantly a tool to regulate already developed markets.[13] SSA countries however face various challenges such as resource constraints (including lack of skilled human resource) and enforcement capacity which always leads to the question as to whether there is a need for tailor-made laws.[14]

Mergers and Acquisitions (M&As) continue to play an integral role in the economic development of Africa. Statistical data points to a surge in M&As in Africa, with the SSA region showing in 2014 an M&A activity level not seen since at least the mid-90s.[15] The benefits from the upsurge in M&A activity include increased FDI, infrastructure improvements, not

---

10 See generally Eleanor M. Fox, 'Antitrust and Regulatory Federalism: Race up, Down and Sideways' (2000) 75 N.Y.U. L. Rev. 1781, 1803.

11 Alexandr Svetlicinii, 'EU-US Merger Control Cooperation: A Model for the International Antitrust?' (2006) 11(3) Journal for Legal Theory and Practice of the Jurists Association of Serbia, 113-126 <http://ssrn.com/abstract=1325695> accessed 15 July 2019.

12 Dina I. Waked, 'Competition Law in the developing world: The why and how of adoption and its implications for international competition law' (2008) 1, Global Antitrust Review 69, 69; see generally Josef Drexl, Mor Bakhoum, Eleanor M. Fox, Michael S. Gal & David J. Gerber (eds), *Competition Policy and Regional Integration in Developing Countries* (Edward Elgar 2012).

13 Waked (Ibid) 73.

14 Ibid 79.

15 Javier Blas and Andrew England, 'M&A activity hots up in Africa as investors bet on growth' *Financial Times* (2 December 2014) <http://www.ft.com/cms/s/0/47dee88a-795c-11e4-a57d-00144feabdc0.html#axzz3OhsEWIfR.> accessed 15 July 2019.

to mention the probability of human resource development and more opportunities for employment. Though the biggest deals are still driven by the natural resource base, there is an increased spending power of the middle class, an improving political climate and an increasing focus on infrastructure development raising optimism for greater economic diversification and sustained economic growth.[16] It is therefore logical that more SSA countries would seek to adopt merger regulation systems in order to have a better grasp on the increased M&A activity in their territories.

Most SSA competition laws are modelled on the provisions of the developed jurisdictions. The EU model has been adopted as the model of choice for many developing jurisdictions and SSA is no exception.[17] Both the European Union and the United States seek an enhancement of economic efficiency and consumer welfare.[18] However, whereas the US system increasingly places greater emphasis on efficiency the European Union tends to balance efficiency considerations with non-efficiency objectives that are critical to the integration of the European Community.[19] This is one of the reasons that make the EU system the model of choice for a number of SSA countries which are also members of Regional Economic Communities (RECs).[20] Developing countries however incorporate deviations which focus specifically on the development objective that is central to their competition laws. The incorporation of public interest in the substantive analysis is the core divergence.

The focus of this study will be on Eastern and Southern Africa (ESA). The ESA countries in focus are Zambia, Zimbabwe, Kenya, Mauritius, Botswana, Tanzania, Malawi, Seychelles and Namibia. The Common Market of Eastern and Southern Africa (COMESA) merger regulations are

---

16 Carolyn Cohn and Susan Fenton, 'Sub-Saharan Africa M&A deals, debt issuance surge in 2013' *Reuters* (London, 16 January 2014) <http://in.reuters.com/article/2014/01/16/africa-deals-idINL5N0KQ1FF20140116.> accessed 15 July 2019; *see also* Mthuli Ncube, 'Mergers and Acquisitions in Africa' (AFDB 2012) <http://www.afdb.org/en/blogs/afdb-championing-inclusive-growth-across-africa/post/mergers-and-acquisitions-in-africa-10163/.> accessed 15 July 2019.

17 Fox (n 10) 1799.

18 Eleanor M. Fox, 'US and EU Competition Law: A Comparison' in J. David Richardson and Edward M. Graham (eds), *Global Competition Policy* (Peterson Institute for International Economics 1997), 339.

19 Ibid. 353-354.

20 *See generally* Josef Drexl, 'Economic Integration and Competition Law in Developing Countries' in Josef Drexl, Mor Bakhoum, Eleanor M. Fox, Michael S. Gal & David J. Gerber (eds), *Competition Policy and Regional Integration in Developing Countries* (Edward Elgar 2012) 231-252.

also included. There are more countries in the SSA region that have adopted competition policies including merger provisions but are yet to undertake implementation. The countries in focus have however implemented their merger regulations with some having reasonable experience in enforcement. The analysis is also restricted to Anglophone countries. The inclusion of the COMESA merger regulation brings the regional perspective into the discussion. The fact that six out of the nine countries in focus are also members of COMESA will facilitate an analysis of the interaction between the regional and national merger regulation systems.[21] The availability of published information (decisions, reports, guidelines and regulations) on which to base the analysis has also largely instructed the choice of jurisdictions.

1.2 Policy Objectives of Merger Regulation

Merger regulation is virtually never adopted as a standalone set of rules. It is a vital component of a country's or region's competition policy. The policy objectives of merger regulation are therefore tied to the objectives behind the adoption of a competition policy. Competition policies are adopted to fit into various political and socio-economic settings, be it the need to control cartelist behaviour, to enhance consumer welfare, to protect public interests, to facilitate regional integration or to act as a catalyst for economic development especially for developing countries.

One of the core intentions behind competition law from a consumer welfare point of view is the allocation of economic resources in an efficient way through protection and promotion of competition in the market. From the total welfare perspective, an ideal situation involves a balance of not only the static (allocative and productive efficiency) but also dynamic efficiency.[22] Policy considerations are however very dynamic. They evolve to meet the needs of the pervasive political and socio-economic circumstances. Therefore, though an efficient distribution of economic resources

---

21 Zambia, Zimbabwe, Kenya, Mauritius, Malawi and Seychelles are part of COMESA.

22 OECD, 'The Objectives of Competition Law and Policy' CCNM/GF/COMP(2003)3, 9 <http://www.oecd.org/daf/competition/2486329.pdf> accessed 15 July 2019. The OECD conducted a survey of competition law objectives across various jurisdictions (including some Sub-Sahara Africa jurisdictions) and virtually all jurisdictions include this as primary or core objectives of their competition policy.

may be a main objective across the board, these specific political and socio-economic considerations have to be taken into account.

A good starting point in the understanding of the evolution of competition policy objectives would be to look at the reasons that led to the implementation of antitrust rules including the current goals in the United States, which is widely regarded as the birthplace of competition law implementation and enforcement and is still very influential in the global development of competition law.

Antitrust regulation was already on the international agenda from the onset of discussions on an international trade organization in the 1940s. Very few jurisdictions had competition policies in place. The policy objectives behind these initiatives for a multilateral antitrust regime, and how they relate to the increasingly converging competition policy standard, are therefore important for understanding the evolution of antitrust.

Another vital perspective as regards competition policy development that currently touches not only on Sub-Saharan Africa but also other developing and emerging markets is that of regional integration and the creation of regional economic communities. Regional integration is in most cases also accompanied by competition policies meant to safeguard the liberated internal markets. In order to understand the policy perspective of a regional community, the European Union is instructive from the point of view of a developed economic community, more so because it is the preferred integration model adopted by emerging and developing markets.

From the national perspective, the adoption of competition law by Sub-Saharan African jurisdictions can be considered from a trade, industrial and government policy context. Trade liberalization and privatization and the ensuing effect of opening up the markets to investment led to the adoption of facilitating policies including competition policy. However, the main objective reflected in most of the competition policies is that of economic development and the need to make the national markets more competitive.

An understanding of these various policy viewpoints would be invaluable in putting the developing and emerging jurisdiction perspectives in context. The objectives behind the policies adopted in Sub-Saharan Africa RECs such as COMESA and SADC as well as the various country perspectives, analysed within the matrix of the various international viewpoints, are vital for understanding the policy structure of the SSA merger regulation climate.

1.3 Research Objectives and Questions

The main objective of merger regulation is to ensure that the post-merger firm does not inhibit competition in the market, consequently ensuring that economic efficiency is maintained.[23] The proliferation of merger regulation systems in emerging markets has however been a point of concern owing to the ensuing counter-effect to economic efficiency.[24] In addition, questions have been raised regarding the ability of emerging markets to run an efficient merger regulation system in light of their resource and capacity constraints.[25]

The increasing number of merger regulation systems is raising the level of regulatory compliance costs for the concerned undertakings.[26] Add to that the inefficiency of some of the systems and the level of uncertainty goes up[27], possibly dissuading the undertakings from proceeding with their transactions. Some commentators posit that certain developing and emerging markets may be better off not adopting merger regulation systems owing to constraints in effectively operating the system.[28]

The globalization of business has also resulted in increased extraterritorial application of domestic laws.[29] This holds especially true for merger regulation. Owing to the absence of supranational competition law, the application by national jurisdictions of their competition laws to activities occurring outside of their borders where such activities have an effect on their national markets is a more or less accepted feature in international competition law.[30] There are however various factors that determine

---

23 Ibid.

24 Andre Fiebig, 'A Role for the WTO in International Merger Control' (1999-2000) 20 Nw. J. Int'l L. & Bus. 233, 234-237; Eleanor M. Fox, 'Antitrust and Regulatory Federalism: Race up, Down and Sideways' (2000) 75 N.Y.U. L.Rev. 1781, 1803.

25 Louise du Plessis, Lurie Judd and Amy van Buuren, 'Competition law in the developing world: A fish out of water?' (Competition Law, Economics and Policy Conference, October 2011), 4-6 <http://www.compcom.co.za/wp-content/uploads/2014/09/FINAL-PAPER-2011.pdf> accessed 15 July 2019.

26 Andre Fiebig, 'A Role for the WTO in International Merger Control' (1999-2000) 20 Nw. J. Int'l L. & Bus. 233, 234-237.

27 Du Plessis et al. (2011) 4-6.

28 Ibid.

29 See for instance IBA, 'Report of the Task Force on Extraterritorial Jurisdiction' (International Bar Association 2009), 45 <http://tinyurl.com/taskforce-etj-pdf.> accessed 15 July 2019.

30 Ibid.

whether and to what extent a country can exercise extraterritorial jurisdiction.

The exercise of extraterritorial jurisdiction by the United States and the European Union for instance would be much more straightforward compared to Sub-Saharan African jurisdictions. This is because the ability to exercise such jurisdiction, especially in terms of enforcement is linked to the economic strength and market presence of the particular jurisdiction.[31] Competition law is concerned with the regulation of markets. The greater the international weight a market has the easier it will be for that particular country to exercise its extraterritorial jurisdiction.[32]

The SSA jurisdictions would find it easy to exercise prescriptive jurisdiction extraterritorially, in terms of putting in place legislative measures, but they would virtually be unable to exercise any enforcement jurisdiction owing to their weaker economies. The question therefore is how the SSA countries can in such instances protect their domestic markets. Is there some form of leverage they can use to facilitate their exercise of extraterritorial jurisdiction? And what role does comity play in this regard?

Merger regulation needs to facilitate rather than hinder international business. Countries in Eastern and Southern Africa (ESA) need to adopt merger regulations that will facilitate both national and international business and which will at the same time effectively achieve their regulatory mandate.

Some of the relevant questions to ask are therefore: Where do the merger regulation regimes in ESA fall within the global convergence in merger regulation? What is the extraterritorial effect of the ESA merger laws? How do the substantive as well as the procedural merger regulation standards fit the context of ESA? Is there a need for redefined merger regulation systems for ESA? What is the appropriate merger regulation regime?

Factoring in the central role that economic development plays in the ESA competition policies the relevant questions include: Can a nexus be made between the adoption of competition law by the ESA jurisdictions and an increase in economic development? Can an increase in FDI and

---

31 See for instance Jeremy Grant and Damien J. Neven, 'The attempted merger between General Electric and Honeywell; A case of transatlantic conflict' (March 2005) <http://ec.europa.eu/dgs/competition/economist/honeywell.pdf> accessed 22 August 2019. This paper discusses the EU prohibition of a merger that had been cleared in the US.

32 IBA, 'Report of the Task Force on Extraterritorial Jurisdiction' (International Bar Association 2009), 63-64 <http://tinyurl.com/taskforce-etj-pdf.> accessed 15 July 2019.

M&A activity be attributed to the merger regulations? Do the merger regulations enhance or facilitate the ease of doing business?

1.4 Structure of the Thesis and Methodology

Although a broad convergence of merger regulation regimes may be highly beneficial especially from the perspective of international transactions, this work does not necessarily advocate for such an approach in respect of the ESA regimes. It rather explores what is suitable for ESA. The purpose of this study in this regard is to explore what can be done to optimize the already existing ESA merger regimes.

The thesis is divided into the following three parts:

Part 2 starts off with an overview of some key national and regional socio-economic and political characteristics of the ESA region in order to contextualise the discussion of competition policy considerations. From a broader perspective, it analyses some of the important developmental concerns of the ESA region and explores the link between adoption of competition policy and economic development.

Part 3 of the study discusses the international merger regulatory landscape. It starts off by discussing the efforts that had been put into creating a multilateral competition law regime and the subsequent move to foster legal convergence. This is followed by a comparative analysis of the substantive and procedural approaches to merger regulation, extraterritoriality and comity as well as institutional design.

The final part of the dissertation contains a summary of the conclusions and recommendations.

The methodology adopted is a comparative assessment of merger review in the European Union, the United States, South Africa, the United Kingdom and ESA as well as the recommendations, proposals and guidelines of the international institutions i.e. OECD, ICN, UN. The discussion of the substantive standard in South Africa and ESA pays special focus to public interest, which is a vital aspect of the substantive analysis in these jurisdictions. The purpose is to reveal whether or not the merger regulation approach in ESA is optimal and to what extent the approach can be optimised.

2 Competition Policy in Eastern and Southern Africa

2.1 *Introduction*

Although the ESA jurisdictions did not have a comprehensive competition regulatory regime most had in place statutes and policies from as early as the 60s aimed at addressing specific market practices that were of pervasive concern on a sectoral level. However, the adoption of comprehensive competition policies for most of the ESA countries was tied to a transitional period in their social, political and economic development where for instance trade liberalization and privatisation, either 'homegrown' or at the behest of external forces, required the adoption of a corresponding policy framework.

At the regional level, competition policy is in many cases, as is the case with the ESA region, usually tied into a greater regional integration objective.[33] Therefore, an analysis of the policy objectives behind a regional competition regime is better understood against the backdrop of the regional integration objectives.

This section gives an overview of the national and regional socio-economic and political context of the ESA region in order to contextualise the discussion of competition policy considerations.

2.2 *The National Context*

2.2.1 Kenya

Kenya's pre-independence economy has been described as having been fairly basic in the context of industrial development and level of monetization. It was essentially import-based, geared mainly towards the needs of the settler community. The exploitation of natural resources from an economic perspective was also aimed at fulfilling the needs of the settlers. One of the immediate concerns was to regulate the price of commodities. It was deemed necessary to put in place a price control mechanism to ensure that the consumer-base was protected from any drastic changes in

33 Josef Drexl, *op. cit.*, (note 20) 231.

the price of goods and services. This need was met by the enactment of a Price Control Act in 1956.[34]

In its Sessional Paper No. 10 of 1965 on African Socialism and its application to planning in Kenya, the post-independence government espoused its plan to ensure rapid economic development and social progress for all citizens.[35] The desire for 'Africanisation' of the economy and public service was expressed. The government indicated the desire to reorganize and mobilize Kenya's African social heritage and the colonial economic legacy to address poverty, disease and lack of education in order to achieve social justice, human dignity and economic welfare for all.[36]

There was a concern that the concentration of economic power in 'domestic hands' could easily lead to undue influence in political affairs. The government equally recognised the conflicting challenges of ensuring wide distribution of wealth and at the same time not prohibiting methods of large-scale production where they are necessary for efficiency.[37] The proposed methods to enable the diffusion of ownership of large-scale enterprises included state ownership, joint ventures between the state and private investors, cooperatives, companies and partnerships.[38]

In order to protect consumers, the government noted that it would not permit producers to make monopoly profits through monopolistic and unfair marketing practices. The government deemed it necessary to keep the prices of basic commodities down in order to ensure increase in per capita income.[39]

The post-independence government also sought to restructure the economy to make it more export-based. The restructuring also involved increased industrialisation as well as indigenisation to ensure that the native population was integrated into the economic system. In order to control

34 CUTS International, 'Competition Regimes of the World: A Civil Society Report: Kenya' (2006) CUTS Civil Society Report, 245 <https://competitionregimes.com/pdf/Africa/46-Kenya.pdf> accessed 15 July 2019.

35 Government of Kenya, Sessional Paper No. 10 of 1965: African Socialism and its application to planning in Kenya (Sessional Paper 1965) <https://www.knls.ac.ke/images/AFRICAN-SOCIALISM-AND-ITS-APPLICATION-TO-PLANNING-IN-KENYA.pdf> accessed 15 July 2019.

36 Government of Kenya Sessional Paper 1965 paras 1-4.

37 Government of Kenya Sessional Paper 1965 para 41.

38 Government of Kenya Sessional Paper 1965 para 45.

39 Government of Kenya Sessional Paper 1965 para 130.

the high inflow of foreign goods, the government placed high tariffs on imports.[40]

To further reduce reliance on imports, the government put in place an import substitution strategy. This involved in the main the formation of state corporations in the major areas of the economy. Reasons proffered for the establishment of state corporations include accelerated socio-economic development and increasing participation of the indigenous population in the economy.[41]

Kenya, having been one of the first countries to sign a structural adjustment plan in 1980 with the World Bank, was required to adopt liberal as well as increasingly outward-oriented trade and industrial policies as a condition to accessing development funding and technical assistance. This was within the context of the three main structural adjustment conditions; deregulation, liberalisation and privatisation.[42] Persisting concerns regarding poor performance, wasteful expenditure as well as highly concentrated and near monopoly markets occasioned by the state corporations necessitated a comprehensive review of the state-owned enterprises which was carried out in 1982 by a Working Party on Government Expenditures. It was recommended that the government reduce its direct involvement in the economy so that there can be more private sector investment. It was considered that such a liberalised economic environment would only work where there is an institution in place to ensure that there is effective competition in the market.[43]

The working party proposals together with related recommendations in Session Papers that called for progressive removal of price controls and reduced government control in the economy led to the passing into law in 1988 of the Restrictive Trade Practices, Monopolies and Price Control (RTPM) Act.[44] The RTPM Act established the Monopolies and Prices Commission which was a department of the Ministry of Finance. The competition authority was therefore not an independent institution. The

---

40 CUTS Civil Society Report Kenya 2006 245.

41 Government of Kenya Sessional Paper 1965 para 17.

42 Geoffrey Gertz, 'Kenya's Trade Liberalization of the 1980s and 1990s: Policies, Impacts, and Implications' (2008) Background paper commissioned by the Carnegie Endowment, 3 <http://carnegieendowment.org/files/kenya_background.pdf> accessed 15 July 2019.

43 CUTS Civil Society Report Kenya 2006 pp. 245-246; See also Gertz (2008), 3-4.

44 The Restrictive Trade Practices, Monopolies and Price Control Act, Laws of Kenya Chapter 504. (RTPM Act).

RTPM Act addressed restrictive trade practices, control of monopolies and concentrations of economic power as well as retaining some price control functions.[45]

The increasing liberalisation of the market meant that the residual price control functions in the RTPM Act needed to be lifted to spur more effective competition. It was also considered that the competition authority needed to be independent and autonomous in order to effectively carry out its functions. The RTPM Act underwent a series of amendments to bring it more in line with the increasingly liberal and diverse economy. This culminated with the enactment of the current statute in 2011, the Competition Act of Kenya. The Act in section 3 sets out its objective as the enhancement of the '…welfare of the people of Kenya by promoting and protecting effective competition in markets and preventing unfair and misleading market conduct throughout Kenya..' in order to, inter alia, increase economic efficiency, promote innovation, protect consumers and create an investment friendly environment.

It established an independent and autonomous competition authority. The new Act did away with the price control functions and introduced consumer welfare provisions. The Act also addresses three other major areas: restrictive trade practices, mergers and control of unwarranted concentration of economic power.[46]

2.2.2 Zambia

Zambia's pre and post-independence socio-economic and political status was largely shaped by copper, which remained the country's economic mainstay for the ensuing decades. The discovery of copper deposits in the 1920s is considered as the most significant economic development in Zambia. However, Zambia's copperbelt has been described as 'an island of comparative plenty in a vast sea of rural poverty'. [47]

At the time of independence in 1964, it is estimated that mining accounted for around 50 percent of the GDP, with 90 percent of foreign exports as well as national income arising from copper. Other sectors,

45 RTPM Act.

46 Competition Act of Kenya, No. 12 of 2010.

47 Howard Simpson, *Zambia: A Country Study* (Scandinavian Institute of African Studies 1985) 11-13. <http://www.diva-portal.org/smash/get/diva2:277702/FULLTEXT01.pdf> accessed 15 July 2019.

mainly agriculture and manufacturing, accounted for less than 20 percent of the GDP. The economy was highly imbalanced with an inordinate reliance on copper. This imbalance extended to the distribution of the benefits, with African social development lagging behind.[48]

The impact of the colonial era socio-economic and political policy has been summarised thus:[49]

> The whole economy was made to hinge on the mining and export of copper. Capitalist agriculture grew in step with the demands for maize by the large urban working class. Manufacturing industry languished thoroughly, due to unchecked and rampant competition from imports from South Africa, Southern Rhodesia and Britain. All industrial activity and commercial agriculture was concentrated along the line of rail which ran through the Southern, Central and Copperbelt provinces. Peasant production of food and other simple commodities was irreparably damaged, and peasant society totally debilitated, by the phenomenal migration of labour from rural to urban areas, induced by the colonial regime. Great regional imbalances arose between the towns and the countryside proper. Monetization of the peasant economy and the growth of wage labour brought the benefits of some "modern" basic consumer goods and some aspects of the social infrastructure to a big proportion of the population. Society became stratified along colour and class lines, leading to tremendous social inequalities between sections of the population.

Naturally, the post-independence regime sought to rectify this. National development plans were put in place between 1966 and 1979 which sought to diversify the economy to reduce reliance on copper, narrow the rural-urban income disparity by improving agricultural productivity, raising education and social welfare levels. The diversification of the economy to reduce reliance on copper proved to be more challenging. [50]

The government restructured the economy to have more direct control over economic activity, which had so far been private and foreign-owned. This process, which was part of what was termed 'Zambianisation', was in line with the then socialist policy, with the government seizing majori-

48 Simpson (1985) 11-13.

49 M R Bhagavan, 'Zambia: Impact of Industrial Strategy on Regional Imbalance and Social Inequality' (1978) Scandinavian Institute of African Studies p 14 <https://www.files.ethz.ch/isn/97149/44.pdf> accessed 15 July 2019.

50 Simpson (1985) 27-28.

ty control over the largest mining, industrial, transport and commercial enterprises. The state-controlled economy, which was still heavily reliant on copper whose prices were falling, proved to be highly inefficient and in need of reform.[51]

In late 1991, Zambia adopted its structural adjustment program, which was part of the wider International Monetary Fund (IMF) requirements for financial support to developing countries. It was estimated that by this time about 80 percent of Zambia's main industries were under state control.[52] Naturally, one of the main conditions of the structural adjustment program was privatisation and increased trade liberalisation.[53] Competition policy was seen as a necessary tool to regulate a liberalised economy.[54]

Zambia's Competition and Fair-Trading Act was enacted in 1994 and came into force on 15 February 1995 and was operationalised in April of 1997. The Act sought inter alia to prohibit anticompetitive trade practices, regulate mergers, regulate monopolies and concentration of economic power and protect consumers. It also put in place the Zambia Competition Commission as the appropriate regulatory authority. The 1994 Act was repealed and replaced by the Competition and Consumer Protection Act of 2010 which enhanced the merger and consumer protection provisions and established a Competition and Consumer Protection Tribunal.[55] The Act sets out in its preamble the objective of safeguarding and promoting competition as well as protecting consumers from unfair trade practices.

51 Simpson (1985) 28.

52 UNCTAD, 'Competition Policy, Trade and Development in the Common Market for Eastern
and Southern Africa' (1999) UNCTAD Series on Issues in Competition Law and Policy, Geneva <https://unctad.org/en/Docs/poitcdclpm18.en.pdf> accessed 15 July 2019.

53 Zambia and IMF, 'Enhanced Structural Adjustment Facility: Policy Framework Paper, 1999-2001' (1999) <https://www.imf.org/external/np/pfp/1999/zambia/> accessed 15 July 2019.

54 CUTS International, 'Competition Regimes of the World: A Civil Society Report: Zambia' (2006) CUTS Civil Society Report, 303. <https://competitionregimes.com/pdf/Africa/59-Zambia.pdf> accessed 15 July 2019.

55 CUTS Civil Society Report Zambia 2006 303-304.

2.2.3 Zimbabwe

Pre-independence, the focus of the settler community in Zimbabwe was on the development of commercial agriculture, with the prospecting for minerals not having yielded the expected commercially viable amounts.[56] The choice of commercial agriculture as an appropriate base for industrial development led to the passing of laws between 1930 and 1956 which would see indigenous communities dispossessed of their land to make way for commercial level agriculture by the settlers. This meant that at independence, agriculture was the most highly developed economic sector, with the most arable land in the hands of the settlers. Industrial input was focused on meeting the needs of the agricultural sector.[57]

Around the time when Britain was ceding control of its colonies in Sub-Saharan Africa, Zimbabwe, then known as Rhodesia and still under the control of the settlers, made a Unilateral Declaration of Independence (UDI) in 1965.[58] Following the UDI, the government in power sought to strengthen self-reliance following a string of international sanctions. The government adopted policies that saw increased intervention and state control of the major economic sectors, import-substitution to promote domestic production, price controls and other measures aimed at ensuring economic stability considering the increased international isolation. However, the indigenous majority were still excluded from the mainstream economy.[59]

---

56 Frank Barry, Patrick Honohan and Tara McIndoe-Calder, 'Postcolonial Ireland and Zimbabwe: Stagnation before Convergence' (2009) IIIS Discussion Paper No. 291, Institute for International Integration Studies <https://papers.ssrn.com/sol3/papers.cfm?abstract_id=1610301> accessed 15 July 2019.

57 Benson Zwizwai, Admore Kambudzi and Bonface Mauwa, 'Zimbabwe: Economic Policy-Making and Implementation: A Study of Strategic Trade and Selective Industrial Policies' 225-252 in Charles C. Soludo et. al. (eds), *The Politics of Trade and Industrial Policy in Africa: Forced Consensus?* (The International Development Research Centre 2004) <https://www.idrc.ca/sites/default/files/openebooks/125-6/index.html> accessed 15 July 2019.

58 For information on the UDI see <https://www.nationsencyclopedia.com/knowledge/Unilateral_Declaration_of_Independence.html> accessed 15 July 2019. The Unilateral Declaration of Independence (UDI) of Rhodesia from the United Kingdom was signed on November 11, 1965, by the administration of Ian Smith, whose Rhodesian Front party opposed an immediate transfer to black majority rule in the self-governing British colony.

59 Daniel Makina, 'Historical Perspective on Zimbabwe's Economic Performance: A Tale of Five Lost Decades. Journal of Developing Societies' (2010) 26 Journal

Therefore, although the few years following the UDI saw relative stability and economic growth, this progress was from the perspective of the settlers and there was increased agitation from the indigenous African majority for independence. Zimbabwe finally achieved internationally recognised independence in 1980 with Robert Mugabe becoming the first prime minister.[60]

It is noted that the focus of the independence government was more on ownership rather than economic expansion. State corporations were put in place to take control of the strategic economic sectors. National policies centred on expanding social services and redistribution of land to the disenfranchised indigenous majority. However, the lack of proper economic policies began to be felt with budget deficits, spiralling inflation, high unemployment, declining foreign exchange reserves and an overall under-performing economy becoming the norm. The independence government determined the way out to be via external financial aid. However, the financial aid came with its conditions. IMF and other main donors required the adoption by Zimbabwe of a structural adjustment program. Zimbabwe adopted an enhanced structural adjustment program (ESAP) in 1991.[61]

The main goal of the ESAP was to transform Zimbabwe into a more open and market-driven economy. Some of the more concrete measures included the adoption of trade liberalizing policies, including privatization of parastatals, as well as increased deregulation of certain core sectors. Competition policy was considered a necessary measure to realise the benefits of the economic reforms.[62]

A study conducted in 1991 revealed that there are indeed existing restrictive business practices such as market power-enhancing barriers to trade and collusive agreements. The need for promoting market efficiency and protecting competition led to the passing in 1996 of the Competition Act, which came into force in 1998. It sets out the main objective as the promotion and maintenance of competition in the economy of Zimbabwe. The act adopts the *per se* and rule of reason approach to prohibiting restrictive business practices. It also sets out provisions for the regulation of mergers.

---

of Developing Societies 1 99–123 <https://doi.org/10.1177/0169796X1002600105> accessed 15 July 2019.

60 Benson Zwizwai et al. (2004) 4-6.

61 Benson Zwizwai et al. (2004) 7.

62 World Bank Group, 'Structural Adjustment and Zimbabwe's Poor' (2012) <http://lnweb90.worldbank.org/oed/oeddoclib.nsf/DocUNIDViewForJavaSearch/15A937F6B215A053852567F5005D8B06> accessed 15 July 2019.

The Competition Act established the Competition and Tariff Commission which is responsible for the administration of competition law and policy in Zimbabwe.[63]

2.2.4 Tanzania

When Tanzania gained independence from Britain in 1961, the independence government took over a largely agriculture-dependent market economy, with agriculture contributing more than 50 percent to the GDP. The structure of the economy, as is the case for most SSA countries today, was mainly geared towards production and export of raw materials and importation of processed goods. The post-independence market economy and the main means of production were still largely under the control of the British and Asians. It is noted that the period between 1961 and 1967, the independence government opted to retain this imbalanced capitalist structure, with the majority of the indigenous Tanzanian population not benefiting socially and economically from independence.[64]

This however changed in 1967, when Tanzania adopted a socialist policy. This included the state taking control of the previously market-oriented economy and nationalizing all the main means of production in the country. State corporations were established to take control of the previously privately held enterprises. The socialist policy is later regarded as the main reason for Tanzania's economic under-performance. As noted by Ngowi, the state corporations were,

> typically characterized by inadequate managerial and technical skills; embezzlement; capacity under-utilization; reliance on government subsidies; non-payment of taxes; over-employing; protected from im-

63 CUTS International, 'Competition Regimes of the World: A Civil Society Report: Zimbabwe' (2006) CUTS Civil Society Report, 306-310 <https://competitionregimes.com/pdf/Africa/60-Zimbabwe.pdf> accessed 15 July 2019.

64 Honest Prosper Ngowi, 'Economic development and change in Tanzania since independence: The political leadership factor' (2009) 3 African Journal of Political Science and International Relations 4 pp. 259-267 <http://www.academicjournals.org/app/webroot/article/article1379789169_Ngowi.pdf> accessed 15 July 2019; see also Martin Mandalu, DR Thakhathi, and Hofisi Costa, 'Investigation on Tanzania's Economic History since Independence: The Search for a Development Model' (2018) 4 World Journal of Social Sciences and Humanities 1 pp. 61-68 <http://pubs.sciepub.com/wjssh/4/1/4> accessed 15 July 2019.

> ports; and monopolistic in nature. As a result they became loss-making entities that depended on government subsidies for their survival. Inefficiencies drove down producer prices and there was high effective protection of the import-substituting industrial sector. Trade controls, instead of exchange rate adjustment, were used as a means of adjusting to external shocks. Suppression of private business limited opportunities for entrepreneurship. Control of prices, exchange rate, interest rate, imports and exports added to the already hostile business and investment climate.[65]

The socialist policies however greatly benefitted the indigenous majority, with a lot of investment going to social services such as education and health. Moving into the eighties, there was an acknowledgement by the government of the failure of the socialist policies to yield the anticipated economic gains. The mid-eighties saw a change in political leadership in Tanzania and with it major reforms which included a shift from the socialist policies to a market-based economy.[66]

Like in many SSA countries, the Tanzania government sought external aid, principally from the IMF, to support the economic recovery. In 1986, Tanzania adopted a structural adjustment program which was part of the conditions attached to the IMF funding. Reforms included privatisation of the state corporations, easing of entry restrictions in the majority of economic sectors, removal of price controls and deregulation in a number of industries.[67]

As part of the ongoing structural adjustments, a government task force was established in 1990 to look into policies and institutional frameworks that can be put in place to regulate Tanzania's market economy. One of the regulatory frameworks that was put in place was the Fair Trade Practices Act which was enacted in 1994 to regulate competition law. The Act inter alia regulated restrictive business practices, misuse of market power, control of monopolies and concentration of economic power via mergers and acquisitions. Various shortcomings in the Act were identified including absence of a competition test, excessive ministerial power

65 Ngowi (2009) 263.
66 Ngowi (2009) 265; Mandlu et al (2018) 66.
67 Ngowi (2009) 265.

and inadequate safeguards for the independence, accountability and transparency of the competition law.[68]

The Act was reviewed in 1994 and 2001 with the current version being the Fair Competition Act of 2003. The Fair Competition Act establishes the Fair Competition Commission which is independent of the relevant ministry. Its object is to inter alia, 'enhance the welfare of the people of Tanzania as a whole by promoting and protecting effective competition in markets and preventing unfair and misleading market conduct throughout Tanzania'.[69]

2.2.5 Mauritius

Prior to gaining independence in 1968, Mauritius had been under the colonial rule of three European powers: the Netherlands, France and in the latter years Britain. Economically, Mauritius depended primarily on its sugar-cane fields, which are argued to have been introduced by the Dutch and later nurtured and exploited by the French and the British. At independence, the country's economy was dependent on sugar for over 90 percent of its export earnings.[70]

From the social perspective, Mauritius has a very high cultural diversity; Mauritians of Indian descent making up most of the population followed by the Creoles (Mauritians of African descent). It has been argued that prior to the Dutch colonising the island around 1658, it was largely uninhabited. Large scale migration into the island is noted to have been intended to meet the labour needs of the European settlers.[71]

Post-independence, there were several socio-economic concerns that needed to be addressed. Racial inequality for instance led to the social

---

68 CUTS International, 'Competition Regimes of the World: A Civil Society Report: Tanzania' (2006) CUTS Civil Society Report pp. 288-292 <https://competitionregimes.com/pdf/Africa/56-Tanzania.pdf> accessed 15 July 2019.

69 CUTS Civil Society Report Tanzania 289.

70 Louis YeungLamKo, 'The Economic Development of Mauritius Since Independence' (1998) School of Economics, University of New South Wales, 4 <http://wwwdocs.fce.unsw.edu.au/economics/Research/WorkingPapers/1998_6.pdf> accessed 15 July 2019; see also Milo Vandemoortele with Kate Bird, 'Progress in economic conditions: Sustained success against the odds in Mauritius' (2011) Overseas Development Institute, 4-7 <https://www.odi.org/sites/odi.org.uk/files/resource-documents/11579.pdf> accessed 15 July 2019.

71 Vandemoortele and Bird (2011) 4.

and economic exclusion of the Creoles. There was also overdependence on sugarcane, with the control of the plantations being in the hands of a few. There were also high unemployment rates coupled with high population growth. Other concerns included a decline in export earnings, poor balance of payments, reduced output and a ballooning external debt.[72]

Mauritius adopted a structural adjustment program in the 1980s as a condition precedent to a loan from the IMF and is credited as having, to a large extent, succeeded in implementing structural adjustment in SSA.[73] Various factors including a sound macroeconomic management policy, a flexible exchange rate policy which favoured competitive prices, structured (and improved) policies for export processing zones, streamlining of the near-capacity sugar industry, and investment in education and inclusive social welfare policies to reduce the social imbalance.[74] Efforts to further diversify the economy to include service industries such as tourism and financial services as well as streamlining the manufacturing sector also contributed to the economy's success. Overall, Mauritius GDP grew by 4.6% annually for the period between 1977 and 2008.[75] The service sector, primarily financial services and tourism, has grown to become the main contributor to the GDP, standing at approximately 74 percent.[76]

In 1980, Mauritius enacted the Fair Trading Act which was largely meant to protect consumers from misleading trade practices as well as preventing the charging of prices beyond those fixed by statute. One of the justifications given for price control was that lack of competition in most sectors hence the need to cushion consumers from excessive prices. The intention was for the price controls to be removed gradually as the markets become more competitive.[77]

As a consequence of various changes in the economy especially privatisation, increased trade liberalisation and the gradual removal of price controls, it was felt that a robust competition policy was needed to pre-

---

72 Vandemoortele and Bird (2011) 5.

73 Philip English, 'Mauritius: Reigniting the Engines of Growth A Teaching Case Study' (2002) Teaching Notes, 3-4 <http://documents.worldbank.org/curated/en/936011468757482849/Teaching-notes> accessed 15 July 2019.

74 English (2012) 3-4.

75 Vandemoortele and Bird (2011) 6.

76 For statistics see Mauritius: Economic Outline <http://www.mauritiustrade.mu/en/trading-with-mauritius/mauritius-economics-outline> accessed 15 July 2019.

77 CUTS International, 'Competition Regimes of the World: A Civil Society Report: Mauritius' (2006) CUTS Civil Society Report, 254-259 <https://competitionregimes.com/pdf/Africa/48-Mauritius.pdf> accessed 15 July 2019.

vent cartelist behaviour form capturing the market.[78] The Competition Act, which was passed in 2003, was considered a necessary policy tool to enhance competition in Mauritius. It however never entered into force. One of the reasons proffered for the 2003 Act not entering into force was that there was a change of government which resulted in proposals for a new Act. It was also argued that a lot of interference from private sector interests had undermined the 2003 Act.[79]

The Act currently in force is the Competition Act of 2007 (entered into force in 2009). It established the Mauritius Competition Commission and regulates various restrictive business practices (such as collusive agreements and non-collusive horizontal agreements). It also provides for merger control.[80]

2.2.6 Malawi

Malawi's economy at the time of independence shares many similarities with several SSA countries. There were high poverty levels affecting the largely rural based African population. There was also a lack of skilled human resource, exacerbated by a burgeoning uneducated population. The lack of mineral resources led to an over reliance on agriculture and pressure for land. Therefore, at the time of independence in 1964, the economy was predominantly dependent on agricultural export earnings. However, although facing similar socio-economic challenges as most other SSA countries at the time of independence, Malawi is noted to have experienced a period of accelerated economic growth in the first decade under the independence government. In addition to the rapid economic growth, there was increased employment, an improved investment climate and an increase in agricultural output.[81]

---

78 Reshma Peerun-Fatehmamode, Sunil Bundoo and Kheswam Jankee, 'Competition Scenario in Mauritius' (2006) CUTS International <http://www.cuts-ccier.org/7up3/pdf/CRR-Mauritius.pdf> accessed 15 July 2019.

79 Siven Pillay Rungien, 'Competition in Paradise: A look at the competition law and enforcement activities of Mauritius' (2011) Queen Mary University Global Antitrust Review 4, 165-166 <http://www.icc.qmul.ac.uk/media/icc/gar/gar2011/GAR-journal-2011_10_rungien.pdf> accessed 15 July 2019.

80 Mauritius Competition Act 25/2007.

81 Happy M. Kayuni, 'Malawi's Economic and Development Policy Choices from 1964 to 1980: An Epitome of 'Pragmatic Unilateral Capitalism' (2011) 20 Nordic Journal of African Studies 2, 112–131 <http://www.njas.helsinki.fi/pdf-files/vol20

The period of growth however hit its peak towards the end of the 1970s. Malawi remained very fragile to shocks to its agricultural sector. The two decades from the beginning of the 1980s were marked with various challenges including falling per capita income and a decline in agricultural output. Malawi adopted its structural adjustment programme in the early 1980s under the advise of the World Bank.[82]

Although facing adverse economic challenges, the 1980s and 1990s were marked with increased trade liberalisation. The government also began to commit more resources to social development such as education. However, the structural adjustment programs to a large extent failed to meet their objectives. It is argued that the structural adjustment program did not address the underlying structural problems such as the rapidly increasing population coupled with poor land distribution and a decrease in the soil's productive capacity.[83]

In spite of the failure of the policy initiatives to reverse the negative trend in socio-economic development, the government continued to pursue trade liberalisation and privatisation of state enterprises in various sectors.[84] It is in the 1990s that Malawi adopted its competition policy. The Malawi Competition and Fair Trading Act was enacted in 1998 and came into force in 2000. The Act inter alia seeks to:

> encourage competition in the economy by prohibiting anti-competitive trade practices; to establish the Competition and Fair Trading Commission; to regulate and monitor monopolies and concentrations of economic power; to protect consumer welfare; to strengthen the efficiency of production and distribution of goods and services; to secure

---

num2/kayuni.pdf> accessed 15 July 2019; see also David Booth, Diana Cammack, Jane Harrigan, Edge Kanyongolo, Mike Mataure and Naomi Ngwira, 'Drivers of Change and Development in Malawi' (2006) Overseas Development Institute Working Paper 261 <https://www.odi.org/publications/1318-drivers-change-and-development-malawi> accessed 15 July 2019 .

82 Booth et al (2006) 5-6; IMF, 'Malawi: Economic Development Document' (2017) IMF Country Report No. 17/184 <https://www.imf.org/en/Publications/CR/Issues/2017/07/05/Malawi-Economic-Development-Document-45037> accessed 15 July 2019.

83 Booth et al (2006) 4-7; IMF Malawi Country Report (2017) 4-6.

84 CUTS International, 'Competition Regimes of the World: A Civil Society Report: Malawi' (2006) CUTS Civil Society Report, 249-253 <https://competitionregimes.com/pdf/Africa/47-Malawi.pdf> accessed 15 July 2019.

the best possible conditions for the freedom of trade; to facilitate the expansion of the base of entrepreneurship.[85]

Malawi also enacted a Consumer Protection Act which came into force in 2003 with the aim of protecting consumers from unfair trade practices.[86]

2.2.7 Botswana

From an economic perspective, Botswana can be analysed from two broad perspectives; the period before and the period after the discovery of diamonds. Pre-independence, Botswana was used by the British and later South Africa mainly for geo-political reasons as a means of safeguarding access to the interior of Africa. There was no real interest in the exploitation of its natural resources. There were further disincentives to invest in the territory as a result of various uncertainties regarding its status as a colonial protectorate. As a result, no extensive administrative structures were set up within Botswana. A number of the pre-colonial indigenous socio-political structures therefore remained prominent even at independence, with tribal chiefs having a level of influence on leadership at the national level. There was therefore a mix of colonial administrative structures as well as the indigenous structures.[87]

Botswana gained independence in 1966. At independence, Botswana's economy was largely dependent on a poorly performing agricultural sector (in particular beef production) which accounted for roughly 40 percent of the GDP. Botswana also faced most of the socio-economic hardship experienced by many of the newly independent African states such as a

85 Competition and Fair Trading Act of Malawi, Act No. 43 of 2008.

86 Consumer Protection Act of Malawi, Act No. 14 of 2003.

87 Daron Acemoglu, Simon Johnson and James A. Robinson, 'Botswana: An African Success Story' in Dani Rodrik (Ed.), *In Search of Prosperity: Analytical Narrative on Economic Growth* (Princeton University Press 2003); Valentin Seidler, 'Why did Botswana end up with Good Institutions: The Role of Culture and Colonial Rule' (2010) Vienna University for Economics and Business: Institute for Economic and Social History, 3-7 <https://ssrn.com/abstract=3051011> accessed 15 July 2019; Lewis H. Gann and Peter Duignan, *Burden of Empire: An Appraisal of Western Colonialism in Africa South of the Sahara* (Hoover Institution Press 1967); John Alan Robinson, and Neil Parsons, 'State Formation and Governance in Botswana' (2006) 15 Journal of African Economies 1, 100-140 <https://scholar.harvard.edu/jrobinson/publications/state-formation-and-governance-botswana> accessed 15 July 2019.

poorly educated population largely dependent on subsistence agriculture. Botswana was for the most part dependent on international development assistance.[88]

However, unlike other SSA countries, Botswana did not adopt policies that seek to promote import substitution. Botswana also avoided the wave of nationalisation of private enterprises. The government did not create state corporations to take over key sectors in the economy. For this reason, Botswana is noted to have avoided many of the economic inefficiencies suffered by states that adopted these policies. Indeed, Botswana is one of the very few developing countries that have not been part of the IMF structural adjustment programs.[89]

The discovery of diamonds in 1967 was a big turning point and ushered in a period of rapid economic growth associated with the exploitation of this resource. It shifted Botswana from an agricultural-based to a predominantly mineral-based economy. Currently, mining averages about 40 percent of Botswana's GDP with manufacturing and agriculture now contributing substantially less to the GDP in comparison. The challenge however is how to diversify the economy and reduce reliance on mineral exports, whose earnings are projected to drop.[90]

Due to good economic and governance policies as well as political stability, Botswana is one of the few countries that have not fallen victim to the 'resource curse' which has seen many developing countries fail to benefit from their natural resources as a result of bad governance and corruption.[91]

In 2005 Botswana adopted a National Competition Policy. It was acknowledged in the policy that Botswana has, since independence, maintained a very open economy and has sought to strengthen the functioning of markets. However, there were concerns regarding the emergence of certain private sector anti-competitive practices. Other considerations included 'the increasing dominance of foreign companies in the Botswana

88 Michael Lewin, 'Botswana's Success: Good Governance, Good Policies, and Good Luck' (2019), 1 <https://www.researchgate.net/publication/265285982> accessed 15 July 2019.

89 *See generally* Lewin (2019); *See also* Patrick Imam, 'Effect of IMF Structural Adjustment Programs on Expectations: The Case of Transition Economies' (2007) IMF Working Paper <https://www.imf.org/en/Publications/WP/Issues/2016/12/31/Effect-of-IMF-Structural-Adjustment-Programs-on-Expectations-The-Case-of-Transition-Economies-21449> accessed 15 July 2019.

90 Lewin (2019) 87.

91 Lewin (2019) 83-84.

economy; the need to safeguard and promote the growth and development of citizen-owned small and medium enterprises; and other Government policy initiatives such as the diversification of the economy.'[92] It was further noted that the competition policy is a strategic tool to:

> promote free entry in the market place by investors and all firms, irrespective of their size; the attraction of both domestic and foreign investment flows; innovation and transfer of technology from intellectual property rights-holders; unfettered competition; acceptable business behaviour and conduct; fair business practice; efficiency; competitiveness; and consumer welfare.[93]

Botswana first adopted a Competition Act in 2009. The 2009 Act was repealed and replaced by the Competition Act of 2018. The 2009 Act established the Competition Authority which was responsible for the day to day implementation and enforcement of the Competition Act. The Act also established in parallel a Competition Commission which served as the governing body of the Competition Authority as well as the adjudicative body. The Act regulated restrictive business practices as well as control of mergers.[94] The 2018 Act changed the name of the Competition Authority to the Competition and Consumer Authority. A Competition and Consumer Board was established and replaced the Competition Commission as the governing body of the Competition and Consumer Authority. The 2018 Act also established the Competition and Consumer Tribunal which is the dedicated adjudicative body. The 2018 Act also introduced criminal liability for cartel conduct, specified particular types of conduct regarded as abusive of dominance and introduced financial penalties for failure to notify mergers falling within the notification thresholds.[95]

2.2.8 Seychelles

Seychelles is a small island (archipelago) economy whose first settlers were the French (1770). It was thereafter colonized by the British in 1811 un-

---

92 Botswana Ministry of Trade and Industry, National Competition Policy of Botswana (2005) <https://www.competitionauthority.co.bw/sites/default/files/National%20Competition%20Policy%20Botswana%202005.pdf> accessed 15 July 2019.

93 National Competition Policy of Botswana (2005) para 2.6.

94 *See generally* Botswana Competition Act, No. 17 of 2009.

95 *See generally* Botswana Competition Act, No. 4 of 2018.

til gaining independence in 1976. It was during the colonization period that most of the physical and administrative structures were put in place. Economically, there was a clear divide between the settlers who owned most of the land and assets, and the migrants from mainland Africa who constituted most of the low-income working class.[96]

Subsequent socio-economic and political developments in the ensuing years led to the formation of two main political parties: The Seychelles People's United Party (SPUP) which was backed by the proletariat and the Seychelles Democratic Party (SDP) which was backed by the elite. The SPUP agitated for wealth distribution as well as independence while the SDP pushed for a maintenance of the status quo. Seychelles gained independence in 1976 with the head of the SDP ascending into power before being ousted a year later and the SPUP seizing power.[97]

The SPUP government embarked on a process of wealth redistribution, with the government acquiring large tracts of land to facilitate this effort. The government subsequently set up state corporations covering most of the economic sectors such as transport, hospitality, manufacturing, tourism, education and financial services. These state corporations essentially became monopolies. The state also relied heavily on borrowing from banks to meet its commitments. The effect was a decline of the private sector which was unable to effectively compete against the state corporations. Therefore, although the economy grew in the 1980s and 1990s this was against the backdrop of overdependence on debt finance, with debt averaging above 40 percent of the GDP.[98]

Seychelles to date is largely dependent on its tourism industry. In order to expand the sector, the government embarked in the 1990s on a mix of policies such as increased privatization and tax incentives in order to attract more foreign investors. There were some gains made in this sector as well as other sectors such as fisheries where the government had adopted similar policies to attract foreign investors. However, the overreliance on debt finance proved unsustainable. By the late 1990s, the government was increasingly unable to service its debt. It is noted that by the end of the year 2001, external debt had risen to over 50 percent of the GDP.[99]

96 Sawkut Rojid, Ahmed Afif, and Emilio Sacerdoti, 'Seychelles: How Classic Policies Restored Sustainability' (2013) World Bank, 1 <https://www.worldbank.org/content/dam/Worldbank/document/Africa/Seychelles/sc-how-classic-policies-restored-sustainability.pdf> accessed 15 July 2019.

97 Rojid et al. (2013) 1-2.

98 Rojid et al. (2013) 2.

99 Rojid et al. (2013) 2-21.

Between 2006-2008 a series of events including rising food and energy prices and the economic crisis which negatively impacted the tourism industry led to the government being unable to honour its external debt payments. It is around this time that the government-initiated discussions with the IMF, World Bank and other institutions in order to develop a structural adjustment program. Some of the immediate priorities included:[100]

Elimination of currency and price controls as well as liberating trade in the market in order that market forces drive trade; and

Reversing budget deficits and reducing external indebtedness.

As part of its program to transform the economy into a more liberal, market-oriented one the government began adopting various policies to safeguard the market. This included the Fair Trading Commission Act and the Fair Competition Act which were both enacted in 2009 with the Fair Competition Act coming into operation in 2010. The purpose of the Fair Trading Commission as noted in its preamble includes, 'to safeguard the interests of consumers, to monitor and investigate the conduct of business enterprises, to promote and maintain effective competition in the economy.'[101] The Fair Competition Act addresses the three main types of competition law concerns: restrictive (horizontal and vertical) agreements, abuse of dominance and anti-competitive mergers.[102]

2.2.9 Namibia

Namibia's pre-independence political economy can be divided into two main time periods; the period between 1884 and 1915 when the country was under German rule and the period between 1919 and 1990 when the country was under the control of South Africa. The period under German occupation was mainly marked with largescale land dispossession and introduction of private ownership to what was a predominantly pastoral indigenous population with a communal land ownership system. It is noted that by 1902, only 38 percent of the total land area remained in the hands of the indigenous population. Most of the previously pastoral communities were forced to take up poorly paying labour jobs. By 1913, around 90 percent of the livestock in established police zones were owned

100 Rojid et al. (2013) 21-27.

101 *See generally* Mauritius Fair Trading Commission Act, No 17 of 2009.

102 *See generally* Mauritius Fair Competition Act, No 18 of 2009.

by the settlers. The settlers had established an export economy focused mainly on agriculture and mining.[103]

South Africa's control of the Namibian territory from 1919 was intended to be a transition period in which Namibia would gradually obtain its independence. South Africa however established itself as a 'colonial power' with the indigenous population largely facing the pre-existing problem of poor human development and land dispossession. South Africa instituted a system of apartheid similar to the one existing in the home country. The native population were confined to native reserves and their movement out of these reserves was restricted. Thus, a system by which the indigenous population were reduced to serfs and practically forced to work on farms, mines and industries set up by the settlers was put in place.[104]

During the period between 1960 and 1979 there was a significant increase in GDP driven largely by investments in the mining sector, which was the most active economic sector and the biggest contributor to the economy. The period from 1980 to just before independence in 1990 saw a decline in GDP caused mainly by a poorly performing mining sector as well as poor weather conditions that affected the agricultural sector. There was also substantial investor uncertainty in the years leading to independence which caused a decline in investment. After Namibia gained independence from South Africa in 1990, the ensuing political stability resulted in a return of investor confidence and a resurgence of investment activity.[105]

Namibia is classified as a small middle-income country and is noted to be one of the few SSA countries that have seen their GDP increase by more than 5 times on average in the last 30 years. This is attributed to policies that effectively address development challenges such as infrastructure, health and education. However, lack of economic diversification and overreliance on the mining sector leaves Namibia vulnerable to external developments.[106]

---

103 Wolfgang Werner, 'A Brief History of Land Disposession in Namibia' (1993) 19 Journal of Southern African Studies 1 <https://www.tandfonline.com/doi/abs/10.1080/03057079308708351> accessed 15 July 2019.

104 *See generally* Tekaligne Godana and John E. Odada, 'Sources of Growth in Africa: A Case Study of Namibia' (2002) <http://citeseerx.ist.psu.edu/viewdoc/download?doi=10.1.1.590.3047&rep=rep1&type=pdf> accessed 15 July 2019.

105 Godana and Odada (2002) 16.

106 IMF, 'Namibia: Selected Issues' (2014) IMF Country Report No. 14/41, 10-11 https://www.imf.org/external/pubs/ft/scr/2014/cr1441.pdf accessed 16 July 2019.

As a middle-income country, Namibia is not eligible for the Bretton Woods international development association funding. Namibia is therefore one of the few SSA countries that were not part of the structural adjustment programs of the Bretton Woods institutions.[107]

Namibia adopted its competition policy in 2003 with one of the core objectives being to boost competitiveness in the economy. It is noted that the government had recognised the necessity of a competition policy to address certain market practices that were affecting the competitiveness of the Namibian economy. The government with the assistance of the EU Commission prepared a study which resulted in the drafting of a Competition Bill in 1996. A committee was formed to further discuss the bill with all relevant stakeholders included, leading to the enactment of the Competition Act in 2003.[108] The Act establishes the Namibia Competition Commission and sets out a number of objectives including: promoting the efficiency of the economy, providing consumers with competitive prices and product choices, advancement of social and economic welfare. It also includes a public interest objective, that is, increasing the ownership stakes of historically disadvantaged persons.[109]

As noted by a former Chief Executive Officer of the Namibia Competition Commission, 'as the Commission pursues fair competition, it in fact creates an enabling environment for factors of competitiveness to manifest themselves, leading to productivity and sustained national economic development. It is thus envisaged that with the well working competitiveness markets, the economy would see lower prices, better quality goods, new product ranges, and innovation in production and distribution, leading to a socio-economic and consumer welfare as defined in the Competition Act'[110]

Substantially the Act addresses restrictive business practices including restrictive agreements and abuse of dominance. It also provides for the regulation of mergers.

---

107 World Bank, 'World Bank Annual Report' (2007), 2 <http://siteresources.worldbank.org/EXTANNREP2K7/Resources/English.pdf> accessed 16 July 2019.

108 CUTS International, 'Competition Regimes of the World: A Civil Society Report: Namibia' (2006) CUTS Civil Society Report, 265-268 <https://competitionregimes.com/pdf/Africa/50-Namibia.pdf> accessed 16 July 2019.

109 Namibia Competition Act ss 2 and 4.

110 Mihe Gaomab, 'Competition Policy and Competitiveness in Namibia', 3 <http://www.nacc.com.na/cms_documents/703_competition_policy_and_competitiveness.pdf> accessed 16 July 2019.

2.2.10 Summary

Outside of the forces that shaped global market dynamics and led to the globalization of markets in the 20th century, the countries in SSA present many similarities in the evolution of their socio-economic and political climate. Three broad time periods are evident:

1. The period before colonial occupation where land ownership was communal and production was basic and largely subsistence, geared more towards consumption than trade.
2. The period of colonisation where settlers divided up the territories, subdued the indigenous populations and introduced a system of private ownership and capitalistic exploitation of resources. The native populations had their socio-economic and political structures disrupted, were excluded from ownership and means of production and were in many cases relegated to a low-income labour force.
3. The period after independence where the newly liberated countries were met with the choice of either maintaining the pre-independence socio-economic structures or developing policies aimed at ensuring a more even distribution of resources, means of production and other human development factors.

The choice for many post-independence governments was the adoption of policies that saw state control and nationalization of many of the previously privately-owned enterprises as a means to enable an equitable distribution of resources. Other measures such as import substitution were aimed at stimulating production in the local market. This is in addition to other policies targeting human development factors such as education and health. This is the case for instance with Kenya, Zambia, Tanzania, Seychelles, Zimbabwe and Malawi.

The outcome of these policies however for most of these jurisdictions was gross inefficiency leading to market failure. Except for Botswana, Mauritius and Namibia, the other ESA jurisdictions introduced structural adjustment programs at the behest of international donor institutions as a condition attached to access to development funds and technical assistance. It was within this matrix of trade liberalization, deregulation and privatisation that a package of policies, which included comprehensive competition policies, were introduced. Although not part of a negotiated structural adjustment program, Mauritius also adopted competition and consumer protection policies as part of a policy framework to support its liberalization and privatisation efforts. In the case of Botswana, which had strived to maintain an open economy since independence, a main concern was the emergence of private-sector anti-competitive practices, especially by foreign enterprises. Namibia highlighted boosting competitiveness of the economy as one of their main reasons for adopting its competition policy.

In terms of objectives of competition policy, the main themes are promoting market efficiency, enhancing social and consumer welfare and facilitating economic growth and development.

2.3 The Regional Context

2.3.1 Introduction

The need for integration in Africa has been expressed over the years through the crafting of various objectives and the creation of a number of legal instruments and institutions to meet these objectives. Though the ultimate intention has always been to create a socially, politically and economically integrated Africa, the focal objectives have evolved over time in response to various circumstances and changes within Africa and globally.

The quest for integration can be said to have begun in the early 20th century with the espousing of the Pan Africanist ideals that advocated for *inter alia* the civil and political rights for Africans as well as encouraging the venturing by Africans into educational, commercial and industrial enterprise as a means of alleviating the poor condition of Africans globally.[111] The initial objectives were largely political, seeking to ensure that Africans were granted a level playing field in terms of having their own voice and seeking their own ideals.

The efforts of the Pan-African movement are credited with the conclusion in 1963 of the Organization of African Unity (OAU) Charter establishing the OAU, which is the predecessor of the current African Union (AU).[112] At its inception the central objective of the OAU was to ensure that after the liberation of most African States the right to self-determination was protected.[113] With increasing globalisation, economic develop-

111 Marika Sherwood, 'Pan-African Conferences, 1900-1953: What did 'Pan-Africanism' Mean?' (2012) 4 The Journal of Pan African Studies 10, 106-126 <http://www.jpanafrican.com/docs/vol4no10/4.10Pan-African.pdf> accessed 16 July 2019.

112 *See* AU in a Nutshell <https://au.int/en/au-nutshell> accessed 16 July 2019.

113 Charter of the Organization of African Unity (OAU Charter) 479 U.N.T.S. 39 <https://www.sahistory.org.za/archive/charter-organization-african-unity-479-u

ment was acknowledged as a core aspect of self-determination and resulted in the increased focus on economic integration as a catalyst for uniting Africa.[114]

One of the core intentions of the OAU had always been to foster economic cooperation among the Member States.[115] This intention was subsequently expressed over the years that followed through the signing of various declarations and conclusion of treaties that aimed at fostering economic cooperation and development among the Member States.

The most concrete step towards the economic integration of Africa under the ambit of the OAU was the signing of the Treaty Establishing the African Economic Community (AEC Treaty) in 1991.[116] The AEC Treaty provides for a six-stage plan towards the eventual achievement of an African Economic Community (AEC).[117]

One of these stages was set in motion on the 10th of June 2015 when the heads of state of three regional economic communities (RECs), the Common Market for Eastern and Southern Africa (COMESA), the East African Community (EAC) and the Southern African Development Community (SADC), signed a declaration launching the biggest free trade area in Africa as well as opening a Tripartite Free Trade Area (FTA) Agreement for signature. This was followed a week later by the launching of negotiations within the AU for the establishment of a Continental FTA.[118] The Continental FTA Agreement was adopted and opened for signature on 21 March 2018.

---

nts-39-entered-force-sept-13-1963> accessed 16 July 2019. The preamble reflects this intention.

114 See, e.g., Organization of African Unity: Declaration on African Cooperation, Development, and Economic Independence, I.L.M 12(4): 996-1013. The preamble for instance expressed the concern over the widening gap in economic development between Africa and the developed world.

115 OAU Charter art 1 and 2

116 Treaty establishing the African Economic Community (AEC Treaty), 30 I.L.M. 1241 (1991).

117 AEC Treaty art 6(2). In respect of the third stage the AEC Treaty provides that 'At the level of each regional economic community and within a period not exceeding ten (10) years, establishment of a Free Trade Area through the observance of the time-table for the gradual removal of Tariff Barriers and Non-Tariff Barriers to intra-community trade and the establishment of a Customs Union by means of adopting a common external tariff.'

118 Africa Union, 'The African Union Assembly launches the Continental Free Trade Area (CFTA) negotiations' (17 June 2015) <https://au.int/sw/node/29332> accessed 16 July 2019.

While the conclusion of the Tripartite FTA Agreement and the Continental FTA Agreement is certainly a bold step towards the creation of the AEC, questions still remain as to the effectiveness of the RECs in achieving their objectives. The FTA Agreements also present their own challenges. The discussion will mainly focus on COMESA, EAC and SADC as well as the Tripartite FTA Agreement. An overview of the Continental FTA Agreement will be presented.

2.3.2 The Regional Economic Communities

Regional integration has been largely accepted in Africa as a way to achieve economic development and sustainable growth. The AU for instance recognises eight RECs, which together cover more or less the whole of Africa. Many RECs in Africa are however lagging behind in the implementation of their objectives. The price volatility on the global market and its effect on the relatively nascent natural-resource based economies in Africa highlights the need for the RECs to expedite their integration efforts in order to bolster and increase regional economic activity. The conclusion of such Agreements by the Member States of the EAC, COMESA and SADC is in this regard highly laudable. One, however, has to take a step back and consider how effective the three RECs are in meeting their own objectives.

The core objective of the three RECs is naturally to achieve social, political and economic integration but the level of integration sought varies. Whereas on the one hand SADC and COMESA intend to eventually achieve a Monetary Union with a single currency, the EAC has the far more ambitious objective of establishing a Political Federation. The three RECs however have common objectives which if harmonised could facilitate the tapping of the great potential within the Tripartite FTA.

2.3.2.1 COMESA

COMESA is the largest of the three RECs with a membership of 21 Northern, Eastern and Southern African states.[119] The origin of COMESA goes back to the 1982 Treaty Establishing the Preferential Trade Area for

119 COMESA Member States are Burundi, The Comoros, Egypt, The Democratic Republic of Congo, Djibouti, Eritrea, Ethiopia, Kenya, Libya, Madagascar,

Eastern and Southern African States (PTA Treaty), which was concluded under the ambit of the OAU.[120] The PTA Treaty sought the enhancement of co-operation and development among the Member States in the fields of trade, customs, agriculture, industry, natural resources, transport, monetary affairs and communications.[121] Member States were required to inter alia bring down and eventually eliminate customs duties on imports from within the PTA and establish common rules of origin (RoO) for products eligible for preferential treatment. The ultimate objective of the PTA was the establishment of an economic community for the Eastern and Southern African states.[122]

The transition of the PTA into a Common Market was set in motion with the ratification of the COMESA Treaty on 8 December 1994. The main objectives of COMESA as set out in the COMESA Treaty are geared towards sustainable growth and development within the Member States and jointly among the Member States. This objective is to be met through the creation of an economically liberalised environment that promotes domestic, cross-border and foreign investment, adoption of common policies and programs and the adoption of common positions with regards to the international agenda.[123] The ultimate aim is the implementation of specific measures that will result in the realisation of the AEC.

The COMESA Treaty sets out undertakings in various economic fields which the Member States are required to meet, some of which were subject to fixed timelines. As regards cooperation in respect of trade liberalisation and development for instance, the COMESA Treaty set a timeline of 10 years from its entry into force for the creation of a Customs Union. Within this period, customs duties and similar charges on imports from the Member Countries were to be eliminated. It also entailed the removal of Non-Tariff Barriers (NTBs) and the establishment of a Common External Tariff (CET) for goods coming from third countries.[124] This in turn necessitated the adoption within this period of various requirements such

---

Malawi, Mauritius, Rwanda, Seychelles, Sudan, Swaziland, Uganda, Zambia, Zimbabwe, Tunisia and Libya.

120 Treaty Establishing the Preferential Trade Area for Eastern and Southern African States (PTA Treaty), 21 ILM 479 (1981) article 29; See also Treaty Establishing a Common Market for Eastern and Southern Africa (COMESA Treaty), 33 I.L.M. 1067 (1994) preamble.

121 PTA Treaty art 3.

122 PTA Treaty art 3.

123 COMESA Treaty art 3.

124 COMESA Treaty, art 45.

as RoO, rules on dumping, restrictions on subsidies and rules on competition.[125] The COMESA Treaty also requires the Member States to cooperate in monetary and financial matters with the highly ambitious eventual goal of establishing a Monetary Union characterised by a common currency that would facilitate easier cross-border trade.[126]

Another fundamental undertaking was geared towards addressing the persistent problem of poor infrastructure. The Member States undertook to establish coordinated and complementary transport and communications policies as well as to expand and improve the current facilities and create new ones.[127] Industrial development, which is intrinsically linked to functional infrastructure, is also acknowledged as a critical development area. The Member States are required to adopt an industrial strategy that takes into account aspects such as specialisation and complementarity of industries while having regard to various comparative advantages.[128] The support of small and medium enterprises, food and agricultural industries, the promotion of industrial Research and Development (R&D), increased private sector participation and the improvement of the investment climate in the Common Market are among the many factors identified as necessary in enhancing industrial development.[129]

Various other critical development areas targeted for achievement by the Member States are: cooperation in the development of energy; efficient and sustainable use of natural resources; protection and preservation of the environment; promotion of scientific and technological progress; cooperation in agriculture and rural development and the progressive adoption of measures to facilitate the free movement of persons, labour and services.

The disparity in terms of economic development between some of the Member States is recognised as a critical integration challenge. The Member States therefore agreed to take measures to address this disparity through cooperating in capacity building for these regions in areas such as infrastructure, industrial development and agriculture.[130]

The COMESA FTA was launched in 2000. To date however not all the Member States are party to the FTA.[131] The Democratic Republic of

---

125 COMESA Treaty art 46-62.
126 COMESA Treaty art 4(4).
127 COMESA Treaty art 84-98.
128 COMESA Treaty art 99.
129 COMESA Treaty art 100.
130 COMESA Treaty art 144.
131 COMESA, 'Final Communiqué of the Eighteenth Summit of the COMESA Authority of Heads of State and Government (COMESA 18th Summit)' (31

Congo, Ethiopia, Uganda, and Eritrea have expressed their commitment to join and are at various stages of preparing accession instruments.

The Customs Union was launched in 2009, which was already beyond the agreed-upon 10-year timeline.[132] A three-band CET was set at 0% for imports of raw materials and capital goods, 10% for imports of intermediate products and 25% for imports of finished products. The 0% on raw materials is because they are important for production and the cost therefore affects competitiveness of the end products. The 25% on finished products is explained as a measure to protect domestic products from the stiff competition of foreign products.[133]

COMESA has adopted various instruments and measures meant to give full effect to the Customs Union but timelines remain largely unmet and the implementation is still low. Member States expressed various concerns including: local industries and revenues being affected by the imported goods; loss of decision-making capacity on various policy areas; some countries facing serious economic and industrial problems hence requiring time for their own economies to recover; insufficient capacity, information and coordination. One concern expressed that touches on the issue of overlaps is the fact that the EAC, a number of whose members are also members of COMESA, already has a customs union.[134]

The COMESA Secretariat pointed out that the real reasons for the non-implementation include: National policies that are incompatible with the customs union; some countries having existing free trade agreements with third countries that include duty free provisions hence making it difficult to subsequently introduce a CET; some domestic industry stakeholders feeling threatened by competition from imports, and a general lack of prioritisation of regional integration requirements as well as institutional, technical and financial constraints in some Member States.[135]

The inadequacy of existing infrastructure in the COMESA region has been noted as one of the key hindrances to the region's economic progress. Various infrastructure projects that have been identified as key in meeting the COMESA Treaty objectives have been initiated. They broadly

---

March 2015) <http://dhanaanmedia.com/wp-content/uploads/2015/03/150331_Final-communique_March-2015_new.pdf.pdf> accessed 5 March 2017.

132 Sindiso Ngwenya et al, 'Key Issues in Regional Integration' (2013) 2, 131 <https://www.comesa.int/wp-content/uploads/2019/03/key-issues-on-intergration-ii_final_final_cutout_print.pdf> accessed 16 July 2019.

133 Ngwenya et al (2013) 79.

134 Ngwenya et al (2013) 134-135.

135 Ngwenya et al (2013) 135.

cover transport, energy, and Information and Communications Technology (ICT).[136] The approach to the development of roads and railways envisions the construction of inter-regional corridors.[137] A Djibouti Corridor Authority was for instance set-up to oversee the implementation of the Djibouti Corridor which links Djibouti, South Sudan, Sudan and Ethiopia.[138] As regards energy, the regional Association of Energy Regulators for Eastern and Southern Africa (RAERESA) was set up in 2009 to streamline cooperation efforts towards sustainable energy development. The current projects are targeted at hydro-electric, geothermal and wind energy, including various proposed regional interconnection projects.[139] The COMESA Infrastructure Fund was set up to raise capital to aid the funding of these proposed projects and is reported to currently have a capitalisation of around USD 22 million.[140] There are however no concrete timelines for the finalisation of the various projects.

Regarding ICT, an association of ICT regulators in the COMESA region (ARICEA) was formed in 2003. One of its objectives is to coordinate cross-border ICT regulatory issues.[141] To this end an ICT Policy and Model Bill was approved as well as various regulatory guidelines touching on for instance interconnection, satellite and wire services, licensing, cyber security being concluded.[142] The status of the expansion and modernisation

136 See for instance COMESA, 'COMESA Region Key Economic Infrastructure Projects' (2013) <https://europa.eu/capacity4dev/file/16076/download?token=46F3PgO7> accessed 16 July 2019 (COMESA Infrastructure Report).

137 COMESA Infrastructure Report para 4.1.

138 Japan International Cooperation Agency, The Data Collection Survey for Djibouti Corridor: Final Report <http://open_jicareport.jica.go.jp/pdf/12302642_01.pdf> accessed 22 August 2019.

139 COMESA Infrastructure Report paras 3.2 and 4.2; See also Tinashe Mushakavanhu, 'Kenya is building Africa's biggest wind energy farm to generate a fifth of its power, Quartz Africa' (2015) <http://qz.com/444936/kenya-is-building-africas-biggest-wind-energy-farm-to-generate-a-fifth-of-its-power/> accessed 16 July 2019.

140 COMESA Infrastructure Report para 5; See also IPAN, 'COMESA Infrastructure kitty hits $22 million' (2015) <http://www.ipan.co.za/?p=314> accessed 16 July 2019.

141 See ARICEA Constitution <https://ariceaweb.org/index.php?option=com_content&view=article&id=4&Itemid=13> accessed 16 July 2019.

142 COMESA, 'Report of the 8th Annual General Meeting of Regulators of Information and Communication for Eastern and Southern Africa (ARICEA)' (2012), 22

of actual regional ICT infrastructure is however uncertain. Various ICT projects had been conceptualised under the ambit of a regional telecommunications project (COMTEL Project) seeking to for example increase fibre-optic linkages, but the funding remains a major hindrance to their implementation.[143] ARICEA also reports facing challenges in attracting private sector participation in its programs.[144]

All these factors point to a significant NTB concern, not to mention a number of lingering tariff issues. These challenges aside, reports point to a slow but somewhat steady achievement of some integration objectives. The operationalisation of the Regional Payment and Settlement System (REPSS) for instance will go a long way in cutting down financial and transaction costs in the region once all the Member States commit to participate in it.[145] As regards actual trade, reports indicate that intra-COMESA trade increased from USD 19.2 billion in 2013 to USD 22 billion in 2014, with a likelihood of seeing further increases once all Member States participate in the FTA.[146]

2.3.2.2 EAC

The EAC Member States are Kenya, Uganda, Tanzania, Rwanda, Burundi and South Sudan. South Sudan was admitted to the EAC in February 2016. With the exception of Tanzania and South Sudan, all the other Member States are also part of COMESA. The EAC was established with the entering into force of the Treaty for the Establishment of the East African Community (EAC Treaty) in the year 2000.[147] The main objective

---

<https://ariceaweb.org/attachments/article/18/8th%20ARICEA%20AGM%20final%20report%20with%20annexes%20(2).pdf> accessed 16 July 2019.

143 COMESA Infrastructure Report para 6.3. Very little information exists about the COMTEL Project with some previous reports indicating that most Member States chose to pursue their own ICT development objectives

144 ARICEA Report (2012) 4.

145 See COMESA's Regional Payment and Settlement System (REPSS) Goes Live <https://www.bou.or.ug/bou/media/statements/COMESA_REPSS.html> accessed 16 July 2019.

146 COMESA 18th Summit Communiqué (2015) 8.

147 See History of the EAC <https://www.eac.int/eac-history> accessed 16 July 2019, The EAC had however previously been in place with a customs union between Kenya, Uganda and the then Tanganyika (now Tanzania) in the 1920 as well an earlier EAC which was dissolved in 1977. Subsequent efforts to reintegrate the three states led to the reestablishment of the EAC.

of the EAC is the development of policies and programmes to foster cooperation among the Member States in political, economic, social and cultural fields, research and technology, defence, security and legal and judicial affairs.[148]

The EAC has a four-stage integration plan; the establishment of a Customs Union, a Common Market, a Monetary Union and eventually a Political Federation.[149] The first three stages are similar to COMESA and SADC objectives. The objective of a Political Federation however makes the EAC the most ambitious REC in Africa. The EAC Treaty neither defines what the Political Federation entails nor elaborates further on specific steps for its achievement. A committee set up in 2004 to oversee the fast-tracking of the East African Federation specified that it would entail the drafting of a Federal Constitution, creation of the office of a Federal President and the eventual establishment of a Federal Government.[150] It is therefore presumed that the individual Member States would evolve into the constituent states. Two institutions that have been in place since 2001 and that are regarded as building blocks of the political federation are the East African Court of Justice and the East African Legislative Assembly. The committee's recommendation was for an integration approach that allows for the overlapping of the four stages so that parallel activities can take place to enable an expedited establishment of the Political Federation.[151] The proposed timelines for the political federation have however proven to have been too ambitious.

In terms of economic integration however, the EAC is lauded as having made the most significant strides among the eight RECs in Africa.[152] Of the three Tripartite FTA RECs, the EAC Customs Union was the first to be established. It should however be noted that unlike SADC and COMESA that included a FTA as a transition phase to a Customs Union, the first stage for the EAC was the establishment of a Customs Union. Its establishment was therefore pivotal to the setting into motion of the integration objectives. The Customs Union Protocol was concluded in 2004 with the

148 EAC Treaty art 5(1).

149 EAC Treaty art 5(2).

150 EAC Secretariat, 'Report of the Committee on Fast Tracking East African Federation' (2004) <http://repository.eac.int/handle/11671/1966> accessed 16 July 2019 (EAC Secretariat Committee Report).

151 EAC Secretariat Committee Report (2004) para. 5.3.

152 AfDB, 'African Development Report 2014: Regional Integration for Inclusive Growth' (2014), 11 <http://www.afdb.org/fileadmin/uploads/afdb/Documents/Publications/ADR14_ENGLISH_web.pdf> accessed 16 July 2019.

aim of inter alia eliminating tariffs on imports from the Member States, elimination of NTBs and the establishment of a CET for third countries. Rwanda and Burundi joined the customs union in 2008.[153] All internal tariffs are to date reported to have been eliminated.[154]

A three-band CET similar to the COMESA CET was also established, broadly set at 0% for meritorious goods, raw materials and capital goods, 10% for intermediate goods and 25% for consumer goods with a few products classified as sensitive goods going above the 25% rate.[155] The CET rates are already fully operational with the most recent amendments on various qualifying goods having come into effect at the beginning of July 2018.[156] The Member States have in addition established a Single Customs Territory (SCT) which commenced at the beginning of 2014 and is in the process of implementation.[157] The main import of the SCT is to allow the assessment and collection of tax revenues at the first point of entry of imports thus facilitating the faster movement of the goods within the territory.[158]

---

153 See EAC, Customs <https://www.eac.int/security/index.php?option=com_content&id=29:eac-portal> accessed 16 July 2019.

154 Ibid, The elimination had however been gradual in respect of various goods from Kenya to Uganda and Tanzania to enable their producers to adjust to the increased competition from the Kenyan imports. See also Evarist Mugisa et al, 'An Evaluation of the Implementation and Impact of the East African Community Customs Union' (2009), 13 <https://www.academia.edu/27637527/An_Evaluation_of_the_Implementation_and_Impact_of_the_East_African_Community_Customs_Union> accessed 16 July 2019.

155 Mugisa et al (2009) 8.

156 EAC Gazette Notice No. 8 of 2018 <https://www.eac.int/documents/category/gazette> accessed 16 July 2019; Ernst and Young, 'The East African Community amends customs duties and common external tariffs' (2018) <https://www.ey.com/Publication/vwLUAssets/The_East_African_Community_amends_customs_duties_and_common_external_tariffs/$FILE/2018G_010349-18Gbl_Indirect_East%20African%20Community%20amends%20customs%20duties%20and%20external%20tariffs.pdf> accessed 16 July 2019.

157 EALA, 'Report of On-Spot Assessment on the EAC Single Customs Territory' (2014) <http://www.eala.org/documents/view/on-spot-assessment-of-the-eac-single-customs-territory-sct> accessed 16 July 2019 (EALA Report).

158 EALA Report (2014) 1; EAC Secretariat, 'Annual Progress Report of the Council to the Summit of EAC Heads of State for the period December 2013 to November 2014' (2015) <http://www.eac.int/index.php?option=com_content&view=article&id=1807:annual-progress-report-of-the-council-to-the-16th-ordinary-heads-of-state-summit-fo

A report published by the EAC Secretariat in December 2014 revealed that a number of NTBs have been resolved.[159] A time-bound program has additionally been put in place for the elimination of various remaining unresolved NTBs. Some of the NTBs identified for elimination include: government sanctioned or tolerated practices such as export subsidies and government monopolies; restrictive customs and administrative entry procedures such as arbitrary customs classifications and surcharges; technical barriers such as non-harmonised standards and charges such as special duties and administrative fees. There are also concerns raised over issues such as arbitrariness, discrimination and costly procedures.[160] The main arguments made to justify these NTBs centre around safeguards on health, security, safety and revenue loss and the protection of local industries and consumers.[161]

The EAC Common Market Protocol entered into force in July 2010 and broadly provides for the freedom of movement of labour, goods, services and capital.[162] The protocol is regarded as being quite ambitious and its implementation wanting.[163] The Member States are reported as all having restrictions that affect inward investments originating from within the EAC, with new restrictions on capital movement being introduced contrary to the requirements under the Protocol.[164] It is also noted that key laws, principally sectoral, within the Member States have several measures that restrict the movement of services. Most of these measures favour the local service providers over service providers from the other Member States

---

r-the-period-december-2013-november-2014-&catid=146:press-releases&Itemid=194> accessed 14 September 2015.

159 EAC Secretariat, 'Status of Elimination of Non-Tariff Barriers in the East African Community' (2014) <http://repository.eac.int/bitstream/handle/11671/416/NTBs%20Vol%207%20-%20compressed.pdf?sequence=1&isAllowed=y> accessed 16 July 2019 (NTB Report).

160 NTB Report (2014) 25.

161 NTB Report (2014) 20.

162 EAC Common Market: Overview <https://www.eac.int/common-market> accessed 16 July 2019.

163 World Bank and EAC Secretariat, 'East African Common Market Scorecard 2014: Tracking EAC compliance in the movement of Capital, Services and Goods' (2014) <http://documents.worldbank.org/curated/en/799871468194049251/Main-report> accessed 16 July 2019 (EAC Common Market Scorecard).

164 EAC Common Market Scorecard (2014) 3; Kenya's laws reportedly make it easier to move capital while Tanzania's and Burundi's are the most restrictive.

contrary to the national treatment principle. The other measures favour service providers from outside the EAC. [165]

In respect of the Monetary Union, a Committee consisting of the Central Bank Governors of the Member States reported that some progress had already been made in the harmonisation of banking regulations, payment systems and monetary and exchange rate policy.[166] Other priority areas identified by the Committee include harmonisation of ICT aspects, integration of the payment systems and harmonisation of reporting standards of which work is reported to be in progress.[167] The Monetary Union Protocol was signed in 2013 and has thus far been ratified by all the five Member States.[168] The next steps include the creation of a Monetary Institute and a Statistics Bureau as well as one tasked with surveillance, compliance and enforcement.[169]

The EAC is reported to be the most economically uniform REC, with economic disparities in terms of fiscal policy, inflation, reserves and revenue to expenditure recording significant reductions since 2000.[170] The value of intra-EAC trade has also seen significant improvement with the period between 2008 and 2013 indicating a 84% increase from USD 3,148.7 million in 2008 to USD 5,805.6 million in 2013.[171]

---

165 EAC Common Market Scorecard (2014) 3-4.

166 UNECA, 'Towards a Common Currency in the East African Community (EAC) Issues, Challenges and Prospects' (2012) <https://www.uneca.org/sites/default/files/PublicationFiles/towards_a_common_currency_in_the_eac-2012.pdf> accessed 16 July 2019 (UNECA Report).

167 UNECA Report (2012) 9-10, 47-48.

168 Christabel Ligami, 'Uganda Ratifies the Monetary Union' (The East African, 7 February 2015) <http://www.theeastafrican.co.ke/news/Uganda-ratifies-the-monetary-union/-/2558/2616360/-/g05itfz/-/index.html> accessed 16 July 2019.

169 EAC Annual Progress Report (2015) 2; Ligami (2015).

170 Mo Ibrahim Foundation, 'Regional Integration: Uniting to Compete' (2014) <http://static.moibrahimfoundation.org/downloads/publications/2014/2014-facts-&-figures-regional-integration-uniting-to-compete.pdf> accessed 16 July 2019 (Mo Ibrahim Foundation Report).

171 EAC Secretariat, 'East African Community Trade Report' (2013), 32 <https://www.eac.int/documents/category/trade-investment-reports> accessed 16 July 2019.

2.3.2.3 SADC

The SADC Treaty[172] was signed in August of 1992 and currently brings together 15 Member States.[173] Eight of the Member States are also part of COMESA and one the EAC. The main Treaty objectives are similar to those of the EAC and COMESA, seeking to achieve economic development, peace and security, and growth, alleviate poverty and enhance the standard and quality of life.[174] A number of Protocols have to date been concluded to give effect to the SADC Treaty objectives including those on trade, trade in services, energy, finance and investment and movement of persons. The SADC integration plan is similar to that of COMESA, involving a transition from a FTA, a Customs Union, a Common Market and finally to a Monetary Union with the eventual adoption of a single currency.

A Regional Indicative Strategic Development Plan was prepared and signed by the Member States to provide a roadmap for the achievement of the various SADC objectives.[175] The timeframes that the Member States set were for the FTA to be formed by 2008, the Customs Union by 2010, the Common Market by 2015, the Monetary Union by 2016 and the Single Currency by 2018.[176]

One of the core aims of the Protocol on Trade which entered into force in 2001 was for the establishment of the FTA.[177] 13 of the 15 Member States are currently party to the FTA with the Democratic Republic of

---

172 Treaty of the Southern African Development Community, 32 ILM 116.

173 The Member States are: Angola, Botswana, DR Congo, Lesotho, Madagascar, Malawi, Mauritius, Mozambique, Namibia, Seychelles, South Africa, Swaziland, Tanzania, Zambia and Zimbabwe.

174 SADC Treaty art 5; see also SADC Objectives <http://www.sadc.int/about-sadc/overview/sadc-objectiv/> accessed 12 February 2017.

175 SADC, 'Regional Indicative Strategic Development Plan (RISDP)' (2001) <http://www.sadc.int/files/5713/5292/8372/Regional_Indicative_Strategic_Development_Plan.pdf> accessed 14 October 2018. A revised RISDP was finalised in 2015 to take into account the reallocation of the existing resources towards the achievement of the most important objectives within the 2015-2020 period. It however does not deviate from the scope and purpose of the original RISDP (see 35th SADC Summit Report, p. 18).

176 See SADC Integration Milestones <http://www.sadc.int/about-sadc/integration-milestones/> accessed 22 August 2019.

177 Protocol on Trade in the SADC Region (1996), art 2 <http://www.sadc.int/files/4613/5292/8370/Protocol_on_Trade1996.pdf> accessed 22 August 2019.

Congo and Angola reportedly set to join.[178] The minimum conditions for the establishment of the FTA were achieved in 2008 when 85% of intra-SADC trade was at zero duty following a tariff phase-down initiative that commenced in 2001. Maximum trade liberalisation was reportedly being achieved in 2012 following the phasing-down of tariffs on sensitive products.[179] There are however various derogations subsequent to 2012 that indicate that maximum liberalisation is in reality yet to be achieved. Mozambique, Malawi, Zimbabwe, and Tanzania for instance require more time to achieve various tariff commitments. The SADC Secretariat indeed highlights that the main action points include the outstanding tariff phase-down commitments, NTBs, problems relating to the RoO, customs and trade facilitation issues as well as liberalisation of trade in services as required under the Protocol on Trade in Services.[180]

The transition from the FTA to the Customs Union did not proceed according to the agreed timeframe and is proving to be quite a challenge for the Member States. This in turn means delayed implementation of the Common Market and the Monetary Union.[181] The biggest challenge identified in this regard is the establishment of the CET which requires the convergence of the various Member State tariff policies. It is notable however that five of the Member States (Botswana, Lesotho, Namibia, South Africa and Swaziland) are already part of a Southern African Customs Union (SACU), an institution separate from and predating the SADC[182], thus providing additional harmonisation and integration challenges.

One positive step towards the achievement of monetary integration was the launching of the SADC Integrated Regional Electronic Settlement System (SIRESS) which to date includes 11 Member States. The SIRESS has had a positive impact in ensuring secure and harmonised settlement

---

178 Seychelles acceded to the FTA in May 2015, See <http://www.seychellestradeportal.gov.sc/trade-agreements> accessed 22 August 2019.

179 See <http://www.sadc.int/about-sadc/integration-milestones/free-trade-area/> accessed 22 August 2019.

180 SADC Secretariat, '35th Summit of SADC Heads of State and Government' (2015) <http://www.sadc.int/news-events/news/35th-sadc-summit-brochure/> accessed 22 August 2019 (35th SADC Summit Report); Services are recognised as generating 57% of the regions GDP. The priority sectors for the liberalisation of trade in services are communication, construction, energy, finance, tourism and transport.

181 See <http://www.sadc.int/about-sadc/integration-milestones/customs-union/> accessed 22 August 2019.

182 See <https://www.tralac.org/images/docs/12054/introduction-to-siress-sabf-presentation-to-sadc-industrialisation-wekk-2017.pdf> accessed 22 August 2019.

of cross-border payments. The milestone for a single currency has however not been achieved.[183]

SADC however indicates some positive figures in terms of intra-regional trade. SADC's intra-regional trade records the most development amongst the RECs in Africa, accounting for 44% of Africa's intra-regional trade as of 2011.[184] Looking at the international picture however, intra-regional trade still has a long way to go. The highest percentage of SADC trade is still with the Asia Pacific Economic Cooperation (APEC) and the European Union (EU).[185]

2.3.2.4 The overlaps challenge

As already noted, one of the core challenges faced by the three RECs is the fact that most of the participating countries belong to more than one REC. This has resulted in instances of functional overlaps and duplication of integration efforts. One particular aspect of the overlaps concern that touches on the Tripartite FTA is the fact that COMESA, EAC and SACU already have Customs Unions in place, with the SADC Customs Union still in the pipeline. Member States belonging to both EAC and COMESA for instance already have the challenge of having to apply two conflicting CETs.

Belonging to more than one FTA may be beneficial in terms of integrating into the Tripartite FTA owing to the fact that measures to remove tariffs and NTBs would already be in place. However, belonging to a Customs Union entails the adoption of a CET which is incompatible with the Tripartite FTA because it would mean putting up a tariff barrier in respect of goods coming from FTA states that are not part of the Customs Union and are thus regarded as third countries.

The concern over various issues arising from the membership overlaps is one of the key issues that led to the formation of the EAC-COMESA-SADC Tripartite (The Tripartite).

183 35th SADC Summit Report 56.

184 Mo Ibrahim Foundation Report (2014) 19.

185 See <http://www.sadc.int/about-sadc/overview/sadc-facts-figures/> accessed 22 August 2019.

2.3.3 The EAC-COMESA-SADC Tripartite

2.3.3.1 Background

The Tripartite was established in 2005 in order to look into ways in which the three RECs could coordinate and harmonise their efforts towards regional integration, especially in the areas of trade, customs, free movement of people and infrastructure development.[186]

The first Tripartite Summit was held in October 2008 bringing together the Heads of State and Government of COMESA, EAC and SADC. The main objective was to chart out how the three RECs can move towards deeper cooperation in their efforts towards trade and economic liberalisation, including joint programmes targeting free movement of persons and infrastructure development.[187] Indeed, as already noted before, the key challenge highlighted at the first Summit was that of overlapping memberships of countries that are already part of a Customs Union and that are negotiating terms for joining an alternative Customs Union or those that are negotiating terms of two separate Customs Unions.[188] The Tripartite was therefore recognised as the best avenue to address this concern.

The need for a road map for establishing the Tripartite FTA was also highlighted progress made towards inter alia harmonising RoO, establishment of one-stop border posts, and the elimination of NTBs on the Tripartite level was also noted.[189] One of the early achievements of the Tripartite has been the successful implementation of a web-based scheme for reporting, tracking and elimination of NTBs that has enabled stakeholders to efficiently report NTBs and monitor the progress in their resolution.[190]

One of the core recommendations in the first Summit was for the establishment of the Tripartite FTA within a five-year period as well as for the adoption of a roadmap for its achievement. It was also recommended that a Memorandum of Understanding between the three RECs be

---

186 See COMESA-EAC-SADC Tripartite <https://www.eac.int/tripartite> accessed 16 July 2019.

187 COMESA, EAC and SADC, 'First COMESA-EAC-SADC Tripartite Summit Report' (2008), para 9 <http://repository.eac.int/handle/11671/1633> accessed 16 July 2019 (1st Tripartite Summit Report).

188 1st Tripartite Summit Report (2008) para 4.

189 1st Tripartite Summit Report (2008) para 23.

190 See Non-Tariff Barriers: Reporting, Monitoring and Eliminating Mechanism <http://www.tradebarriers.org/about> accessed 16 July 2019.

concluded, setting out the broad cooperation objectives as well as the legal and institutional framework for the Tripartite process and a coordination mechanism.[191] The Memorandum of Understanding between the three RECs came into force much later in January 2011.

The draft agreement including its annexes was conveyed to the Member States of the three RECs for review and proposals in December 2009.[192] The revised version was made available in 2010 for purposes of deliberation at the second Summit.[193]

The second Summit was held in June 2011. A three-pillar development approach was adopted at this Summit: market integration, infrastructure development, and industrial development. Three key milestones towards the Tripartite FTA were also achieved at this Summit; a declaration launching the negotiations for the establishment of the COMESA-EAC-SADC Tripartite FTA was signed and the roadmap for the establishment of the Tripartite FTA and the Tripartite FTA negotiating principles, processes, and institutional framework were adopted.[194]

The Tripartite FTA promises a market comprising 632 million people (57% of Africa's population) with a total Gross Domestic Product (GDP) of USD 1.3 trillion as at 2014 which was roughly 58% of Africa's GDP.[195] Africa's GDP figures for the past few years have generally displayed a positive trend, with real GDP growth averaging 5% a year since the turn of the century.[196]

---

191 1st tripartite Summit Report para 44 and 104.

192 Aileen Mallya, 'COMESA-EAC-SADC Tripartite Framework: State of Play' (2011), 3-5 <https://www.researchgate.net/publication/271524706_COMESA-EAC-SADC_Tripartite_framework_state_of_play> accessed 16 July 2019.

193 Draft agreement establishing the COMESA, EAC and SADC Tripartite Free Trade Area (2010) <http://www.tralac.org/wp-content/blogs.dir/12/files/2011/uploads/Draft_Tripartite_FTA_Agreement_Revised_Dec_2010.pdf> accessed 20 July 2018.

194 COMESA, EAC and SADC, 'Communiqué of the Second COMESA-EAC-SADC Tripartite Summit' (2011), 1 <http://repository.eac.int:8080/handle/11671/550> accessed 16 July 2019.

195 COMESA, EAC and SADC, 'Communiqué of the Third COMESA-EAC-SADC Tripartite Summit' (2015) <http://www.sadc.int/files/5914/3401/0196/Communiqu_of_the_3rd_COMESA_EAC_SADC_Tripartite_Summit.pdf> accessed 23 April 2018.

196 AFDB, 'Tracking Africa's Progress in Figures' (2014), 20 <http://www.afdb.org/en/knowledge/publications/tracking-africa%E2%80%99s-progress-in-figures/> accessed 16 July 2019; see also AfDB et al, 'Africa Economic Outlook 2015: Regional Development and Spatial Inclusion' (2015), 9

Trade figures likewise reflect progressive improvement. The value of exports outside of Africa has experienced encouraging growth; from a figure of USD 148 billion in 2000 to USD 657 billion in 2012, with the 2014 figure of USD 552 billion indicating some decline from the 2012 figures.[197]

The negotiations as set out in the negotiating principles are to be conducted in two phases. Phase one negotiations being in respect of trade in goods aspects i.e. tariff liberalisation, RoO, dispute resolution, customs procedures and simplification of customs documentation, transit procedures, NTBs, trade remedies, technical barriers to trade and sanitary and phytosanitary measures. It was also agreed that negotiations on movement of business persons were also to be part of the phase one negotiations but as a parallel and separate track. Phase two negotiations are in respect of trade in services, cooperation in trade and development, competition policy, intellectual property (IP) rights and cross border investment. The Agreement was to be finalised once the phase one negotiations were concluded.[198] According to the roadmap, the phase two negotiations would be part of a built-in agenda once the Agreement was finalised.

The Tripartite FTA was finally launched on the 10th of June 2015 at the third Tripartite Summit in Cairo.[199] The Agreement was opened for signing and a post-signature implementation plan was adopted. It was also directed that the outstanding issues from the phase one negotiations be completed and that negotiations on the phase two be commenced.

2.3.3.2 The Tripartite FTA Agreement

The Agreement formalises the commitment to establish the FTA and gives a legal basis and framework for the participating countries to implement

---

<http://www.africaneconomicoutlook.org/fileadmin/uploads/aeo/2015/PDF_Chapters/Overview_AEO2015_EN-web.pdf> accessed 16 July 2019.

197 AfDB Tracking Africa's Progress (2014) 42; see also AfDB et al Africa Economic Outlook (2015) 6; The trade data can also be found on the International Trade Centre (ITC) website <http://www.trademap.org/Country_SelProduct_TS.aspx> accessed 16 July 2019.

198 See Guidelines for Negotiating the Tripartite Free Trade Area among the Member/Partner States of COMESA, EAC and SADC (2011), para 2 <http://www.tralac.org/images/docs/5284/tfta-negotiating-principles-12062011.pdf> accessed 16 July 2019; see also Roadmap for Establishing the Tripartite FTA. <http://www.trademarksa.org/sites/default/files/publications/Roadmap%20for%20TFTA%20Negotiation%20-%2012.06.2011.pdf> accessed 16 July 2019.

199 Third Tripartite Summit Communiqué 1.

the objectives of the Tripartite. The intention as reflected in the preamble to the Agreement is for the Tripartite FTA to evolve into a single Customs Union.[200]

The specific objectives are stated to be the progressive elimination of tariff and non-tariff barriers, the liberation of trade in services, cooperation on customs and trade-related areas, implementation of trade facilitation measures as well as putting in place the institutional framework for implementing and administering the Tripartite FTA.[201]

The principles governing the Agreement include variable geometry, flexibility and special and differential treatment, transparency, building on the *acquis*, single undertaking with regard to the various phases of the Agreement, Most Favoured Nation Treatment (MFN), National Treatment, reciprocity, substantial liberalisation, and consensus-based decision making.[202]

Participating countries may conclude preferential trade agreements with third countries provided that reciprocity is accorded to other participating countries. One aspect however that could affect the unity of the Tripartite FTA is the fact that the Agreement allows participating countries to enter into preferential agreements among themselves. Although such agreements are required to be on MFN basis and in accordance with the objectives of the Agreement, sanctioning such multiplicity within the FTA may ultimately complicate the integration into a single FTA which is an overarching objective of the Agreement.[203] It is not clear from the Agreement what nature of preferential agreements among the participating countries is contemplated. Unless some exceptional circumstances are provided for, it ultimately makes no sense from the perspective of the Tripartite FTA territory for participating countries to conclude among themselves preferential agreements consisting only of aspects that are within the scope of the Agreement. Such agreements would not be 'preferential' in respect of the excluded participating countries because of reciprocity and non-discrimination. One can however picture a situation where derogations are

---

200 Agreement Establishing a Tripartite Free Trade Area among The Common Market For Eastern And Southern Africa, The East African Community And The Southern African Development Community, preamble, <https://www.tralac.org/news/article/7646-signed-agreement-establishing-a-tripartite-free-trade-area-among-comesa-the-eac-and-sadc.html> accessed 16 July 2019 (The Tripartite Agreement).

201 The Tripartite Agreement art 5.

202 The Tripartite Agreement art 6.

203 The Tripartite Agreement part II.

made in the Agreement in accordance with the special and differential treatment principle. This could be for instance to facilitate preferential agreements aimed at assisting the weaker countries to integrate better into the Tripartite FTA.

The principles of Variable Geometry and flexibility, special and differential treatment are specifically geared towards addressing the different levels of development among the participating countries.[204] The Agreement defines variable geometry as 'the principle of flexibility which allows for progression in cooperation amongst members in a larger integration scheme in a variety of areas and at different speeds'.[205] This is however having due regard to the principle of building on the *acquis*, by which the progress already achieved among the three RECs is meant to be built upon and consolidated.[206]

Some commentators have expressed the concern that the principle of *acquis* would result in an effort for additional and separate trade arrangements.[207] The reasoning is that if the Agreement allows the RECs to maintain preferential terms between their Member States, then participating countries that are not party to such arrangements would have to negotiate their own terms on the basis of the Agreement.[208] This would therefore be contrary to the idea of an all-inclusive system as envisioned in the creation of the Tripartite, in addition to exacerbating rather than resolving the overlaps challenge.

---

204 The Tripartite Agreement art 6; The differences in economic development among the participating countries is also highlighted in the preamble to the Agreement.

205 The Tripartite Agreement art 1.

206 The Agreement does not define the term *acquis*. The term had however been explained in context earlier on in the negotiating principles for the Tripartite FTA. Building on the acquis of the existing REC FTAs in terms of consolidating tariff liberalisation in each REC FTA was one of the overarching principles guiding the negotiations. See Guidelines for Negotiating the Tripartite Free Trade Area among the Member/Partner States of COMESA, EAC and SADC (2011).

207 Gerhard Erasmus, 'The Agreement preceding the Agreement: how the negotiating principles decided the Tripartite FTA game plan', cap 2 in Hartzenberg T et al (eds) *Cape to Cairo: Exploring the Tripartite FTA agenda* (tralac 2013) <http://www.tralac.org/publications/article/5548-cape-to-cairo-exploring-the-tripartite-fta-agenda.html> accessed 16 July 2019.

208 Ionel Zamfir, 'The Tripartite Free Trade Area project Integration in southern and eastern Africa' (2015), 6-7 <http://www.europarl.europa.eu/RegData/etudes/BRIE/2015/551308/EPRS_BRI(2015)551308_EN.pdf> accessed 16 July 2019.

From a different perspective however, it was expressed in the Tripartite Trade Negotiations Forum that Member States that belong to an already existing FTA would not need to renegotiate tariff terms between them. They would simply have to consolidate their liberalisation levels to the agreed-upon Tripartite FTA standard, with the eventual result being that all participating countries will be harmonised to the Tripartite FTA standard.[209] Such an application of the principle of building on the *acquis* suggests that the intention is to make it easier to converge towards the Tripartite FTA. Additionally, article 30(7) of the Agreement provides, 'In the event of inconsistency or a conflict between this Agreement and the treaties and instruments of COMESA, EAC and SADC, this Agreement shall prevail to the extent of the inconsistency or conflict.' It may therefore be argued that the overriding objectives of the Agreement, inter alia the creation of a single FTA, take precedence and the principle of *acquis* would be applicable to the extent that it does not interfere with this objective. One may additionally question the validity of any preferential agreements in light of the reciprocity and non-discrimination principles.

The scope of the Agreement covers trade in goods and services as well as other trade-related matters i.e. competition policy, cross-border investment, trade and development, and IP rights.[210] The core areas of harmonisation and cooperation are set out in a more or less general manner with the intention being that the member countries will conclude protocols and annexes to the Agreement to give full effect to its provisions.

Liberalisation of trade in goods is addressed in Part Three of the Agreement. Finalisation of the trade in goods aspects as noted in the roadmap was the main undertaking on which the conclusion of the Agreement was to be based. Trade in goods is in fact the backbone of the Agreement. It is however noted in the Agreement that there are outstanding aspects of the phase one negotiation in respect of elimination of customs duties, trade remedies and RoO that the participating countries undertake to conclude as part of a built-in agenda.[211] The failure to come to an agreement on the core trade in goods aspects of the FTA especially on elimination of

209 Bridges Africa, 'Launch of African Tripartite FTA now set for June' (2015) <http://www.ictsd.org/bridges-news/bridges-africa/news/launch-of-african-tripartite-fta-now-set-for-june> accessed 16 July 2019.

210 The Tripartite Agreement art 3.

211 The Tripartite Agreement art 44.

customs duties and RoO prior to the adoption of the Agreement has led to its workability as a comprehensive instrument being questioned.[212]

Participating countries are required to desist from imposing new import duties or charges having equivalent effect except as stipulated in the Agreement.[213] This however only applies to goods that are subject to trade liberalisation. The criteria and conditions for goods that shall be eligible for preferential treatment have however not been finalised owing to outstanding issues on RoO. Based on the report of the Technical Working Group (TWG) on RoO, some of the outstanding aspects are rather fundamental to comprehensive RoO.[214] The RoO have indeed been one of the significant harmonisation challenges, especially since SADC RoO markedly differ from those of COMESA and EAC.[215]

The report indicates that there was lack of agreement between SACU Member States and the other Member States as to what criteria of origin should be adopted, specifically in the case of materials that do not originate from within the Tripartite FTA. The SACU Member States had expressed preference for the use of agreed common rules for the launch of a Partial Tripartite FTA, opting to leave out any determination based on value addition on non-originating materials. The other Member States preferred the use of agreed common rules as well as 35% value-added on the ex-factory cost as interim RoO of the Tripartite FTA.[216]

The Agreement further provides that duties are to be eliminated progressively in accordance with schedules on elimination of import duties, the negotiation of which is not complete.[217] The goal that has been set is

---

212 Gerhard Erasmus, 'The Tripartite Free Trade Agreement: Results of Phase One of the Negotiations' (2015), 8-9 <http://www.tralac.org/publications/article/7803-the-tripartite-free-trade-agreement-results-of-phase-one-of-the-negotiations.html> accessed 16 July 2019.

213 The Tripartite Agreement art 9(1) and (2).

214 COMESA, 'Report of the 9th Meeting of the Technical Working Group on Rules of Origin' (2015), 16-19 <http://www.comesa.int/index.php?option=com_content&view=article&id=1440> accessed 16 July 2019 (COMESA RoO Report).

215 Erasmus G (2015), p. 19.

216 COMESA RoO Report (2015) paras 12-17. The value addition criterion is in respect of (raw) materials that do not originate from within the FTA. The proposal therefore advocates for an added value that is not less than 35% of the ex-factory cost of the finished product in the case of non-originating materials. Common rules here refers to rules that are the same across the three RICs and for which it was agreed no further negotiations would need to be undertaken.

217 The Tripartite Agreement art 9(3).

for 100% tariff liberalisation under the Tripartite FTA. The benchmark for countries that are yet to fully liberalise their tariffs within their RECs or those in existing REC FTAs is at 60-85% upon entry into force of the Agreement. The Tripartite FTA negotiations are however built on consensus-based decision making. Various countries have submitted their tariff offers but not all tariff offers are ready, meaning negotiations are set to continue.[218] This essentially means that the Agreement as it currently is provides no definitive guidance as to how the participating countries should go about liberalising trade in goods. The section dealing with the liberalisation of trade in goods, which is a core aspect of the Agreement, is in effect not operable.

The participating countries should also eliminate and refrain from imposing NTBs as well as quantitative restrictions on trade on other participating countries. The Agreement however details exceptional circumstances in which quantitative restrictions can be applied.[219]

Participating countries undertake to cooperate in terms of customs and mutual administrative assistance in the implementation of the Agreement. They should also put in place measures to facilitate trade through standardisation of trade and customs documentation and information is also prioritised.[220]

Trade remedies are also subject to ongoing negotiations.[221] Interim measures were however adopted to facilitate the conclusion of the Agreement. Anti-dumping, countervailing and safeguard measures may be applied on the basis of the existing provisions of the RECs for Member States belonging to the same REC or on the basis of World Trade Organization (WTO) rules in respect of inter-REC issues.[222] The Agreement incorporates a built-in agenda by which guidelines on the implementation of the trade remedies are expected to be concluded. The core provisions on anti-dumping, countervailing and safeguard measures as well as preferential standards

218 Bridges Africa (2015); See also Erasmus (2015) 17.

219 The Tripartite Agreement art 11. The exceptions are those contained in Article XI.2 of GATT 1994, the WTO Agreement on Safeguards, Articles 17 and 18 of the Agreement which deal with anti-dumping, countervailing and safeguard measures and annex II of the Agreement which deals with trade remedies. The annex on trade remedies is however one of the areas in which outstanding issues still exist.

220 The Tripartite Agreement part IV.

221 The Tripartite Agreement art 44.

222 The Tripartite Agreement art 16 (1).

are however suspended pending the finalisation of the annex on trade remedies.[223]

The Agreement points to a heavy reliance on WTO rules on trade remedies which are regarded as difficult to implement, more so for many African countries. The inclusion of WTO rules rather than a *sui generis* trade remedies regime was at the insistence of Egypt and South Africa, which already have active domestic trade remedies regimes.[224] This is also reflected in their proposals in the course of the trade remedies negotiations. South Africa, Egypt, and Malawi for instance proposed the retention of a part incorporating the global safeguard measures under Article XIX of the General Agreement on Tariffs and Trade (GATT) 1994 as well as the WTO Agreement on Safeguards.[225] The EAC however proposed that this part be deleted. Egypt in addition expressed the desire for a system that would allow an affected country to proceed with an appropriate countervailing measure without prejudice to the fact that consultations with the allegedly subsidising country may be proceeding.[226]

The rights and obligations under the WTO agreements on technical barriers to trade (TBT) and sanitary and phytosanitary measures (SPS) are reaffirmed in Part Six of the Agreement. The provisions do not point to any outstanding aspects in this regard. The participating countries are also permitted to establish special economic zones to speed up development. Where the circumstances require, participating countries are allowed to adopt measures geared towards the protection of infant industries. An infant industry is defined as 'a new industry of national strategic importance that has not been in existence for more than five years, and that is experiencing high start-up costs and difficulties competing with like imports.'[227] The only outstanding aspect in this part of the Agreement is in respect of guidelines which are to be developed in respect of measures to alleviate severe balance of payment and external financial difficulties.

The Agreement also provides generally for cooperation in financial areas, trade policies and negotiations, research and statistics. The institutions charged with the implementation of the Tripartite FTA, including a dis-

223 The Tripartite Agreement art 16 (2) and (3).

224 Erasmus G (2015) 20; See also Ousseni Illy, 'Trade remedies in Africa: experiences, challenges and prospects' (2015) <http://www.ictsd.org/bridges-news/bridges-africa/news/trade-remedies-in-africa-experiences-challenges-and-prospects> accessed 16 July 2019.

225 The Tripartite Agreement Annex on Trade Remedies 2.

226 The Tripartite Agreement Annex on Trade Remedies 1-2.

227 The Tripartite Agreement art 24.

pute settlement body responsible for the administration of the dispute settlement are set out in Part Eight and Nine of the Agreement.

Defaulting countries may be subjected to sanctions as determined by the Tripartite Summit on recommendation of the Tripartite Council of Ministers. A participating country may withdraw from the Agreement subject to it discharging its existing obligations under the Agreement.

A two-year timeline from the entry into force of the Agreement has been put in place for the conclusion of a protocol on trade in services as well as on competition policy, cross-border investment, trade and development, and IP rights, which constitute phase two of the negotiation agenda.[228] Going by the negotiations during the drafting of the Agreement, it is expected that the protocol on IP rights will draw upon some of the WTO's Agreement on Trade-Related Aspects of Intellectual Property Rights (TRIPs) flexibilities. The annex on IP rights in the draft Agreement for instance had a provision encouraging participating countries to fully exploit the flexibilities contained in the Doha Declaration on TRIPs and public health to facilitate access to medicines.[229]

Another exclusion from the Agreement is in respect of the movement of business persons in spite of the fact that it was originally included as part of the phase one negotiation. As indicated before the plan was for negotiations on the movement of business persons to be part of phase one but as a parallel and separate track. It was eventually agreed that movement of business persons should not be included in the Agreement.[230] A separate agreement is now being negotiated under the aegis of the Tripartite Technical Committee on the movement of business persons.[231] Some of the provisions being considered include short-term and long-term temporary movement, identification of a business person, entry, stay, exit as well as a multi-entry multi-visa concept.[232]

---

228 The Tripartite Agreement art 45.

229 The Tripartite Agreement Annex on Intellectual Property Rights para 7, <http://www.tralac.org/images/Resources/Tripartite_FTA/TFTA%20Annex%2009%20IPR%20Revised%20Dec%202010.pdf> accessed 18 November 2018.

230 See generally COMESA, EAC and SADC, 'Report of 3rd TTC-MBP, Tripartite Agreement on Movement of Business Persons' (2014) <https://tis.sadc.int/files/8614/1640/5306/Draft_Tripartite_Agreement_on_Business_Persons.pdf> accessed 18 November 2018 (MBP Report).

231 MBP Report (2014); See also COMESA, 'E-COMESA Newsletter' (12 November 2014) <http://www.comesa.int/attachments/article/1379/e-comesa_newsletter_435.pdf> accessed 12 October 2018.

232 MBP Report (2014).

The concept of a built-in agenda from the WTO perspective is in respect of continuing review or further negotiation of specific aspects in already binding agreements.[233] Its use in the Agreement is however different from this. The built-in agenda was initially targeted for phase two negotiations. It was envisioned that they would commence after the trade in goods negotiations had been concluded and the Agreement finalised. The current built-in agenda is now in respect of outstanding phase one aspects as well as the phase two negotiations. As already noted, the outstanding phase one aspects include core trade in goods issues which bring to question whether the Agreement in its current state is binding.[234]

One questions how this concept of a built-in agenda can be reconciled with the principle of a single undertaking as used in Article 6 of the Agreement. The principle of single undertaking is not defined in the Agreement. According to the WTO, a single undertaking would mean that virtually every item of the negotiation is part of a whole and indivisible package and cannot be agreed separately. "Nothing is agreed until everything is agreed".[235] There is however a derogation from this principle under the Doha Ministerial Declaration. Article 47 of the Ministerial Declaration provides that "agreements that are reached at an early stage may be implemented on a provisional or a definitive basis". There is no such derogation under the Tripartite Agreement. The principle of single undertaking as it was used in the negotiating framework had been specifically focused on trade in goods. The Agreement however provides that it is with regard to the various phases of the Agreement. If we go by the WTO definition of a single undertaking, one may very well argue that there is no agreement. Even if we assume that the derogation applies there is no conclusive trade in goods agreement that can be said to have been reached at an early stage.

The overall feeling one gets is that the Agreement was rushed in order to have it ready within an already extended timeline. The entry into force of the Agreement requires 14 ratifications. Participation by accession is also provided for.[236] So far 22 countries have signed the Agreement[237]. Egypt,

233 See WTO: Built-in Agenda: Work set out in existing agreements, <https://www.wto.org/english/thewto_e/minist_e/min99_e/english/about_e/04agen_e.htm> accessed 16 July 2019.

234 See also Erasmus (2015) 14.

235 See WTO: How the negotiations are organised, <https://www.wto.org/english/tratop_e/dda_e/work_organi_e.htm> accessed 16 July 2019.

236 The Tripartite Agreement art 40 & 41.

237 Erasmus (2015) 8.

Kenya, Uganda, Botswana, Burundi, Namibia, Rwanda, Eswatini, Zambia and South Africa have deposited their instruments of ratification.[238]

One big concern here is that the three RECs will continue to pursue their own individual integration agenda hence further complicating the harmonisation and integration into a single FTA. The need for renegotiation of customs aspects by the countries that are already in Customs Unions is expected to further delay the entry into force of the Agreement.

The anticipation had been that the Agreement would be a game changer in view of some of the challenges faced by the three RECs. However, a lot of work still needs to be done before it can be considered to be a game changer. What is critical is for all the 26 countries to participate in the FTA. Insufficient participation would mean an additional REC hence defeating the whole purpose of the Tripartite FTA. Given the difficulties the three RECs have experienced in liberalising their markets a lot of political goodwill and commitment is needed in order to make the Tripartite FTA a reality in the foreseeable future.

2.3.4 The Continental Free Trade Area

The promise of the Continental Free Trade Area (CTFA) is a market that brings together 1 billion people with a combined GDP of around USD 3.4 trillion. The objectives of the CFTA include: the creation of a single continent-wide market for goods and services, expanding intra-African trade, enhancing competitiveness through scale production, continental market access and better resource allocation. The CFTA also seeks to address the multiple and overlapping REC memberships.[239] It is however not clear how the potential overlaps between the CFTA and the Tripartite FTA will be addressed or whether they will create an additional layer of overlaps. The provisions of both Agreements are very similar as are the challenges to be faced as addressed above. The existence of the two Agreements thus appears to exacerbate and add a layer to rather than resolve the challenge of overlaps.

---

238 See COMESA News, 'New Deadline set for Ratification of Tripartite Free Trade Area' (2021) <https://www.comesa.int/new-deadline-set-for-ratification-of-tripartite-free-trade-area/> accessed 4 May 2021.

239 See African Union, CFTA: Continental Free Trade Area <https://au.int/en/ti/cfta/about> accessed 16 July 2019.

So far 54 countries have signed onto the CFTA Agreement, majority of which are also signatories to the Tripartite FTA Agreement. 22 ratifications are required for the agreement to enter into force. On 29 April 2019 the 22-country threshold was reached, triggering the entry into force of the CFTA 30 days later on the 30 May 2019.[240] There is in addition a high probability that the Tripartite FTA Agreement will as well soon enter into force. It is not clear what measures will be put in place to address the largely similar and overlapping objectives and negotiations that are to take place in the context of the two Agreements.

Like the Tripartite FTA Agreement, negotiations in the areas of competition policy and intellectual property constitute phase two of the negotiations.[241] It is however interesting to note that the CFTA Agreement also includes protocols on trade in goods and services as well as a protocol on dispute settlement. This means that the signatories have committed themselves to these protocols irrespective of the fact that negotiations in these areas, particularly on tariffs and rules of origin, is not complete. This would therefore raise the question of whether the CFTA Agreement can be implemented considering it has entered into force before the negotiations are complete.[242]

These discussions should also be put in the context of global trade. Europe remains Africa's largest trading partner. This presents a challenge to regional integration because the EU negotiates for Economic Partnership Agreements (EPAs) on terns that in some cases may conflict with integration objectives. Some critics go as far as to label it a *'divide and conquer'* approach.[243] China has however surpassed the USA as Africa's single largest trading partner, indicating the increased competition for the

240 Agreement Establishing the African Continental Free Trade Area (CFTA Agreement), art 23 <https://au.int/en/treaties/agreement-establishing-african-continental-free-trade-area> accessed 16 July 2019;; See also TRALAC, 'AfCFTA Agreement enters into force' (2019) <https://www.tralac.org/resources/by-region/cfta.html.> accessed 16 July 2019.

241 CFTA Agreement art 7.

242 For a brief discussion see Gerhard Erasmus, 'South Africa to ratify Tripartite FTA and Continental Free Trade Area Agreements' (2018) <https://www.tralac.org/blog/article/13467-south-africa-to-ratify-tripartite-fta-and-continental-free-trade-area-agreements.html#_ftnref3> accessed 16 July 2019.

243 Stephen McDonald et al, 'Why Economic Partnership Agreements undermine Africa's Regional Integration' (2013), 4 <https://www.wilsoncenter.org/publication/why-economic-partnership-agreements-undermine-africas-regional-integration> accessed 16 July 2019.

African market.[244] Intra-Africa trade continues to post encouraging figures, with the SADC region responsible for the bulk of intra-African trade.[245]

2.3.5 Summary

Regional integration has largely been embraced in Africa to realise economic development and sustainable growth. The recent entry into force of the CFTA Agreement as well as the formalisation by the Member States of the EAC, COMESA and SADC of the Tripartite FTA Agreement is therefore highly laudable. However, though the CFTA Agreement and the Tripartite FTA present an opportunity to set in motion the eventual establishment of an African Economic Community, the reality is that there are considerable challenges that need to be overcome before the Tripartite FTA can be actualised.

The overall picture shows that a lot more still needs to be done. Africa's share of global trade still remains quite low, with an export value of about 3% as at 2014.[246] There is still a high dependence on commodities and natural resources showing very little improvement in terms of economic diversification.[247] This is in part as a result of a lack of the necessary infrastructure, technological development and technical expertise needed to enable the proper exploitation of the resources.[248]

If the objective of social, political and economic integration and development in Africa is to be achieved a lot more work needs to be done.

---

244 AfDB (2014) 42; see also AfDB et al (2015) 6.

245 AfDB (2014) 43; see also Bernard Busuulwa, 'Intra-African trade rises as market access between blocs improves' (The East African, 29 August 2015) <http://www.theeastafrican.co.ke/business/Intra-African-trade-up-as-market-access-between-blocs-improves-/-/2560/2850908/-/14qd2iy/-/index.html> accessed 16 July 2019.

246 Figure courtesy of the International Trade Centre (ITC) data <http://www.trademap.org/Country_SelProduct_TS.aspx> accessed 16 July 2019.

247 AfDB (2014) 42.

248 UNECA, 'Economic Report on Africa 2008: Africa and the Monterrey Consensus: Tracking Performance and Progress' (2008), 133 <http://www.uneca.org/publications/economic-report-africa-2008> accessed 16 July 2019; UNCTAD, 'Economic Development in Africa Report 2009: Strengthening Regional Economic Integration for Africa's Development' (2009), 15 <http://unctad.org/en/Docs/aldcafrica2009_en.pdf> accessed 16 July 2019.

2.4 The Competition Policy Perspective

2.4.1 Introduction

One of the definitions proffered for competition is 'the activity or condition of striving to gain or win something by defeating or establishing superiority over others.'[249] In the business context, it has been described as striving to gain or win 'the custom and business of people in the market place' or as a process of rivalry between firms that are seeking to win customers. This rivalry is widely regarded as a fundamental aspect of an open market society. In its most basic form, this process of rivalry is geared towards private gain. A producer will primarily seek to maximize the profits from his product whereas the consumer seeks to maximize utility of the product.[250]

Yet, as Kenneth Train (1991) observes, through this process of firms on the one hand seeking to maximize their profits (even in disregard of social welfare) and on the other hand consumers seeking to maximize their utility, the welfare of society at large is ultimately maximized. This 'invisible hand' that 'molds privately motivated actions into socially desirable outcome' is considered a rationale for free markets and a guardian of social welfare.[251]

The result of optimal competition in this regard should be an increase in efficiency and ultimately social welfare. However, whereas from the perspective of economic theory the ultimate effects of optimal competition are widely accepted, competition policy is to a great extent a function of its context.[252] Fox (2001) opines that it cannot be expected that different jurisdictions will have identical policy concerns.[253] Whish and Bailey (2012) observe that 'competition policy does not exist in a vacuum: it is an

249 See Oxford Dictionary definition.

250 Richard Whish and David Bailey, *Competition Law* (7th edn, OUP 2012) 3-5.

251 Kenneth Train, *Optimal Regulation: The Economic Theory of Natural Monopoly* (the MIT Press 1991) 1.

252 Eleanor Fox, *The Competition Law of the European Union in Comparative Perspective: Cases and Materials* (West, 2nd edn, 2009) 5.

253 Eleanor Fox, 'The Kaleidoscope of Antitrust and its significance in the World Economy: Respecting Differences' in Barry E. Hawk (ed.), *Annual Proceding of the Fordham Corporate Law Institute Conference on International Antitrust Law & Policy* (Juris 2001), 597-603.

expression of the current values and aims of society and is as susceptible to change as political thinking generally.'[254]

This is certainly the case in the context of the ESA jurisdictions which reflect a number of objectives beyond efficiency and welfare gains. These include economic growth and development and social or public interest goals such as levelling the playing field for historically disadvantaged persons. Competition policy is also regarded as a necessary instrument for the promotion of regional integration. Even the conception of what constitutes welfare gains from a developing economy perspective may be a function of the particular context of the developing economy.[255]

2.4.2 The Birth of Antitrust in the United States

The United States is widely regarded as the birthplace of modern antitrust law. The statutory cornerstone of US Antitrust is the 1890 Sherman Antitrust Act.[256] The Act was conceived towards the end of the 19th century, a period when the United States had experienced an unprecedented expansion of her industries.[257] The 19th century was not only a period of great industrial expansion but also one of socio-economic restructuring, with the Civil War (1861 to 1865) playing a significant part in reshaping industrial organization.

War time contracts heralded large scale expansion in some manufacturing sectors which were integral to the war.[258] At the time, however, this expansion did not result in harmful concentration of industries. The early post war period was still marked by competition in most of the industries, with some sectors experiencing an intensification of competition.[259]

---

254 Whish and Bailey (2012) 20.

255 *See* Josef Drexl, 'Consumer Welfare and consumer harm: adjusting competition law and policies to the needs of developing jurisdictions' in Michal Gal et. al (eds), *The Economic Characteristics of Developing Jurisdictions: Their Implications for Competition Law* (Edward Elgar 2015).

256 Section 1 of the Sherman Act prohibits contracts, combinations or conspiracies that are in restraint of trade. Section 2 prohibits monopolization and attempts at monopolization.

257 Hans B. Thorelli, *The Federal Antitrust Policy* (Johns Hopkins Press, Baltimore 1955) 55.

258 Ibid. at 56. Industries such as shoe manufacture, firearms and manufacture of sewing machines gravitated towards bigness.

259 Ibid 55-57.

The post-war period also saw some industries gravitate towards big business because of the conditions created by the war. This 'bigness' was however not the result of competitors coming together. It was attributed to large-scale technical units that were initially designed to cater to the wartime needs.[260] Indeed, one key political and socio-economic change because of the war was the shifting of power from the agrarian South to the industrialist and nationalist North, the South having been left in a post-war political and economic depression.[261]

One industry that benefited from the post-war expansion and which is often cited as one of the key instigators of the birth of US antitrust is the railroads.[262] However, though the railroads experienced expansion to cater for the wartime transportation needs, the railroad expansion and standardization was still a vital aspect of the economic development and had proceeded outside the context of the war.[263]

The tendency in the later part of the 19th century towards mass production is what led in some cases to barriers to entry and created a conducive environment for combinations to thrive. The failure to rein in the railroad and some other industries led to more agitation from not only the farmers but also other interest groups against the monopolistic practices and increasingly against industrial combination.[264]

Thorelli argues that Congress was of the view that the ultimate beneficiary of competition was the consumer; with the immediate beneficiary being the small business proprietors who needed to be shielded from the big business interests. He posits that in this way the Sherman Act embodied what could be referred to as a social purpose.[265] The concern for consumers and small businesses was also at the heart of the 1914 Clayton Act. The Act was *inter alia* intended to prevent small firms from being barred from the market by the bigger firms.[266]

260 Ibid.
261 Ibid.
262 Ibid.
263 Ibid.
264 Ibid.
265 See Eleanor M. Fox and Robert Pitofsky, 'Goals of US Competition Policy' in J. David Richardson and Edward M. Graham (eds), *Global Competition Policy* (Peterson Institute for International Economics 1997). where farmers, small proprietors, consumers and those who suffered inequality of condition, wealth and opportunity are idenitified as victims for whose benefit the Sherman Act was passed.
266 Thorelli (1955) 236.

It was through the Clayton Act that merger regulation was introduced in the United States.[267] Merger activity had begun earlier with the 1879 Standard Oil trust arguably being the merger that heralded the first wave of US merger activity.[268] The first wave of mergers of the late 19th century and early 20th century resulted in the creation of large monopolistic firms.[269] This wave is arguably attributed to a period of retardation of industrial growth in the United States, with the mergers being an avenue for producers to maintain their profits in light of declining demand and increased competition.[270] The second wave of mergers saw the shift from monopolistic structures to oligopoly, with the smaller firms at the forefront of this merger wave, hence shifting the balance of control in favor of a more open market.[271]

The link between economic power and political power was another point of concern in the development of US policy. The 1950 amendment to section 7 of the Clayton Act[272] was intended to curtail the concentration of economic power, the goal being to keep economic power dispersed hence keeping political power in check.[273]

Another shift in US policy was experienced in the 1970s, with the pendulum swinging from the small business interests in favor of consumer interests. Economically efficient conduct which increased the welfare of the consumer began to be treated as legally sound. Antitrust regulation became non-interventionist, with transactions that were viewed as economically inefficient being highly likely to be prohibited. Economic efficiency is indeed widely regarded as the pervasive antitrust objective in the US.[274]

267 Section 7 of the Clayton Act, as amended in 1950 and 1980, prohibits mergers and acquisitions that are likely to result in a substantial lessening of competition or tend to create a monopoly.

268 Derek C. Bok, 'Section 7 of the Clayton Act and the Merging of Law and Economics' (1960) 74 Harv. L. Rev 228, 229.

269 Ibid.

270 Ralph L. Nelson, *Merger Movements in American Industry* (Princeton University Press, 1959) 71,72.

271 Bok (1960) 230.

272 Ibid 236, The amendment was effected through the Celler-Kefauver Act which introduced the prohibition of mergers whose effect may be to substantially lessen competition or tend to create a monopoly.

273 Ibid.

274 Ibid 237.

2.4.3 The European Union

Regional integration usually seeks to achieve certain political and socio-economic objectives of the countries at play. The European Union integration for instance, was first and foremost driven by the need to avoid a recurrence of the 20th century Europe wars.[275] This main political objective of peace was to be buttressed by subsequent political and economic integration objectives aimed at bolstering the unity of the Member States and increasing the competitiveness of the Union as a whole.[276]

Competition law played a critical role in the deliberations for an integrated Europe. The Schuman Declaration of 1950[277], in which the then French minister for foreign affairs Robert Schuman proposed the formation of the European Coal and Steel Community (ECSC)[278] contained proposals that reflected the integral role of competition law, and indeed merger regulation, in helping to achieve the objective of maintaining peace in Europe. The proposal was to pool the production of coal and steel in France and Germany under a supranational authority, with the subsequent economic ties being regarded as critical in avoiding a recurrence of war, especially in these two 'industries of war'.[279]

Schuman stated that, 'In contrast to international cartels, which tend to impose restrictive practices on distribution and the exploitation of national markets, and to maintain high profits, the organization will ensure the fusion of markets and the expansion of production'.[280]

Article 65 and 66 of the now expired ECSC Treaty contained provisions of direct bearing to supranational competition regulation. Article 65, which is like the current Article 101 of the TFEU, sought to ensure that cartels did not disrupt competition in the common market through fixing prices, output controls or market allocation. Article 66 contained provisions that submitted prospective concentrations which fell under

---

275 *See for instance* Drexl (2012) 236.

276 This objective is reflected in the preamble and Article 2 of the Treaty on European Union; *See also* Willem F. Duisenberg, 'The Past and Future of European Integration: A Central Banker's Perspective' (1999) Per Jacobsson Lecture <http://www.imf.org/external/am/1999/lecture.htm.> accessed 23 August 2019.

277 The Schuman Declaration – 9th May 1950 <http://europa.eu/about-eu/basic-information/symbols/europe-day/schuman-declaration/index_en.htm.> accessed 23 August 2019.

278 Ibid, The ECSC effectively being the first supranational European institution.

279 Ibid, Coal and steel were integral in the manufacture of weapons.

280 Ibid.

the Treaty's regulatory ambit to the authorization of a High Authority established under the Treaty. The intention being to prevent *inter alia* the influencing of prices, the curtailing of production or marketing, the impairment of competition in the market for the relevant products.

The detailed nature of these two articles and the inclusion of similar provisions in subsequent Treaty texts is indicative of the vital role that competition law continues to play in the efforts towards an integrated Europe.

Supranational merger control was first applied in the EU in 1999 following the 1989 EC Merger Regulation, which has subsequently been replaced by the 2004 EC Merger Regulation.

2.4.4 Eastern and Southern Africa

2.4.4.1 National Perspective

Competition policy operates within a matrix of interrelated policy measures which are mainly socio-economic. A good starting point in contextualizing competition policy in the ESA region is to consider trade, industrial and government policy.

From a trade policy standpoint, trade liberalization has played an important role in stimulating increased investment in SSA, by making it possible for investors to exploit the opportunities available in the increasingly open markets. Research indicates that the current reforms in trade liberalization are of a unilateral nature, though there is an increased effort towards reforming to comply with regional and international trade agreements.[281] Trade liberalization has not necessarily resulted in a balance of trade in favour of the SSA countries[282], but it has necessitated the adoption of related policies meant to facilitate the objectives of the trade policy.

Opening the markets and creating new opportunities for investment likewise brings into discussion privatization policy in SSA. Privatization

281 Charles Ackah and Oliver Morrissey, 'Trade Policy and Performance in Sub-Saharan Africa since the 1980s' (2005) Centre for Research in Economic Development and International Trade, University of Nottingham, 1 <https://www.nottingham.ac.uk/credit/documents/papers/05-13.pdf> accessed 23 August 2019. This should however be considered against a backdrop of the structural adjustment programmes that were implemented by a majority of SSA countries and which included trade liberalization as one of the core conditions.

282 Ibid 2-5.

programs in SSA commenced roughly around the same time that the countries started to adopt trade liberalization policies, indicating the need to couple liberalized markets with avenues for investment. Research indicates that the privatization wave began with the small and medium-sized enterprises in the early 1990s and spread to larger companies in the latter part of the 90s.[283] The greatest difficulty has however been experienced in the utilities sector, with data indicating that it has largely been unsuccessful.[284] This lack of success has been attributed *inter alia* to improper regulatory frameworks, insufficient skills and know-how, vested interests in 'strategic companies', lack of political consensus and capacity constraints.[285]

One of the constraints identified as a drawback to liberalization is the lack of adoption or implementation of competition policies.[286] Competition law is however increasingly being adopted as a tool to facilitate trade and other economic policies. COMESA for instance has 21 member states. Of these 14 have competition laws. The number however goes down to 10 when considering those with competition authorities. And out of these 10 countries the authorities are at various stages of implementing or enforcing the competition laws. SADC on its part consists of 15 member states, 8 of which are also members of COMESA. Of the 15, 9 have operational competition regimes. The others are at various stages of adopting and implementing competition laws.[287]

The national competition laws as well reflect objectives geared towards economic development, with a special focus on developing the national markets and making them more competitive. Creating an environment that facilitates local and foreign investment is also seen as a core objective

---

283 Jean-Claude Berthelemy, Celine Kauffmann, Marie-Anne Valfort and Lucia Wegner, 'Privatisation in Sub-Saharan Africa: Where do we stand?' (OECD 2004) 119-120 <http://www.oecd.org/dev/emea/privatisationinsub-saharanafricawheredowestand.htm> accessed 23 August 2019.

284 Ibid. See also generally Kate Bayliss and Terry McKinley, 'Privatising Basic Utilities in Sub-Saharan Africa: The MDG Impact' (UNDP 2007) <http://www.ipc-undp.org/pub/IPCPolicyResearchBrief3.pdf> accessed 15 September 2019.

285 Ibid.

286 Osman Suliman and Ghirmay Ghebreysus, 'Determinants of Privatisation in Selected Sub-Saharan African Countries: Is Privatisation Politically Induced?' (2001) 26(2) Journal of Economic Development 45.

287 Gladmore Mamhare, 'Southern African Development Community (SADC) regional competition policy' in Josef Drexl, Mor Bakhoum, Eleanor M. Fox, Michael S. Gal and David J. Gerber (eds), *Competition Policy and Regional Integration in Developing Countries* (Edward Elgar 2012).

of adopting competition laws. They also express the need to meet regional integration goals.[288]

2.4.4.2 The Case of South Africa

Much like most Sub-Saharan Africa countries, South Africa's economy was built on a foundation of reliance on extractive industries and natural resources, primarily diamond and gold. Successive governments sought to reduce this reliance by putting in place economic policies aimed at enhancing farming and manufacturing industries. Other themes such as dominance of state-owned enterprises in vital aspects of the economy, import substitution and putting in place market controls (such as price caps) were also dominant themes in South Africa. However, one predominant theme which ties to the socio-economic and political structure of South Africa (and which traces similarities to many pre-colonial Sub-Saharan African countries) is the legacy of economic inequalities.[289]

The indigenous population was kept out of the formal economy. Vital aspects of economic development such as means of production, arable land ownership, government subsidies for farming were all reserved for the settler communities. This resulted in very highly concentrated ownership of capital. All these factors played a vital role in the development of South Africa's competition law framework.[290]

South Africa's competition policy framework is the most advanced in Sub Saharan Africa. Its modern antitrust framework traces its roots to 1923 when the Board of Trade and Industries was granted an advisory role in relation to competition policy. It was under the auspices of the Board of Trade and Industries that a report recommending the adoption of a general competition legislation led to the enactment of the Regulation of Monopolistic Conditions Act in 1955. As its title suggests, the legislation was aimed at addressing monopolies, adopting a rule of reason approach

---

288 See for instance Kenya Competition Act s 3; National Competition Policy for Botswana (2005); Namibia Competition Act s 2; Tanzania Competition Act s 3.

289 OECD, 'South Africa: Peer Review of Competition Law and Policy' (2003), 9-11 <http://www.oecd.org/southafrica/34823812.pdf> accessed 16 July 2019.

290 OECD South Africa Peer Review (2003) 9-17.

to addressing such monopolistic conditions based on a public interest standard.[291]

Although the Board of Trade and Industries was responsible for the administrative processes revolving around monopoly cases, ultimate discretion was placed in the hands of the Minister of Trade and Industry to determine which cases would be investigated and what relief would be provided. It is however notable that in the 20 years the statute was in force only 18 investigations were initiated by the Minister. The biggest downside to this statute, apart from its limited applicability to only monopoly situations, was the sweeping discretion it granted the Minister.[292]

This sweeping discretionary power was partly the subject of an inquiry launched in 1975 to assess the effectiveness of the 1955 law. It was noted particularly that the Ministerial discretion made the enforcement of the statute highly susceptible to political influence. The commission of inquiry recommended among other things a new competition body with an independent enforcement function and decision-making tribunal as well as the extension of its scope to cover mergers. The recommendations led to the enactment of the 1979 Maintenance and Promotion of Competition Act which established a Competition Board with an extended mandate to investigate mergers. The Competition Board used its investigative power to come up with 75 formal reports. The appointment of the Board was however still effected through the Minister. The new statute however still did not address residual concerns such as the absence of explicit prohibitions as well as maintaining the undefined public interest as the substantive standard of analysis. Further, the Competition Board was not truly independent as it was composed of individuals serving official functions in other government ministries.[293]

The post-apartheid period saw further changes made to South Africa's competition law framework. Renewed dialogue on the most appropriate competition law framework began and in 1997 the Department of Trade and Industry published Proposed Guidelines for Competition Policy. The guidelines sought to particularly address a number of shortcomings of the 1975 statute as well as pursuing various goals that go beyond econo-

291 Republic of South Africa, 'Board of Trade and Industries Act', No 28 of 1923 and No 19 of 1944; Republic of South Africa, 'Regulation of Monopolistic Conditions Act' No 24 of 1955.

292 Philip Sutherland and Katharine Kemp, *Competition Law of South Africa* (Service Issue 18, LexisNexis 2014) cap 3.

293 Ibid.

mic efficiency. These included the lack of a proper definition of public interest, economic distortions resulting from the unequal distribution of resources in the apartheid era as well as ensuring equal opportunity to participate in the economy. In the main, the guidelines called for more comprehensive merger regulation provisions (including an appropriate pre-notification regime), a more robust and independent administrative authority as well as stronger prohibitions against anti-competitive conduct. Further, in order to address the historical concentration of ownership, stronger divestiture powers were also proposed.[294]

This eventually led to the adoption in 1998 of the Competition Act. The Act established three increasingly independent administrative and judicial bodies (the Competition Commission, the Competition Tribunal and the Competition Appeal Court). Although the primary purpose remains the enhancement of economic efficiency and the promotion and maintenance of competition in South Africa, the Act also seeks to address historical injustices that prevented most of the population from adequately participating in the economy. In this regard, the Act specifically addresses employment and socio-economic welfare, opportunities for SMEs to participate in the economy and the increasing of ownership stakes for historically disadvantaged people.[295]

Given several similarities between the pre- and post-colonial socio-economic and political structures and South Africa's unique situation, the South African competition law framework can serve as a useful guide for a number of Sub-Saharan Africa countries looking to implement their own competition laws.

2.4.4.3 Regional perspective

Both at a national and regional level, the main themes of competition policy are promoting market efficiency, enhancing social and consumer welfare and facilitating economic growth and development. At the regional level, promoting regional integration is one of the key objectives of competition policy. Regional economic integration is also regarded as a catalyst

294 Republic of South Africa, 'Maintenance and Promotion of Competition Amendment Act, No 5 of 1986; See also Ben Fine and Zavareh Rustomjee, *The Political Economy of South Africa – From Minerals-Energy Complex to Industrialisation* (Hurst and Company 1996) cap 3.

295 Sutherland and Kemp (2003) cap.3.

for economic development in Sub Saharan Africa. Looking at COMESA, for instance, the economic objectives are all geared towards sustainable growth and development within the Member States and jointly among the Member States. The integrative objective is to be achieved through creating an environment that promotes domestic, cross-border and foreign investment, adoption of common policies and programs and the adoption of common positions with regards to the international agenda. The aim is the implementation of specific measures that will result in the realization of the economic community.[296]

Similar objectives are observable in the SADC Treaty[297], the main difference being that the SADC chooses cooperation and harmonization of measures rather than the creation of binding supranational provisions. Article 5 of the SADC Treaty lists the objectives which are to be achieved through, *inter alia*, the harmonization of the political and socio-economic policies of the Member States, improvement of economic management and performance through regional cooperation and promoting the coordination and harmonization of the international relations of Member States.

Article 55 of the COMESA Treaty sets out the foundation for the development of the COMESA competition policy and the subsequent COMESA Competition Regulations. Article 55(1) requires Member States to proscribe conduct that has the effect of negating free and liberalized trade within the common market.

Currently, the COMESA Competition regime is the most active and well-established regional competition regime in Africa. Its foundation was set out in Article 55 of the COMESA Treaty, which provided the foundation for the development of the COMESA competition policy and the subsequent COMESA Regulations. Article 55(1) requires Member States to proscribe conduct that has the effect of negating free and liberalized trade within the common market. This is therefore the principal objective of the competition policy.

From an efficiency perspective, Article 55(2) however allows conduct[298] that would in normal circumstances be considered anticompetitive in

296 COMESA Treaty art 3.

297 Treaty of the Southern African Development Community (SADC Treaty) art 5 <http://www.sadc.int/files/9113/5292/9434/SADC_Treaty.pdf.> accessed 23 August 2019.

298 Article 55(2) specifically provides as follows: 'The Council may declare the provisions of paragraph 1 of this Article inapplicable in the case of: any agreement or category thereof between undertakings; any decision by association of undertakings; any concerted practice or category thereof; which improves production

instances where such conduct 'improves production or distribution of goods or promotes technical or economic progress and has the effect of enabling consumers a fair share of the benefits', thus highlighting the goal of economic growth and development through a balancing of the pro and anti-competitive effects of the conduct in question.

Article 55(3) specifically mandates the Council of Ministers to make Regulations to realize this objective. The Council of Ministers set the ball rolling in 2004 when they invoked Article 55(3) and consequently promulgating the COMESA Competition Regulations of 2004. The COMESA Competition Commission, which is established under Article 6 of the COMESA Competition Regulations, became operational on 14 January 2013 and currently plays a very active role in regulating competition in the region including the assessment of mergers. Its mandate is in respect of conduct that has an appreciable effect on trade between Member States and restricts competition in the Common Market. Notifiable mergers are those that fall within the notification thresholds and that have a 'regional dimension', that is, where: (a) both the acquiring firm and target firm or either the acquiring firm or target firm operate in two or more Member States; and (b) the threshold of combined annual turnover or assets provided for is exceeded.[299]

The EAC also has a competition regime in place. The EAC Competition Act was enacted by the East African Legislative Assembly in 2006.[300] The EAC Competition Act became effective on the 1 December 2014 and has been ratified by all the EAC Member States. In February 2016, the EAC Council of Ministers approved the appointment of 5 Commissioners to head the Competition Authority.[301] A secretariat has also been put in place.[302] The EAC Competition Authority has already began operations

or distribution of goods or promotes technical or economic progress and has the effect of enabling consumers a fair share of the benefits: Provided that the agreement, decision or practice does not impose on the undertaking restrictions inconsistent with the attainment of the objectives of this Treaty or has the effect of eliminating competition.' This provision draws from Article 101(3) of the TFEU.

299 COMESA Competition Regulations art 16,18 and 23.

300 Gazette of the East African Community No. 002 Vol AT 1-003 (September 2007) <https://www.eac.int/documents/category/gazette> accessed 16 July 2019.

301 See EAC, Five Commissioners of the EAC Competition Authority sworn in at the EAC <https://www.eac.int/press-releases/605-1048-346-five-commissioners-of-the-eac-competition-authority-sworn-in-at-the-eac> accessed 16 July 2019.

302 Adam Ihucha, 'EAC Competition Authority to Start Operations in July' (The East African Standard 18 June 2016) <https://www.theeastafrican.co.ke/business/

and is currently conducting market studies to assess the EAC competition climate as well as the prevalence of anti-competitive practices.[303] The Competition Authority is however yet to begin the assessment of mergers.

This inevitably raises the question of jurisdictional overlaps with the COMESA Competition Commission. Article 10(2) of the COMESA Treaty specifies that a regulation shall be binding on all Member States in its entirety. This means that no further step would need to be taken on at the Member State level to give effect to the provisions of the COMESA Regulations. Furthermore, Article 3 of the COMESA Regulations provides, *inter alia*, that the Regulations shall apply to all economic activities having an effect within the Common Market and to conducts covered by parts 3, 4 and 5[304] of the COMESA Regulations which have an appreciable effect on trade between Member States. Additionally, the Article provides that the COMESA Regulations have primary jurisdiction, 'over an industry or a sector of an industry which is subject to the jurisdiction of a separate regulatory entity (whether domestic or regional) if the latter regulates conduct covered by Parts 3 and 4 of these Regulations'.

The EAC Treaty also provides that Regulations made pursuant to the Treaty shall be binding on the Member States.[305] The EAC Competition Act, which is the equivalent of a regulation made pursuant to the EAC Treaty, also applies to economic activities and sectors having a cross-border effect between its Member States.[306] The Act similarly addresses restraints by enterprises, abuse of dominance and mergers and acquisitions in more or less the same way as the COMESA Regulations do.

The Act equally establishes the EAC Competition Authority which has broad investigative powers, power to prohibit or approve the regulated conduct and arrangements and a duty to receive merger notifications and approve or disapprove mergers.[307] In other words, it has the same powers

EAC-competition-authority-to-start-operations-in-July-/2560-3255818-pwwagnz/index.html> accessed 16 July 2019.

303 James Anyanzwa, 'East Africa competition watchdog begins operations, market studies ongoing' (The East African, 28 March 2018) <https://www.theeastafrican.co.ke/business/East-Africa-competition-watchdog-operations-market-studies/2560-4361580-1rqaquz/index.html> accessed 16 July 2019.

304 These parts are in respect of anti-competitive business conduct and practices, mergers and acquisitions and consumer protection.

305 EAC Treaty art 16.

306 Ibid.

307 Article 42 and Parts II, III, IV, VII and VIII of the EAC Act.

and functions within its area of operation as the Competition Commission under the COMESA Regulations.

Even more specifically conflicting is the fact that the EAC Competition Act vests in the EAC Competition Authority exclusive original jurisdiction over violations of the Act with its resolutions and decisions being binding on the authorities of the Member States and their subordinate courts. The right of appeal from the decisions of the Authority lies in the East African Court of Justice[308] whose decisions are also final and binding[309] as are the decisions of the COMESA Court of Justice.

There is no such risk of such a conflict with the SADC given its regional integration model. The SADC approach is one of enhancing co-operation between the Member States through harmonizing various political and socio-economic policies rather than adopting substantive directly applicable rules.[310] The SADC approach to competition policy therefore aims at ensuring the Member States adopt at the national level measures aimed at prohibiting unfair business practices and promoting competition rather than adopting a supranational authority to enforce the regional competition policy.[311]

It is not yet certain how COMESA and EAC will deal with this overlap. It can however be reasonably expected that they will enter into negotiations to conclude a Memorandum of Understanding.

At the supra-regional level, the importance of competition policy is recognized in both the Tripartite FTA Agreement and the CFTA Agreement. Both Agreements place competition policy high on their agenda for their next phase of negotiations.[312] One question in this regard is whether there will be a push for a supra-regional competition regulator and what impact this will have on the existing regional frameworks.

---

308 Established under Article 9 of the EAC Treaty.

309 EAC Treaty art 35.

310 See SADC Treaty art 5; Protocol on Trade in the SADC Region art 25; see generally SADC Declaration on Regional Cooperation in Competition and Consumer Policies (2009) <http://www.sadc.int/documents-publications/show/SADC_Declaration_on_Competition_and_Consumer_Policies.pdf.> accessed 16 July 2019.

311 SADC Treaty, Protocol on Trade.

312 The CFTA Agreement's protocol on trade in services already contains provisions by which State Parties to the Agreement should: (1) ensure that suppliers enjoying a monopoly position within their territories do not abuse their monopoly in the supply of services in the relevant market; and (2) cooperate with other State Parties with a view to eliminating anti-competitive practices in the supply of services.

2.4.5 Competition policy objectives

Having the politico-economic objectives of regional integration in mind makes it easier to contextually frame the regional competition policy objectives. The preamble to the COMESA Regulations sets out the specific objectives. These can be condensed to the following main objectives:

1. Promotion of regional integration[313];
2. Economic and market efficiency;
3. Economic growth and development; and
4. Consumer welfare.

Section 3 of the EAC Competition Act sets out the following objectives:

1. Enhancing the welfare of the people in the EAC;
2. Enhancing the competitiveness of Community enterprises in world markets by exposing them to competition within the Community;
3. Creating an environment which is conducive to investment in the Community;
4. Bringing the Community's competition policy and practice in line with international best practices;
5. Strengthening the Partner States' role in relevant international organizations.

One of the main economic objectives of regional integration in the context of trade liberalization is the removal of barriers to trade.[314] Anti-competitive conduct is one of the main non-tariff barriers to trade.[315] The effect of private barriers to market access can be as effective as the government barriers in hindering effective market access. The removal of tariff barriers

313 David J. Gerber, *Global Competition: Law, Markets and Globalization* (Oxford University Press 2010), 182, in the context of promotion of EU integration.

314 This is reflected in Article 4 of the COMESA Treaty which among other things requires the Member States to abolish all non-tariff barriers to trade among themselves, establish a common external tariff and co-operate in customs procedures and activities; See also SADC Protocol on Trade Article 3 and 6 and EAC Treaty Article 75 on the need to eliminate non-tariff barriers to trade. Also reflected in Article 5 and 10 of the Tripartite FTA Agreement and Article 2 of the CFTA Agreement.

315 *See* Drexl (2012) 234; *See also* Diane P. Wood, 'Antitrust: A Remedy for Trade Barriers?' (1995), 2 Asian Law Program, Japan Information Access Project, Washington, D.C., <http://www.justice.gov/atr/public/speeches/0170.pdf> accessed 16 July 2019, which succinctly captures the effect of anti-competitive conduct as a private barrier to trade.

should be accompanied by effective competition policy to prevent anti-competitive barriers from seizing the newly freed market.[316]

Competition policy also promotes economic and market efficiency through incentivizing competition and creating room for innovation and expansion.[317] The removal of the artificial market entry barriers placed by anti-competitive measures means that more market players can access the market. This in turn encourages entrepreneurship and efficient investment of resources for optimal growth and development.[318]

Anti-competitive conduct also has an adverse impact on consumer welfare. The biggest consumer interest on the market is the availability of sufficient substitutes for products on the market at competitive prices. Cartels for instance have the effect of raising prices of the products on the market and restricting optimal output of the products.[319]

Consumers on the market are a largely unorganized group. They have little bargaining power, lack knowledge of their rights and the avenues for enforcing them and the existing information asymmetries make it difficult for them to tackle such anti-competitive conduct.[320] The necessity for effective competition policy complemented by the necessary consumer protection policy can therefore not be wished away.

2.4.5.1 Economic development

One of the main objectives espoused by ESA jurisdictions in favour of the adoption of competition law is that it spurs economic development. It is regarded as an avenue to bolster international, regional and local economic activity by creating a conducive environment for investment in the market. From the perspective of globalised business, it is an avenue

---

316 Wood (1995) 3.

317 Gerber (2010) 3.

318 Lawrence J. White, 'The Role of Competition Policy in the Promotion of Economic Growth' (2008) Essay presented at the Competition Policy Research Center of the Fair Trade Commission of Japan's International Symposium, 5-7 <http://web-docs.stern.nyu.edu/old_web/emplibrary/competition%20policy%20and%20growth.ljw%20draft%203-30-08.pdf> accessed 16 July 2019.

319 *See* Pradeep S. Mehta, Siddhartha Mitra and Cornelius Dube, *Competition Policy and Consumer Policy: Complementarities and Conflicts in the Promotion of Consumer Welfare* 56, UNCTAD, The Effects of Anti-competitive Business Practices on Developing Countries and their Development Prospects (United Nations Publication 2008).

320 Ibid 67.

to increase FDI.[321] The reduced (and in some instances eliminated)[322] barriers to international trade also serve as a motivating factor for many countries to implement competition laws to prevent the establishment of private frontiers that curtail the efficiency of the global market and which would as well result in their own national markets being less attractive for investment.[323]

However, the increased adoption of competition laws comes at a cost, especially to transnational business enterprises. From their perspective, more regulation means more compliance costs. Therefore, competition law, in serving its function to ensure that market efficiency is maintained, should also ensure that it as much as possible facilitates rather than hinders the ease of doing business.

One of the main questions that arises is whether a link can be made between the adoption of competition law by the ESA jurisdictions and an increase in economic development. This is however keeping in mind that economic development and FDI depend on many other socio-economic factors as well as other policy and regulatory choices.

Economic development does not lend itself easily to specific and concrete competition policy choices. Further, creating a link between economic development and the adoption of competition policies, in terms of specific economic markers of a competition policy's success, is considerably challenging.[324] Some scholars advocate for a human development approach for developing countries, suggesting that competition policy should focus on those sectors that have the greatest impact on human development such as agriculture and health. These sectors would in this regard serve as test cases for the effectiveness of the competition policy on development and eventually instruct the need to expand its application.[325]

---

321 Waked (2008) 1.

322 For instance, in the case of Regional Economic Communities where trade tariffs between the member states are eliminated.

323 Fox (1997) 19-20.

324 Simon J. Evenett, 'Would Enforcing Competition Law Compromise Industrial Policy Objectives?' in Douglas H. Brooks & Simon J. Evenett (eds), *Competition Policy and Development in Asia* (Palgrave Macmillan, 2005) 47; see also P.A.M. Jacobs & Simon van Norden, 'Why Are Initial Estimates of Productivity Growth So Unreliable?' (2016) 47 J. MACROECONOMICS 200.

325 Aditya Bhattacharjea, 'Who Needs Antitrust? Or, Is Developing-Country Antitrust Different? A Historical-
Comparative Analysis', in Daniel Sokol, Thomas K. Cheng & Ioannis Lianos (eds), *Competition Law and Development* (OUP 2013), 52-53.

Fox (2012) highlights the need for inclusivity and empowerment of people to participate effectively in the economy when making development-focused policy choices. Fox notes specific characteristics of developing countries that need special consideration when making such policy choices including: high levels of concentration, scarcity of human and financial capital, pervasive presence of the state in the economy, high entry barriers, marginalization of the majority from effective participation in the economy and rampant corruption. Therefore, competition policy choices that can measurably impact on these factors would have a positive effect on development. Particularly, Fox highlights the conclusions of the Spence (World Bank) Growth Report which emphasized the importance of inclusivity and the distribution of wealth and opportunity for the growth of developing countries.[326]

In the context of priority setting, Fox and Gal (2015) propose that the focus should be on markets that most affect the welfare of the population, particularly the weakest and poorest. These include agriculture, financial services and infrastructure. Fox and Gal note that the overarching goal should be efficient inclusive development. i.e. 'focusing on market access issues which affect the ability of the weaker parts of the society to take part and participate in the market on a larger scale than their current conditions allow them.'[327]

2.4.5.1.1 Economic Statistics

2.4.5.1.1.1 Foreign Direct Investment

Statistics point to a FDI inflow of USD 46 billion to Africa in 2018, attributed largely to increased demand and better prices for commodities as

---

326 Eleanor M. Fox, 'Competition, development and regional integration: in search of a competition law fit for developing countries' in Josef Drexl, Mor Bakhoum, Eleanor M. Fox, Michael S. Gal & David J. Gerber (eds), *Competition Policy and Regional Integration in Developing Countries* (Edward Elgar 2012) 273-290.

327 *See* Michal S. Gal and Eleanor M. Fox, 'Drafting competition law for developing jurisdictions: learning from experience' in Michal Gal et. al (eds), *The Economic Characteristics of Developing Jurisdictions: Their Implications for Competition Law* (Edward Elgar 2015), 320. See also Mor Bakhoum, 'The informal economy and its interface with competition law and policy' in Michal Gal et. al (eds), *The Economic Characteristics of Developing Jurisdictions: Their Implications for Competition Law* (Edward Elgar 2015) 190.

well as non-resource-based investments in some countries. FDI inflows to the East African region was for the most part unchanged for the 2017-2018 period, standing at USD 9 billion. Despite reduced FDI inflows, Ethiopia remains the largest FDI recipient in East Africa. Improvements in the private enterprise and foreign investment climate as well as an improved Ease of Doing Business ranking saw Kenya's FDI inflows increase by 27 percent. The same period also saw increased FDI inflow across the border in Tanzania and Uganda. Both Tanzania and Kenya have adopted a policy allowing 100 percent foreign ownership of listed companies, in a bid to boost investment. In Southern Africa, FDI inflows saw a significant recovery in 2018. The country-specific statistics however showed stark differences with the largest inflows going to South Africa while Angola experienced decreased investment.[328]

The figure and table below provide some FDI inflow statistics for Sub-Saharan Africa, including some specific statistics for the reviewed ESA jurisdictions.

328 UNCTAD, 'World Investment Report: Special Economic Zones' (2019) 36-38 <http://unctad.org/en/PublicationsLibrary/wir2016_en. https://unctad.org/en/PublicationsLibrary/wir2019_en.pdf> accessed 23 August 2019.

Figure 11: FDI inflows (in USD billion) to SSA (without South Africa) and the world, 1980-2006[329]

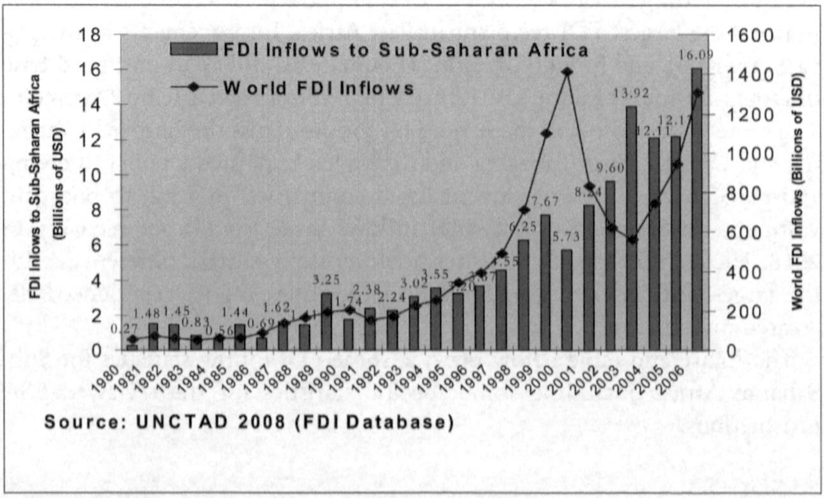

Table 11: FDI inflows (in USD million) for the ESA Region and the reviewed ESA Jurisdictions, 2010-2015

	2010	2011	2012	2013	2014	2015
Eastern Africa[330]	4 520.2	4 779.0	5 474.1	6 789.8	7 927.8	7 808.2
Southern Africa[331]	3 521.2	9 136.5	8 101.0	11 035.9	17 540.4	17 900.1
South Africa	3 635.6	4 242.9	4 558.8	8 300.1	5 770.6	1 772.4
Botswana	218.4	1 371.1	487.2	398.5	515.2	393.6
Kenya	178.1	335.2	258.6	514.4	1 050.7	1 437.0
Zimbabwe	165.9	387.0	399.5	400.0	544.8	421.0
Zambia	633.9	1 110.0	2 433.4	1 809.8	3 194.8	1 653.0

329 United Nations Industrial Development Organization, 'Foreign Direct Investment in Africa: Determinants and Location Decisions' (2009) 6 <https://open.unido.org/api/documents/4818201/download/Foreign%20Direct%20Investment%20in%20Sub-Saharan%20Africa%20-%20Determinants%20and%20Location%20Decisions> accessed 23 August 2019.

330 Includes Comoros, Djibouti, Eritrea, Ethiopia, Kenya, Madagascar, Mauritius, Mayotte, Seychelles, Somalia, Uganda and Tanzania.

331 Includes Angola, Botswana, Lesotho, Malawi, Mozambique, Namibia, South Africa, Swaziland, Zambia and Zimbabwe.

Seychelles	210.8	207.4	261.4	170.3	230.0	194.5
Mauritius	430.0	433.4	589.0	293.3	418.4	208.3
Tanzania	1 813.3	1 229.4	1 799.6	2 087.3	2 049.3	1 531.5
Namibia	793.0	1 119.8	1 133.4	800.5	431.8	1 077.8
Malawi	97.0	128.8	129.5	119.5	130.0	142.5

Courtesy of UNCTAD World Investment Report 2016

Table 3 shows that although the individual country statistics fluctuate substantially over the years, the region-wide statistics indicate a steady increase in FDI inflows into the Eastern and Southern Africa region. Figure 1 as well reveals that FDI into Sub-Saharan Africa has over a long-term period seen a steady increase.

Analysts have pinned the fluctuations to the continued reliance on commodities, with the bulk of investment still focused on natural resource-based industries. However, there has been a notable improvement in private consumption, as well as increased investment in infrastructure with the role of the services sector as well as manufacturing seeing an increase.[332]

The longer-term growth in investment has been linked to increased structural changes, with progress in five main structural areas being identified as key to ensuring long-term progress: governance, diversification, infrastructure, human development and business enablement.[333]

Regulatory hurdles fall within the business enablement criterion. The World Bank for instance regularly undertakes a survey on the ease of doing business, with one of the main measures involving considering global indicators of regulatory governance. The five aspects of good regulatory practices covered include the transparency of rulemaking, public consultation in rulemaking, impact assessments, challenging regulations and accessing the laws and regulations.[334]

332 Ernst and Young, 'Navigating Africa's Current Uncertainties' (2016) 3 <https://www.tralac.org/images/docs/9673/ey-attractiveness-program-africa-2016.pdf> accessed 18 July 2019.

333 Ernst and Young (2016) 7-8.

334 World Bank Group, 'Global Indicators of Regulatory Governance' <http://rulemaking.worldbank.org/~/media/WBG/CER/Documents/Global-Indicators-of-Regulatory-Governance-Project-Summary.pdf?la=en> accessed 19 September 2019.

Many the reviewed ESA jurisdictions score poorly on these indicators.[335] On the question of transparency of rulemaking for instance, key questions such as making proposed drafts of regulations publicly available or whether an obligation to publish such proposed texts exists. For Botswana, Malawi, Mauritius, Seychelles, Namibia, Zimbabwe, Zambia, Tanzania score negatively or have inconclusive information on this question. The same countries score poorly on the question of whether an impact assessment is conducted of proposed laws. South Africa scores quite well, with Kenya posting decent results on the issue of transparency in rule making and impact assessment.

On the question of access to laws and regulations, a number of the countries surprisingly score well on the question whether the websites and registries where the laws can be accessed is updated regularly. This may be so for the actual statutes but cannot be reconciled with the huge challenge faced in accessing detailed and up to date information on merger regulation, especially when it comes to properly elaborated decisions.

While data revealing a direct link between merger regulation to the FDI inflows may not be easily obtained, these indicators on business enablement through transparency and accountability reveal that the information asymmetry existing within the reviewed ESA jurisdictions as far as merger regulation is involved does pose a challenge to the ease of doing business.

2.4.5.1.1.2 Cross-border M&A

M&A trends in Africa still display a bias for natural resources, with deals in energy, mining and utilities continuing to lead the way. Statistics indicate that in 2014/2015 energy, mining and utilities accounted for 24 percent of the deal value in Africa and 17 percent of the total deal volume. The fall in commodity prices has however led to fewer big deals, which in turn has resulted in smaller deals in the consumer and financial services taking centre stage. The pharma, medical and biotech sector, although constituting only 2 percent of deal value grew by 20 percent between 2013 and 2015. Telecommunications is also expected to remain a resilient deal market given the large number of customers in Africa and the need to ensure infrastructure is maintained. South Africa (which remains the

335 The data is accessible at <http://rulemaking.worldbank.org/> accessed 23 August 2019.

biggest M&A market in Africa), Nigeria and Kenya continue to attract the most M&A activity in Sub Saharan Africa.[336]

The East African region has proven to be particularly attractive to investors owing to very positive GDP figures, as well as providing avenues for investment away from the traditional energy and natural resources. These include deals in the financial sector, construction and pharma, offering a diversity of opportunities which may be smaller in value size but offer growth and expansion opportunities.[337]

Several obstacles to an improved M&A climate have been identified, including political risks, economic uncertainty, currency volatility and security risks. However, the top concern identified by most investors is regulatory uncertainty in as far as compliance and integrity is concerned. Transparency and completeness of information have also been ranked as a significant obstacle to M&A activity.[338] This naturally brings to mind the merger regulation challenges identified in many of the reviewed ESA jurisdictions, particularly the insufficiency of published information which contributes to regulatory uncertainty and raises questions on transparency.

2.4.5.1.2 Summary

The adoption of competition law within a context of economic development is not entirely peculiar to the developing jurisdictions. In the US, antitrust law developed in an economic environment that was undergoing great industrial expansion. In the European Union the aim was to ensure that the common market objective was not hampered by cartelist behaviour.

The difference however is that whereas the US and the European Union adopted competition law to 'regulate' economic development, the jurisdictions in Sub-Saharan Africa are adopting competition laws with the view to spur economic development, both from the regional economic integration perspective and the individual national perspective. Competition

336 See <http://dealdriversafrica.mergermarket.com/overview-ma-activity-in-africa> accessed 23 August 2019.

337 See <http://dealdriversafrica.mergermarket.com/feature-east-africa> accessed 23 August 2019.

338 See <http://dealdriversafrica.mergermarket.com/survey-findings-continued> accessed 23 August 2019.

laws are regarded as an avenue to attract (foreign) investment into the markets.

Economic development is however dependent on a myriad of policy choices as well as other political and socio-economic factors. The ability to attract foreign investment will also be largely influenced by how these factors are addressed. From the point of view of business enablement, competition law and in particular merger regulation should indeed as far as possible ensure that regulatory uncertainty does not arise. Merger regulation should facilitate as much as possible the ease of doing business. However, the priority for ESA should be on inclusive economic development, where, as Fox and Gal (2015) explain, the focus is on market access where the weaker parts of the effectively enabled to meaningfully participate in the market on a large scale.

2.6 *Conclusion*

The economic, social and political characteristics of developing countries invariably raise the question whether they should adopt competition policies. There are numerous proponents as well as opponents for the adoption of such policies in developing countries. The immediate argument in support of adoption of a competition policy framework is the expected gains in terms of economic efficiency, consumer welfare as well as economic growth and development.

Yet the unique characteristics of developing countries often raise the question whether competition policy would be an appropriate and effective policy choice for the achievement of these gains. One of the recurring arguments in this regard is in respect of constrained resources. Developing jurisdictions are often cited as lacking the necessary resources in terms of financial capacity as well as antitrust and economic expertise within the enforcement agencies as well as the judiciary. The resource shortfall is therefore seen as considerably hampering the ability of developing jurisdictions to effectively implement a competition policy framework. Insufficient financial resources are considered to interfere with enforcement particularly where certain cases involve intensive investigation of anti-competitive effects.[339] In terms of expertise, developing country agencies that

339 See Gal and Fox (2015) 296, 311–314. See also Michal S. Gal, 'When the Going Gets Tight: Institutional Solutions When Antitrust Enforcement Resources Are Scarce' (2010) 41 Loy. U. Chi. L.J. 417, 423–425.

adopt a more efficiency-based approach arguably find it difficult to carry out the sophisticated economic evaluation of anti-competitive conduct given their constrained human resource capability.[340]

One counter-argument highlighted is the fact that many competition agencies rarely start operations when fully constituted and with sufficient resources.[341] They therefore have to slowly build capacity first through market analysis, followed by advocacy and eventually effective enforcement. It is only after such capacity has been built that the effectiveness of the agency can be assessed.[342]

Another oft-cited argument against the adoption of competition policies by developing countries is the absence of political will, or worse still, a hostile political environment. Weak rule of law and lack of independence of the enforcement agencies and judiciary are regarded as severely hampering the effectiveness of competition policies. These ingredients are highly likely to contribute to a situation of regulatory capture, thereby severely hampering the efficiency and enforcement of competition policy.[343] Where this is combined with a lack of competition culture, it can lead to a serious impediment to competition policy.[344] In this regard, the advocacy role of competition authorities plays an integral part in ensuring the importance of competition policy is appreciated.

The fact that most markets in developing countries are underdeveloped can also prevent even the most effectively implemented competition policy

---

340 David J. Gerber, 'Adapting the Role of Economics in Competition Law: A Developing Country Dilemma' in Michal S. Gal et al. (eds), *The Economic Characteristics of Developing Jurisdictions: Their Implications for Competition Law* (Edward Elgar 2015).

341 See Tim Büthe and Gabriel T. Swank, 'The Politics of Antitrust and Merger Review in the European Union: Institutional Change and Decisions from Messina to 2004' (2006) Harv. Ctr. for Eur. Stud.,Working Paper No. 142 17-20, highlighting the point that even the EU's Directorate General for Competition commenced operations amidst lots of scepticism and considerably lean staff.

342 See William Kovacic and Marianela Lopez-Galdos, 'Lifecycles of Competition Systems: Explaining Variation in the Implementation of New Regimes' (2016) 79 Law and Contemporary Problems 4, 97.

343 Stephen Weymouth, 'Competition Politics: Interest Groups, Democracy, and Antitrust Reform in Developing Countries' (2016) 61 Antitrust Bull. 296-316.

344 Allan Fels and Wendy Ng, 'Rethinking Competition Advocacy in Developing Countries' in Daniel Sokol, Thomas K. Cheng & Ioannis Lianos (eds), *Competition Law and Development* (OUP 2013), 182-183; see also David Lewis,'Embedding a Competition Culture: Holy Grail or Attainable Objective?' in Daniel Sokol, Thomas K. Cheng & Ioannis Lianos (eds), *Competition Law and Development* (OUP 2013) 228, 230–235.

from achieving its objective. It has been argued that even a development-focused competition policy cannot spur development where the appropriate market structures are absent, more so where there is government interference in economic activity as well as, in some cases, exemptions for state-run enterprises.[345]

Yet, these very same concerns regarding adoption of competition policies by developing countries are regarded by some as a strong imperative for the adoption of such policies. Because of high concentration levels and high barriers to entry, Gal particularly highlights that absent appropriate regulation, market forces in a small economy will in many cases not be enough to sustain competitive discipline among firms in the economy. Accordingly, competition policy is necessary in determining market structure, conduct and the intensity of competition.[346] Gal also points out that given the relative weakness of market forces in small economies, and a much weaker self-correcting tendency, there are higher costs associated with improperly designed and inadequately implemented competition laws. Thus, the natural conditions of many small market economies which have a suppressive effect on competition increase the need for the adoption of appropriate competition policies.[347]

Competition policies are especially important for developing countries that adopted policies for deregulation, privatisation, trade liberalization as well as regional integration as they help with efficient resource distribution. Deregulation and privatisation potentially expose existing and potential competitors as well as consumers to abuse of dominance by the

345 Avner Greif, *Institutions and the Path to the Modern Economy: Lessons from Medieval Trade* (Cambridge University Press 2006); Barak D. Richman, 'Contracts and Cartels: Reconciling Competition and Development Policy' in Daniel Sokol, Thomas K. Cheng & Ioannis Lianos (eds), *Competition Law and Development* (OUP 2013) 155, 164–166; Eleanor M. Fox and Deborah Healey, 'When the State Harms Competition: The Role for Competition Law' (2014) 79 Antitrust L. J. 769, 775–95; Marco Botta, 'Does the EU Competition Law Model Satisfy the Needs of the Emerging Economies? Lessons from the Countries Without a "Carrot"' in Karolina Podstawa and Laura Puccio (eds), 'Framework for Economic Development in EU External Relations' (2012) European University Institute Working Paper, 2251, 2262; William E. Kovacic, 'Getting Started: Creating New Competition Policy Institutions in Transition Economies' (1997) 23 Brook. J. Int'l L. 403, 450; Armando E. Rodriguez & Malcolm B. Coate, 'Competition Policy in Transition Economies: The Role of Competition Advocacy' (1997) 23 Brook. J. Int'l L. 365, 367–69.

346 Gal (2003) 45.

347 Gal (2003) 5.

incumbent. A robust competition policy would be necessary to prevent abuses of the restructured markets. Trade liberalization potentially leads to not only a robust domestic market, it also exposes the economy to international competition. Therefore, trade liberalization as well as regional integration and the consequential elimination or reduction of barriers to trade present a strong case for robust national and regional competition policies to protect the newly liberated national and regional markets from anti-competitive practices that may lead to barriers to trade.

Developing countries also argue that competition policy helps to promote the international competitiveness of their domestic industries. It has been argued that a competitive domestic market forces firms to use resources in the most efficient way, in essence allowing them to become more experienced in conducting business in a competitive climate. This would consequentially prepare the domestic firms to compete in an increasingly globalised market.[348]

Developing countries, particularly in Sub-Saharan Africa, also argue that competition policy provides an avenue to correct historical social injustices by promoting the equal distribution of resources to previously side-lined members of the society, enabling them to effectively participate in the economy.[349]

In sum, the dialogue should not be whether developing countries should adopt competition policies. Rather, what is the most effective competition policy framework to address the unique characteristics of developing countries. In this regard, context should dictate form.

---

348 Frank Emmert, Franz Kronthaler, Johannes Stephan, 'Analysis of statements made in favour of and against the adoption of competition law in developing and transition economies' (2005) Institut Für Wirtschaftsforschung Halle Report, 23-26 <https://www.iwh-halle.de/fileadmin/user_upload/publications/iwh_sonderhefte/SH_05-1.pdf> accessed 17 July 2019.

349 Ibid.

3 The Merger Regulation Landscape

3.1 Efforts towards a multilateral regime

Antitrust regulation has always been a vital component of the international trade discourse, but has in the same breath always fallen short of international consensus on a multilaterally binding regime. What is however notable is the evolution of the scope of global antitrust with the increasing globalization. Looking at the Havana Charter in the late 1940s, the focus was on hardcore cartels which were viewed as a threat to a global economy. The focus then shifted to the need to provide assistance to developing countries in establishing functional antitrust regimes to enable them respond better to the needs of the converging global economy.

Merger regulation also began to emerge as a core area for global legal regulation, reflecting the need to facilitate the transactions of the increasingly pervasive multinational corporation.

This Chapter briefly tracks the efforts towards developing an international regime. It highlights the unsuccessful efforts to create a single international regime and the gradual shift towards seeking convergence and facilitation of competition law development and adoption in developing regimes.

3.1.1 The Havana Charter

The first attempt to conceive an international antitrust regime was embodied in the Havana Charter in the late 1940s. The Havana Charter was an initiative of the then United Nations Conference on Trade and Employment. The intention behind the Havana Charter was the creation of the International Trade Organization (ITO). The General Agreement on Tariffs and Trade (GATT) which was concluded a few months prior to the commencement of negotiations for the Havana Charter, was ideally intended to be an interim measure pending the conclusion of the Havana Charter.[350]

---

350 The GATT years: From Havana to Marrakesh

Considering the complex socio-economic and political context of the period during which the Havana Charter was being negotiated, it could be described as having been nothing short of ambitious. The Havana Charter envisioned an international regime that would go beyond the traditional trade aspects. It sought to address more specific issues such as employment, an international investment perspective of economic development and reconstruction, inter-governmental commodity agreements and restrictive business practices.[351]

Negotiations for the Havana Charter began in 1947, two years after the end of the Second World War. The Havana Charter was envisioned to be the starting point of a peace-time global economic and political dispensation.[352] The depth of international cooperation sought by the Havana Charter, considering the persisting post-war tensions and the looming cold war, was indeed laudable.

International economic cooperation had already been one of the core agenda items of a post-war global dispensation. This is for instance reflected in the Atlantic Charter, a non-binding commitment reached in August 1941 by the US and Great Britain, with one of the core principles being 'the fullest collaboration between all nations in the economic field, with the object of securing for all improved labour standards, economic advancement and social security'. More concretely, it is considered that the draft of the ITO was the result of a 1945 bilateral Anglo-American proposal on commercial policy, with the US and Britain both having considered the need for a multilateral trading system.[353]

Ambitious as it may have seemed, the Havana Charter largely failed to materialise owing to the refusal of the US, which was its main proponent,

---

<http://www.wto.org/english/thewto_e/whatis_e/tif_e/fact4_e.htm#rounds.> accessed 23 August 2019.

351 See Havana Charter, article 1.

352 Richard N. Gardner, *Sterling-dollar diplomacy in current perspective: the origins and the prospects of our international economic order* (Columbia University Press 1980) 355-358.

353 For detailed discussion see Clair Wilcox, 'The London Draft of a Charter for an International Trade Organization' (1947) 37 Am. Econ. Rev. 529; Richard Toye, 'Developing Multilateralism: The Havana Charter and the Fight for the International Trade Organization, 1947–1948' (2003) 25 International History Review 282-305; Jean-Christophe Graz, 'The Havana Charter: when state and market shake hands' in Rainer Kattel, Jayati Ghosh & Erik Reinert (Eds), *Handbook of Alternative Theories of Economic Development* (E. Elgar, 2016) 281-290; Ivan D. Trofimov, 'The Failure of the International Trade Organization (ITO): A Policy Entrepreneurship Perspective' (2012) 5 Journal of Politics and Law 56.

to ratify it. There are different opinions proffered for the US rejection of the Havana Charter. One of the oft-cited reasons is the concessions that needed to be made in respect of lesser developed countries. The need to take into consideration these countries in the crafting of a multilateral framework became increasingly apparent. Their main concern was that the proposed multilateral framework was too focused on the needs of the developed countries and failed to take into consideration the unique developmental needs of the lesser developed countries. Quite interestingly, it was the US that proposed the introduction of provisions on economic development into the Havana Charter in response to concerns expressed by the lesser developed countries.[354]

In spite of a majority of the developed country participants having coalesced to many of the economic development concessions, a change of the US administration as well as an increasingly protectionist agenda in the face of the looming cold war meant that there was a shift in priorities for the US, with the Havana Charter becoming a victim of these shifting priorities.[355]

Chapter 5 of the Havana Charter envisioned the adoption of provisions on restrictive trade practices, the aim being to seek co-operation among the Member States of the ITO in the prevention of business practices that restrain competition, limit market access, or foster monopolistic control, whenever such practices are detrimental to the expansion of production or trade and the attainment of a world economy.[356]

The specific restrictive practices that the Havana Charter sought to prohibit were mainly instructed by a proposal by the United States which primarily sought to curb cartelist behavior.[357] The proposal referred to situations in which undertakings come together with the objective of fixing prices, allocation of markets, curtailing production, suppressing innovation and excluding rivals.[358] The proposal posited that such behavior may be of greater detriment to world trade than government restrictions.[359]

---

354 Toye (2003); Graz (2016) 282-284.

355 Graz (2016) 282-284).

356 Havana Charter art 46.

357 Department of State, 'Proposal for Expansion of World Trade and Employment' (1945, Commercial Policy Series 79) 4-5 <http://www.worldtradelaw.net/misc/ProposalsForExpansionOfWorldTradeAndEmployment.pdf.download#page=4> accessed 21 December 2018.

358 Ibid.

359 Ibid.

The Havana Charter would have empowered the ITO to carry out investigations on complaints by Member States, request for information, conduct studies on its own initiative or on request of a Member State along with other powers that a normal competition authority would be expected to have.[360] The ITO would then make recommendations to the respective Member State(s) regarding what remedial action was to be taken.[361] The Havana Charter did not preclude and in fact encouraged the adoption of national measures to deal with restrictive trade practices.

3.1.2 The WTO Initiatives

The failure of the Havana Charter notwithstanding, competition policy remained a vital component of the international trade agenda. Negotiations on international commerce proceeded under the General Agreement on Tariff and Trade (GATT) which had been signed not long before the negotiations on the Havana Charter had commenced.[362] The GATT is credited with having presided over a period of very fruitful global trade liberalization.[363] However, unlike the case with the Havana Charter, the provisions on restrictive trade practices were not included in the GATT. This however did not preclude further discussions on the need to address restrictive trade practices within the international trade perspective. In 1958 the GATT contracting states passed a resolution recommending the formation of a Group of Experts to investigate competition policy concerns, noting that 'the activities of international cartels and trusts may hamper the expansion of world trade and interfere with the objectives of GATT.'[364]

In 1960, the Group of Experts, consisting of experts from 12 contracting states[365] while noting that 'business practices which restrict competition

360 Havana Charter ch 5.

361 Ibid.

362 The GATT years: From Havana to Marrakesh <http://www.wto.org/english/thewto_e/whatis_e/tif_e/fact4_e.htm#rounds.> accessed 23 August 2019.

363 Ibid.

364 Restrictive Business Practices: Arrangements for Consultations, Decision of 18 November 1960, BISD 9S/28, <http://www.worldtradelaw.net/misc/rbp1.pdf.download> accessed 16 July 2019. See also, Report of Experts, Restrictive Business Practices: Arrangements for Consultations of 2 June 1960, L/1015, BISD 9S/170 <http://www.worldtradelaw.net/misc/rbp2.pdf.download> accessed 16 July 2019.

365 Austria, Canada, Denmark, Federal Republic

in international trade may hamper the expansion of world trade and the economic development in individual countries and thereby frustrate the benefits of tariff reduction and removal of quantitative restrictions or may otherwise interfere with the objectives of the General Agreement on Tariffs and Trade' recommended a comity-based approach to addressing these concerns. It was evident that international cooperation was necessary to address restrictive trade practices.[366]

The Group of Experts recommended that, 'at the request of any contracting party a contracting party should enter into consultations on such practices on a bilateral or a multilateral basis as appropriate. The party addressed should accord sympathetic consideration to and should afford adequate opportunity for consultations with the requesting party, with a view to reaching mutually satisfactory conclusions, and if it agrees that such harmful effects are present it should take such measures as it deems appropriate to eliminate these effects.'[367]

The fast evolving international trade environment was eventually no longer sustainable under the GATT.[368] This was also reflected by the number of countries that had signed GATT by 1994 (in comparison to the 1947 agreement), a large number of which included developing countries.[369] The need for a new institution to handle the complex issues of increasingly globalized trade led to the birth of the WTO in January 1995.[370]

Within the WTO context, other international trade agreements, particularly the General Agreement on Trade in Services (GATS) and the Agreement on Trade Related Aspects of Intellectual Property Rights (TRIPS), have provisions that have a bearing on competition policy aspects of international trade.

Article 8 of the GATS for instance provides that 'Each Member shall ensure that any monopoly supplier of a service in its territory does not, in

---

of Germany, France, Japan, Kingdom of the Netherlands, Norway, Sweden, Switzerland, United Kingdom, and
United States.

366 Report of Experts: Restrictive Business Practices: Arrangements for Consultations (1960) para 7.

367 Ibid.

368 Ibid.

369 WTO, The 128 countries that had signed GATT by 1994 <http://www.wto.org/english/thewto_e/gattmem_e.htm.> accessed 23 August 2019.

370 *See* WTO, The First WTO Ministerial Conference <http://www.wto.org/english/thewto_e/minist_e/min96_e/min96_e.htm.> accessed 23 August 2019.

the supply of the monopoly service in the relevant market, act in a manner inconsistent with that Member's obligations'.

Article 9 further calls for the recognition of restrictive business practices and calls for members to adopt a proactive comity approach to eliminate such practices, quite like the 1960 recommendation of the Group of Experts. Specifically, it provides that:

1. Members recognize that certain business practices of service suppliers, other than those falling under Article VIII, may restrain competition and thereby restrict trade in services.
2. Each Member shall, at the request of any other Member, enter into consultations with a view to eliminating practices referred to in paragraph 1. The Member addressed shall accord full and sympathetic consideration to such a request and shall cooperate through the supply of publicly available non-confidential information of relevance to the matter in question. The Member addressed shall also provide other information available to the requesting Member, subject to its domestic law and to the conclusion of satisfactory agreement concerning the safeguarding of its confidentiality by the requesting Member.'

In relation to the TRIPS Agreement, Article 8.2 provides that 'Appropriate measures, provided that they are consistent with the provisions of this Agreement, may be needed to prevent the abuse of intellectual property rights by right holders or the resort to practices which unreasonably restrain trade or adversely affect the international transfer of technology.'

Article 40.1 of the TRIPS Agreement acknowledges that 'some licensing practices or conditions pertaining to intellectual property rights which restrain competition may have adverse effects on trade and may impede the transfer and dissemination of technology.'

Article 40.2 of the TRIPS Agreement details the right of Member States to take the necessary measures to address competition law concerns: '…a Member may adopt, consistently with the other provisions of this Agreement, appropriate measures to prevent or control such practices, which may include for example exclusive grantback conditions, conditions preventing challenges to validity and coercive package licensing, in the light of the relevant laws and regulations of that Member.'

Article 40.3 of the TRIPS Agreement requires Member States to take a positive comity approach to addressing such anti-competitive practices: 'Each Member shall enter, upon request, into consultations with any other Member which has cause to believe that an intellectual property right owner that is a national or domiciliary of the Member to which the request for consultations has been addressed is undertaking practices in violation of the requesting Member's laws and regulations on the subject matter of this Section, and which wishes to secure compliance with such legislation, without prejudice to any action under the law and to the full freedom of an ultimate decision of either Member.'

Some scholars have criticized the lack of guidance within the TRIPS Agreement in relation to the absence of standard of assessment of anti-competitive practices (for instance dominance or substantial lessening of competition) as well as the lack of guidance on appropriate remedies.[371]

The agenda for an international antitrust regime, championed to a large extent by the European Union, came up again at the 1996 Singapore Conference, where the intention to commence an investigative study on the antitrust policy areas that require WTO attention was expressed.[372] The presence of interspersed provisions on control of anti-competitive practices in various areas, especially in the GATS and TRIPS Agreements, was as well taken note of.[373] This exploratory approach to antitrust is also reflected in the Ministerial Declaration pursuant to the Singapore Conference where it was decided that a Working Group on the Interaction between Trade and Competition Policy (WGTCP) would be established to explore the issues raised by the Members as regards antitrust policy 'relating to the interaction between trade and competition policy, including anti-competitive practices, in order to identify any areas that may merit further consideration in the WTO framework'.[374]

Competition policy was again up for discussion in the Doha Conference in 2001. Article 23 of the Doha Ministerial Declaration recognized 'the case for a multilateral framework to enhance the contribution of competition policy to international trade and development...'. Further, based on the results of the WGTCP, a concrete undertaking was made in the ministerial declaration to provide 'strengthened and adequately resourced assistance' in terms of technical assistance and capacity building for developing and least developed countries.[375] The work set out for the WGTCP at this conference was to focus on core principles of competition policy

371 Robert D. Anderson and Peter Holmes, 'Competition Policy and the Future of the Multilateral Trading System' (2002) 5 Journal of International Economic Law 2, 531–563.

372 WTO, Press Brief on Competition Policies <http://www.wto.org/english/thewto_e/minist_e/min96_e/comppol.htm.> accessed 23 August 2019.

373 Ibid.

374 Singapore WTO Ministerial 1996: Ministerial Declaration WT/MIN(96)/DEC.

375 Doha WTO Ministerial 2001: Ministerial Declaration WT/MIN(01)/DEC/1.

and to provide support to the competition institutions of the developing countries, with full regard to the needs of developing and least developed members. The focus was therefore not on modalities for negotiation of a supranational competition rule-set but was more on assistance and capacity building especially for the developing and least developed members.

Article 23 of the Doha Ministerial Declaration further called on negotiations to take place after the Fifth Session of the Ministerial Conference in relation to the multilateral competition framework, that is, at the 2003 Cancún Conference. The need for assistance to developing and least developed Members was also reiterated at the Cancún Conference in 2003. There was however still no clear decision to negotiate on the terms for a supranational competition regime.[376] The failure to make headway in relation to competition law was mainly due to resistance by developing countries. It is noted that the objections expressed by the developing countries were not of a technical nature, but rather, political.

Three main issues have been highlighted as having led the developing countries to refuse the negotiations on competition policy:

1. The negotiations on competition policy were tied, as a single undertaking arising from the Singapore Ministerial Declaration, to other negotiations such as on investment, government procurement and trade facilitation. The developing countries were not ready to negotiate based on a single undertaking.
2. There were already concurrent negotiation burdens (such as the Cotonou Agreement for the African, Pacific and Caribbean countries and the Free Trade Area of the Americas negotiations for the Latin American countries). Developing countries were therefore hesitant to stretch their negotiating capacity to areas where they lacked the necessary technical expertise.
3. The developing countries were concerned about an increase in their regulatory burden and costs of compliance in relation to a multilateral competition framework.

There was also a concern among developing countries that they would lose their investigative and prosecutorial independence if a multilateral competition framework is put in place.[377]

---

376 Cancún WTO Ministerial 2003: Draft Cancún Ministerial Text JOB(03)/150/Rev.2.

377 Taimoon Stewart, 'The Fate of Competition Policy in Cancun: Politics or Substance?' (2004) 31 Legal

Negotiations on interaction between trade and competition policy was altogether dropped from the WTO agenda in a decision adopted by the WTO General Council in August 2004, rendering the WGTCP inactive.[378]

3.1.3 The United Nations Restrictive Business Practices Code

The failure of the Havana Charter to take off did not dampen the efforts to conclude a multilaterally agreed set of competition law principles under the auspices of the UN In 1980 the set of Multilaterally Agreed Equitable Principles and Rules for the Control of Restrictive Business Practices, commonly referred to as the UN Set was concluded.[379] One of the driving forces behind the UN Set was the developing countries push to rein in anti-competitive business conduct of multinationals.[380] This is reflected in the 1980 resolution of the UN Conference on Restrictive Business Practices and in the objectives of the UN Set which indicate the inclination to give special attention to the needs of the developing countries.[381]

The UN Set targets restrictive business practices that seek to negate the benefits of a liberalized trade environment with a specific focus on those practices that affect 'trade and development of developing countries'.[382]

Of interest is the fact that the UN Set contains principles which, though very general in nature, address the regulation of mergers on the multina-

---

Issues of Econ. Integration 7, 7; WTO, Day 5: Conference ends without Consensus, <http://www.wto.org/english/thewto_e/minist_e/min03_e/min03_14sept_e.htm> accessed 17 July 2019; Robert D. Anderson and Anna Caroline Müller, 'Competition Law/Policy and the Multilateral Trading System: A Possible Agenda for the Future' (2015) E15 initiative on Strengthening the Global Trade and Investment System for Sustainable Development <http://e15initiative.org/publications/competition-lawpolicy-and-the-multilateral-trading-system-apossible-agenda-for-the-future/> accessed 17 July 2019; Anu Bradford, 'International Antitrust Negotiations and the False Hope of the WTO' (2007) 48 Harvard International Law Journal 2, 410-412. See also Josef Drexl, 'International Competition Policy after Cancún: Placing a Singapore Issue on the WTO Development Agenda' (2004) 27 World Competition Law and Economics Review 3, 419-457.

378 WTO, Decision Adopted by the General Council on 1 August 2004 WT/L/579.

379 The United Nations Set of Principles and Rules on Competition TD/RBP/CONF/10/Rev.2 (1980) (UN Set).

380 Eleanor M. Fox, 'Competition Law and the Agenda for the WTO: Forging the links of Competition and Trade' (1995) 4(1) Pac. Rim Law & Pol.y, 3-4.

381 UN Set 3, 9.

382 Ibid.

tional level. This can be seen for instance in the objectives, which talk of *inter alia* 'attaining greater efficiency in international trade and development...through... control of the concentration of capital and/or economic power'.

Under the section on principles and rules for enterprises[383], the UN Set encourages enterprises to refrain from acts which through the abuse or acquisition of dominant position of market power via inter alia 'mergers, takeovers, joint ventures or other acquisitions of control, whether of a horizontal, vertical or a conglomerate nature' would limit market access and restrain competition, again with specific focus on the developing countries.[384]

The UN Set is however not legally binding. It puts forward a set of principles which it recommends and encourages states and enterprises to adopt. It opts for a cooperative and consultative approach among states towards addressing the issue of restrictive business practices. It therefore does not contain any enforcement mechanisms or sanctions.

3.1.4 Efforts to foster legal convergence

The work towards a binding multilateral antitrust regime may have been so far unsuccessful but the initiatives that emanated from those efforts have resulted in very effective consultative and cooperative approaches towards the global development and convergence of competition laws.

The WGTCP for instance in the course of its active mandate received many submissions on competition policy issues from WTO Members and international organizations, not to mention the working documents prepared for the WGTCP on various policy aspects and the annual reports they issued.[385] The WGTCP is currently inactive but the WTO Secretariat still remains available to respond to request for technical assistance in the area of trade and competition policy.

The UN, as indicated in previous chapters, has also consistently contributed towards the global development of competition policy. Under the auspices of UNCTAD, a competition and consumer policies program was set up to provide a forum for intergovernmental deliberations, research, policy analysis, data collection and provision of technical assistance to de-

383 Ibid 13, 14.

384 Ibid.

385 All their working documents are available on the WTO website.

veloping countries.[386] One of the bodies established to facilitate this mandate is the Intergovernmental Group of Experts on Competition Law and Policy (IGE), which facilitates discussions on ways of improving worldwide cooperation on competition policy implementation and enhancing convergence and consensus building.[387] It is not a rule making body and thus carries out its mandate on a voluntary basis.[388]

The OECD also plays a big part in the development of competition law in terms of fostering international cooperation, country reviews, capacity building on various antitrust law aspects, judicial training and policy briefings.[389] The scope of the OECD is in this regard not limited to the OECD member states. The OECD endeavors to disseminate its work globally through a forum in which officials from OECD Member and selected non-member competition authorities take part in roundtable discussions and peer reviews of competition laws. The OECD also publishes guidelines and recommendations aimed at steering greater harmonization of competition law.[390]

Of importance is the Recommendation of the OECD Council on Merger Review as well as the OECD Policy Roundtable report on the Standard for Merger Review.[391] The OECD recommendation on merger review, primarily aimed at OECD Members, addresses four main aspects:

1. In relation to merger notification and review procedures, it is expected that they are effective, efficient and timely. There should be sufficient access to information, the process should be cost-effective and decisions should be reached within a reasonable timeframe. It is also

386 UNCTAD: Mandate and Key Functions <http://unctad.org/en/Pages/DITC/CompetitionLaw/ccpb-Mandate.aspx.> accessed 22 September 2019.

387 UNCTAD: Intergovernmental Deliberations <http://unctad.org/en/Pages/DITC/CompetitionLaw/Intergovernmental-Deliberations.aspx.> accessed 22 August 2019.

388 Ibid.

389 OECD: Competition Global Relations <http://www.oecd.org/daf/competition/competitionglobalrelations.htm.> accessed 22 August 2019.

390 OECD: Competition <http://www.oecd.org/daf/competition/.> accessed 22 August 2019.

391 OECD, 'Recommendation of the Council on Merger Review'(2005) <https://www.oecd.org/competition/mergers/40537528.pdf> accessed 19 September 2019; OECD: Standard for Merger Review (OECD Policy Roundtables 2009) DAF/COMP(2009) available at <https://www.oecd.org/competition/mergers/45247537.pdf> accessed 17 July 2019. The OECD Merger Review Standard and Recommendation on Merger Review are discussed further in the next chapter within the context of the substantive merger regulation standards.

recommended that rules, policies, practices and procedures should be transparent and publicly available. The merging parties should also be given the opportunity to consult with the competition authority.
2. OECD Members should as far as possible seek to co-operate and coordinate their review processes in relation to transnational mergers.
3. OECD Members should ensure that the competition authorities are adequately resourced and have enough powers to effectively carry out their mandate.
4. OECD Members should seek to regularly review their merger laws and practices.

The OECD further encourages non-member countries to implement this recommendation.

Regarding the standard for merger review, the OECD principally focuses on the country experience in relation to the country experiences with the change from the dominance test to the substantial lessening of competition test. It is noted that most countries have undertaken this change without any significant impact on legal certainty and that convergence on a common substantive test may benefit international cooperation.

One of the highly effective initiatives for the achievement of international competition law convergence is the International Competition Network (ICN). The ICN was the brainchild of the International Competition Policy Advisory Committee (ICPAC) which in 2000 issued a report recommending a Global Competition Initiative.[392] The ICPAC was a US initiative formed in 1997 to review various global competition law concerns affecting the US and make recommendations to the Assistant Attorney General in charge of the Antitrust Division of the US Department of Justice.[393] This eventually led to the formation of the ICN in 2001.[394] In its final report, the ICPAC recommended the continued use of the already existing international organizations (WTO, OECD, UNCTAD) but, noting

---

392 The ICPAC Final Report (2000) <http://www.justice.gov/atr/icpac/finalreport.html.> accessed 22 August 2019 Chapter 6 titled 'Preparing for the Future' discusses the need for the Global Competition Initiative as well as the limitations of the existing avenues.

393 Charter of the International Competitiveness Advisory Committee (1997) <https://www.justice.gov/atr/charter-international-competitiveness-advisory-committee> accessed 17 July 2019, ICPAC was disbanded in the year 2000 following completion of its mandate.

394 ICN: History <http://www.internationalcompetitionnetwork.org/about/history.aspx.> accessed 22 August 2019.

their inherent limitations, and advocating a better suited avenue.[395] The logic behind the initiative was the realization that countries are willing to cooperate but should not be bound by an international regime.[396] Competition authorities use the ICN as a specialized platform for convergence and for tackling practical competition regulation concerns with a specific focus on competition law enforcement.[397] It carries out this mandate through five working groups one of which focuses mainly on mergers. The ICN working group on mergers has published several reports and recommendations touching on various aspects of merger review.[398]

In relation to international cooperation, the ICN has published a Framework for Merger Review Cooperation. The ICN explains that the Framework 'is intended to facilitate effective and efficient cooperation between and among ICN member agencies by identifying each agency's liaison officers and possible ways to exchange information. The framework includes (i) creating the contact list of liaison officers who are in charge of the contact person in the participating agencies, and (ii) the ways to contact and exchange information with other relevant agencies.'[399]

The ICN has also published a Practical Guide to International Enforcement Cooperation in Mergers. This Guide 'is intended to serve as: (i) a voluntary and flexible framework for interagency cooperation in merger investigations; (ii) practical guidance for agencies seeking to engage in such cooperation; and (iii) practical guidance for merging parties and third parties seeking to facilitate cooperation.'

The ICN is not a rule-making body. It makes recommendations based on consensus, leaving the decision on implementation to the various competition authorities.[400]

---

395 ICPAC Report (n 392).

396 Ibid.

397 ICN: About <http://www.internationalcompetitionnetwork.org/about.aspx.> accessed 22 August 2019.

398 For overview see <https://www.internationalcompetitionnetwork.org/document-library/?keyword=&groups=16&types=12> accessed 17 July 2019. There is a detailed analysis of some of the ICN core recommendations on merger regulation in the next chapter within the context of the substantive merger regulation standards.

399 See ICN Framework for Merger Review Cooperation <https://www.internationalcompetitionnetwork.org/portfolio/icn-framework-for-merger-review-cooperation/> accessed 17 July 2019.

400 See Overview of ICN <https://www.internationalcompetitionnetwork.org/about/> accessed 17 July 2019.

The approach taken by UNCTAD, OECD and ICN towards competition law convergence is to a large extent similar. Their scheme of operation is highly consultative and inclusive, bringing together views, interests and opinions of both developing and developed state parties. Based on contributions from and discussions with agents from participating countries they propose in the form of guidelines and recommendations model provisions which they intend to be instructive on the laws of the interested states.

3.2 The Merger Review Procedure

3.2.1 Introduction

From the perspective of the transacting parties and their lawyers, the procedural requirements of merger regulation are of most concern. In many jurisdictions, parties to a proposed merger are required to notify the competition authority and to submit all the necessary information for the authority to decide as to whether the transaction should be prohibited or approved. The transaction is therefore dependent on the decision reached by the competition authority. This task becomes quite onerous, costly and time consuming where multiple jurisdictions are involved and the transacting parties are required to comply with many different procedural requirements. Convergence of procedural requirements is therefore where an immediate and welcome impact would be felt by transacting parties.

Most jurisdictions employ a mandatory pre-merger notification system. Parties seeking to consummate a merger that falls within the notification threshold would therefore require the approval of the competition authority to proceed with or complete the transaction. A handful of jurisdictions employ a voluntary pre-merger notification system. However, even where a voluntary system is employed, most parties opt to pre-notify or discuss the merger with the competition authority to avoid the risk of post-merger repercussions such as divestiture of assets.[401] Pure post-merger notification systems are practically non-existent because they would result in substan-

401 See generally Jean-François Bellis and Porter Elliott (eds), *Merger Control: Jurisdictional Comparisons* (2nd edn, Thomson Reuters 2014).

tial legal uncertainty for the merging parties as well as limiting the options available for effective remedies.[402]

Jurisdictional reach, notification thresholds, information requirements and decision timelines are some of the main issues that transacting parties need to pay keen attention to. The extent of the jurisdiction is especially important because it may not only require the parties to notify their transactions in countries not directly affected by their merger but it may also extend the reach of the competition authority beyond the confines of its territorial border.

This Chapter looks at the merger regulation procedure in the European Union, the United States and South Africa which require pre-merger notification as well as the United Kingdom which employs a voluntary pre-merger notification system. The aim is to draw comparison with the ESA procedural practices, to highlight what lessons can be learnt and facilitate the determination of an optimal procedural approach for the ESA jurisdictions.

3.2.2 Defining concentration

3.2.2.1 The concept of control

Article 3(1) of the EU Merger Regulation defines a concentration as arising where there is a lasting change of control resulting from:

(a) the merger of two or more previously independent undertakings or parts of undertakings, or
(b) the acquisition, by one or more persons already controlling at least one undertaking, or by one or more undertakings, whether by purchase of securities or assets, by contract or by any other means, of direct or indirect control of the whole or parts of one or more other undertakings.

Recital 20 of the EU Merger Regulation states that 'it is expedient to define the concept of concentration in such a manner as to cover operations bringing about a lasting change in the control of the undertakings concerned and therefore in the structure of the market.'

402 Katri Paas-Mohando, 'Choice of merger notification system for small economies' (2013) 34(10) E.C.L.R. 548, 550; Inter-American Development Bank and OECD, 'Merger Control Laws and Procedures in Latin America and the Caribbean' (discussion paper 2005), 7 <http://www.oecd.org/dataoecd/41/57/38835612.pdf> accessed 23 August 2019.

The European Commission in its Jurisdictional Notice[403] explains, with reference to various decisions of the EU Courts, that an Article 3(1)(a) merger may also occur where there is no legal merger but where a combination of the activities of previously independent undertakings leads to the creation of a single economic unit.[404] A single economic unit is characterised by a permanent, single economic management.[405]

A change of control is the triggering occurrence that results in a concentration. Article 3(2) of the EU Merger Regulation explains that control is constituted by factors such as rights, contracts or any other means which confer the 'possibility of exercising decisive influence' on an undertaking. This can be through owning or having the right to utilise the assets of the undertaking or having a decisive influence on the voting, constitution or the decisions of the organs of the undertaking. Persons or undertakings holding or having the power to exercise such (contractual) rights would therefore be regarded as acquiring control over an undertaking.[406]

The concept of control is therefore a qualitative rather than a quantitative one and can arise *de jure* or *de facto*.[407] Control is more often gained through the acquisition of shares or assets of the target undertaking. It can also be contractual, where the control over management and resources conferred is similar to that under an asset or share acquisition.[408] Other exceptional contractual arrangements such as long-term supply agreements as well as other structural links which lead to economic dependence may also be regarded as conferring control.[409] Changes of control would also be deemed to arise where undertakings that were previously under sole control shifts to joint control and vice versa.[410]

The European Commission further clarifies that the concept of control under the EU Merger Regulation may differ from that in other areas of European Union and national laws such as taxation, prudential rules, air transport or the media. Such interpretations are regarded as not neces-

403 Commission Consolidated Jurisdictional Notice under Council Regulation (EC) No 139/2004 on the control of concentrations between undertakings (2008/C 95/01) (EU Jurisdictional Notice).

404 EU Jurisdictional Notice, para 10.

405 Ibid.

406 EU Merger Regulation art 3(3).

407 EU Jurisdictional Notice paras 7 and 16.

408 Ibid paras 17 and 18.

409 Ibid para 20.

410 Ibid paras 83-90.

sarily decisive *vis-a-vis* the concept of control under the EU Merger Regulation.[411]

The US Clayton Act and the Hart-Scott-Rodino Antitrust Improvements Act[412] (HSR Act) do not elucidate the concept of concentration.[413] Section 7 of the Clayton Act prohibits the acquisition, directly or indirectly, of *the whole or any part* of the assets, the stock or other share capital of an undertaking where the acquisition or the use of the stock (such as by exercising voting rights or granting proxies) would lead to a substantial lessening of competition. It goes without saying that the acquisition of the whole of the stock, assets or other share capital would enable the exercise of decisive influence over an undertaking. Section 7 has indeed been noted to be interpreted in a way that covers changes in control. However, the pre-merger notification requirement in the United States is not restricted to transactions that result in a change in control or the exercise of a decisive influence. What is more important is the value of the transaction. Where the transaction triggers the notification thresholds under the HSR Act it becomes notifiable whether or not it results in a change of control.[414]

There is no definition of concentration in the SA Competition Act. However, the SA Competition Act lists instances in which control over a firm will be deemed to have been established. Section 12(1) of the SA Competition Act states that 'a merger occurs when one or more firms directly or indirectly acquire or establish direct or indirect control over the whole or part of the business of another firm'. This may be through the acquisition or leasing of shares or assets, an amalgamation, or combination of the firms.[415] Control over a firm can be established *inter alia* by: holding more than half of the issued share capital of the target firm; having a majority voting right or the ability to control such a majority directly or

411 Ibid para 23.

412 Hart-Scott-Rodino Antitrust Improvements Act, 15 U.S. Code § 18a (Clayton Act, s 7a). The HSR Act incorporated the acquisition of assets as also leading to a merger, thereby sealing a loophole that existed under the Clayton Act. It also introduced the pre-merger notification requirement for transactions that meet the prescribed thresholds.

413 The concept of control is however present in the HSR Rules but in the context of determining what constitutes a person for purposes of determining a notifiable transaction. (16 C.F.R. s 801.1).

414 Clayton Act s 7a; Douglas Broder, *US Antitrust Law and Enforcement* (2nd edn, OUP 2012), 116.

415 SA Competition Act s 12 sub-s 1(b).

indirectly; ability to appoint or veto a majority of the directors; through a holding company; or being in a position to materially influence the policy of the firm in a similar way that a person in control would.[416]

The South Africa Competition Appeal Court has nonetheless stated that the section 12(2) lists instances of control that are not exhaustive and do not define how a change of control might take place.[417] The South Africa Competition Tribunal has made the point that control not only arises in 'bright line' situations where a majority ownership is achieved, but could also arise in instances where that bright line is not crossed and the majority right is not met.[418] The Tribunal has indeed displayed an inclination to treat section 12(2)(g) which is in respect of the ability to exercise 'material influence' as a catch-all provision for the exercise of control; more so for those instances when the bright line is not crossed, but an exercise of some form of economic or commercial leverage in nonetheless achieved.[419] An exercise of material influence is therefore regarded as being possible even in the absence of a majority stake or of decisive influence.[420] In the *Ethos Private Equity Fund* case the Tribunal gave the example of public companies where there is no clear majority but some shareholders may still be able, in certain circumstances, to exercise a majority voting right at a general meeting.[421]

The UK Enterprise Act defines a merger as taking place where 'two or more enterprises…have ceased to be distinct enterprises'[422] It further provides that two enterprises cease to be distinct where they are brought under common ownership or control.[423] Common control broadly arises in legal arrangements where the enterprise for instance belongs to a group of companies or is indirectly controlled by the same person(s).[424] The UK Enterprise Act further provides that the ability to directly or indirectly control or exercise material influence over the policy of an enterprise, even where a controlling interest does not arise, may still be treated as

416 SA Competition Act s 12 sub-s 2.

417 *Distillers Corporation (SA) Ltd / SFW Group Ltd and Bulmer (SA) (Pty) Ltd / Seagram Africa (Pty) Ltd*, 08/CAC/May01, 27 November 2001, 18.

418 *Ethos Private Equity Fund IV/Tsebo Outsourcing Group (pty) Ltd* 30/LM/Jun03, 3 October 2003, paras 42 and 43.

419 Ibid para 32.

420 Ibid paras 32-45.

421 Ibid para 44.

422 UK Enterprise Act s 23 sub-ss 1(a) and 2(a).

423 UK Enterprise Act s 26 sub-s 1.

424 UK Enterprise Act s 26 sub-s 2.

having control over the enterprise.[425] There are therefore three levels of control under UK merger regulation; material influence, *de facto* control (ability to control the enterprise's policy absent a controlling interest) and de jure control i.e. a controlling interest.[426] The CMA further explains that the policy of an enterprise in this context means 'the management of its business, and thus includes the strategic direction of a company and its ability to define and achieve its commercial objectives'.[427] Having material influence over policy can arise in various cases for instance exercising voting rights, ability to influence the board or the right to block or veto special resolutions. The CMA may examine a 15% or more shareholding to determine whether there is material influence.[428]

Material influence under UK merger regulation is therefore broader than decisive influence under EU merger regulation. This means that some transactions which would not be treated as mergers in the European Union may still be regarded as the same in the United Kingdom.[429]

In terms of classifying which transactions will be considered as mergers or notifiable for regulatory purposes, we see that the United States, South Africa and the United Kingdom all have a lower standard in terms of the level of control over the target firm. They therefore exercise a broader transactional reach.

3.2.2.1.1 Assessment of Joint Ventures

The concept of control also requires special consideration in relation to how the various jurisdictions assess joint ventures and whether they meet the criteria for assessment under the merger provisions. Article 3(4) of the EU Merger Regulation for instance provides that, 'The creation of a joint venture performing on a lasting basis all the functions of an autonomous economic entity shall constitute a concentration within the meaning of paragraph 1(b)'.

As previously noted, Article 3(1)(b) of the EU Merger Regulation provides that a concentration may arise where there is a lasting change of

425 UK Enterprise Act s 26 sub-s 3.

426 See also Competition and Markets Authority, Mergers: Guidance on the CMA's Jurisdiction and Procedure (2014), paras 4.12-4.30 (UK Procedural Guidance).

427 UK Procedural Guidance para 4.14.

428 Ibid paras 4.16-4.21.

429 UK Procedural Guidance para 4.14.

control resulting from 'the acquisition, by one or more persons already controlling at least one undertaking, or by one or more undertakings, whether by purchase of securities or assets, by contract or by any other means, of direct or indirect control of the whole or parts of one or more other undertakings.'

The European Commission has further published a notice addressing the concept of a 'full-function' joint venture under the EU Merger Regulation (EC Joint Venture Notice).[430] Essentially, a joint venture needs to satisfy two main criteria to be captured under Article 3 of the EU Merger Regulation:

1. There needs to be joint control where the controlling parties can exercise decisive influence over the venture.
2. The joint venture must be 'full-function' meaning that it must perform on a lasting basis all the functions of an autonomous economic entity. The EC Joint Venture Notice further clarifies that 'this means that a joint venture must operate on a market, performing the functions normally carried out by undertakings operating on the same market. In order to do so the joint venture must have a management dedicated to its day-to-day operations and access to sufficient resources including finance, staff, and assets (tangible and intangible) in order to conduct on a lasting basis its business activities within the area provided for in the joint-venture agreement.[431]

Where the joint venture leads to a co-operation between the joint venture partners that impacts their competitive behaviour, the assessment of the joint venture will include an assessment of any anti-competitive coordination issues that may arise under Article 101(1) and 101(3) of the TFEU.[432]

The United States does not adopt any special rules relating to the treatment of joint ventures. The value of the transaction as well as the net sales and assets of the parties to the joint venture will be highly instructive of whether it is notifiable under the HSR Act. A joint venture will be notifiable if it results in the direct or indirect acquisition[433] of any voting securities, non-corporate interests[434] or assets where:

---

430 Commission Notice on the concept of full-function joint ventures under Council Regulation (EEC) No 4064/89 on the control of concentrations between undertakings (98/C 66/01) (EC Joint Venture Notice).

431 EC Joint Venture Notice para 12.

432 EC Joint Venture Notice para 16.

433 Acquisitions include mergers and consolidations *see* 16 C.F.R. s 801.2.

434 16 C.F.R. s 801.1.

1. both the acquiring and acquired persons are engaged in commerce or any activity affecting commerce in the United States; and
2. the prescribed thresholds under the HSR Act are met.[435]

If the joint venture results in the formation of a new entity, then the new entity will be treated as the acquired person and each of the joint venture parties contributing to the formation of the new entity will be treated as the acquiring persons.[436]

In the United Kingdom, a joint venture would fall under the UK Enterprise Act:

1. where two or more enterprises cease to be distinct, meaning the joint venture (whether through acquisition or the formation of a new enterprise) is brought under common ownership or control through material influence, *de facto* control or de jure control; and
2. the relevant thresholds are met.[437]

In South Africa, to the extent that a joint venture arises from 'one or more firms directly or indirectly acquiring or establishing direct or indirect control over the whole or part of the business of another firm'[438] and the relevant thresholds are met, the joint venture would be notifiable under the SA Competition Act.

The South Africa Competition Commission has further issued a practitioner guide in relation to the applicability of the merger regulation provisions to joint ventures.[439] The South Africa Competition Commission essentially clarifies that the definition of a merger in the SA Competition Act is broad enough to cover joint ventures.[440] Particularly, the South Africa Competition Commission states that only those joint ventures that result in a change of control and meet the threshold would be notifiable.[441] In this regard, the South Africa Competition Commission specifies which kind of joint venture transactions are examined:

---

435 The notification thresholds are addressed in detail in chapter 9.

436 HSR Rules 16 CFR § 801.40.

437 The notification thresholds are addressed in detail in chapter 9.

438 SA Competition Act, s 12(1).

439 Competition Commission of South Africa, Practitioner Update: The application of merger provisions of the Competition Act 89 of 1998, as amended, to joint ventures, <http://www.compcom.co.za/wp-content/uploads/2014/09/Practitoner-Update-Joint-Ventures-Published-version.doc> accessed 17 July 2019.

440 SA Practitioner Update on Joint Ventures para 13.

441 SA Practitioner Update on Joint Ventures para 14.

(a) Where two or more firms jointly form a new entity for a specific purpose; and
(b) Where two or more firms acquire joint control over an existing firm or business thereof.[442]

3.2.2.3 The ESA Perspective

All the ESA jurisdictions in focus classify mergers based on change of the controlling interest. A merger is therefore deemed to arise where;

i) One or more undertakings directly or indirectly obtain control over the (whole or part of) the business of another undertaking. This is the case in Namibia, Kenya, Botswana, Seychelles, Zimbabwe and COMESA. The wording is similar to that used to define mergers in South Africa and the European Union.[443]
ii) It brings (undertakings) together under common ownership and control. This is the definition used in Mauritius and Zambia and is similar to the UK definition of enterprises 'ceasing to be distinct'.[444]
iii) It gives rise to a change of control. This is the definition in Tanzania.[445]

The conventional ways in which a change of control is effected also apply in the ESA jurisdictions that are in focus. This is *inter alia* via acquisition of shares and assets, holding the majority voting rights and the right to appoint or veto the appointment of the majority of directors. In terms of the threshold for a change of control, the ability to exercise material influence is the standard used in Botswana, Kenya, Mauritius and Zambia.[446] Zimbabwe defines a controlling interest as *inter alia* an interest that enables the holder to exercise any control over the activities or assets of

---

442 SA Practitioner Update on Joint Ventures para 15.

443 Botswana Competition Act s 52 sub-s 1; Kenya Competition Act s 41 sub-s 1; Namibia Competition Act, s 42 sub-s 1; COMESA Competition Regulations art 23(2); Zimbabwe Competition Act, s 2 sub-s 1; Seychelles Competition Act s 1 sub-s 2.

444 Mauritius Competition Act, s 47 sub-s 1; Zambia Competition Act s 24 sub-s 1; Zambia Merger Guidelines para 8; UK Enterprise Act s 26 sub-s 1.

445 Tanzania Competition Act s 2.

446 Botswana Competition Act s 52 sub-s 2; Kenya Competition Act s 41 sub-ss 2-3; Namibia Competition Act s 42 sub-ss 2-3; COMESA Competition Regulations art 23 (1) and (2); Zimbabwe Competition Act s 2 sub-s 1; Mauritius Competition Act s 47 sub-s 3; Tanzania Competition Act s 2; Zambia Competition Act s 24 sub-ss 2-3; Seychelles Competition Act s 1 sub-s 2.

another undertaking. Any control can indeed be very widely construed to include situations that fall below the bright line.[447]

The COMESA defines a controlling interest in an undertaking as inter alia 'any control whatsoever over the activities or assets of the undertaking.' In this case the wording may also be construed widely to include cases falling below the bright line.[448] However, it is clarified in the COMESA merger guidelines that control is to be defined in the sense of decisive influence.[449]

Malawi and Tanzania do not clarify their position on the issue of what level of control can be regarded as a controlling interest. Seychelles points to certain obvious cases such as acquiring of majority stake but leaves open to guidance by the Commission on other instances in which change of control shall be deemed to occur.[450]

Just as is the case in the European Union, a number of the jurisdictions also specify that the question of control depends on qualitative rather than quantitative criteria.[451] Botswana for instance highlights financial arrangements that lead to a high level of dependency on the lender as possibly giving rise to material influence. Additionally, situations where minority shareholders have a right to veto decisions of strategic importance to the undertaking or any other means by which an acquirer may influence the policy of the target undertaking may give rise to a controlling interest.[452] Kenya also points out that the ability to influence key commercial decisions materially will be regarded by the authority as an acquisition of indirect control and will be treated similarly to decisive influence for analytical purposes.[453] Similar instances in which material influence may be de facto exercised over an enterprise by means of influencing strategic commercial arrangements e.g. financial, veto rights are also reflected in Mauritius, Namibia and Zambia.[454]

Although the COMESA merger guidelines specify that control arises where the ability to exercise decisive influence is conferred, they further

447 Zimbabwe Competition Act s 2 sub-s 1.
448 COMESA Competition Regulations art 23(2).
449 COMESA Merger Guidelines para 2.5.
450 Seychelles Merger Guidelines para 2.5.
451 EU Jurisdictional Notice paras 7 and 16; Botswana Merger Guidelines para 3.5; Mauritius Merger Guidelines para 2.4; Seychelles Merger Guidelines para 2.4.
452 Botswana Merger Guidelines paras 3.6 et seq.
453 Kenya Merger Guidelines paras 22 et seq.
454 Mauritius Merger Guidelines paras 2.12 et seq; Namibia Merger Guidelines paras 3.6 et seq.; Zambia Merger Guidelines paras 4 et seq.

highlight instances by which a minority interest may enable the exercise of a decisive influence. The factors highlighted are more or less those taken into consideration in determining material influence. of the COMESA merger guidelines also take into consideration the ability to influence strategic commercial behaviour, specifically appointment of senior management, the budget or business plan or strategic commercial policy. In effect, COMESA as well considers situations that fall below the bright line.[455]

3.2.2.3.1 The assessment of joint ventures in ESA

Kenya, Zambia and COMESA subsume joint ventures under their merger regulation provisions and provide further clarification in the merger guidelines. Quite interestingly, a number of the ESA jurisdictions have adopted the 'full-function' concept of joint ventures with a formulation that is very similar to the European Union.

The Kenya Competition Act does not have any specific provisions in relation to joint ventures. Nevertheless, in the Kenya Merger Guidelines, the Competition Commission of Kenya notes that:

> For a joint venture to constitute a ‚merger' within the meaning of Section 41 of the Act, it must be a ‚full-function' joint venture. This means that it must perform, for a long duration (typically 10 years or more) all the functions of an autonomous economic entity, including:
> (a) operating on a market and performing the functions normally carried out by undertakings operating on the same market; and
> (b) having a management dedicated to its day-to-day operations and access to sufficient resources including finance, staff and assets (tangible and intangible) in order to conduct for a long duration its business activities within the area provided for in the joint-venture agreement.[456]

The Competition Authority of Kenya further notes that joint ventures established for a 'purposefully finite period' (such as a construction project) will not be viewed as having a long duration.

In addition to the guidance in the Kenya Merger Guidelines, the Competition Authority of Kenya in February 2021 published draft Joint Venture Guidelines which were open for comment from stakeholders until

455 COMESA Merger Guidelines para 2.8.
456 Kenya Merger Guidelines paras 30-34.

March 2021.[457] The draft Joint Venture Guidelines reiterate the full-function requirement captured in the Kenya Merger Guidelines. The draft guidelines however elaborate on a number of aspects that are not currently included in the Kenya Merger Guidelines.

They introduce a definition of a joint venture as:

> integration of operations between two or more separate firms, in which the following conditions are present: (i) the enterprise is under joint control of the parent firms; (ii) each party makes a substantial resource contribution to the joint enterprise; (iii) the enterprise exists as a business entity separate from its parents; and (iv) the joint venture creates significant new enterprise with a direct market access, in terms of new productive capacity, new technology, new products, or entry into a new market.[458]

They also incorporate the concept of greenfield joint ventures which are defined as joint venture arrangements aimed at engaging in a new business venture separate from and unrelated to the activities undertaken by the parties to the joint venture. It is further explained that greenfield joint ventures are formed in situations where local or foreign entities collaborate with other local domiciled entities to develop a new product separate from the products and services provided by the parent entities. Parties to greenfield joint ventures are advised to seek advisory opinions from the Competition Authority of Kenya before implementation.[459]

In relation to notification, given that joint ventures do not conform to the usual target and acquirer format of a merger, the draft Joint Venture Guidelines require the necessary documentation to be submitted separately by the joint venture parent entities and by the joint venture vehicle. Given the potential a joint venture has to change the competition dynamics in the country, the draft Joint Venture Guidelines propose to have the parent entities submit the relevant asset and turnover figures not just in relation to their business in Kenya but globally.[460] There is also an acknowledgement of the impact of e-commerce on the economy. It is proposed that an

---

457 Competition Authority of Kenya, Joint Venture Guidelines under the Competition Act No. 12 of 2010 (Kenya Joint Venure Guidelines) <https://www.cak.go.ke/sites/default/files/Draft%20Joint%20Venture%20Guidelines%20Under%20the%20Competition%20Act%20No%2012%20of%202010.pdf> accessed 25 June 2021.

458 Kenya Joint Venture Guidelines para 10.

459 Kenya Joint Venture Guidelines para 11 and section 4.

460 Kenya Joint Venture Guidelines para 20.

assessment will consider aspects of big data and digital economy dynamics of entry and access to data in transactions likely to involve big data even where data is not the main component of the transaction.[461]

The COMESA Competition Regulations do not have any specific provision for joint ventures. The COMESA Merger Guidelines however have a similar definition of a full-function merger to Kenya, with the exception that a long duration is deemed to be five or more years. The exclusion of joint ventures formed for a 'purposefully finite period' mirrors the exclusion in the Kenya Merger Guidelines.[462]

The Zambia Competition Act defines an 'enterprise' to include a joint venture for purposes of defining a merger. Section 24(1) of the Zambia Competition Act defines a merger as occurring,

> where an enterprise, directly or indirectly, acquires or establishes, direct or indirect, control over the whole or part of the business of another enterprise, or when two or more enterprises mutually agree to adopt arrangements for common ownership or control over the whole or part of their respective businesses.' Section 24(2) further provides that a merger as contemplated in section 24(1) includes instance 'where a joint venture occurs between two or more independent enterprises.

In relation to mergers arising out of mutual arrangements between enterprises that lead to common ownership, the Zambia Merger Guidelines provide that a mutual arrangement may arise in the case of a joint venture. For a joint venture to be considered as a mutual arrangement 'each enterprise must make a substantial contribution to the implementation of a common project, and it must be a separate business – and usually a separate legal entity – but is jointly owned and controlled by the parent enterprises.'[463]

The Zambia Merger Guidelines likewise include the concept of a full-function joint venture. Full-function joint ventures that meet the merger notification thresholds have to be notified to the Zambia Competition Commission. The Zambia Merger Guidelines similarly define a full-function joint venture as one that 'performs on a lasting basis all the functions of an autonomous economic entity, competing with other enterprises in

461 Kenya Joint Venture Guidelines para 23.1.
462 COMESA Merger Guidelines paras 2.11-2.15.
463 Zambia Merger Guidelines paras 8-9.

a relevant market, and has sufficient resources and staff to operate independently on the relevant market.'[464]

In relation to Mauritius, Namibia, Seychelles, Botswana, Tanzania, Malawi and Zimbabwe, neither the merger regulation provisions of their competition statutes nor the merger guidelines provide for any definition or special treatment for joint ventures. It may however be presumed that where a joint venture satisfies all the criteria of a merger, it would be subsumed under the merger control provisions.

3.2.3 Notification Thresholds

3.2.3.1 The European Union

In addition to a transaction resulting in a lasting change of control as per article 3, the EU Merger Regulation further requires a 'community dimension' for the transaction to fall within its jurisdiction.[465] Mergers with a community dimension are exclusively under the jurisdiction of the European Commission.[466]

Article 1(2) and 1(3) of the EU Merger Regulation provide two sets of cumulative thresholds required for the achievement of a community dimension. Article 1(2) requires that both an aggregate worldwide and an aggregate community-wide turnover threshold of the undertakings be met. The aggregate worldwide turnover is set at EUR 5 billion or more and the community-wide turnover is set at EUR 250 million or more. However, whereas the aggregate worldwide turnover is in respect of all the undertakings concerned, the aggregate community-wide turnover is in respect of at least two of the undertakings concerned. In the event that more than two-thirds of the aggregate community-wide turnover is realised by each of the concerned undertakings in one Member State, it will be regarded as falling within the Member States jurisdiction i.e. a domestic transaction.[467]

Article 1(3) targets those transactions that do not fall under the Article 1(2) community dimension but which nonetheless would substantially affect at least three Member States. The turnover thresholds are thus set

464 Zambia Merger Guidelines para 12.
465 EU Merger Regulation art 1(1).
466 EU Merger Regulation art 21.
467 EU Merger Regulation art 1(2); EU Jurisdictional Notice para 125.

at a lower level.[468] One of the intentions here is to eliminate the need for multiple notifications in those countries, which in turn cuts down transaction costs for the parties.[469] The two-thirds domestic transaction threshold applies in this case as well.

For the purposes of determining the turnover, not only are the undertakings directly concerned considered, but also those undertakings falling within a group of undertakings i.e. under common control.[470] The undertakings concerned could be each of the merging entities or in the case of an acquisition the acquiring undertaking(s) as well as the target undertaking.[471]

The notification requirement will be triggered provided that these thresholds are met and the transacting parties qualify as undertakings concerned, irrespective of whether the transaction in question takes place outside of the EU or that the undertakings concerned are located or carry on a significant part of their business outside the EU.[472]

Transactions seeking to create concentrations with a community dimension are required to be pre-notified to the European Commission. In terms of determining jurisdiction, the operative date is taken to be the date of the conclusion of a binding legal agreement, the announcement of a public bid, the acquisition of a controlling interest or the date of the first notification.[473]

3.2.3.2 The United States

The HSR Act prohibits the direct or indirect acquisition[474] of any voting securities, non-corporate interests[475] or assets of any other person 'unless

468 Aggregate worldwide turnover of EUR 2,500 million or more for all undertakings concerned; combined aggregate turnover of EUR 100 million or more for all undertakings concerned in each of at least 3 Member States; aggregate turnover of EUR 25 million or more for each of at least two of the undertakings concerned in each of at least 2 of the 3 Member States and an aggregate Community-wide turnover of EUR 100 million or more in respect of each of at least two of the undertakings concerned.

469 EU Jurisdictional Notice para 126.

470 EU Merger Regulation art 5(4); EU Jurisdictional Notice para 130.

471 EU Merger Regulation art 3(1); EU Jurisdictional Notice para 132 and 133.

472 Whish and Bailey (2012) 499.

473 EU Merger Regulation art 4(1); EU Jurisdictional Notice paras 154-156.

474 Acquisitions include mergers and consolidations *see* 16 C.F.R. s 801.2.

475 16 C.F.R. s 801.1.

both persons (or in the case of a tender offer, the acquiring person) file notification' if; (i) both the acquiring and acquired persons are engaged in commerce or any activity affecting commerce and (ii) as a result of the acquisition the acquiring person would hold an aggregate total amount of the voting securities and assets of the acquired person in excess of the prescribed monetary thresholds.[476] The FTC notes that this provision in essence prescribes three main tests for the determination of jurisdiction; the commerce test, the size of the person test and the size of the transaction test.[477]

The commerce test requires that the parties be engaged in commerce or any activity affecting commerce. Commerce is defined to include interstate commerce, commerce with foreign nations, commerce in any territory of the United States, in the District of Columbia, inter-territory commerce, between any territory and any state or foreign nation, or between the District of Columbia and any state or territory or foreign nation.[478] Both the transacting parties therefore need to have a commercial link to the United States. Commerce itself is regarded as any exchange of money for goods or services, irrespective of whether it is for profit or not.[479]

The HSR Rules define a person as 'an ultimate parent entity and all entities which it controls directly or indirectly'. A person therefore includes a group of interconnected entities. Control in this case means a 50 percent plus interest in respect of voting securities, or a right to 50 percent plus of the profits or of the assets in case of a dissolution.[480] The term entity is given a broad definition which includes natural persons, corporations, partnerships, joint ventures, trusts etc. An ultimate parent entity is one which is not controlled by any other entity. Where an ultimate parent entity is foreign then any entity under its control will be regarded as a foreign person.[481] The concept of an entity in this respect however excludes

---

476 Clayton Act s 7a (a) the thresholds are subject to annual fiscal adjustments to reflect changes in gross national product.

477 FTC, To File or not to File: When you must file a Premerger Notification Report Form (September 2008) <ftc.gov/bc/hsr> accessed 23 September 2019 (FTC Premerger Notification Guide).

478 16 C.F.R. s 801.1; *see also* Clayton Act s1; Federal Trade Commission Act s4.

479 Christopher Lynn Sagers (ed), *Handbook on the Scope of Antitrust* (American Bar Association 2015), 15.

480 16 C.F.R. s 801.1.

481 Ibid. In the case of a corporation, this means that it is neither incorporated or organised under the laws of the US nor does it have its principal offices in the US. If a natural person this means neither a citizen nor a resident of the US.

countries or governments as well as their agencies whether foreign or US. [482]

The monetary thresholds can be regarded as two-fold; (i) directed at the net sales or assets of the parties (the size of the person test) and (ii) directed at value of the actual transaction i.e. the acquisition of voting securities, non-corporate interests or assets (the size of the transaction test). According to the thresholds adjusted for 2021:[483]

1) acquisitions of voting securities, non-corporate interests or stock with an aggregate value of more than USD 368 million by persons engaged in commerce or any activity affecting commerce in the US would be notifiable; or
2) Where the aggregate value of the acquired voting securities, non-corporate interests or assets falls between USD 92 million and USD 368 million and:
   (a) The target has annual net sales or total assets of USD 18.4 million or more and the acquirer has annual net sales or total assets of USD 184 million;
   (b) The target does not have sales but has total assets of USD 18.4 million or more and the acquirer has annual net sales and total assets of USD 184 million; or
   (c) The target has annual net sales or total assets of USD 184 million or more and the acquirer has annual net sales or total assets of USD 18.4 million or more.

In summary the jurisdiction of the HSR Act over a specific transaction principally falls on whether or not; (i) the transaction is a qualifying acquisition, (ii) the parties are engaged in commerce or any activity affecting commerce (iii) the transacting parties exceed the threshold size in terms of

482 16 C.F.R. s 801.1. An entity is defined as 'any natural person, corporation, company, partnership, joint venture, association, joint-stock company, trust, estate of a deceased natural person, foundation, fund, institution, society, union, or club, whether incorporated or not, wherever located and of whatever citizenship, or any receiver, trustee in bankruptcy or similar official or any liquidating agent for any of the foregoing, in his or her capacity as such; or any joint venture or other corporation which has not been formed but the acquisition of the voting securities or other interest in which, if already formed.'

483 Clayton Act s 7a *read together with* Revised Jurisdictional Thresholds for Section 7A of the Clayton Act, Federal Register / March 2021 <https://www.federalregister.gov/documents/2021/02/02/2021-02110/revised-jurisdictional-thresholds-for-section-7a-of-the-clayton-act.> accessed 25 June 2021.

assets and commercial activity in or into the US and (iv) the actual value of the transaction exceeds the threshold.

The HSR Rules provide for various exceptions. These include *inter alia*:

(a) Acquisition of goods and services in the ordinary course of business;[484]
(b) Acquisitions solely for the purpose of investment;[485]
(c) Intra-person acquisitions, for instance a merger of two majority owned subsidiaries;[486] and
(d) Acquisition of foreign assets and voting securities of a foreign issuer.[487]

The exemption of acquisition of foreign assets will however require further consideration of the sales generated in or into the United States by the target firm exceeded USD 92 million in its most recent fiscal year.[488] If it does exceed this amount then it will only be exempt if four cumulative criteria are met:[489]

(a) Both the acquirer and the target are foreign persons;
(b) The aggregate sales of the acquirer and target in or into the US are less than USD 184 million in their most recent fiscal years;
(c) Their aggregate total assets in the United States are less than USD 184 million; and
(d) The transaction's value does not go beyond USD 368 million.

The exemption on an acquisition of foreign voting securities by a US person shall not apply where the assets held by the target in the United States have an aggregate value that exceeds USD 92 million or the aggregate sales in or into the US in the target's most recent fiscal year exceeded USD 92 million.[490]

Where the acquisition of the foreign voting securities is by a foreign person, the exemption will not apply if the foreign person will gain control of a target with aggregate assets or sales in or into the US exceeding USD 92 million. The transaction will however still be exempt if the four cumulative criteria above are met.[491]

A transaction falling below the notification thresholds may however still be subject to investigation. The investigation can be carried out before or

---

484 16 C.F.R. s 802.1.
485 16 C.F.R. s 802.9.
486 16 C.F.R. s 802.30.
487 16 C.F.R. s 802.50 and s 802.51.
488 16 C.F.R. s 802.50(a).
489 16 C.F.R. s 802.50(b).
490 16 C.F.R. s 802.51(a).
491 16 C.F.R. s 802.51(b) and (c).

after consummation and the same remedies are available as is the case with reportable mergers.[492]

3.2.3.3 South Africa

The SA Competition Act classifies mergers into three different categories; small mergers, intermediate mergers and large mergers.[493] Therefore, in addition to determining whether the transaction qualifies as a merger, the parties need to determine which category they fit into. As noted previously, a merger arises 'when one or more firms directly or indirectly acquire or establish direct or indirect control over the whole or part of the business of another firm'[494]

An acquiring firm is defined as a firm that has or would directly or indirectly acquire or establish direct or indirect control over the whole or part of the business of another firm.[495] A target firm is defined as one that would be transferring direct or indirect control to or would be under the direct or indirect control of the acquiring firm.[496]

Whether a merger is small, intermediate or large is determined by where it falls in respect of a lower and higher threshold of combined turnover

---

492 OECD, Investigations of Consummated and Non-notifiable Mergers: United States DAF/COMP/WP3/WD(2014)23, para 3 <https://www.ftc.gov/system/files/attachments/us-submissions-oecd-other-international-competition-fora/consummated_mergers_us_oecd.pdf> accessed 23 August 2019.

493 SA Competition Act s 11.

494 SA Competition Act s 12 sub-s 1(a).

495 SA Competition Act s1 sub-s 1(i). The exact phrasing of this definition in the Act does contain some ambiguity and redundancy. The exact definition provides that 'acquiring firm' means a firm: (a) that, as a result of a transaction in any circumstances set out in section 12, would directly or indirectly acquire, or establish direct or indirect control over, the whole or part of the business of another firm; (b) that has direct or indirect control over the whole or part of the business of a firm contemplated in paragraph (a); or (c) the whole or part of whose business is directly or indirectly controlled by a firm contemplated in paragraph (a) or (b);' A reading of sub-section c of the definition for instance may be understood to mean that the acquiring firm is a firm that is directly or indirectly controlled by itself.

496 SA Competition Act s1 sub-s 1(i)(xxxxi). A firm includes a person, a partnership or a trust (s1(1)(xi). A person is deemed to include every legal entity capable of conducting business, including a natural person. (Sutherland and Kemp (2014) para 9.2.2).

and assets.[497] A small merger falls at or below the lower threshold, an intermediate merger between the lower and higher thresholds and a large merger lies at or above the higher threshold.[498] There is no requirement to notify small mergers and they may be implemented without approval unless the Commission is of the opinion that the merger may substantially lessen competition or cannot be justified on public interest grounds. They may nonetheless be voluntarily notified.[499] Intermediate and large mergers must be notified and cannot be consummated without the required approval. The Commission is responsible for investigating both intermediate and large mergers. In the case of intermediate mergers, the Commission must either approve (with or without conditions) or prohibit the merger after completing the assessment. However, after investigating a large merger, the Commission must refer the merger, together with a recommendation, the Competition Tribunal and the Minister of Economic Development. The Commission does not have the authority to reach a determination in respect of large mergers. [500]

The current guidelines on thresholds (Threshold Guidelines) came into operation in April 2009.[501] The lower and higher thresholds are currently set at:[502]

(a) R600 million and R6.6 billion for any combination of the assets or annual turnover of the acquiring and transferred firms in, into or from South Africa respectively; or
(b) R100 million and R190 million for either the assets or the annual turnover of the transferred firms in, into or from South Africa respectively.

The transferred firm is defined in terms of the business or assets (including the firm itself) that is or would come under the direct or indirect control of the acquiring firm.[503] Therefore only the value of the transferred business or assets is relevant for the determination. The valuation of the assets and the turnover is in terms of their gross values rather than net values. The Threshold Regulations further specify that where the acquiring and transferred firms are part of a group of companies then the combined

497 SA Competition Act s 11.
498 Ibid.
499 SA Competition Act s 13.
500 SA Competition Act s 13A.
501 Determination of Merger Thresholds and Method of Calculation, GN 216 (6 March 2009) (SA Threshold Guidance).
502 SA Threshold Guidance s 2 and s 3.
503 SA Threshold Guidance s 1.

assets or turnover in South Africa of the whole group shall be taken into account. Turnover or assets derived from intra-group transactions are however excluded.[504]

3.2.3.4 The United Kingdom

In addition to the enterprises ceasing to be distinct, a transaction in question needs to meet certain threshold requirements to qualify as a relevant merger in the United Kingdom.[505] The thresholds are classified as the turnover test and the share-of-supply test. These two tests are not cumulative. The achievement of either of the two in addition to the enterprises ceasing to be distinct will give rise to the relevant merger situation. The turnover test requires that the value of the turnover of the target enterprise in the United Kingdom exceeds GBP 70 million.[506] If post-merger there will be enterprises that cease to be distinct and those that remain under the same ownership and control, the relevant turnover is determined by deducting the turnover arising from those enterprises that remain under the same ownership or control. This means that intra-group transactions are also excluded in the United Kingdom.[507] Where all enterprises cease to be distinct then a deduction is made of the turnover with the highest value in the United Kingdom.[508]

The share of supply test requires that as a result of the merger, both the acquiring and target enterprises will realise a 25% stake or increment in their supply or acquisition of relevant goods or services in the United Kingdom or in a substantial part of it.[509]

As noted at the beginning of the chapter, notification in the United Kingdom is voluntary. This is irrespective of whether a relevant merger situation has arisen.[510] This however does not bar the CMA from initiating the review of a relevant merger situation.[511] The CMA has a market intelligence function through which it can gather information on relevant merger situations which have not been notified and which raise competi-

504 SA Threshold Guidance s 8.
505 UK Enterprise Act s 23.
506 UK Enterprise Act s 23; See also UK Procedural Guidance para 4.3.
507 UK Procedural Guidance para B19.
508 UK Enterprise Act s 28; See also UK Procedural Guidance paras 4.48 - 4.50.
509 UK Enterprise Act s 23; See also UK Procedural Guidance para 4.3.
510 UK Procedural Guidance para 6.1.
511 UK Procedural Guidance paras 6.59 and 6.60.

tion concerns. It also relies on complaints received from third parties. In the worst-case scenario, the parties to a relevant merger situation even run the risk of an already consummated merger being terminated if it raises serious competition concerns.[512] There are three avenues through which the parties may involve the CMA:[513]

(i) Where the parties feel that a genuine competition issue arises, they can seek informal advice from the merger unit of the CMA. It is usually in respect of confidential transactions i.e. not yet in the public domain but which are past the hypothetical stage.

(ii) Where the parties intend to make a formal notification, they may first engage the CMA in pre-notification discussions. Apart from clarifying various issues arising out of the proposed merger thus facilitating a smoother notification and review period, these discussions also facilitate the determination of whether the transaction falls within a community dimension and hence whether a referral to the Commission is due.

The parties may also submit a formal notification where the proposed merger is already publicly known.

3.2.3.5 Eastern and Southern Africa

Except for Malawi and Mauritius, all the highlighted ESA jurisdictions employ a mandatory pre-notification system. Therefore, in addition to the change of control requirement, mergers qualify for review where they meet the notification thresholds.[514]

Just like the United Kingdom, Malawi and Mauritius exceptionally employ a voluntary notification system.[515] However, unlike the United Kingdom, Malawi has no set notification thresholds. Mauritius employs a market share-based threshold. The United Kingdom has turnover and share of supply thresholds which are used to determine whether a relevant merger situation has arisen. The CMA's market intelligence function empowers it to investigate relevant merger situations. The Commissions in Malawi and Mauritius similarly have the power to investigate mergers that

512 UK Procedural Guidance paras 6.5-6.21.
513 UK Procedural Guidance paras 6.22-6.58.
514 See Annex.
515 Ibid; UK Procedural Guidance para 6.1.

may result in a substantial lessening of competition.[516] The repercussions of failing to notify a merger that eventually turns out to be anticompetitive or liable for prohibition is quite serious in all three jurisdictions. In the United Kingdom, such mergers may be liable for termination. In Malawi, the Act provides that such transactions will have no legal effect in addition to giving rise to an offense punishable by either a fine or in the worst-case scenario imprisonment. It is however highly unlikely that imprisonment will ensue in the case of a merger offence.[517] In Mauritius, both structural remedies (for example blocking mergers and divestment) as well as behavioural remedies may be employed.[518]

It is therefore clear that irrespective of the fact that notification is voluntary, parties to mergers that are likely to have adverse effects on competition would be highly motivated to seek the authorities' approval. The UK's CMA gives parties the chance to seek informal advice, to engage in pre-notification discussions or to make a formal notification. Malawi and Mauritius as well give the parties the option to contact the Commission for guidance as well as to make applications for negative clearance.[519]

In respect of the jurisdictions employing mandatory pre-merger notification, the thresholds are mainly based on assets and turnover.

COMESA in addition naturally requires a regional dimension to be met. Pursuant to Art. 23(3)(a) of the COMESA Competition Regulations, both undertakings must be operational in at least two Member States. Therefore, the acquiring and/or target firms need to operate in two or more Member States. This is like the European Union's community dimension requirement. In relation to merger regulation jurisdiction, Article 3(3) of the COMESA Competition Regulations provides that 'These Regulations shall have primary jurisdiction over an industry or a sector of an industry which is subject to the jurisdiction of a separate regulatory entity (whether domestic or regional)'. Therefore, where the 'regional dimension' is satisfied and the merger thresholds are met, the COMESA Competition Commission shall have primary jurisdiction. This naturally raises concerns over jurisdictional overlap with the EAC Competition Act which also provides for exclusive original jurisdiction.[520]

516 Ibid.

517 UK Procedural Guidance paras 6.5-6.21.

518 Mauritius Remedies and Penalties Guidelines part 4.

519 Malawi Merger Guidelines para 6.1; Mauritius Merger Guidelines para 2.5.

520 EAC Competition Act Article 44(1).

At inception, the COMESA merger regulations presented various challenges. The merger notification threshold had been set at zero which essentially meant that any transaction globally in respect of which the transacting parties had a regional presence in the Common Market had to be notified. This was regardless of the assets or turnover generated within the Common Market. In addition to this there was uncertainty around the provision on filing fees which required parties to pay a rather large sum of money. The provisions also captured transactions where the presence in the region of either the acquiring or the acquired party was sufficient to trigger notification. This meant that transactions where the acquiring party is within the Common Market and the acquired party is outside of the Common Market (and has no business within the Common Market) also had to be notified. All these challenges meant the COMESA merger regulations extended a very large and unnecessary extraterritorial footprint. The COMESA Competition Commission however made amendments to the regulations in 2014 introducing notification thresholds, clarifying the issue of filing fees as well as ensuring a sufficient nexus of a transaction to the Common Market by focusing attention on operations within the Common Market.[521]

Unlike the European Union which also considers worldwide turnover and assets, COMESA focuses only on assets and turnover in the Common Market with the aim of capturing those transactions with an appreciable effect on trade within the Common Market.[522] Again, like the European Union, where at least two-thirds of the assets or turnover of the parties is achieved in one Member State the jurisdiction to review the merger will fall on that Member State.[523]

---

521 See COMESA Competition Regulations ss 23-24; COMESA, Rules on the Determination of Merger Notification Thresholds and Method of Calculation <https://www.comesacompetition.org/wp-content/uploads/2015/04/Amendments-to-the-Rules-to-the-Determination-of-Merger-Thresholds-and-Method-of-Calculation-adopted-by-COM-26-March-2015.pdf> accessed 17 July 2019 ; See also Vincent Angwenyi, Competition Law and Regional Integration: The Common Market for Eastern and Southern Africa (COMESA) MIPLC Master Thesis Series (2012/2013) pp 40-45 available at SSRN: <https://ssrn.com/abstract=2406825> accessed 26 July 2017; Webber Wentzel Competition E-Alert - 10 April 2015 <http://www.polity.org.za/article/further-refinements-to-comesas-merger-control-regime-2015-04-10> accessed 26 July 2017; Annex; EU Merger Regulation art 1(1).

522 COMESA Merger Guidelines paras 3.5-3.6.

523 Ibid; Annex; EU Merger Regulation art 1(2); EU Jurisdictional Notice para 125.

Some of the jurisdictions also apply a market share-based threshold, like the UK's share-of-market-supply test.[524] Botswana for instance has, in addition to its asset and turnover threshold, a share of supply threshold of 20 percent of the goods or services in Botswana. Where the merging parties meet this threshold following implementation, they are required to notify the transaction. Mauritius and Seychelles also have market share tests of 40 and 30 percent respectively.[525]

In Kenya, the asset and turnover thresholds are further classified based on specific industries. These are specifically categorised as the health care, carbon-based mineral and oil sectors. The merger guidelines do not give any specific policy objectives for the singling out of these specific industries other than the broad objectives of consumer welfare protection and safeguarding of competition.[526]

3.2.4 Merger Assessment Process

3.2.4.1 The European Union

3.2.4.1.1 The Case Referral system

The EU Merger Regulation provides for a system by which a proposed merger may be referred by the Commission to a Member State authority or vice versa prior to or after the submission of a notification.[527] The parties to a proposed merger may, prior to making a notification, inform the Commission that the effects of a proposed merger would to a significant extent be felt within a Member State and should therefore be examined by that Member State. The Commission may subsequently decide whether to refer the case in whole or part to the competition authority of the relevant Member State for a determination of the case based on the Member States national law.[528] The parties may also make a pre-notification submission to the Commission seeking the examination by the Commission of an Article 1(3) transaction i.e. one that falls short of the community dimension but which would nonetheless affect at least three Member States. If none of

524 UK Enterprise Act s 23; See also UK Procedural Guidance para 4.3.

525 See Annex.

526 Kenya Merger Guidelines para 38.

527 The COMESA case referral system is briefly discussed later in the Chapter.

528 EU Merger Regulation art 4(4).

the Member States objects to the referral then the transaction would be brought under the jurisdiction of the Commission through the making of a formal notification.[529]

Similarly, the Commission may itself make a post-notification referral in whole or in part of a concentration to the relevant Member State authority. The considerations in this respect are whether the concentration would affect a significant part of a distinct market within that Member State or whether such a market does not make up a substantial part of the common market.[530] The Member States may also request the Commission to review a concentration that does not have a community dimension but which may nonetheless affect trade between Member States and may significantly affect competition within the Member State(s) submitting the request.[531]

The Commission in its case referral guidance explains that the referral of cases should be carried out having regard to three main principles:[532]

(i) To ensure that a case in question is handled by the more appropriate authority with due consideration to where the significant impact of the transaction on competition is felt as well as the capacity of the authority to handle the case;

(ii) To ensure that the benefits of the one-stop-shop approach where a single authority addresses the case is maintained hence achieving efficiency and avoiding duplicate and fragmented enforcement approaches as well as conflicting treatment from multiple authorities. Therefore, whereas referral could lead to a fragmentation of cases, such an outcome should be avoided as much as possible; and

(iii) To ensure that legal certainty in respect of jurisdiction over a certain case is maintained. Therefore, referrals should be considered only in circumstances where compelling reasons dictate a departure from the original jurisdiction.

529 EU Merger Regulation art 4(5).

530 EU Merger Regulation art 9(1) and (2).

531 EU Merger Regulation art 22(1).

532 Commission Notice on Case Referral in respect of Concentrations (2005/C 56/02), para 8-14.

3.2.4.1.2 Procedure for Notification

Like the UK, the Commission does provide an avenue for parties to engage in informal and confidential pre-notification discussions.[533] The Commission notes that this allows it and the parties to discuss jurisdictional and other legal issues, to discuss the scope of the informational requirements, to zero in on key competition concerns at an early stage as well as ensuring the completeness of the notification forms.[534]

The Commission also employs a simplified procedure in respect of transactions that do not raise significant competition concerns within the European Economic Area.[535] Transactions qualifying for this procedure include: (a) joint ventures with turnover and assets of less than EUR 100 million in the EEA; (b) mergers that do not involve any horizontal market overlaps or vertical relationship; (c) where the undertakings have a combined market share of less than 20% in competing markets or less than 30% in vertical markets; (d) where the transaction entails a change from joint to sole control; and (e) mergers where the combined market share for all competing undertakings is less than 50% or where the increase in the HHI would be less than 150.[536] Such transactions benefit from a short form decision where they would be declared compatible with the internal market within a 25-day period from the date of notification.[537]

The Commission's normal investigation is divided into two phases. Once the notification is made, the phase one investigation commences. The notification itself is in a prescribed form and requires the submission of detailed information from the parties as well as supporting documents.[538] In the cases of acquisition of joint control the acquiring parties

---

533 DG Competition: Best Practices on the Conduct of EC Merger Proceedings (20/01/04) <http://ec.europa.eu/competition/mergers/legislation/proceedings.pdf> accessed 23 September 2019 (EU Best Practices Guidelines), para 5.

534 EU Best Practices Guidelines paras 6-9.

535 Commission Notice on a simplified procedure for treatment of certain concentrations under Council Regulation (EC) No 139/2004 (2013/C 366/04) (Simplified Procedure Notice).

536 Ibid para 5.

537 Ibid para 26. The Commission however reserves the right to revert to the normal procedure.

538 See generally Implementing Council Regulation (EC) No 139/2004 on the control of concentrations between undertakings, (EC) No 802/2004 (EU Implementing Regulation). The information submitted by the parties is subject to a professional secrecy obligation and must therefore be treated in confidence, see EU Merger Regulation art 17.

are required to submit a joint notification. In other cases, it is the acquiring party that makes the notification.[539] The timeline for the phase one process is 25 days. At the end of this phase the merger may be cleared unconditionally, cleared subject to remedies or where it still raises competition concerns be submitted to a phase two investigation.[540] The phase two investigation involves a detailed consideration of the effects on competition. The timeline is therefore longer i.e. 90 days (extendable by a maximum of 20 days) from the opening of phase two investigations. In both the phase one and two investigations the Commission ensures that the parties are updated and informed of the progress. At the end of the phase two investigations a final decision is made. The Commission clears the merger unconditionally, approves it subject to remedies or prohibits it. The publication of both phase one and two decisions is done on the Commission website. The parties reserve a right of appeal to the General Court and ultimately to the Court of Justice of the European Union.[541]

3.2.4.2 The United States

The FTC and the DOJ also provide the parties with an opportunity to engage in pre-notification discussions. This is particularly useful where the merger involves complex substantial issues.[542] The notification in the United States is filed in prescribed form by the acquiring and target parties with both the FTC and the DOJ. The form is as well accompanied by various supporting documents (including voluntary information) all of which is subject to a confidentiality requirement.[543] Once the filing is

539 EU Merger Regulation art 4(2); EU Implementing Regulation art 2.

540 European Commission, Competition: Merger Control Procedures (2013) <http://ec.europa.eu/competition/publications/factsheets/merger_control_procedures_en.pdf> accessed 18 September 2019. (EC Procedure Factsheet); EU Merger Regulation, article 8.

541 EC Procedure Factsheet.

542 Broder (2012) 174-175. See Michel G. Egge and Jason D. Cruise, 'Practical guide to the U.S. merger review process' (2014) Concurrences N° 1, 3 <https://www.lw.com/thoughtLeadership/practical-guide-us-merger-review-process-012014> accessed 23 August 2019; See also Skadden, Arps, Slate, Meagher & Flom LLP, 'Merger Control 2016 – USA Law & Practice' (contribution to Chambers and Partners Global Practice Guides) <http://www.chambersandpartners.com/guide/practice-guides/location/272/8096/2500-200> accessed 23 August 2019.

543 FTC, '

done, a 30-day waiting period begins to run.[544] There is an option for an early termination of the waiting period where it is requested for, all the parties made complete submission and the two Agencies have reviewed the transaction and decided that no enforcement action is required. The FTC notes that early termination is granted for most transactions when requested. Otherwise, the parties may proceed with the proposed merger once the waiting period has expired and the agencies have not raised any issues.[545]

Both the DOJ and the FTC carry out the preliminary substantive review. If they are of the view that there should be further investigation, they undertake a clearing procedure where they decide which of the two Agencies will carry out the investigation. Prior to this clearance the parties usually engage both agencies.[546] If determined that a further investigation is required, the relevant agency will request the parties to the transaction to submit additional information and documents, i.e. the second request. This is comparable to a phase two investigation in the European Union. The second request extends the waiting period by a maximum of 30 days (or 10 days in the case of a cash tender offer).[547]

What is the Premerger Notification Program?: An Overview', 6 (March 2009) <https://www.ftc.gov/sites/default/files/attachments/premerger-introductory-guides/guide1.pdf> accessed 23 September 2019 (FTC Premerger Notification Overview); Clayton Act s 7a sub-s h.

544 Clayton Act s 7a sub-s b(1)(a). In case of cash tender offers it is a 15-day waiting period. The waiting period begins to run subject to a completed notification being filed. If not completed there has to be a statement for reasons of non-compliance.

545 Clayton Act s 7a sub-s b (2); FTC Premerger Notification Overview 10; Egge (2014) para 14.

546 FTC Premerger Notification Overview 11. This is to avoid duplication and confusion and is based on an agreement between the two Agencies. See also Egge (2014) para 13.

547 Clayton Act s 7a sub-s e. Any further extension can only be granted by the District Court.

Once the substantive investigation is complete a final determination is made by the relevant agency to either:[548]

(i) allow the transaction to proceed i.e. take no further action where no evidence of a probable substantial lessening of competition is found. The DOJ and the FTC do not grant approvals or clearances in the strict sense of the word. A public statement is usually issued with the outcome of the investigations.[549] This however does not bar the enforcement agencies from later instituting any post-merger enforcement action.

(ii) institute injunctive relief proceedings at the District Court to bar the transaction from proceeding where the transaction raises competition concerns and is likely to result in a substantial lessening of competition.

(iii) negotiate a settlement with the parties.

Instituting injunctive relief or negotiating a settlement is based on the premise that the parties intend to proceed with the transaction if the agencies find that it would violate the antitrust laws. The parties may however also opt to abandon the transaction.

3.2.4.3 South Africa

As is the case with the European Union and the United States, the Competition Commission may avail an opportunity prior to notification for the merging parties to engage with it if they so request for guidance.[550] The legal services division also provides non-binding advisory opinions on the basis of a written request by the parties seeking guidance.[551] A notification is required in the case of intermediate and large mergers and is as well accompanied by detailed information and supporting documents.[552]

---

548 Clayton Act s 7a sub-s f; See also FTC Premerger Notification Overview 13-14.

549 OECD, Investigations of Consummated and Non-notifiable Mergers: United States para 20.

550 Bowman Gilfillan, 'Merger Control 2016: South Africa Law & Practice' (contribution to Chambers and Partners Global Practice Guides) <http://www.chambersandpartners.com/guide/practice-guides/location/272/8560/2429-200> accessed 23 August 2019.

551 Info available on the SA Competition Commission website <http://www.compcom.co.za/file-a-merger/.> accessed 23 August 2019.

552 SA Competition Act s13A. A copy of the notice should also be sent to the registered trade union or to the employees affected where such trade union does

The Competition Commission in turn is required to send copies of the merger notices to the Minister of Trade and Industry (the Minister) and the Tribunal.[553] The Minister has a right to intervene and participate in intermediate and large mergers in order to make public interest representations.[554] Where the transaction falls under the jurisdiction of the banking statutes a notice must also be sent to the Minister of Finance. The Minister of Finance may make a public interest intervention to seize jurisdiction of such transactions that require consent under banking statutes.[555]

The Competition Commission requires a single joint notification to be made by either the primary acquiring or primary target firm. A request may however be made by one of the primary firms for a separate filing.[556] In the case of small mergers under scrutiny, the Commission may require a notification from the parties. In such a case, it will serve them in prescribed form and the parties will have a 20-day window to fulfil the requirements.[557] The Commission has a five (for large mergers) to ten business day timeline to inform any filing party of a complete or incomplete filing.[558]

According to the SA Competition Act, once a completed notification is filed, an initial period for consideration of 20 days for small and intermediate mergers and 40 days for large mergers begins to run.[559] This period is not suspended even where the Commission requests for additional information. The only time the period is suspended is in cases where the Commission issues a demand for corrected information. Where the parties file corrected information, the initial period begins to run anew. The parties are however permitted to appeal the demand for corrected information or a finding that the merger is within jurisdiction or falls within a certain category to the Tribunal.[560] In the case of small and intermediate mergers,

---

not exist. Notified trade unions or employees may apply to the Commission in order to participate in the merger proceedings. See Rules for the Conduct of Proceedings in the Competition Commission, Proclamation No. 12, GG 22025, 01/02/2001 (SA Commission Rules) rule 37.

553 See Sutherland and Kemp (2014) para 9.3.10. The primary responsibility over large mergers lies with the Tribunal.

554 SA Competition Act s 18; SA Commission Rules rule 35.

555 SA Competition Act s 18; SA Commission Rules rule 36.

556 SA Commission Rules rule 26-28.

557 SA Commission Rules rule 25.

558 SA Commission Rules rule 30.

559 SA Commission Rules rules 24 and 29.

560 SA Commission Rules rules 24, 31-33. Filing of false or misleading information is not penalised. The Commission simply requests for corrected information.

the Commission may extend the initial period by a maximum of 40 days. The initial period for a large merger can be extended by a maximum of 15 days. Whereas the extension of time for small and intermediate mergers is in the Commission's sole discretion, it should be with the consent of the parties and the Tribunal in the case of large mergers.[561]

The Commission has however published service standards that reflect a more realistic picture of the turnaround times that are to be expected as well as categorizing the review of mergers into phases in respect of their relative complexity.[562] Accordingly, mergers are categorised into three phases, with phase three being further categorised into intermediate and large mergers. The phase one and phase two turnaround times are 20 and 45 days respectively, reflecting the relative non-complexity of the mergers. Phase three turnaround is 60 days for intermediate mergers and 120 days for large mergers where the issues to be considered are complex.[563]

Parties seeking to protect the confidentiality of submissions are required to file a prescribed form where they provide details of the information that is to be kept confidential. The duty of the Commission and Tribunal to maintain the confidentiality of information is therefore not a general rule and is pegged on the claim made by the party seeking to protect its information.[564]

The Commission may approve, approve with conditions or prohibit a small or intermediate merger.[565] The Commission also retains the power to revoke an approval decision it has made and prohibit a proposed merger where there is evidence of deceit, breach of obligations or incorrect

---

In addition, where it is determined that the merger does not fall within the Commission's jurisdiction a refund of the filing fee will be due (Rule 33). However, where parties abandon a merger, the fee is forfeited (Rule 34).

561 SA Competition Act ss 14-14A; SA Commission Rules rules 38 and 41.

562 Competition Commission of South Africa, M&A Service Standards (2015) <http://www.compcom.co.za/wp-content/uploads/2014/09/Service-Standards_2015_Final.pdf> accessed 23 August 2019 (SA Service Standards).

563 SA Service Standards 5.

564 SA Competition Act s 44.

565 SA Competition Act ss 13-14; SA Commission Rules rules 38 and 40. Failure by the Commission to either extend the initial period or issue a decision within the 20-day period will be regarded as an approval of the merger.

information.[566] An aggrieved party naturally has the right of appeal to the Tribunal and ultimately to the Competition Appeals Court.[567]

The Commission cannot approve or prohibit a large merger. It makes a referral to the Tribunal recommending the approval, conditional approval or prohibition of the proposed merger. The Tribunal therefore has the jurisdiction to make the decision.[568] Although there are timelines within which the Tribunal must take certain steps after the filing of a referral, there is no prescribed maximum time frame for the making of the ultimate decision.[569] An aggrieved party may appeal the Tribunal's decision to the Competition Appeal Court. The parties may naturally opt to abandon a merger.

3.2.4.4 The United Kingdom

Parties contemplating filing a merger notice in most cases start off by engaging the CMA in pre-notification discussions on jurisdiction aspects and the scope of information to be included in the voluntary notification. The parties usually submit drafts of their voluntary notification at this stage. There is no requirement for all the parties to notify. Customarily, the acquiring party undertakes the notification.[570] Once the parties formally submit their merger notice, the CMA assesses the notification and if complete confirms to the parties the start of the first phase timeline i.e. 40 days.[571] If the CMA begins an investigation on its own initiative, the timeline will begin to run once the CMA has confirmed to the parties that it has received sufficient information from them to proceed with its inves-

566 SA Competition Act s 15; SA Commission Rules rule 40.

567 SA Competition Act ss 16-17; Rules for the Conduct of Proceedings in the Competition Tribunal, GN 22025 vol. 428, 01/02/2001 (SA Tribunal Rules) rule 32.

568 SA Competition Act ss 14A and 16; SA Commission Rules rule 41; SA Tribunal Rules rule 35.

569 SA Tribunal Rules rule 35. The Commission may seek the revocation of an approval or a conditional approval made by the Tribunal (see SA Tribunal Rules rule 37).

570 UK Procedural Guidance paras 6.49-6.58; see also Debevoise & Plimpton LLP, 'Merger control in the UK (England and Wales): overview' (Practical Law Global Guide 2015/16) <global.practicallaw.com/0-500-7317> accessed 18 September 2019.

571 UK ERR Act sch. 8; UK Procedural Guidance 38.

tigation.[572] Given the voluntary nature of the process the parties have no obligation to suspend their transaction in the course of the investigations. The CMA may therefore in some cases take interim measures to prevent or reverse any pre-emptive action that the parties may take or have taken.[573]

During the phase one investigation and substantial examination the CMA continually engages with the parties in order to gather information and discuss the state of play of the investigation. The CMA has a statutory obligation to maintain the confidentiality of all information that is subject to restrictions on disclosure.[574] The CMA may also invite comments from or directly contact interested third parties in order to get their views on the transaction.[575] If the parties fail to comply with a notice issued by the CMA requiring them to provide information or documents or to give evidence as witnesses, the 40 day period may be extended for as long as compliance remains outstanding or until the CMA cancels the extension.[576] At the end of phase one the CMA may clear the transaction unconditionally, clear it subject to undertakings or refer it to a phase two investigation where substantial competition concerns arise.[577]

The statutory timeline for the phase two full investigation is 24 weeks and can be extended at the discretion of the CMA for another eight weeks.[578] The result of a full investigation is unconditional clearance, clearance subject to undertakings or a prohibition. Where the parties opt to abandon the proposed merger at either phase one or phase two the CMA terminates the investigation.[579] The parties retain a right of appeal to the Competition Appeal Tribunal.[580]

572 UK Procedural Guidance 39. The own-initiative investigation affects even completed transactions and they risk being referred to a full investigation for remedial action. Completed transactions do not receive any favourable treatment (UK Procedural Guidance para 6.20).
573 UK Enterprise Act s 73 as read with UK ERR Act s 30; UK Procedural Guidance 38.
574 UK Enterprise Act ss 237-238.
575 UK Procedural Guidance 39.
576 UK ERR Act sch. 8 (s34ZB).
577 UK Procedural Guidance 40.
578 UK Enterprise Act s 39; UK Procedural Guidance 97 and para 13.11.
579 UK Procedural Guidance paras 13.10-14.11.
580 UK Enterprise Act s 120.

3.2.4.5 Eastern and Southern Africa

3.2.4.5.1 Pre-Notification Guidance

Just like with the European Union, the United States, South Africa and the United Kingdom, a number of the ESA jurisdictions also avail the opportunity for the transacting parties to engage the competition authorities in pre-notification discussions for purposes of seeking guidance on their transaction.

The COMESA merger guidelines highlight the importance of these consultations in ensuring quick assessment once the notification is formally made, as well as helping to avoid unnecessary notifications.[581] The COMESA Commission may also provide comfort letters confirming that a merger is not notifiable. The parties may therefore submit a request accompanied by relevant information and accompanying documents and within 21 days receive confirmation on whether a formal notification will be necessary.[582] The Kenya Competition Authority also avails the opportunity for the parties to seek an advisory opinion on whether or not their transaction is notifiable.[583]

Malawi places specific importance on consultations with the parties especially because notification is voluntary and the consequences for the parties of failure to notify a notifiable transaction could be dire if the transaction were to be prohibited. The Malawi Commission also provides comfort letters. Parties may also apply for negative clearance. This application is subject to a less rigorous process than the formal notification.[584]

Mauritius and Seychelles as well avail the opportunity to the parties to make an application to their respective Commissions for guidance prior to notification.[585] The Zambia Commission also gives the parties a chance to engage it in pre-notification consultations to determine whether the merger is to be notified as well as to clarify preliminary issues in case the

581 COMESA Merger Guidelines para 4.1.

582 Ibid paras 4.2 et seq.

583 Kenya Merger Guidelines para 40.

584 Malawi Merger Guidelines paras 6.1.2 et seq.

585 Mauritius Competition Commission Rules of Procedure GN 161/2009, rule 7 <http://www.ccm.mu/English/Documents/Legislations/Rules-of-Procedure-2009-051112.pdf> accessed 23 August 2019 (Mauritius Procedure Rules); Seychelles Merger Guidelines, para 2.5.

merger needs to be formally notified. The Zambia Commission also avails the option of a negative clearance for the parties.[586]

Given the vital nature of pre-notification consultations it can be presumed that the authorities in Botswana, Namibia, Tanzania and Zimbabwe also provide the parties with the opportunity to engage them in these consultations.

3.2.4.5.2 COMESA Case Referral System

In a similar way to the EU case referral system, the COMESA Competition Regulations provide an avenue for a Member State to request the Commission to refer a merger to its competition authority for determination on the national level where the Member State is of the opinion that the merger would disproportionately affect competition within its jurisdiction. The Commission may thereafter deal with the case itself or refer the whole or part of the case to the Member State.[587] However, unlike the EU, there is no specific guidance as to whether the Commission may itself, after receipt of a notification, refer a merger in whole or partly to the competent Member State authority.

3.2.4.5.3 Procedure for Notification

Once a transaction has been notified one of the immediate concerns for the parties is the length of time it will take for a final determination to be made. The table below gives an overview of the main timelines in the various ESA jurisdictions:

Table 8: Merger Review Timelines

JURISDICTION	*REVIEW TIME*
COMESA (COMESA Competition Regulations, Arts 24 & 25)	– Notification no later than 30 days after decision to merge – Commission decision to issue within 120 days from receipt of complete notification (extendible to a period not exceeding 30 days cumulatively for phase 1 and 2 determinations) – Phase 1 determination for non-problematic mergers to issue within 45 days (extendible within the 30 day cumulative period. Also

586 Zambia Merger Guidelines para 19 and paras. 27 et seq.

587 COMESA Competition Regulations art. 24(8) and 24(9); EU Merger Regulations art 9(1) and 9(2).

	affected by suspension of time for delays in complying to requests for more information) – Phase 2 determination for problematic mergers to issue within the remainder of the 120-day period (extendible within the 30 day cumulative period) – Appeals to decisions to be submitted within 30 days after publication of decision
Botswana (Botswana Competition Act, s 56-58)	– Determination within 30 days after receipt of notification – In case of request for more information the 30 days begin to run after receipt of such information – If determined that hearing should be held in respect of the merger, within 30 days from conclusion of the hearing – All timelines above extendible to a maximum of 60 days
Kenya (Kenya Competition Act, s 44 & 45)	– Determination within 60 days after receipt of notification – In case of request for more information the 60 days begin to run after receipt of such information – If determined that a hearing conference should be held in respect of the merger, within 30 days from conclusion of the hearing conference – All timelines above extendible to a maximum of 60 days
Malawi (Competition and Fair Trading Act, s 39)	– Determination within 45 days from receipt of application for authorizing order – In case of request for more information the 45 days begin to run after receipt of such information
Namibia (Namibia Competition Act, s 44 & 45)	– Request for more information to be made by Commission within 30 days from receipt of notification – Determination within 60 days after receipt of notification – In case of request for more information the 30 days begin to run after receipt of such information – If determined that a conference should be held in respect of the merger, within 30 days from conclusion of the hearing conference – All timelines above extendible to a maximum of 60 days
Tanzania (Fair Competition Act, s 11)	– Notice of complete or incomplete filing issued by Commission within 5 days of filing of application – After issuance of notice of complete filing, review to be completed by Commission within 14 days – In case further review is required, it is to be completed within 90 days. – The 90 days is extendible to a maximum of 30 days – A delay in obtaining information from the parties may extend the periods as per the Commission's considerations
Zambia (Competition and Consumer Protection Act, s 32)	– Determination to be made within 90 days from date of receipt of complete notification (in case of delayed submission of information period is extendible commensurate to the delay) – 90-day period extendible by up to 30 days – Phase 1 investigation conducted within first 35 days. If no serious competition issues arise merger will be cleared. – If at the end of phase 1 serious competition issues arise, review proceeds to phase 2 for in depth analysis.

	– Final decision issued at the end of phase 2 (within the 90 days unless there is an extension)
Zimbabwe (Competition Act, s 34A & 36(5))	– Notification to Commission to be made within 30 days from conclusion of a merger agreement or from acquisition of controlling interest by one party in another. – Determination to be made *'as expeditiously as possible'*
Seychelles	– Not clarified in the Act or Guidelines
Mauritius	– Not clarified in the Act or Guidelines

The merger review timeline data reveals that most of the jurisdictions have a maximum statutory review timeline of 120 days. This includes extensions and on the assumption that the parties make a complete filing and promptly comply with any requests for further information from the competition authorities. COMESA has the longest statutory review timeline at 150 days, with Malawi and Botswana having the shortest at 90 days. Zimbabwe merely provides for the completion of merger reviews as expeditiously as possible, in effect leaving the transacting parties with a lot of uncertainty regarding the timeline for review. Seychelles and Mauritius do not provide any information on timelines in their statutes or guidelines, thus highlighting the challenge of insufficiency of publicly available information that is vital for parties to assess with a level of predictability the review process of the authorities.

In comparison, the European Union has a maximum statutory review timeline of 135 days, with transactions qualifying for the simplified procedure taking 25 days.[588] The US maximum statutory review timeline is 60 days.[589] South Africa's timelines vary based on the category of merger and are divided into three broad phases. The phase one and phase two turnaround times are 20 and 45 days respectively, reflecting a relative non-complexity of the mergers. Phase three turnaround is 60 days for intermediate mergers and 120 days for large mergers where the more complex issues.[590]

The categorization of transactions into phases is as well vital in ensuring that non-problematic transactions are promptly reviewed and allowed to proceed expeditiously. The European Union, the United States and South Africa all categorise their review into phases based on whether issues warranting further review arise. COMESA and Zambia as well categorise their

588 Simplified Procedure Notice para 26; EC Procedure Factsheet.

589 Clayton Act s 7.

590 SA Service Standards 5.

review into phases. The rest of the ESA jurisdictions do not specify in their guidelines whether they employ a phased approach.

3.2.4.5.4 Confidential Information

Confidentiality of information is as well not an automatic statutory requirement in the majority of the ESA jurisdictions. COMESA and Mauritius for instance require the parties to specify and give reasons why certain information should be kept confidential. Parties cannot request blanket confidentiality. Tanzania allows the parties to claim confidentiality over the whole or any part of material submitted. South Africa and Kenya as well require the parties to specifically claim confidentiality. Such claims however do not necessarily lead to automatic treatment of information as confidential. The authorities retain the discretion on whether to treat information as confidential.

Zambia requires the parties to submit confidential information separately with an explanation as to why it should be treated with confidence. The Zambia Competition Commission however reserves the right to decide what constitutes confidential information.[591]

Botswana has a broad confidentiality requirement that does not require the parties to make any claim or request and that arises automatically subject to some conditions.[592] Namibia provides for a restriction on the use of confidential information by employees of the Commission. There is however no general guidance on the treatment of confidential information.[593] Seychelles, Malawi and Zimbabwe do not provide specific guidance on the confidentiality of information received from the merging parties.

591 COMESA Merger Guidelines paras 5.7 et seq.; SA Competition Act s 44; Kenya Competition Act s 20; Mauritius Procedure Rules rule 31; Tanzania Competition Act s 76; Zambia Merger Guidelines paras 19-21.

592 Botswana Competition Act s 74.

593 Namibia Competition Act s 10.

3.2.4.5.5 Final Determination

Once the assessment of the proposed merger is complete the authorities will naturally approve it unconditionally, approve it subject to conditions or undertakings from the parties or prohibit the merger.[594]

A number of the authorities also reserve the right to revoke an approval where there is failure to comply or where the decision was based on misleading or incorrect information. The COMESA Competition Regulations reserve the right of the Commission to amend or revoke an order but without specifying any reasons.[595]

The parties also have the right of appeal from the decisions of the authorities. In Botswana, an appeal is made to the High Court with a further right of appeal to the Court of Appeal on a point of law or on a decision as to the penalty amount. In Kenya and Zambia decisions are subject to review by a Competition Tribunal with a further right of appeal to the High Court, with the High Court's decision being final. In Malawi appeals are made to a High Court judge in chambers. Parties in Mauritius reserve the right to appeal to the Supreme Court. In Seychelles, the parties may appeal to a Competition Tribunal and ultimately to the Supreme Court.

Tanzania as well grants appeals to a Competition Tribunal whose decisions are final. This may seem to be a restriction of access to the courts. The Tribunal in Tanzania is however granted similar powers to those of a High Court. Appeals in Zimbabwe are made to an Administrative Court constituted under the Act. Namibia peculiarly grants the power to review decisions to the Minister with further recourse to the courts. Decisions from the COMESA Commission may be appealed to a specially constituted Board of Commissioners.[596]

---

594 Botswana Competition Act s 60; Kenya Competition Act s 46 sub-s 1; Malawi Competition Act s 39 sub-s 2; Mauritius Competition Act s 61 sub-s 2 and s 63; Namibia Competition Act s 47; Seychelles Competition Act s 28; Tanzania Competition Act s 13 sub-s 1; Zimbabwe Competition Act s 36; Zambia Competition Act s 34; COMESA Competition Regulations art 26(7).

595 Botswana Competition Act s 62; Kenya Competition Act s 47 sub-s 1; Namibia Competition Act s 48 sub-s 1 and s 52; Seychelles Competition Act s 30; Tanzania Competition Act s 13 sub-s 4; Zimbabwe Competition Act s 38; Zambia Competition Act s 35; COMESA Competition Regulations art 26(11).

596 Botswana Competition Act ss 67-71; Kenya Competition Act ss 48-49; Malawi Competition Act s 48; Mauritius Competition Act s 67; Namibia Competition Act s 49; Seychelles Competition Act ss 50-52; Tanzania Competition Act ss 83-85; Zambia Competition Act ss 60 and 75; COMESA Competition Regulations art 26(12).

3.2.5 Market Definition

3.2.5.1 Role of Market Definition in Merger Control

Defining the relevant market in many cases sets the stage on which the substantive merger analysis is to be conducted and determines the scope of the analysis. The European Commission for instance expresses the view that, 'market definition is a tool to identify and define the boundaries of competition between firms. It serves to establish the framework within which competition policy is applied by the Commission…'[597] The OECD as well views it as 'providing the analytical framework for the ultimate inquiry of whether a particular conduct or transaction is likely to produce anticompetitive effects.'[598]

There are various viewpoints about the main purpose of market definition. One common aspect that emerges is market power. The purpose behind seeking to set the boundaries of the market is linked to the determination of where market power lies.[599] The OECD expresses the view for instance that 'the main goal of market definition is to assess the existence, creation or strengthening of market power, which is defined as the ability of the firm to keep the price above the long-run competitive level.'[600] The ICN points out that in a number of cases market definition is regarded as a first step in the evaluation of whether a transaction creates market power.[601] It is seen as a means to screen out situations that do not require the attention of the competition authorities.[602]

The standard notion therefore is that defining the market is the starting point in terms of conducting merger analysis.[603] This notion is however being reconsidered in some markets where the industries have evolved to give rise to a number of instances which may not necessarily be properly

---

597 Notice on the definition of relevant market for the purposes of Community competition law, OJ (1997) C 372/5 para 2 (EC Market Definition Notice).

598 OECD: Market Definition, DAF/COMP(2012)19, Overview <http://www.oecd.org/daf/competition/Marketdefinition2012.pdf> accessed 26 August 2018 (OECD Market Definition Guidance).

599 See for instance Paul Geroski, 'Thinking creatively about markets' (1998) 16 International Journal of Industrial Organization 6, 677-695.

600 Ibid 11.

601 ICN, Project on Merger Guidelines, ch. 2 para 1.7 <https://www.internationalcompetitionnetwork.org/portfolio/merger-guidelines-report/> accessed 18 September 2019 (ICN Merger Guidelines Report).

602 OECD Market Definition Guidance 28.

603 Ibid 22.

addressed by way of the traditional market definition approach.[604] This point is made in part 4 of the US Horizontal Merger Guidelines where it is stated that 'the Agencies' analysis need not start with market definition. Some of the analytical tools used by the Agencies to assess competitive effects do not rely on market definition, although evaluation of competitive alternatives available to customers is always necessary at some point in the analysis.'

This is as well a testament to the effects-based approach of the SLC test where multiple factors are taken into consideration and depending on the case in question one factor or the other may be more probative. Some critics go as far as considering market definition as superfluous where one moves from a dominance-based analysis to a case-by-case effects-based analysis. From their perspective, market definition is primarily necessary for determining dominance, which focuses on criteria such as market shares and concentration.[605]

Where market share and concentration levels, which are traditionally viewed as indicators of market power, still play a central role then a structural approach, which starts off with a clear delineation of market boundaries, would put market definition as the cornerstone of merger analysis.

The European Commission as well employs an effects-based approach meaning that market definition is one factor within a multi-factor matrix and therefore not an end in itself. However, given that the creation and strengthening of a dominant position is still the prime example of a significant impediment to effective competition, structural considerations based on the analysis of market share and concentration levels admittedly still play an important part in setting the boundaries of the relevant market.[606] Its position should however not be overstated. Market definition is seen as a way to delineate the market to enable the European Commission to better appreciate the operation of competition in the market.[607] The

---

604 Ibid. See also ICN Merger Guidelines Report 3. Some of the markets highlighted as not being properly captured by the traditional market definition paradigm are those for differentiated products, bidding markets, two sided markets etc.

605 Emanuela Arezzo, 'Is there a Role for Market Definition and Dominance in an effects-based Approach?' In: Mackenrodt MO., Gallego B.C., Enchelmaier S. (eds) *Abuse of Dominant Position: New Interpretation, New Enforcement Mechanisms?* MPI Studies on Intellectual Property, Competition and Tax Law, vol 5. (Springer 2008).

606 EC Market Definition Notice para 10.

607 Lindsay and Berridge (2009) para 3-001.

focus is ultimately on the main goal which it to predict what effect the transaction is likely to have on competition in the market.[608] The position of market definition was aptly captured by then Commissioner Mario Monti when he stated that:

> market definition is not an end it itself but a tool to identify situations where there might be competition concerns. As in most other competition jurisdictions around the world, our competitive analysis focuses on market power. We use market definition and market shares as an easily available proxy for the measurement of the market power enjoyed by firms. In effect, the main objective of defining a market is to identify the competitors of the undertakings concerned by a particular case that are capable of constraining their behaviour... market definition is a cornerstone of competition policy, but not the entire building. Market definition is a tool for the competitive assessment, not a substitute for it. What is ultimately important is to understand the nature of the competitive situation facing the firms involved in a certain practice or in a proposed merger. The market definition is a first - and very important - step in the analysis.[609]

Although South Africa also uses the multi-factor analysis the authorities typically follow the standard approach of beginning with market definition though making it clear that this does not bar the use of alternative analytical frameworks.[610] The Competition Tribunal of South Africa has indeed expressed the view that the role of market definition should not be overstated, especially in cases where other analytical factors may be more probative.[611] A similar view has been expressed by the Appeal Court in South Africa which has stated that an appraisal of the effects of a merger need not be 'preceded by a proper definition of the market' in the *Medicross Healthcare* case.[612] There is as well an acknowledgement of the fact

---

608 Joaquin Almunia, Policy Objectives of Merger Control, speech made on September 8, 2011 <http://europa.eu/rapid/press-release_SPEECH-11-561_en.htm?locale=en> accessed 26 August 2019.

609 Mario Monti, 'Market definition as a cornerstone of EU Competition Policy' speech made on 5 October, 2001, <http://europa.eu/rapid/press-release_SPEECH-01-439_en.htm?locale=en> accessed 26 August 2019.

610 OECD Market Definition Guidance 377.

611 *Primedia Ltd v Competition Commission* 39/AM/May06, 9 May 2008, para 66.

612 *Medicross Healthcare Group (Pty) Ltd v Competition Commission* 55/CAC/Sep05, para 25.

that there are instances where the markets in question are not amenable to a standard market definition approach.[613]

The European Commission rightly points out that the kind of competition question being addressed has a bearing on the relevant market even where the methodology used to define the market is the same. Thus, the relevant market in the case of merger regulation will be based on a prospective analysis whereas in the case of abuse of dominance it will be based on past conduct. The scope of the two markets may therefore be different.[614]

On the back of the view that a more structured approach favours market definition as a starting point for merger analysis where aspects such as market shares and concentration levels play a central role, one may argue that such an approach would be ideal for Sub-Saharan African jurisdictions. A structured analysis carried out within a defined framework may help nascent merger regulation regimes in markets that are not very diversified to develop analytical competence.

This section therefore takes a look at the standard approach to market definition as well as highlighting some of the markets that do not conform to the traditional market definition approach. This is within the context of a comparative overview of the practice in the US, EU and South Africa. The aim is to subsequently put into perspective the approach taken by the authorities in Sub-Saharan Africa.

3.2.5.2 The Concept of Substitutability

Defining the relevant market invariably hinges on the ability of a consumer finding a substitute for the product or service in question in the relevant market.

It is based on substitutability that the European Commission for instance provides concise definitions of what it considers to be the relevant product and geographic markets:

> A relevant product market comprises all those products and/or services which are regarded as interchangeable or substitutable by the

613 OECD Market Definition Guidance 377-384.

614 EC Market Definition Notice para 12.

> consumer, by reason of the products' characteristics, their prices and their intended use.[615]
>
> The relevant geographic market comprises the area in which the undertakings concerned are involved in the supply and demand of products or services, in which the conditions of competition are sufficiently homogeneous and which can be distinguished from neighbouring areas because the conditions of competition are appreciably different in those areas.[616]

Substitutability is likewise the core determinant of market definition in the US. The US Horizontal Merger Guidelines for instance provide that the focus of market definition is solely on demand substitution factors, this being the ability of customers to switch to alternative products in response to a price increase or even reduction in quality or service, as well as the reaction of suppliers to such changes.[617] The US Supreme Court in its decision in *United States v Brown Shoe Co*[618] stated that 'the outer boundaries of a product market are determined by the reasonable interchangeability of use or the cross-elasticity of demand between the product itself and substitutes for it', a position which has been approved and used by the Competition Tribunal of South Africa.[619] The European Commission's definition of the product market has as well been reiterated by the Competition Tribunal of South Africa in its decision in *Massmart Holdings Ltd and Jumbo Cash and Carry.*[620]

The European Commission's definition also touches on the aspect of interchangeability, which has been singled out by the Court of Justice as highly probative in the definition of the relevant product market. In *United Brands* for instance, the Court of Justice, in response to an argument by the applicant that bananas belong to the same market as other fresh fruit, stated that it fell on whether bananas could be 'singled out by such special features distinguishing it from other fruits that it is only to a limited extent interchangeable with them and is only exposed to their

---

615 EC Market Definition Notice para 7.

616 Ibid para 8.

617 US Horizontal Guidelines 7.

618 *Brown Shoe Co., Inc. v. United States* 370 U.S. 294 (1962), 325.

619 *Nestle (SA) (Pty) Limited & Pets Products (Pty) Limited* Competition Tribunal case no 21/LM/Apr01, 18 June 2001, para 21 where the Competition Tribunal expressed its preference for the US Supreme Courts position in this regard.

620 *Massmart Holdings Ltd and Jumbo Cash and Carry (Pty) Limited* Competition Tribunal case no 39/LM/Jul01, 10 October 2001, para 8.

competition in a way that is hardly perceptible.'[621] It has however been noted that the practical measurement of interchangeability can be quite problematic. Defining the relevant market as a whole is acknowledged as quite a complex endeavour.[622]

However, unlike the US where the focus is predominantly on demand side substitution, the European Commission classifies demand and supply side substitutability as well as potential competition as the three main sources of competitive constraints for firms.[623] Similar to the US position, the European Commission regards demand substitution 'as the most immediate and effective disciplinary force on the suppliers of a given product, in particular in relation to their pricing decisions.'[624]

The ability of customers to switch with relative ease to alternative products, which is also central to the South African analysis[625], is crucial in the determination of whether the merging firms will be subject to sufficient competitive pressure.

The focus is on very close substitutes, i.e. those which consumers easily and readily switch to.[626] The US Agencies point out that a broad definition that includes relatively distant products can be misleading.[627]

Supply substitutability on its part is focused on the ability of the producers within the market to convert or switch to producing the product in question in response to a price increase by the hypothetical monopolist.[628] Where producers are able to put into effect such a switch with relative ease i.e. without incurring huge costs or risks, the consequence would be the exertion of competitive pressure on the hypothetical monopolist. Mario Monti in his capacity as the then EU Commissioner for competition pointed out that supply substitutability is important 'when its effects are equivalent to those of demand substitution in terms of effectiveness and immediacy. This would be the case if such producers already have the required capacity in place.'[629]

---

621 United Brands Case (1978) para 22.

622 Whish and Bailey (2012) 30. The concept of interchangeability is as well briefly discussed.

623 EC Market Definition Notice para 13.

624 EC Market Definition Notice para 13.

625 SA Ten Year Review (2009) 16.

626 Lindsay and Berridge (2009) para 3-006.

627 US Horizontal Guidelines para 4.

628 EC Market Definition Notice para 20.

629 Monti (2001).

From a procedural point of view, the European Commission highlights the flexibility of its approach, specifying that there is no strict hierarchy of information sources or evidence that is relied on in the process of determining substitutability. Rather, an open approach in which all the information available relevant to the case in question will be used.[630] The US Agencies also highlight the need to be flexible in the application of the market definition principles, thus allowing for the complexities that may arise to be taken into account.[631]

The Cellophane Fallacy

In the course of determining the relevant product market, it is advised to exercise caution in circumstances where a monopolist is already charging a monopoly premium. The consumers would in this case already be at the point at which any further price increase by the monopolist would lead them to stop buying from the monopolist.[632] An application of the hypothetical monopolist test at this point would result in the misleading conclusion that there is a sufficient level of substitutability in the market. This concern was indeed realised in the US Supreme Court decision in *United States v. E.I. du Pont*[633] where the court mistakenly included in the relevant market other wrapping products which were viewed as interchangeable with cellophane without regard to the fact that DuPont was already charging a monopoly premium hence creating the false impression of substitutability at the margin.[634]

The European Commission as well takes notice of this concern by providing that:

> Generally, and in particular for the analysis of merger case, the price to take into account will be the prevailing market price. This may not be the case where the prevailing price has been determined in the absence of sufficient competition. In particular for the investigation of abuses of dominant positions, the fact that the prevailing price might already have been substantially increased will be taken into account.[635]

630 Ibid para 25.

631 US Horizontal Guidelines para 4.

632 Whish and Bailey (2012) 32.

633 *United States v. E.I. du Pont de Nemours & Co.*, 351 U.S. 377 (1956).

634 OECD Market Definition Guidance 328-329. The Cellophane Fallacy was first pointed out by Stocking and Mueller in George W. Stocking and Willard F. Mueller, *The Cellophane Case and the New Competition* (1955) 45 American Economic Review 29, 53-54.

635 EC Market Definition Notice para 19.

The Competition Tribunal of South Africa as well acknowledges the concern in respect of the *E.I. du Pont* decision, stating that:

> Admittedly, the 'cellophane fallacy effect' should be borne in mind when using demand elasticities to determine market power or the extent of the relevant market, as any profit-maximising firm with a degree of market power will set prices at a level where demand for its product is elastic (otherwise it would raise prices further). Using elasticities that are based on elastic demand pricing are therefore misleading, as substitution at monopoly prices is much more likely than at competitive levels.[636]

Geographic market

The European Commission's definition of the relevant geographic market focuses on the homogeneity of conditions of competition in a particular area as the distinguishing factor in delimiting the market. This definition arises from the Court of Justice decision in *United Brands* where the court stated that:

> The opportunities for competition under article 86 (article 102 TFEU) of the treaty must be considered ... with reference to a clearly defined geographic area in which it is marketed and where the conditions of competition are sufficiently homogeneous for the effect of the economic power of the undertaking concerned to be able to be evaluated.

The US Agencies on their part look at how the willingness or ability of consumers to substitute to other products or the willingness or ability of suppliers to supply the consumers is affected by the geographic limits.[637] In the context of globalization and internationalization of business, the authorities in the European Union, the United States and South Africa all point to the need to determine whether a geographic market is national, regional or international.[638] Factors such as language, tariff and non-tariff barriers, regulatory limitations, lack of sufficient economies of scale, volatility are regarded as having a decisive role in determining whether

---

636 *Distillers Corporation (SA) Limited & Stellenbosch Farmers Winery Group Ltd* Competition Tribunal case no 08/LM/Feb02, 19 March 2003, paras 134-136.

637 US Horizontal Guidelines para 4.2.

638 See discussion in Whish and Bailey (2012) 39; US Horizontal Guidelines para 4.2; Sutherland and kemp (2014) para 10.5.2.

a market can be regarded as international.[639] The authorities in the European Union and the United States additionally point out that transport costs can have a big impact on setting the bounds of the geographic market.[640]

3.2.5.3 Determining substitutability: The Hypothetical Monopolist Test

In order to determine substitutability for the purposes of defining the relevant market, most competition authorities use the hypothetical monopolist test (HMT) which was first applied in the US. Under the HMT, the competition authority will continuously add the closest competing product to those offered by the merging firms and then ask whether customers would switch to the seller of the next closest competing product within the defined market.

One of the early conceptions of the reasoning behind the HMT was proffered by Adelman who stated:

> No matter how the boundaries may be drawn in terms of products or areas, there is a single test: If, within the purported market, prices were appreciably raised or volume curtailed, would supply enter in such amounts as to restore approximately the old price and output? If the answer is "yes," then there is no market, and the definition must be expanded. If the answer is "no," the market is at least not wider. If it would be "no" even on a narrower definition, then the narrower definition must be used. Any other scheme of definition, is not so much "wrong" as meaningless.[641]

Further building on the reasoning espoused by Adelman, Sullivan stated that:

> To define a market in product and geographic terms is to say that if prices were appreciably raised or volume appreciably curtailed for the product within a given area, while demand held constant, supply from other sources could not be expected to enter promptly enough and in large enough amounts to restore the old price or volume. If

639 US Horizontal Guidelines para 4.2; See Sutherland et al. (2014) para 10.5.2 for the considerations in the South African perspective.

640 US Horizontal Guidelines para 4.2; Whish and Bailey (2012) 39.

641 Morris A. Adelman, 'Economic Aspects of the Bethlehem Opinion' (1959) 45 Va. L. Rev. 684, 688.

> sufficient supply would promptly enter from other geographic areas, then the "defined market" is not wide enough in geographic terms; if sufficient supply would promptly enter in the form of products made by other producers which had not been included in the product market as defined, then the market would not be wide enough in defined product terms. A "relevant market," then, is the narrowest market which is wide enough so that products from adjacent areas or from other producers in the same area cannot compete on substantial parity with those included in the market.[642]

The concept of a hypothetical monopolist was first formalised in the 1982 US Merger Guidelines which stated that:

> a market is as a product or group of products and a geographic area such that (in the absence of new entry) a hypothetical, unregulated firm that made all the sales of those products in that area could increase its profits through a small but significant and non-transitory increase in price (above prevailing or likely future levels).[643]

The concept of a hypothetical monopolist was further refined in the 1992 US Merger Guidelines, which provided that:

> If, in response to the price increase, the reduction in sales of the product would be large enough that a hypothetical monopolist would not find it profitable to impose such an increase in price, then the Agency will add to the product group the product that is the next-best substitute for the merging firm's product . . . . The price increase question is then asked for a hypothetical monopolist controlling the expanded product group. This process will continue until a group of products is identified such that a hypothetical monopolist over that group of products would profitably impose at least a "small but significant and nontransitory" increase ["SSNIP"], including the price of a product of one of the merging firms.[644]

---

642 Lawrence A. Sullivan, *Handbook of the Law of Antitrust* (West Publishing Company, 1977) 41.

643 U.S. Department of Justice, Merger Guidelines § II n.6, reprinted in 4 Trade Reg. Rep. (CCH) ¶ 13,102 (June 14, 1982).

644 Department of Justice & Federal Trade Commission, Horizontal Merger Guidelines, reprinted in 4 Trade. Reg. Rep. ¶ 13,104, at § 1.11 (1992).

The HMT is explained in the current US Guidelines as follows:

> The hypothetical monopolist test requires that a product market contain enough substitute products so that it could be subject to post-merger exercise of market power significantly exceeding that existing absent the merger. Specifically, the test requires that a hypothetical profit-maximizing firm, not subject to price regulation, that was the only present and future seller of those products ("hypothetical monopolist") likely would impose at least a small but significant and non-transitory increase in price ("SSNIP") on at least one product in the market, including at least one product sold by one of the merging firms.[645]

The European Commission as well employs the HMT. In respect of demand-side substitutability for instance, the European Commission points out that the determination 'can be viewed as a speculative experiment, postulating a hypothetical small, lasting change in relative prices and evaluating the likely reactions of customers to that increase. The exercise of market definition focuses on prices for operational and practical purposes, and more precisely on demand substitution arising from small, permanent changes in relative price'.[646]

South Africa similarly employs a HMT, with the consideration likewise being whether undertakings engaged in the production of the same products and operating within the same area would be able to profitably maintain a small but significant non-transitory price increase.[647]

Applying the HMT test: The relevant product and geographic market

The United States approach to defining the relevant product market is to start off by singling out the products of the merging parties and broadening the market by adding the next best substitute to the point where the HMT is satisfied.[648]

This approach is likewise applied in South Africa and within the European Union.[649] The authorities will start off with a narrow market and if

645 US Horizontal Guidelines 9.

646 EC Market Definition Notice para 15.

647 Competition Commission and Competition Tribunal of South Africa, 'Ten years of enforcement by the South African Competition Authorities: Unleashing Rivalry' (2009), 16 <http://www.compcom.co.za/wp-content/uploads/2014/09/10year.pdf> accessed 16 September 2019 (SA Ten Year Review).

648 US Commentary on the Horizontal Merger Guidelines 5.

649 SA Ten Year Review 16; EC Market Definition Notice paras 16-18.

the hypothetical monopolist will not be able to profitably implement the small but significant price increase then substitute products are added and the test repeated to the point where the hypothetical monopolist would still find it profitable.[650] The same approach is favoured when it comes to determining the geographic market. This means starting off in the area where the merging parties compete in respect of the relevant products and expanding this area as long as the HMT is satisfied.[651]

The US Guidelines however acknowledge the difficulty of capturing the relevant market in precise bounds.[652] The Competition Tribunal of South Africa has analogised defining the relevant market to defining an elephant. Giving a precise definition of the elephant may be difficult but one would not fail to recognise an elephant if it were before them.[653] Mario Monti, a former EU Commissioner, has likewise expressed the view that definitions of the relevant market are made 'only when strictly necessary'.[654]

3.2.5.4 Challenges to market definition

As noted at the beginning of this chapter there are markets that cannot be properly captured using the standard market definition approach. They require a nuanced approach to defining the market. This is the case with differentiated product markets for instance. Differentiated products would prima facie be viewed as close substitutes due to similar uses. They are however differentiated on the basis of various characteristics such as branding, price, quality, location, consumer preferences or any other factors. The greater the differentiation between the products the weaker their link in terms of substitutability.[655] Depending on the degree of differentiation it may be difficult to employ the HMT especially where it is difficult to have clear distinctions between the products. In such cases the level of diversion i.e. diversion ratio between the two products may be a more probative indicator where used together with market share and concentration levels.[656]

---

650 Lindsay and Berridge (2009) para 3-006.

651 US Commentary on the Horizontal Merger Guidelines 6; SA Ten Year Review 16; EC Market Definition Notice paras 16-18.

652 US Horizontal Guidelines para 4.

653 *Mondi Ltd & Kohler Cores and Tubes a division of Kohler Packaging Limited* Competition Tribunal case no 06/LM/Jan02, 20 June 2002, para 37.

654 Monti (2001).

655 See OECD Market Definition Guidance 47-51 for a detailed discussion.

656 OECD Market Definition Guidance 47-51.

Another example is multi-sided markets which involve indirect network effects such that there are two sets of consumers whose interaction through the platform/product is of mutual benefit, ultimately bolstering the utility of the platform.[657] The effect of a change for example in price on one side of the market cannot be considered in isolation from the other side of the market, a factor which would need to be taken into account when employing the HMT for example.

In the case of innovation-intensive markets for instance, quick changes in the market structure that are typical of such industries means market definition requires the time-horizon factor to be taken into account. A strict application of the HMT normally focuses more on static factors such as current demand substitutability hence failing to take into account the dynamic nature in which new products keep getting added to such markets. This could lead to an improper definition of the relevant market.[658]

In these cases, traditional approaches such as looking at market shares and concentration levels may not appropriately capture the relevant market. Other analytical substitutes such as pricing pressure indices, which focus on the propensity of the merging firms to increase prices post-merger, have been proposed as alternatives.[659] Merger simulation models have also been proposed as alternatives, though they do not serve as simple first screens owing to their extensive data requirements. These and other alternative approaches are most certainly not intended to do away with market definition but to complement it or step in in circumstances where market definition may be deficient.[660]

The authorities in the European Union, the United States and South Africa have indeed highlighted these challenges in their merger regulation work.[661] What is clear however is the flexibility of their approach to such challenges, where they adopt the analytical tools that are relevant to the particular case in question.

657 Ibid 54.
658 OECD Market Definition Guidance 57-58.
659 Ibid 59-71.
660 Ibid 71-73, 77-79.
661 Ibid 329-331, 337-340, 377-382.

3.2.5.5 The ESA Perspective

With the exception of Tanzania, the reviewed ESA jurisdictions reflect in their guidelines a more tempered approach to the role of market definition, an approach quite similar to that in the United States, the European Union and South Africa. The Tanzania merger guidelines take the position that the starting point in respect of any type of competition analysis is defining the relevant market.[662] This is reflective of its traditional dominance based test which almost invariably favours a more structured approach within a defined framework that has at its core the definition of the market followed by the determination of the market shares and concentration levels.

The Competition Authority of Botswana expresses the view that that determining market power does require the relevant market to be defined. The guidelines in fact quote the American Bar Association's perspective of market definition as establishing the framework for competition analysis and as setting the first step for market power assessment. However, the guidelines further take the position that it is not an end in itself but a key step in figuring out the competitive constraints, which is similar to the view expressed by then EU Commissioner Monti.[663] The Zambia merger guidelines stress the importance of market definition where market shares and concentration levels play a big role. This may be taken to suggest that where these two factors do not play a central role a well-defined market may not be too important.[664]

Looking at the other Eastern and Southern African jurisdictions market definition is regarded as an almost indispensable part of their review. The Kenya market definition guidelines decisively categorise market definition as the first step in a full competition analysis.[665] The Namibia and Tanzania merger guidelines also regard market definition as the starting point

662 Tanzania Merger Guidelines para 4.2.1.

663 Competition Authority of Botswana Market Definition Guidelines (2014) paras. 2.1 et seq <http://www.competitionauthority.co.bw/sites/default/files/MARKET%20DEFINITION%20GUIDELINES.pdf> accessed 26 August 2019 (Botswana Market Definition Guidelines).

664 Zambia Merger Guidelines para 68.

665 Competition Authority of Kenya, Guidelines on Relevant Market Definition, para. 3 <http://www.cak.go.ke/images/docs/guidelines_for__market_definition1.pdf> accessed 26 August 2019 (Kenya Market Definition Guidelines)

of their analysis.[666] Seychelles terms it as a fundamental step for all its competition investigations.[667] Mauritius regards market definition as vital even where market shares are not being considered, because market definition delineates the sphere of analysis.[668] The Malawi merger guidelines term it as integral but do not specify whether it should be the default starting point.[669] The COMESA merger guidelines provide that market definition will be determined for each merger being assessed.[670]

The determination of the relevant market is more or less uniform across the jurisdictions and reflects a largely standardised approach that is similar to that taken in the European Union and the United States and in line with recommendations of the ICN and the OECD.[671] It also involves a delineation of the relevant product and geographic markets. Within these relevant markets the substitutability of the product in question is analysed both from the supply and demand side. The substitutability is predominantly measured using the hypothetical monopolist test. Other factors taken into consideration when they do arise include temporal markets (i.e. markets that are time dependant e.g. peak and off-peak services as well as seasonal variations) and secondary markets (in respect of markets that arise on the basis of a primary product).[672]

3.2.6 The Substantive Test

The majority of jurisdictions that have a merger regulation framework in place apply one of two major control standards or a combination of both; the dominance test and the substantial lessening of competition (SLC) test.

---

666 Namibia Merger Guidelines para 9.1.

667 Fair Trading Commission of Seychelles Guidelines on the Definition of Relevant Market para 1.2 (Seychelles Market Definition Guidelines).

668 Competition Commission of Mauritius Market Definition and the Calculation of Market Shares (2009) para 1.4 <http://www.ccm.mu/English/Documents/Legislations/CCM2%20-%20Guidelines%20-%20Market%20definition_Nov09.pdf> accessed 26 August 2019 (Mauritius Market Definition Guidelines).

669 Malawi Merger Guidelines para 7.1.2.

670 COMESA Merger Guidelines para 8.3.

671 See ch 8.5.

672 See generally Botswana Market Definition Guidelines; Mauritius Market Definition Guidelines; Kenya Market Definition Guidelines; Seychelles Market Definition Guidelines; Namibia Merger Guidelines part 9; COMESA Market Definition Guidelines; Malawi Merger Guidelines para 7.1.2 et seq; Tanzania Merger Guidelines para 4.2.1.

The ICN refers to these two tests as the competition tests.[673] The various national legislationsapply their merger regulations against the backdrop of a formulation of one of these tests, or a combination of the two.

The UNCTAD Model[674] on its part proposes a hybrid test, prohibiting acquisitions of control where 'the proposed transaction substantially increases the ability to exercise market power…' and 'the resultant market share in the country, or any substantial part of it, relating to any product or service, will result in a dominant firm or in a significant reduction of competition in a market dominated by very few firms.'[675]

A majority of jurisdictions have or are considering reorienting their merger regulation systems from a dominance test to a SLC test, which would eventually lead to the SLC test being the standard substantive test.[676]

The focus of the substantial lessening of competition test is whether a merger is likely to significantly lessen or restrain competition on the market. One key difference between the SLC test and the dominance test is its weaker focus on market structure. The SLC test is therefore viewed as being more flexible in addressing a wider range of anti-competitive concerns. The effect of the merger on existing competitive constraints and the level of post-merger market power play a crucial role under the SLC test.[677] The most influential jurisdiction employing a SLC-type test is the United States. The European Union employs a combination of both tests. The discussion of the SLC test is therefore principally based on these two jurisdictions. The discussion will also include the South African experience in order to bring in an emerging market perspective.

The basic premise of the dominance test is to determine whether a merger is likely to create or strengthen a dominant position. There are however very few jurisdictions that apply a pure dominance test. The European Union for instance changed the substantive test from a broadly defined dominance test to a SLC type test. The dominance test is now subsumed to a Significant Impediment to Effective Competition test (SIEC)

---

673 ICN: Merger Guidelines Workbook (April 2006) 6 <https://www.internationalcompetitionnetwork.org/portfolio/merger-guidelines-workbook/> accessed 18 September 2019.

674 UNCTAD: Model Law on Competition (United Nations 2010).

675 Ibid ch 6(2).

676 *See generally* OECD: Standard for Merger Review (OECD Policy Roundtables 2009) DAF/COMP(2009)21 https://www.oecd.org/competition/mergers/45247537.pdf> accessed 26 August 2019 (OECD Merger Review Standard).

677 OECD Merger Review Standard 16.

with the creation or strengthening of a dominant position being regarded as a prime example of a SIEC.

Germany was the largest dominance test jurisdiction within the European Union until 2013 when the country changed the substantive test to the SIEC test to bring it in line with the EU standard.[678] The creation or strengthening of a dominant position likewise plays a central role under the German SIEC test. The creation or strengthening of a dominant position will therefore be considered from the point of view of the European Union with some comparison to Germany, in order to highlight the nuances brought about by the change from a dominance test to the SIEC test.

The broader objective of the analysis of the United States, European Union and South African substantive approaches is to form a basis of comparison with the approach taken by Sub-Saharan African jurisdictions in order to draw lessons that can be passed on to these nascent jurisdictions.

3.2.6.1 The United States

The operative provision for the regulation of mergers in the United States, which also espouses the substantive standard for assessment, is section 7 of the Clayton Act[679] which prohibits mergers if, 'in any line of commerce or in any activity affecting commerce in any section of the country, the effect of such acquisition may be substantially to lessen competition, or to tend to create a monopoly.'

This provision seems to advocate for a hybrid test but the focus of the Department of Justice (DOJ) and the Federal Trade Commission (FTC) (the agencies), which are the authorities charged with merger control), has been on the substantial lessening of competition.

The Horizontal Merger Guidelines (Guidelines)[680] set out the main points of analysis and the core evidentiary requirements relied on by the agencies in assessing whether a horizontal merger will lead to a substantial lessening of competition. The Guidelines are supplemented by the Com-

678 For a general explanation see for instance The Bundeskartellamt: Legislation <http://www.bundeskartellamt.de/EN/AboutUs/Bundeskartellamt/legislation/legislation_node.html> accessed 26 August 2019.

679 The Clayton Act, 15 U.S.C. § 18.

680 US Horizontal Merger Guidelines (August 19, 2010) <https://www.ftc.gov/sites/default/files/attachments/merger-review/100819hmg.pdf> accessed 26 August 2019 (US Horizontal Guidelines).

mentary on the Horizontal Merger Guidelines (Commentary)[681] which is issued by the agencies. Given the multi-factor approach taken to analyzing mergers the agencies clarify that the Guidelines are in no way intended to be exhaustive.

The prevention or prohibition of the creation, enhancement or entrenchment of or a facilitation of market power is a central theme of the Guidelines. Market power is regarded as the ability to profitably maintain prices above competitive levels for a significant period of time.[682] An enhancement of market power through a merger is linked to the encouraging of one or more firms increasing prices, reducing innovation, reducing output or generally injuring consumers owing to the fettering of competition.[683] Some scholars have advocated an approach under which the focus is on two alternative and independent ways of attaining anticompetitive economic power namely through increasing one's prices, on the one hand, or raising rival costs, on the other.[684]

The Guidelines adopt a five-part structure consisting of: (1) market definition and concentration; (2) potential adverse competitive effects; (3) entry analysis; (4) efficiencies; and (5) failing and exiting assets. It is noted in the Commentary that this five-part structure has become integral to the analysis of mergers. The approach to merger analysis is however integrated and need not follow the specific order of the five parts.[685]

This integrated approach is applied in the context of two broad analytical frameworks: (i) whether, as a result of the merger, an increase in market power would encourage or increase the likelihood of 'coordinated, accommodating, or interdependent behavior among rivals'[686]; (ii) whether the merger would facilitate the exercise by the merged firm of unilater-

681 US Commentary on the Horizontal Merger Guidelines (March 2006) <https://www.ftc.gov/sites/default/files/attachments/merger-review/commentaryonthehorizontalmergerguidelinesmarch2006.pdf> accessed 26 August 2019 (US Commentary).

682 Ibid 1.

683 US Horizontal Guidelines 2.

684 Thomas G. Krattenmaker, Robert H. Lande and Steven C. Salop, 'Monopoly Power and Market Power in Antitrust Law' (1987) 76(2) Georgetown Law Journal 241 The authors argue that judicial precedence has largely bred uncertainty as to whether monopoly power and market power are similar or distinct concepts. They express the view that the two concepts are qualitatively identical and the focus should rather be on a determination based on these two alternative ways in which anticompetitive economic power can be achieved.

685 US Commentary on the Horizontal Merger Guidelines 2.

686 Ibid 2-3.

al market power through, for instance, increasing price or reducing output.[687]

The Guidelines address several common types of unilateral effects while making it clear that it is by no means an exhaustive discussion. The most prominent example is where the only firms in the relevant market merge to form a monopoly.[688] In the proposed merger between *Franklin Electric and United Dominion*[689], the only two domestic producers of submersible turbine pumps in the relevant market sought to effect, through the merging of their subsidiaries (FE Petro and Marley) by way of a joint venture, a merger that would have resulted in the merged entity controlling the entire productive capacity of the submersible turbine pump market. The Court granted a permanent injunction that had been sought by the US government against the merger. The DOJ highlighted the absence of any justifying reason for the transaction other than the achievement of a dominant position by the parties.[690] It was noted that the market already had high barriers to entry as well as low substitutability. Potential market entrants would for instance have to seek design-around alternatives to avoid infringing the patents held by Franklin and Dominion. This was in addition to the fact that Franklin was the only company in the United States approved to sell the submersible pumps. The users of the pumps also rely heavily on the reputation of the manufacturer and the length of time they have been in business. One of the defenses presented by the merging parties was that Marley, which previously held a dominant position in the market for submersible turbine pumps, had not abused its dominance during its dominant years. The Court noted however that as a result of the dominant position, Marley did not improve its products or services due to lack of competition.[691]

Another example of a unilateral effect is the probable pricing strategy of firms offering differentiated products, where the merged firm may opt to raise the price of one or both of their product offerings. The likelihood of sales lost due to price increase in one product are easily diverted to the product of the merger partner, thus offsetting any losses and making the price increase profitable, especially where the product of the merger

---

687 Ibid.

688 US Horizontal Guidelines para 6; US Commentary on the Horizontal Merger Guidelines 25.

689 *United States v. Franklin Electric Co., United Dominion Industries, Ltd., and United Dominion Industries, Inc.*, 130 F. Supp. 2d 1025 (W.D. Wis. 2000).

690 Ibid 1034.

691 Ibid 1036.

partner was the next best choice for the consumers.[692] In the case of the proposed merger between *Interstate Bakeries and Continental Baking*[693] the differentiated product in question was white pan bread. Continental was at the time the largest and interstate the third-largest producer of fresh bread in the United States. Consumer preferences leaned towards the more expensive premium brands rather than the private label supermarket brands, with evidence indicating little competition between the premium and private label brands. Both Interstate and Continental were producers of premium white pan bread. The econometric data additionally indicated the high level of demand cross-elasticity between the two companies with the probability of a price increase post-merger. Based on a conclusion that the merger would result in price increases in five metropolitan areas, the DOJ required the divestiture of brands and related assets in these five areas.

Another probative unilateral effect is the elimination, as a result of the merger, of an avenue for negotiation where buyers would otherwise pit competing sellers against each other. The merger in this case increases the probability of more favorable outcomes for the merged parties.[694] In the proposed merger between *Slidell Memorial and Tenet*[695] the parties were involved in the provision of health care services. Slidell and Tenet were the only full-service acute care hospitals in that geographic market and the merger would have eliminated a competitive option for customers. Insurance companies would have had to contend with a decision to either leave out the merged entity from their offerings (which would have made their packages less attractive to customers who wanted access to the service in the Slidell area) or possibly paying an increased price. The FTC in its analysis in this case concluded that the greater probability was that insurance companies would accede to the price increase. The FTC's ultimate decision was against the merger.

Output squeezes, suboptimal use of capacity, and diversion of capacity to other markets in order to raise prices in the relevant market by a merged firm is also considered a probable unilateral action.[696] The effect of the merger on innovation activities and product variety is also taken into consideration where necessary.

---

692 US Horizontal Guidelines 20.

693 *United States v. Interstate Bakeries Corp. and Continental Baking Co.*, 60 Fed. Reg. 40,195 (Aug. 7, 1995).

694 US Horizontal Guidelines 23.

695 *Tenet Health Care Systems and Slidell Memorial Hospital* (2003). <http://www.ftc.gov/opa/2003/04/lahospmerger.htm> accessed 26 August 2019.

696 US Horizontal Guidelines 23.

The Guidelines also address coordinated effects, where as a result of accommodating reactions among firms the profitability of their market activities is guaranteed.[697] Coordinated interaction can be implemented through an explicit or tacit agreement, the latter where market conditions allow for easy detection and punishment of any defections. The Guidelines also cover an even more remote form of coordination, which edges close to unilateral conduct. It is termed as parallel accommodating conduct where reactions by competing firms are motivated by individual rationality rather than retaliation or deterrence but which nonetheless has anti-competitive effects such as encouraging increases in price.[698] The DOJ and FTC point out that successful coordination would typically fulfil three cumulative criteria: (1) terms of coordination that are profitable to all the coordinating rivals; (2) ways to detect deviations from the coordination; and (3) ability to punish such deviations.[699] In *LaFarge and Blue Circle*[700] the proposed merger was in the cement industry. The post-merger market share of the two firms would have increased above 40% with the top four firms cumulatively controlling 90% of cement supply in the market Transactions were also frequent, relatively small and regular. What this meant was that the probability of post-merger coordination was relatively high with little incentive for firms to deviate from coordination. The FTC in this case opted for a consent order that required a divestiture of cement-related assets.

A merger would therefore be subject to scrutiny where it would result in a market concentration level that would embolden such responses or result in sufficient market transparency to allow for better prediction of these responses.[701] The agencies are usually on the lookout for the following conditions:

(1) the merger would significantly increase concentration and lead to a moderately or highly concentrated market; (2) that market shows signs of vulnerability to coordinated conduct; and (3) the Agencies have a credible basis on which to conclude that the merger may enhance that vulnerability.[702]

---

697 US Horizontal Guidelines 24.

698 Ibid 25.

699 US Commentary on the Horizontal Merger Guidelines 18.

700 *Lafarge S.A.; Blue Circle Industries PLC; Blue Circle North America, Inc.; and Blue Circle, Inc.* (2001), 66 Fed. Reg. 34,682.

701 Ibid.

702 US Horizontal Guidelines 25-26.

Other factors taken into consideration by the agencies include the likelihood of sufficiently significant buyer power to curtail the merging parties' ability to raise prices, the probability of market entry that would deter or counteract negative competitive effects of the proposed merger including the timeliness, sufficiency and likelihood of such entry.

In cases involving failing firms the agencies regard a merger with such a firm as not likely to enhance market power. However, the following circumstances all have to be met:

(1) the inability of the failing firm to meet its financial obligations in the near future;
(2) its inability to reorganize successfully under Chapter 11 of the Bankruptcy Act; and (3) unsuccessful good-faith efforts to elicit reasonable alternative offers that would keep its tangible and intangible assets in the relevant market and pose a less severe danger to competition than does the proposed merger.[703]

The agencies also review partial acquisitions which do not result in effective control but which may result in restrained competition through for instance (i) giving the acquiring firm a position of influence over the target firm, e.g. voting rights, (ii) reducing the acquiring firm's incentive to compete with the target firm, or (iii) enabling the acquiring firm to access sensitive trade information from the target firm.

Regarding non-horizontal mergers, the principal approach is to consider the effect of the merger on perceived potential and actual potential competition.[704] Perceived potential competition is harmed where the merger would eliminate a significant present competitive threat which keeps in check the firms that are already in the market.[705] Actual potential competition is harmed where the merger eliminates the possibility of entry of a competitor resulting in the lost chance for improved market performance.[706] The firms already present in the market would foreclose the market for a perceived potential competitor, for instance by setting a price which deters the potential competitor and at the same time maximizes the merging firms' profits. Where such strategies would not be optimal in deterring entry the merger would harm actual potential competition.[707]

---

703 Ibid 32.

704 Non-Horizontal Merger Guidelines <http://www.justice.gov/sites/default/files/atr/legacy/2006/05/18/2614.pdf> accessed 26 August 2019 (US Non-Horizontal Guidelines).

705 US Non-Horizontal Guidelines para 4.111.

706 Ibid para 4.112.

707 Ibid para 4.12.

The factors taken into consideration include market concentration, the ease or difficulty of market entry, the entry advantage of the potential competitor, market share of the acquiring firm and efficiencies.[708] As regards vertical mergers the agencies may also consider whether there will be a resultant barrier to entry or whether it would facilitate collusion between market participants.[709]

3.2.6.2 The European Union

Merger regulation within the European Union (with a community dimension) is governed by the EU Merger Regulation.[710] The main objective of the EU Merger Regulation is linked to the aims of the TFEU, i.e. the maintenance of an open market economy with free competition in order to safeguard the further development of the internal market.[711] It is contemplated in the EU Merger Regulation recitals that 'the completion of the internal market and of economic and monetary union, the enlargement of the European Union and the lowering of international barriers to trade and investment will continue to result in major corporate reorganisations, particularly in the form of concentrations.'[712] The Council of the European Union further notes the importance of maintaining dynamic competition by ensuring that 'the process of reorganization does not result in lasting damage to competition; Community law must therefore include provisions governing those concentrations which may significantly impede effective competition in the common market or in a substantial part of it.'[713]

Therefore, the recitals already indicate that the *significant impediment to effective competition* (SIEC) is the test employed in the European Union. Article 1(2) and 1(3) of the EU Merger Regulation are the operative provisions in this regard. Article 1(3) provides that, 'A concentration which would significantly impede effective competition, in the common market or in a substantial part of it, in particular as a result of the creation or

---

708 Ibid para 4.21.

709 Ibid para 4.22.

710 Council Regulation on the Control of Concentrations between Undertakings (EC) No 139/2004 OJ L 24/1 (the EU Merger Regulation).

711 EU Merger Regulation rec 2.

712 EU Merger Regulation rec 3.

713 EU Merger Regulation rec 5.

strengthening of a dominant position, shall be declared incompatible with the common market'.

The counterpart under the German Act against Restraints of Competition (Gesetz gegen Wettbewerbsbeschränkungen GWB)[714] which was amended to be in line with the EU position is found in Section 36(1) which prohibits a merger which would significantly impede effective competition particularly where it will lead to the creation or the strengthening of a dominant position.[715] This test is similar to that employed by the EU Merger Regulation save for the common market dimension. The GWB further provides that the prohibition will not apply if the parties demonstrate that the merger will result in improvements in the competitive conditions which outweigh the negative effects.[716]

One of the scholarly interpretations of SIEC establishes, by looking at the component parts of the test, that effective competition is competition which delivers material benefits to consumers.[717]

The European Commission (Commission) has published guidelines on the application of the substantive standard, i.e. the Guidelines on the assessment of horizontal mergers[718] and the Guidelines on the assessment of non-horizontal mergers[719].

The creation or the strengthening of a dominant position, which was the test previously employed in the European Union, still remains a primary consideration in the analysis of significant impediments to effective competition. The previous EU Merger Regulation[720] defined dominance

---

714 Act against Restraints of Competition in the version published on 26 June 2013 (Bundesgesetzblatt (Federal Law Gazette) I, 2013, p. 1750, 3245), as last amended by Article 1 of the law of 1 June 2017 (Federal Law Gazette I, p. 1416). English language translation available at: <http://www.gesetze-im-internet.de/englisch_gwb/englisch_gwb.html> accessed 26 August 2019.

715 Bekanntmachung der Neufassung des Gesetzes gegen Wettbewerbsbeschränkungen (26 Juni 2013 BGBl. I S. 1750, 3245). Translation courtesy of author and Google translate.

716 GWB s 36(1).

717 Alistair Lindsay and Alison Berridge, *The EU Merger Regulation: Substantive Issues* (4th edn, Sweet and Maxwell, 2009).

718 Guidelines on the assessment of horizontal merger under the Council Regulation on the control of concentrations between undertakings, [2004] OJ C 31, 5 (EU Horizontal Merger Guidelines).

719 Guidelines on the assessment of non-horizontal mergers under the Council Regulation on the control of concentrations between undertakings, [2008] OJ C 265, 6 (EU Non-horizontal Merger Guidelines).

720 Council Regulation (EEC) No 4064/89 of 21 December 1989 on the control of concentrations between undertakings. Recital 2 of the Horizontal Merger

as 'a situation where one or more undertakings wield economic power which would enable them to prevent effective competition from being maintained in the relevant market by giving them the opportunity to act to a considerable extent independently of their competitors, their customers and, ultimately, of consumers'.

This definition is similar to the German position which draws parallels between dominance, market power and the ability to act independently of competitive restraints from competitors, customers and consumers. The Bundeskartellamt in its Guidance on Substantive Merger Control[721] makes reference to a decision of the Federal Court of Germany (Bundesgerichtshof) where the court termed a position of dominance as one where the company is not restrained sufficiently by the competitive climate.[722] The Bundeskartellamt also makes reference to the *United Brands* decision[723] where dominance is determined by the ability of an undertaking to behave independently of its competitors, customers and consumers.

The Horizontal Merger Guidelines as well as the Bundeskartellamt Guidance indicate that incompatibility based on the SIEC test will continue to be predominantly dictated by a finding of dominance.[724] Both Guidelines therefore do not attempt to reinvent the wheel. The Horizontal

---

Guidelines makes reference to the definition of dominance under the previous regulations. This definition was established by the European Court of Justice in e.g. Case 322/81 *Michelin v Commission* [1983] ECR. 3461, para. 30; See also Case 85/76 *Hoffmann-La Roche* [1979] ECR. 461, para 38.

721 Guidance on Substantive Merger Control (Bundeskartellamt 2012) <http://www.bundeskartellamt.de/SharedDocs/Publikation/EN/Leitlinien/Guidance%20-%20Substantive%20Merger%20Control.pdf?__blob=publicationFile&v=6.> accessed 26 August 2019 (Bundeskartellamt Guidance). Though the guidelines were published before the amendment of the GWB, the Budenskartellamt already contemplated the change and noted that the current guidance will provide a basis for the next review (hence will still remain applicable, especially because the creation or strengthening of a dominant position will still remain the prime example of a SIEC.) The next update will then be focused on the analytical changes brought about by the SIEC Test.

722 Bundeskartellamt Guidance 3.

723 *See* Case 27/76 *United Brands Company and United Brands Continental Bv v Commission* , [1978] ECR 207 where a dominant position was determined to be 'a position of economic strength enjoyed by an undertaking which enables it to prevent effective competition being maintained on the relevant market by giving it the power to behave to and appreciable extent independently of its competitors, customers and ultimately of its consumers.'

724 Horizontal Merger Guidelines para 4; Bundeskartellamt Guidance para 1; See also GWB s 36(1). This is also indicative of the intention to maintain the jurisprudential experience developed under the previous test as specifically

Merger Guidelines draw principally from the experience under the previous regulations and provide additional guidance in the areas that were perceived to leave gaps under the previous regulations.

According to the Bundeskartellamt the distinction to be made between, for instance, a prohibition for abuse of dominance and a prohibition for creation or strengthening of dominance is that in merger control law the threshold is much lower. A 'threat to the functioning of competition' is sufficient to warrant intervention by the Bundeskartellamt.[725] Mergers for the mere purpose of entrenching dominance without commensurate benefits to the competition climate therefore have a high likelihood of prohibition.

To determine the effects on competition of a merger, the Commission as well as the Bundeskartellamt conducts an assessment of the market pre and post-merger.[726] An assessment is also done of the market situation had the merger not taken place (the counterfactual). They both also take into consideration changes to the market that can be reasonably predicted. The Bundeskartellamt stipulates that any prognoses should be restricted to a forseeable future timespan, which in itself may vary depending on the market conditions from case to case. The aim here is to assess whether the merger would lead to a shift in the market structure to the detriment of the competitive process.[727]

One probative aspect that draws a line of congruence in merger control between the European Union, Germany and the United States is market power. The Commission, as is the case with the Bundeskartellamt and the DOJ/FTC, aims to prevent mergers that would harm consumers by significantly increasing the market power of the merging firms, i.e. the ability of one or more firms to profitably increase prices, reduce output, choice or quality of goods and services, diminish innovation, or otherwise influence parameters of competition.[728]

The creation of a dominant position will be assessed in the light of the magnitude of the market power. The strengthening of a dominant position will result from the change in intensity of competition where high market power was already present.[729] Mergers that would strengthen

---

reflected in para 4 of the Horizontal Merger Guidelines and para 1 of the Bundeskartellamt Guidance.

725 Bundeskartellamt Guidance para 10.

726 EU Horizontal Merger Guidelines para 9; Bundeskartellamt Guidance para 12.

727 Ibid.

728 EU Horizontal Merger Guidelines para 8.

729 Bundeskartellamt Guidance para 13-14.

an already dominant market position tend to attract high regulatory scrutiny. The Bundeskartellamt therefore notes that where a merging party was already a dominant market player, even a marginal increase of market power would constitute a strengthening of a dominant position,[730] with a 'definite negative effect on competition' being the determining factor.

As regards the creation of a dominant position, the former Court of First Instance (CFI, now General Court) in the case of *General Electric v Commission*[731] noted inter alia that: (i) the elimination of competition is not a prerequisite for a finding of a dominant position; (ii) price reductions as a result of competitive pressure from rivals generally point to a lack of a dominant position; and (iii) active competition in a particular market doesn't necessarily mean that there is no dominant position. The essential factor is ability to act independently of competitive pressure.

In respect of the strengthening of a dominant position, the CFI has expressed the interesting view that a merger in a market where one of the parties already holds a monopoly position could not be prohibited.[732] The reasoning is that a monopoly is the ultimate form of a dominant position. A merger in such a market would therefore not affect competition because there is no competition to begin with. The Commission however made the point that where such a market faces liberalization it would be necessary to analyze the effect of the merger on competition. The Commission has as well intervened where such a merger would have an effect on potential competition.[733]

The concept of a strengthening of market dominant position in Germany is however not restricted to market share considerations. Instances where the market standing is improved by other means, such as by acquiring through merger sole control over a previously jointly controlled venture have also been considered by the Bundeskartellamt.[734]

Both the Commission and the Bundeskartellamt target instances of single firm and collective dominance. The Commission notes that single firm dominance has been the most common basis for determining that a merger would result in a SIEC.[735] Collective dominance from an oligopolistic perspective is also covered under the dominance concept.

---

730 Ibid.

731 *General Electric v Commission* Case T-210/01 [2005] ECR II-5575, paras 114, 116, 117 and 215.

732 *EDP v Commission* Case T-87/05 [2005] ECR II-3745.

733 Lindsay and Berridge (2009) 63-64.

734 Ibid.

735 EU Horizontal Merger Guidelines recital 4.

The main elements of the Commission's assessment are; (i) market shares and concentration ratios, (ii) likelihood of anticompetitive effects save for countervailing factors, (iii) likelihood of sufficient buyer power to countervail increased market power, (iv) likelihood of market entry to maintain effective competition in the relevant markets, (v) likelihood of counteracting efficiencies and (vi) failing firm defence. As is the case in Germany and the U.S., the Commission makes it clear that the circumstantial nature of merger regulation and the multifactor analysis needed means that a checklist method is not suitable. The preferred approach is therefore an overall assessment of the competitive effects of a merger.[736]

The Commission's approach to the analysis of market shares and concentration levels at first glance seems to lean on structural considerations, with definite market share and HHI levels/thresholds still playing an important role in establishing safe harbors.[737] One would associate this with a focus on structural aspects which is more in line with a dominance test and not a SLC-type test, which focuses more on effects. This approach can be regarded as being indicative of the significant role that the experience under the previous regime still plays even under the SIEC test. However, given the multifactor approach taken towards merger regulation, an overall assessment eventually leads to the Commission taking an effects-based approach, with market share and concentration levels falling foul of the thresholds not necessarily resulting in a prohibition of a merger. In *T-Mobile Austria and tele.ring*[738] for instance, the merged firms would not have been in a post-merger dominant position. The Commission was however concerned that the merger would have resulted in the elimination of a core competitive force (a maverick firm) namely, tele.ring. The Commission however allowed the merger to proceed on the basis of commitments made by T-Mobile to divest some of the tele.ring assets to another weaker market player (H3G). This divestiture meant that H3G would be able to take up the position that tele.ring had as an important competitive constraint to other market players.[739]

Market share and concentration levels also play an important role in Germany but are as well not the ultimate decisive factor in the Bun-

736 Ibid paras 11-13.

737 EU Horizontal Merger Guidelines paras 14-21.

738 *T-Mobile Austria/tele.ring* case COMP/M.3916. See also Johannes Luebking, 'T-Mobile Austria/tele.ring: Remedying the loss of a maverick' (Competition Policy Newsletter, 2006) <http://ec.europa.eu/competition/publications/cpn/2006_2_46.pdf> accessed 26 August 2019.

739 Luebking (2006) 49-50.

deskartellamt's analysis. Market share levels that meet the prescribed dominance threshold usually lead to a rebuttable presumption of dominance for the company (in the case of single firm dominance) or for the companies (in the case of collective dominance).[740] High market shares are therefore not conclusive but are indicative of the need for further investigation. The overall investigation of the actual state of competition is what is decisive in determining dominance.[741] As regards concentration, the absolute post-merger HHI level and the change in HHI may also be useful, depending on the particular case, in the overall assessment.[742]

The factors taken into account by the Commission in determining whether a horizontal merger will increase the probability of non-coordinated effects[743] include situations in which the merging firms hold large market shares, the firms are close competitors, customers have restricted possibilities of switching suppliers, competitors are unlikely to increase supply to counter a price increase on the part of the merging firms, the merged firms are able to restrict the expansion of competitors or where the merger eliminates an important competitive dynamic, e.g. where the merged firms were competing innovators in a market where innovation is an important competitive force.

In *Aerospatiale-Alenia and De Havilland*[744], the Commission made its first ever prohibition and it was on the basis of non-coordinated or unilateral effects.[745] The Commission noted that the merger would have resulted in a strengthening of the merged firms' dominant position as well as leading to unilateral effects. One of the core deciding factors in this case was the high post-merger market share that would have been realized. All the companies involved were active in the aviation industry. The merger would have put the merged entity in the position of the only provider of a full range of products (small, medium and large aircrafts) on the market

740 Section 19(3) of the GWB places the threshold at a third of the market share. In the case of collective dominance if three or fewer companies reach a combined market share of 50 percent; or if five or fewer companies reach a combined market share of two thirds.

741 Bundeskartellamt Guidance paras 26-27.

742 Ibid.

743 Ibid para 22(a). Non-coordinated effects are deemed to result where the merger would eliminate 'important competitive constraints on one or more firms, which consequently would have increased market power, without resorting to coordinated behavior.'

744 *Aerospatiale-Alenia/De Havilland* Commission decision 91/619/EEC [1991] OJ 334/42.

745 The dominance test was still the substantive standard.

to the detriment of the competitors. Apart from unilateral effects resulting from high combined market shares the merger would also have eliminated the competitive pressure exerted on Aerospatiale-Alenia by De Havilland. The Commission found that these various factors would give the merged entity the ability to act independently of competitors and customers.

The elimination of a close competitor was also a deciding factor in *Volvo and Scania*.[746] Both companies were active in the industry for heavy engines as well as trucks. The Commission in this case divided the product market into various categories, i.e. light, medium and heavy duty trucks as well as city and intercity buses and touring coaches. The focus was however on the market for heavy trucks and buses where the geographic market was determined to be a national one i.e. Sweden, Denmark, Norway, Finland and Ireland. It was found that the two companies were each other's closest competitors and that there would be insufficient post-merger competitive pressure from other market players. The merger would also have resulted in a large increase in market share for the merged firm hence leading to a dominant position in the relevant markets. Possible unilateral effects that were identified in this case were barriers to entry as well as price increases.

The Bundeskartellamt takes into consideration capacities and capacity constraints, customer preferences and switching costs, intellectual property rights and know-how, market phase, access to suppliers and customers, corporate and personal links with other companies, and financial resources.[747] Additional factors that the Bundeskartellamt would take into account are potential competition and barriers to entry, imperfect substitution and countervailing buyer power.

As regards coordinated effects[748] the Commission considers the ease with which competitors are able to reach terms of coordination, the ease with which deviations can be monitored (market transparency plays a critical role), mechanisms that deter deviation from the coordination and the effect or reaction of non-coordinating firms, competitors and customers.[749]

---

746 *Volvo/Scania* [2001] OJ L 143/74.

747 Bundeskartellamt Guidance 10-30.

748 Ibid. para 22(b). Coordinated effects arise where the merger changes 'the nature of competition in such a way that firms that previously were not coordinating their behaviour, are now significantly more likely to coordinate and raise prices or otherwise harm effective competition. A merger may also make coordination easier, more stable or more effective for firms which were coordinating prior to the merger.'

749 EU Horizontal Merger Guidelines para 39–57.

These factors were indeed clarified by the CFI in *Airtours and First Choice*[750] where the court highlighted three factors needed for a determination of a collective dominant position:

i) 'each member of the dominant oligopoly must have the ability to know how the other members are behaving in order to monitor whether or not they are adopting the common policy',
ii) 'the situation of tacit coordination must be sustainable over time, that is to say, there must be an incentive not to depart from the common policy on the market' and
iii) 'it must also be established that the foreseeable reaction of current and future competitors, as well as of consumers, would not jeopardise the results expected from the common policy.'

The Bundeskartellamt goes into more detail in explaining what they consider to be collective dominance and how they handle it. Collective dominance is as well addressed from the perspective of tacit (implied) coordination or outright collusion between dominant undertakings that negates would-be competition between them and renders insubstantial external competitive forces.[751] The ability and incentive to take part in future coordination or to facilitate already existent coordination is the critical factor sought to be determined by the Bundeskartellamt.[752]

Some of these factors were at play in the proposed merger between *Total and OMV*.[753] This case involved the proposed acquisition by Total of 59 petrol stations in Germany from OMV. Both Total and OMV have operations at all levels of the fuel sector in Germany, with Total having the fourth-largest petrol station network in Germany.

The Bundeskartellamt determined that the merger would lead to the strengthening of an oligopolistic dominant position in all the relevant markets which is contrary to section 36(1) of the GWB. The analysis found that Shell, Aral/BP, ConocoPhillips/Jet ExxonMobil/Esso and Total jointly have a dominant position in the relevant markets for petrol and diesel sales through petrol stations according to section 19 (2) of the GWB. The relevant factors here were among others the lack of internal competition, integrated production, transport and storage, mutual dependence through

750 Commission decision *Airtours/First Choice* 2000/276/EC [1999] OJ 93/1.
751 Bundeskartellamt Guidance para 81.
752 Ibid.
753 *Total Deutschland GmbH and OMV Deutschland GmbH*, Case B8 – 175/08 <https://www.bundeskartellamt.de/SharedDocs/Entscheidung/DE/Entscheidungen/Fusionskontrolle/2009/B8-175-08.pdf?__blob=publicationFile&v=3> accessed 26 August 2019.

exchange agreements which was found to result in a great retaliatory potential.

Total's purchase would therefore result in the dominant oligopoly having an increased market share in the relevant markets. Other considerations were the elimination of an active competitor (OMV) and decreased potential for external competition, without a justifying improvement of competition conditions to outweigh the negative effects of the dominance.

Similar to the Commission's position, the Bundeskartellamt notes that tacit collusion requires a stable coordination, where the firms have no motivation to individually go against the collusive trend, especially out of fear of reprisal from the other firms.[754] Investigating for tacit collusion also requires a multi-factor analysis which feeds into an overall assessment of each individual case. Aspects that go towards determining the particular market structure such as combined market share are a good starting point. High market shares among the (would be) coordinating firms would point to the likelihood of insufficient external competitive constraints.[755] As with single dominance, the Bundeskartellamt employs a market share based rebuttable presumption of collective dominance, which is likewise not a conclusive determinant of dominance.[756]

Other factors taken into account by the Bundeskartellamt include the number of competitors, existence of barriers to entry, frequency of interaction between competitors in the market, market transparency, product homogeneity, low buyer power, symmetry between the coordinating firms as well as existing links between them, stable market conditions and actual competitive behavior with the comparative importance of the factors being dependent on the case in question.[757]

Where a merger involves a potential competitor, the Commission pays specific attention to whether the potential competitor 'already exerts a significant constraining influence or there must be a significant likelihood that it would grow into an effective competitive force' or whether there is an insufficient number of other potential competitors to exert sufficient pressure on the merger.[758]

754 Ibid paras 84-87.

755 Ibid paras 88-89.

756 GWB s 19(3). Companies are presumed to be collectively dominant if three or fewer companies reach a combined market share of 50 percent; or if five or fewer companies reach a combined market share of two thirds.

757 Bundeskartellamt Guidance para 90.

758 EU Horizontal Merger Guidelines para 58-60.

The anticompetitive pressure exerted by a merger of downstream firms on the upstream market is also of probative value to the Commission particularly where the upstream market is fragmented. Such a merger may also have foreclosure effects on rivals.[759]

The strength and sufficiency of countervailing buyer power and the ease of market entry (including its likelihood, timeliness and sufficiency) are also taken into account.[760]

In cases where one of the merging parties is a failing firm such that the disruption of the competitive structure is not attributable to the merger, the Commission may opt not to prohibit the merger.[761] The Commission will however look at the following three criteria: (i) the merger will prevent the failing firm from exiting the market in the near future because of financial constraints, (ii) there is no less anti-competitive alternative, (iii) the assets of the failing firm would otherwise inevitably exit the market.[762] The Bundeskartellamt also allows a failing firm defence based on similar criteria. They also take into account an inevitable market exit by the failing firm absent the merger and the lack of a less anti-competitive alternative. They additionally consider the option that the failing firm's market position would either way be largely gained by the acquiring firm.[763]

Though the Commission has also published Non-horizontal Merger Guidelines[764], it clarifies that they are a continuity of the Horizontal Merger Guidelines which are also relevant to the non-horizontal merger situations.[765] The Commission further notes that in certain instances a merger may entail both horizontal and non-horizontal aspects. A key consideration of the Commission as to how a non-horizontal merger may lead to a SIEC is the probability that the merger may change the merging parties' and competitors' 'ability and incentive' to compete in ways that may harm consumers.[766]

The principal non-coordinated effect taken into account by the Commission in the context of non-horizontal mergers is anticompetitive foreclosure, i.e. instances where 'actual or potential rivals' access to supplies

759 Ibid paras 61-63.
760 Ibid paras 64-75.
761 EU Horizontal Merger Guidelines para 89.
762 Ibid para 90.
763 Bundeskartellamt guidance para 184.
764 The two main types of non-horizontal mergers focused on are vertical and conglomerate mergers.
765 EU Non-Horizontal Merger Guidelines para 6.
766 Ibid para 15.

or markets is hampered or eliminated as a result of the merger, thereby reducing these companies' ability and/or incentive to compete.' This may result in an environment where the merging parties or competitors are able to profitably increase prices. The Bundeskartellamt likewise focuses on foreclosure effects, particularly strategies which increase the costs and lower the revenues of competitors or that create or increase barriers to entry.[767]

The principal considerations taken into account by both the Commission and the Bundeskartellamt in the case of coordinated effects are whether the merger will increase the likelihood, ease, stability or effectiveness of coordination.[768]

3.2.6.3 South Africa

Section 12a of the Competition Act 89 of 1998[769] ('SA Competition Act') sets out the substantive test applied by the Competition Commission and the Competition Tribunal (the 'Competition Authorities') in South Africa. The Competition Authorities are required to make a decision on whether the merger is likely to substantially prevent or lessen competition.[770] This entails an assessment of the strength of competition in the relevant market as well as the probability of post-merger competition or cooperation among the firms in the market.[771]

The SA Competition Act sets out a non-exhaustive multi-factor list according to which an assessment of the strength of competition in the relevant market should be carried out. This multifactor effects-based approach is similar to the application of the SLC test in the European Union and the United States. It includes: assessing the level of barriers to entry; looking at the trends and levels of concentration; history of collusion; the level of countervailing power; market characteristics such as growth, innovation

767 Bundeskartellamt Guidance para 133-152.

768 EU Non-Horizontal Merger Guidelines para 18; Bundeskartellamt Guidance para 153-159.

769 Competition Act no. 89 of 1998 <http://www.compcom.co.za/the-competition-act/> accessed 26 August 2019 (SA Competition Act).

770 SA Competition Act s 12a. The test applied under the previous regime was a hybrid test that was based on whether the merger would lead to the creation of monopoly situation/s that were not in the public interest. (a brief discussion is available in the South Africa chapter in the OECD Merger Review Standard).

771 SA Competition Act s12a sub-s 2.

and product differentiation; the nature and extent of vertical integration in the market; considering the failing firm perspective; and whether the merger will cause the exit of an effective competitor.[772] It is further provided that the Competition Authorities should take into consideration pro-competitive benefits such as technological and efficiency gains which are likely to off-set any SLC effects, especially where the same would not be obtained without the merger.[773]

From a developing country perspective, the Competition Authorities also strive to protect market-oriented policy objectives such as deregulation, where state-controlled industries are increasingly liberalized to foster competitiveness. In the proposed *Sasol and Engen*[774] joint venture for instance, the relevant market was the South African petroleum industry, which was subject to a deregulation policy. Engen was already in control of the largest petrol station network in the country, therefore the merger would have resulted in a significant consolidation of the largely vertically integrated industry. The Competition Tribunal expressed the view that the merger would lead to a substantial lessening of competition especially through foreclosure effects. From a policy perspective, it was expressed that the merger would be detrimental to the move to deregulate the market, which would result in recartelization. There were as well no efficiency gains or public interest benefits that would have saved the venture, leading to the transaction's prohibition.

The application of the competition test is characterised by a number of similarities to that in the United States and the European Union. It has indeed been noted that in the implementation of the provisions of the SA Competition Act, the Competition Authorities do indeed take consideration of developments in other jurisdictions and international comparisons are encouraged. The merger regulations in fact have similarities to those of Canada, which is testament to the increasing global convergence on the aspect of the substantive competition test.[775] It is also evidenced by the fact that where a large international merger is involved, the decision of the Competition Authorities is to a large extent influenced by that taken

---

772 Ibid.

773 SA Competition Act s12a sub-s 1(a)(i).

774 *Sasol Limited et al.*, Competition Tribunal case no 101/LM/Dec04, 23 February 2006.

775 OECD, Competition Law and Policy in South Africa: OECD Peer Review (2003), 21 <http://www.oecd.org/southafrica/34823812.pdf> accessed 26 August 2019.

by the counterpart authority especially where close correspondence was maintained.

This was the case for instance in *A P Moller-Maersk and Royal P & O Nedlloyd N.V.*[776] where both the Competition Authorities and the European Commission granted a conditional approval of the proposed merger in their respective jurisdictions. The market in this case was for containerized shipping. The concern had been that the post-merger market share of the new firm in their various trade routes would have risen to above 30%, increasing the likelihood of barriers to entry and foreclosure effects thus contributing to a substantial lessening of competition. An analysis of the market however revealed that there was no acute threat to competition. The limitation to entry in respect of the South Africa/Europe route was for instance noted to have been principally the effect of port constraints. The Competition Authorities considered the adoption of the conditions imposed by the European Commission to be satisfactory in addressing the concerns in South Africa. It is also notable from this merger that the United States approved the merger unconditionally, once again pointing to the preference that Sub-Saharan Africa jurisdictions have for the European Union approach.

As highlighted in the discussion on the United States and the European Union, market power plays a crucial role in determining whether or not to sanction a proposed merger. However, unlike the US and the EU guidelines, the SA Competition Act does not explicitly make the market power link in its merger regulation provisions. Market power is used in the determination of dominance in the SA Competition Act.[777] Market power is itself defined as 'the power of a firm to control prices, or to exclude competition or to behave to an appreciable extent independently of its competitors, customers or suppliers'.[778] One can immediately see the connection between this definition and the definition of dominance under the previous EU Merger Regulations as well as in the *United Brands* decision and the German guidelines. Though there is no specific categorization of the importance of market power in the SA Competition Act, the Competition Authorities have made determinations on proposed mergers on the

776 *A P Moller-Maersk and Royal P & O Nedlloyd N.V.*, Competition Tribunal case no 48/LM/May05 (12 May 2006) and Case No COMP/M.3829 - Maersk/PONL <http://ec.europa.eu/competition/mergers/cases/decisions/m3829_20050729_20212_en.pdf> accessed 26 August 2019.

777 SA Competition Act s 7.

778 SA Competition Act s 1 sub-s (xiv).

basis of post-merger market power, thus confirming the fact that market power and dominance as well plays a part in their application of the SLC test.

In the proposed merger between *Reclamation Group, SA Metal and Machinery Company and Waste Control* for instance, the Commission determined that it would lead to the creation of a dominant firm with market power in the market for ferrous and non-ferrous scrap metal in South Africa. This, according to the Commission, would have led to a substantial lessening of competition. The parties subsequently abandoned the proposed merger.[779]

The Commission also alludes to market power in assessing ease of entry into the market. The Commission states that 'a merger is unlikely to create or enhance market power or to facilitate its exercise if entry into the market is timely'.[780]

The competition enforcers of South Africa are likewise on the lookout for the probability of unilateral as well as coordinated effects post consummation of the merger. In *Pioneer Hi-Bred and Panaar Seed*[781] for instance the Competition Tribunal's decision was based on the likelihood of unilateral and coordinated effects in the market for maize seed in South Africa. Both merging parties had a significant presence in the market for breeding, development, production and sale of improved maize seed varieties in South Africa. Post-merger there would have been only two sizable firms left in the hybrid maize seed market in South Africa, the other firm being Monstanto. Although economic experts had disagreed with the view that there would be a likelihood of post-merger coordination between the two big firms, the Competition Commission expressed the concern that a duopolistic market would significantly increase the chances of tacit coordination. A duopolistic market, according to the Commission, would have increased the symmetry between the merged firm and Monsanto thereby increased the market transparency making monitoring deviations easier.

The decision in this case was however made on the basis of the probable unilateral effects. The Commission had pointed out that there was a risk

779 Competition Commission of South Africa Annual Report 2006/2007, 22-23. <http://www.compcom.co.za/annual-reports/> accessed 26 August 2019.

780 See SA Competition Commission: File a merger <http://www.compcom.co.za/file-a-merger/> accessed 25 September 2019.

781 *Pioneer Hi-Bred International Inc and Pannar Seed (Pty) Ltd v Competition Commission* case no 81/AM/Dec10, 9 December 2011.

of unilateral price effects not likely to be addressed by claimed efficiencies. The Tribunal as well agreed that the merger would result in long-term unilateral price effects (an increase well above the SSNIP threshold) that would harm consumers, as well as eliminating an effective competitor.

What these examples indicate is that where the application of the competition test is concerned, there is increasingly convergence as well as a reliance on the positions in the developed merger jurisdictions for guidance.

3.2.6.4 The Competition Tests from the Eastern and Southern Africa Perspective

3.2.6.4.1 Substantial Lessening of Competition

Of the nine countries in this analysis Malawi, Mauritius, Seychelles and Zambia employ a SLC test. The COMESA merger regulation as well incorporates a SLC test. Tanzania has adopted a dominance test whereas Kenya, Botswana, Zimbabwe and Namibia have opted for a hybrid test that incorporates both the SLC as well as the dominance test.

The premise of the SLC test is whether a proposed merger is likely to lead to a significant lessening or restraining of competition in the market. The test is expressed along the same or similar lines in Malawi, Mauritius, Seychelles and Zambia as well as in the COMESA regulations.[782] The analytical approach as well reflects the multi-factor analysis method that is typical to the SLC test.

The Competition and Fair Trading Act of Malawi (Malawi Competition Act) for instance provides that the effect on competition is determined by reference to all factors affecting competition in the market.[783] The Merger Guidelines further provide that a substantial lessening of competition will be deemed to have occurred where there is a post-merger probability of a significantly greater price level or distorted competition outcomes, which is a function of market power.[784] A non-exhaustive list of factors that is

---

782 Competition and Fair Trading Act of Malawi no 43/1998 (Malawi Competition Act) s 35; Competition Act of Mauritius no 25/2007 (Mauritius Competition Act) s 47 sub-s 4; Fair Competition Act of Seychelles no 18/2009 (Seychelles Competition Act) s38(c); Competition and Consumer Protection Act of Zambia no 24/2010 (Zambia Competition Act) s 30 sub-s 1; COMESA Competition Regulations, gazette vol 17 no 12 art 26(1).

783 Malawi Competition Act s 2 sub-s 5.

784 Competition and Fair Trading Commission: Merger Assessment Guidelines

taken into account is provided and includes the effect of the proposed merger on market structure, barriers to entry, the level of concentration and the dynamic nature of the market (e.g. innovation). The presence of countervailing power, the availability of substitutes and the likely removal of an effective competitor are also considered.[785] This list of factors practically mirrors those taken into account in Zambia which is also non-exhaustive.[786]

The Fair Competition Act of Seychelles (Seychelles Competition Act) as well sets out a non-exhaustive list of factors to be considered in determining whether a proposed merger would result in a substantial lessening of competition. It includes: the effect on the market structure; the degree of control the merging firms have over the market; the availability of alternatives on the market; the likely effect on consumers and on the economy and the existing or potential competition from other firms.[787] The Merger Guidelines further provide that the Commission will regard a lessening of competition as substantial if it 'confers an increase in market power on the merged firm that is significant and sustainable'. The Commission in Zambia expresses the exact same view in respect of market power.[788] A merger that would cause a significant and sustained price increase or a reduction in product quality would thus be considered as likely to result in a substantial lessening of competition.[789]

The Commission in Mauritius merely outlines the need to ensure that there is effective rivalry on the market and that the ensuing benefits to consumers such as on price, quality and choice are protected. Though a direct link between market power and lessening of competition has not been expressly made, the factors taken into account in assessing whether effective rivalry is being maintained are the same as those used to assess changes to market power.[790]

<http://www.cftc.mw/index.php/2013-12-16-13-35-12/guidelines/28-mergers-and-acqusitions-guidelines/file.html> accessed 23 September 2019 (Malawi Merger Guidelines) para 7.1.5.

785 Malawi Merger Guidelines para 7.1.6.

786 Zambia Competition Act s 30 sub-s 2.

787 Seychelles Competition Act s 24.

788 Competition and Consumer Protection Commission: Guidelines for Merger Regulation <http://www.ccpc.org.zm/wp-content/uploads/2016/04/CCPC-Mergers-Guideline.pdf> accessed 26 August 2019 (Zambia Merger Guidelines) para 63.

789 The Fair Trading Commission of Seychelles: Mergers (Seychelles Merger Guidelines) para 4.2.

790 Competition Commission of Mauritius Guidelines: Mergers, para 3.2

Post-merger market power is one of the factors listed in the COMESA Competition Act as requiring mandatory consideration in the determination of whether a merger is likely to occasion a substantial prevention or lessening of competition. The non-exhaustive multifactor list is as well similar to that considered in Seychelles, Zambia and Malawi.[791]

The position taken in these jurisdictions in respect of market power is thus consistent with the perspective of the OECD as well as the position of the United States and the European Union.[792] The United States also underlines the importance of the prevention or prohibition of the creation, enhancement or entrenchment of or a facilitation of market power in curbing a substantial lessening of competition. The European Commission as well targets mergers that would significantly increase the market power of the merging firms i.e. 'the ability of one or more firms to profitably increase prices, reduce output, choice or quality of goods and services, diminish innovation, or otherwise influence parameters of competition'.[793]

3.2.6.4.1.1 Analytical approach

There is congruence not only on the basis of the multi-factor approach of the analysis but also on the theories of harm on which the analysis is based. In respect of horizontal mergers, Zambia, Seychelles, Mauritius, Malawi as well as COMESA consider unilateral effects and coordinated effects. In respect of vertical and conglomerate mergers, the main question is whether the merger will lead to market foreclosure.[794] All these are in the same vein weighed against the counterfactual (i.e. the situation had the merger not taken place) in Zambia, Seychelles, and Mauritius and by

---

<http://www.ccm.mu/English/Documents/Legislations/CCM5%20-%20Guidelines%20-%20Mergers_Nov09.pdf> accessed 26 August 2019 (Mauritius Merger Guidelines).

791 COMESA Competition Regulations art 26(2).

792 OECD Merger Review Standard 16. As previously noted, the OECD specifically highlights the crucial role played by existing competitive constraints as well as the level of post-merger market power in the SLC test.

793 EU Horizontal Merger Guidelines para 8.

794 Zambia Merger Guidelines para 45; Seychelles Merger Guidelines paras 4.5-4.6; Mauritius Merger Guidelines paras 3.26-3.27; Malawi Merger Guidelines paras 3.1, 4.1.2 and 4.2; COMESA Merger Assessment Guidelines, para 8<http://www.comesacompetition.org/wp-content/uploads/2014/10/141121_COMESA-Merger-Assessment-Guideline-October-31st-2014.pdf> accessed 23 September 2019.

the COMESA Commission as is the case with the European Union and Germany.[795]

The bases on which the multi-factor analysis is conducted are invariably similar across the jurisdictions reflecting a more or less harmonised approach to that in the United States and the European Union: (i) market definition (ii) market structure and concentration, (ii) countervailing factors, (iii) countervailing buyer power, (iv) likelihood of market entry to maintain effective competition in the relevant markets, (v) likelihood of counteracting efficiencies and (vi) failing firm defence. These core factors are crucial to merger assessment in any jurisdiction.[796] As is the case in the United States and the European Union, the position tends to be that no one factor is given more consideration than the other and an overall assessment is what will determine the decision taken. As noted in the Zambia Merger Guidelines, 'No specific weight is given to the factors on which the Commission will rely on. When evaluating a transaction, the Commission will perform a balancing act, the outcome of which will be determined for the most part by the specific facts of each case. The factors to be taken into account will be those relevant to the market under review.'[797]

The factors and evidence that is taken into account in determining whether there has been unilateral or coordinated effects are also largely the same as those considered in the United States and the European Union. In respect of unilateral effects most of the factors relate to the probability of the existing competition, the potential entry of new competitors or buyer power as having a constraining effect on the post-merger firm.[798] In respect of coordinated effects the factors revolve around aspects that make it easier for market actors to reach terms of coordination as well as to punish deviation. These include market transparency and stability.[799] The

795 Zambia Merger Guidelines para s78-81; Seychelles Merger Guidelines para 4.5; Mauritius Merger Guidelines para 3.26; COMESA Merger Guidelines para 7.6.

796 Zambia Merger Guidelines para 66; Seychelles Merger Guidelines paras 5-13; Mauritius Merger Guidelines part 3; Malawi Merger Guidelines part 7; COMESA Merger Guidelines sec 8.

797 Zambia Merger Guidelines, para 66; See also COMESA Merger Guidelines para 8.1; Mauritius Merger Guidelines para 3.9.

798 Seychelles Merger Guidelines para 8.11; COMESA Merger Guidelines para 8.15; Mauritius Merger Guidelines paras 3.28-3.38; Zambia Merger Guidelines paras 46-48.

799 COMESA Merger Guidelines paras 8.41-8.65; Seychelles Merger Guidelines para 9; Mauritius Merger Guidelines paras 3.31-3.46; Zambia Merger Guidelines paras 49-51; Malawi Merger Guidelines para 4.1.2.

authorities in a similar way also make it clear that the factors considered depend on the case in question.

3.2.6.4.1.2 Case Studies

A number of the jurisdictions in focus do not regularly publish their detailed decisions that clearly elucidate the reasoning behind a particular determination. A detailed analysis of the analytical approaches is therefore in a number of instances not possible. The purpose of the case studies however is to point out which factors were most probative for the competition authorities in reaching their ultimate decision.

Mauritius

LC Events Co. Ltd (LCE) & Event Strategy Ltd (ECL)[800]

In this case a complaint was made to the Mauritius Competition Commission by LCE (one of the parties to the merger transaction) on the grounds that the purchase by ECL of 33% of the shares in LCE would result in a substantial lessening of competition. Both companies were involved in the provision of events services, e.g. lighting, sound and video management, outdoor tents etc. Both companies were considered to respectively have very strong market positions in the provision of these services in Mauritius.[801]

The detailed investigation involved inter alia a consideration of whether there were any unilateral, coordinated or foreclosure effects. It also included a multifactor assessment of aspects such as market definition and structure and an assessment of likelihood of entry. In respect of unilateral effects the consideration was whether a merger between LCE and ECL being two main competitors would result in the loss of an effective competitor (LCE), hence increasing the likelihood of a post-merger price increase or quality reduction. The subsequent consideration was whether the market would be able to restore competition through for instance the entry of competitors or more competition from the existing competitors.[802]

800 Review of Completed Merger of Event Strategy Ltd & LC Events Co Ltd: Final Report (Competition Commission of Mauritius 25/02/11) <http://www.ccm.mu/English/Documents/Investigations/INV008%20-%20Final%20Report%20Public%20Version.pdf> accessed 25 September 2019 (Event Strategy Report).

801 Event Strategy Report 5-6.

802 Event Strategy Report paras 5.1-5.10.

In order to determine the main market players, a customer survey was conducted. The survey revealed that for 30 to 40 percent of clients the merger would result in a significant loss of substitutes with 17 percent having only one choice for a service provider post-merger.[803] There was however no evidence that there would be any coordinated or foreclosure effects.[804] Therefore, on the basis of unilateral effects, the investigation reached the conclusion that the merger of the two competitors would result in a substantial lessening of competition.

Evidence however indicated no barriers to entry hence it would be reasonable to conclude that there would be sufficient and timely post-merger market entry or expansion of existing market players enabling a restoration of competition subsequent to the weakening of LCE.[805]

The parties however reached an agreement to cancel the transfer of shares and reverse the transaction.[806]

Swan Group & Rogers Group[807]

This merger investigation arose from a request by the Swan Group and the Rogers Group for guidance from the Competition Commission as to whether a merger between them would lead to post-merger anticompetitive effects. The Swan Group companies were Swan Insurance Company Limited (Swan) and the Anglo Mauritius Assurance Society Limited (AMAS). The Rogers Group companies were CIM Insurance Limited (CIL) and CIM Life Ltd (CLL). The relevant markets were determined to be the long-term insurance market and the general insurance market. The Competition Commission assessed the merger based on the impact on competition in these two markets. Swan and CIL were both involved in the general insurance business and a merger between the two would push their combined market share to above 30 percent in the general insurance market. The merger AMAS and CLL which were involved in the

803 Event Strategy Report para 7.14.

804 Event Strategy Report paras 7.16-7.21.

805 Event Strategy Report paras 7.32-7.33.

806 *Event Strategy Ltd & LC Events Co. Ltd* CCM/DS/002.

807 Investigation on the proposed merger of the insurance businesses of Swan Group and Rogers Group: Report of the Executive Director (Competition Commission of Mauritius 13/02/12) <http://www.ccm.mu/English/Documents/News_2012/29.02.12_2.pdf> accessed 26 August 2019 (Swan Group Report).

long-term insurance business would as well have pushed their combined market share to above 30 percent in the long-term insurance market.[808]

In terms of market share, Swan and CIL were the second and third largest companies in the general insurance business and the merger would make them the largest in this market.[809] AMAS and CLL were regarded as being among the four largest companies market share wise in the pensions market and the merger would likely make them the second largest or largest in that market.[810]

The investigation found that the mergers would likely result in a number of unilateral effects, as well as market foreclosure. The unilateral effects were in terms of post-merger price increases as well as a substantial decrease in terms of choice among insurance providers. The foreclosure would ensue from the cessation of supply of certain insurance products or cessation of supply to specific markets. No evidence of a likelihood of coordinated effects was found.[811] AMAS and Swan however made various undertakings inter alia not to increase prices as well as undertaking to continue conducting business with all duly registered brokers and insurers in order to address the concerns.[812] The parties also undertook to continue providing the same type of products and maintain same coverage as well as not lessening the accessibility of their products and services.[813]

The Executive Director of the Commission found these undertakings as well as certain statutory safeguards as sufficient to address the concerns on unilateral effects and foreclosure.[814] The Commission as a whole was also satisfied that the measures were sufficient to address the anticompetitive effects of the mergers.[815]

Holcim Ltd and Lafarge S.A.

Holcim Ltd and Lafarge S.A., both world leaders in the construction sector conducted cement business in Mauritius through their subsidiaries,

808 Swan Group Report paras 1.2 – 1.7.
809 Swan Group Report para 5.3.
810 Swan Group Report para 5.4.
811 Swan Group Report paras 7.4, 7.15 and 7.18.
812 Swan Group Report paras 7.5-7.10.
813 Swan Group Report para 7.19.
814 Swan Group Report para 7.30.
815 Investigation on the proposed merger of the insurance businesses of Swan Group and Rogers Group: Commission Decision CCM/DS/0013

Holcim (Mauritius) Ltd and Lafarge (Mauritius) Cement Ltd.[816] Their proposed merger therefore had an effect on several jurisdictions including Mauritius. Holcim Ltd and Lafarge S.A. made an application for guidance on the merger on the basis of which the investigation was launched.[817]

The merger had multiterritorial effect in several countries including European jurisdictions. The European Commission was hence also involved in the review of the proposed merger. The Competition Commission of Mauritius did in fact seek to collaborate with the European Commission.[818] Apart from collaborating with the European Commission on the investigation the Competition Commission of Mauritius also assessed the approach of the European Commission towards aspect such as market definition and even drew parallels between their approach and its approach.[819]

The investigation encompassed several factors mainly the market definition and a look at the market shares, assessment of the counterfactual, a consideration of barriers to entry, the experience of other jurisdictions in the assessment of the merger and a consideration of the undertakings provided by the parties.

Holcim Ltd and Lafarge S.A were determined to be in the upstream market for the manufacture and export of cement to the Mauritian subsidiaries.[820]

The Competition Commission of Mauritius identified various concerns which were however not subjected to a full-fledged investigation owing to a divestment undertaking given by the parties which was deemed sufficient to address the competition concerns. One of the main concerns that the Commission identified was that the merger, in the absence of the undertakings given by the merging parties, would have eliminated the competitive constraint that the two Mauritian subsidiaries had on each other in the cement market.[821] In the absence of this undertaking the merger would have pushed the market share of the two parties to above

816 Investigation of the Proposed merger between Holcim Ltd & Lafarge S.A.: Report of the Executive Director (Competition Commission of Mauritius 13/05/15) <http://www.ccm.mu/English/Documents/Investigations/INV028-MR-FinalReport.pdf> accessed 26 August 2019 (Holcim Report).

817 Holcim Report para 1.1.

818 Holcim Report para 2.12.

819 Holcim Report para 3.20.

820 Holcim Report paras 5.7 and 5.63.

821 Holcim Report para 6.28.

50% which the Commission considered to be sufficient for the exercise of unilateral market power.[822]

However, as a result of the divestment undertaking being implemented the number of competitors and market structure would be maintained and concentration concerns as well as the risk of substantial lessening of competition would be sufficiently addressed.[823] The Executive Director of the Commission therefore considered the undertakings to be sufficient to address the main competition concerns and recommended that the Commission allows it to proceed.[824] The Commission was indeed convinced with the recommendations of the Executive Director and were satisfied that the undertakings were sufficient to address any substantial lessening of competition concerns.[825]

The European Commission had as well considered the transaction and its effect on the European Union and had found that divestment commitments made by the parties were sufficient to address the competition concerns within the European Union.[826] Though not explicitly indicated the collaboration with the European Commission as well as the substantial consideration of the assessment of the merger in the European Union may have influenced the final opinion of the Executive Director of the Competition Commission of Mauritius.

Malawi

Dhunseri Petrochem and Tea Pte Limited & Global Tea and Commodities Limited[827]

This case involved the application for negative clearance by Dhunseri and Global Tea on account of a prospective acquisition by Dhunseri, a company based in India, of 100% shareholding of three subsidiaries of Global Tea. The three subsidiaries were active in the market for the growing, processing and marketing of tea, macadamia nuts and coffee. The Commission's assessment revealed that the market structure in Malawi would not

822 Holcim Report para 6.32.

823 Holcim Report para 7.87.

824 Holcim Report part 9.

825 Proposed Merger between Holcim Ltd & Lafarge S.A: Decision of the Competition Commission (CCM/DS/0016).

826 Holcim Report para 3.37.

827 Competition and Fair Trading Commission of Malawi Annual Report 2012/2013, 11 <http://www.cftc.mw/index.php/2013-12-16-13-35-12/reports/annual-reports/30-20122013-annual-report.html> accessed 26 August 2019.

be altered as Dhunseri was not based in the country. The Commission also lauded the pro-competitive benefits that would arise, such as the expansion and improvement of the capacity of the acquired companies hence further expanding the already export oriented market of the companies.[828]

Toyota Tsusho Corporation & CFAO Malawi Ltd/Cica Motors Ltd[829]

The impact of the global merger between Toyota and CFAO could be felt in many countries including Malawi, Kenya, Zambia, Tanzania and Mauritius. In Malawi, the transaction involved an application for authorization of an acquisition by Toyota Tsusho, a Japanese company with a subsidiary in Malawi, of 41.99% of the shares of CFAO Malawi and Cica, both subsidiaries of CFAO which is a French company.

An assessment revealed that the merger would reduce competition between the car distributors in Malawi. The car brands distributed by CFAO i.e. Ford and Nissan and by Toyota Malawi, i.e. Toyota were regarded as leading brands which compete on the market. The transaction was however conditionally approved subject to behavioural remedies inter alia that the companies would continue to operate independently. The Commission recognised the public interest in preventing a disruption of supply of certain vehicle brands. The adoption of behavioural remedies meant that the Commission also committed itself to continually monitor compliance.[830]

First Merchant Bank Limited & International Commercial Bank Limited[831]

This merger involved a purchase by First Merchant Bank (FMB) of 100% shareholding in International Commercial Bank Malawi Limited (ICB Malawi). The acquisition was part of plans by FMB to expand into Malawi. The other aspect of the transaction however was the fact that ICB Malawi was facing liquidity problems (i.e. a failing firm scenario) and there was a danger that the customers would be at risk if nothing was done. The Commission's decision to approve the merger was therefore based on the public interest need to protect the depositors from the failing firm as well as the view that the merger would strengthen the banking industry which would benefit the public.[832]

828 Ibid.

829 Malawi 2012/2013 Annual Report 12-13.

830 Ibid.

831 Malawi 2012/2013 Annual Report 16.

832 Ibid.

COMESA

PPC International Holdings Proprietary Limited (PPC International) & CIMERWA Limited (CIMERWA)[833]

An application was made to the COMESA Competition Commission (Commission) on account of the fact that the two companies together conducted business in five COMESA member states i.e. Zambia, Zimbabwe, Rwanda, Uganda and the Democratic Republic of Congo. The transaction therefore met the regional dimension requirements that trigger the jurisdiction of the Commission.[834] Both PPC International, based in South Africa, and CIMERWA, based in Rwanda, are active in the construction sector; specifically the market for manufacture and sale of cement. The relevant market was determined on account of customer interviews.[835]

The determination however was that the merger would not lead to a substantial lessening of competition owing to the fact that the parties were not competitors in the relevant market and therefore there would be no changes to market concentration. There was also no risk of dominance leading to abuse of market power owing to the fact that the merging parties were rather small in the relevant market.[836]

The COMESA Competition Regulations also require a consideration of the effect of transactions to the common market integration objective contained in the COMESA Treaty. It was determined that the merger would not negate free and liberalised trade. The Regulations as well require a consideration of the effect on public interest as part of the substantive analysis. In this regard the Commission determined that the merger would bring in foreign investment, promote competition and foster economic growth and development within Rwanda and the Common Market as a whole. The Commission considered the infrastructure and industrial needs of the common market noting the deficit of cement supply specifically in Rwanda, Burundi, Uganda and the Democratic Republic of Congo. The merger would thus increase efficiency and reduce costs for cement production in the Common Market.[837]

---

833 Decision of the Committee of Initial Determination on the Application for Authorisation of the Merger between PPC International Holdings Proprietary Limited ("PPC International") and CIMERWA Limited ("CIMERWA"), Case File No. CCC/MER/8002/2013.

834 Ibid 2; COMESA Competition Regulations art 23.

835 Ibid.

836 Ibid 3.

837 Ibid 3-4; COMESA Competition Regulations art 26.

CFR Inversiones SPA (CFR) & Adcock Ingram Holdings Limited (Adcock)[838]

This transaction was in respect of an acquisition by CFR, a Chile-based company, of 100% of the issued share capital of Adcock, a South Africa-based company. The regional dimension requirement was met on account of Adcock operating in more than two Member States.[839] Both companies are active in the pharmaceutical sector. The Commission therefore determined the relevant product market to be pharmaceutical products and related services.[840]

Owing to the fact that CFR had no prior business in the Common Market the Commission determined that there was no risk of a substantial lessening of competition or a threat to public interest within the Common Market. The market structure would not be changed. The existing competitive constraints would remain in place and the merger would not enhance dominance of the merged entity in the Common Market. The Commission as well determined that the merger would not create any barriers to trade between the member states or frustrate the single market objective.[841]

The Commission also considered the improved efficiency and increased production that would result from CFR introducing better technology, thus enhancing consumer welfare within the Common Market.[842]

China National Tire and Rubber Co. Ltd (CNRC) & Pirelli and C.S.p.A (Pirelli)[843]

Both Companies in this transaction are established outside of the Common Market i.e. CNRC in China and Pirelli in Italy, but are actively involved in the tyre business within the Common Market, hence the notification to the Commission. The proposed transaction involved an indirect purchase i.e. through a holding company of a 50% to 65% stake in Pirelli by CNRC.[844]

838 Decision of the Committee of Initial Determination Regarding the Merger between CFR Inversiones SPA and Adcock Ingram Holdings Limited, CASE FILE No. CCC/MER/1223/2013.

839 Ibid paras 1-5.

840 Ibid para 7.

841 Ibid para 8.

842 Ibid paras 8-9.

843 Decision of the nineteenth Committee responsible for Initial Determination Meeting Regarding the proposed Merger between China National Tire and rubber Co. Ltd and Pirelli and C.S.p.A, Staff paper No. 2016/03/07/04/JB

844 Ibid paras 1-6.

The Commission determined the relevant market to be the global supply of replacement tyres. In respect of the whole Common Market, the Commission determined that the merger would not change the market concentration as the parties would still not fall among the top three market players subsequent to the merger. However, the merger would lead to a dominant position in the Egyptian market for truck tyres where Pirelli held a market share of 45% and CNRC 15%.[845]

Although the combined market share would place the merged entity in a dominant position in Egypt, the Commission, short of imposing any concrete conditions, maintained the view that as long as the parties exercised care not to abuse their dominant position they would avoid action for abuse of dominance in both Egypt and the Common Market.[846]

The Commission found that the merger would not lead to any input or customer foreclosure. In addition there wouldn't be any barriers to entry nor would existing competition be eliminated. The conclusion was that the merger would have no substantial effect on trade between Member States. Hence there would be neither a substantial lessening of competition nor a negative effect on trade within the Common Market.[847]

Zambia

Toyota Tshusho Corporation (TTC) & CFAO[848]

The effect of this global transaction in Zambia was the indirect acquisition by TTC of CFAO's car distribution subsidiaries in Zambia. The relevant markets were determined to be new saloon, sports utility and light commercial vehicles as well as the market for their spares.

Toyota Zambia however had significant market shares in these markets; 35 percent in saloon vehicles, 58 percent in sports utility vehiclesand 51.7 for light commercial vehicles. CFAO Zambia (then the distributor of the Nissan brand of vehicles) had 15 percent, 9 percent and 20 percent market share respectively. Toyota and CFAO therefore fell among the top three market players in terms of market share.

845 Ibid paras 8-9.

846 Ibid.

847 Ibid paras 10-11.

848 Kondwani Kaonga and Parret Muteto, 'Understanding Competition and Regulation across Borders: A Toyota Tshusho Case Study' (Competition and Consumer Protection Commission of Zambia, 2015) 11 et seq <https://static1.squarespace.com/static/52246331e4b0a46e5f1b8ce5/t/55349f5ee4b047c173df89f9/1429512030611/Parret+Muteto+et+al_Understanding+Competition+and+Regulation+across+borders.pdf> accessed 26 August 2019.

By calculating the concentration ratio pre-and post-merger the Commission found that the market was already largely oligopolistic and highly concentrated and the merger would only serve to further entrench this concentration. In all the relevant markets, the post-merger firm would have been in a dominant position.

The Commission identified the risk of coordinated effects in terms of pricing and product availability. The markets were also subject to high barriers to entry. It was overall determined that there were no pro-competitive benefits to the transaction. The Commission therefore initially prohibited the merger.[849] The merger was however subsequently approved after Nissan terminated its franchise license with CFAO Zambia and granted it to another company.

3.2.6.4.2 Creation or Strengthening of a dominant position

3.2.6.4.2.1 Analytical approach in Tanzania

As noted at the beginning of the chapter, Tanzania is the only country out of the jurisdictions under review that applies a pure dominance test.[850] The dominance test and the substantial lessening of competition test are usually distinguished on the grounds that the former focuses more on structure and the latter employs a multi-factor approach which can be adopted to a particular case in question. The substantial lessening of competition test therefore adopts a broader approach, which subsumes the dominance test. However, as noted in the EU and Germany, prior to the conversion to a substantial lessening of competition type of test the dominance test can evolve to a point where the analytical approach follows a more or less multi-factor analysis similar to a substantial lessening of competition approach. This is however not the case with Tanzania, whose substantive analysis fits the traditional classification of a dominance test model.

The merger guidelines reveal that the analytical approach in Tanzania is very much focused on the structure of the market, with market defini-

849 Mathew Hill, 'Zambia Blocks Local Merger of Toyota-CFAO on Competition Grounds' (29 January 2013) <http://www.bloomberg.com/news/articles/2013-01-29/zambia-blocks-local-merger-of-toyota-cfao-on-competition-grounds> accessed 26 August 2019.

850 The Fair Competition Act of Tanzania no 8/2003 (Tanzania Competition Act) s 11 sub-s 1.

tion and the determination of market shares playing the most important role.[851] The Commission's analytical approach starts with defining the relevant market then determining the market shares of the participants within that market.[852] The guidelines set the decisive post-merger market share at 35 percent. Post-merger firms with a market share of less than 35% will in most cases be approved in the first stage of analysis on the ground that they are unlikely to affect competition and may in fact promote efficiency.[853]

Where the post-merger market share will be in excess of 35 percent then it will be upon the parties to prove to the Commission that the firm acting alone would not be in a position to substantially restrain competition. In order to make this determination, the Commission will consider the number and size of participants in the market, barriers to entry, the level of vertical integration, availability of alternatives on the market, efficiencies and the effect on consumers, competition and the economy at large.[854]

If the Commission determines that a firm holding a market share above 35 percent and acting alone is in a position to substantially restrain competition, then it will be upon the parties to apply to the Commission for an exemption.[855] In this case the Commission will consider various public interest factors including increased efficiency, technical or economic progress and whether the pro-competitive benefits to the public outweigh the anti-competitive detriments. The Commission will also consider whether one of the firms was in a failing firm scenario.[856]

3.2.6.4.2.2 Case Studies

Helios Towers Tanzania Infraco Limited (HTT) & Millicom International Cellular (MIC) Tanzania Limited.[857]

This transaction involved the acquisition by HTT of telecommunications towers and other site assets of MIC in Tanzania. HTT, established in

---

851 Fair Competition Commission of Tanzania Merger Guidelines, para. 4.2.3 <http://www.competition.or.tz/attachments/article/59/fcc_merger_guidelines_tanzania.pdf> accessed 26 August 2019 (Tanzania Merger Guidelines).
852 Tanzania Merger Guidelines 10-11.
853 Tanzania Merger Guidelines 12.
854 Tanzania Merger Guidelines 13-16.
855 Tanzania Merger Guidelines 16.
856 Tanzania Competition Act s 13; Tanzania Merger Guidelines 16-18.
857 Fair Competition Commission of Tanzania Newsletter (April-June 2011) 6

Tanzania, was involved in the provision of telecommunication towers and related site infrastructure to mobile and data network providers and enterprise customers. MIC Tanzania, a joint venture between a Luxembourg-based company (MIC) and the Tanzania Posts and Telecommunications Corporation, was involved in the provision of cellular telecommunication network services in Tanzania.

The Commission identified a number of public interest and pro-competitive benefits that would arise from the merger including job creation, service provision to under-served areas, outsourcing infrastructure management to HTT hence allowing MIC to focus on service provision, reducing installation and operating costs, thus decreasing consumer prices and improved quality of service. HTT was also tipped to bring increased foreign direct investment in the telecommunications sector and with-it technical expertise and new building practices.

The Commission determined that the merger would not prevent, restrict or distort competition in the relevant market and approved it unconditionally.

Uranium One Inc. and Mantra Australia[858]

Uranium One Inc, a Canada-based company, notified the Commission of its intention to acquire Mantra Australia, an Australian firm with a subsidiary in Tanzania. Uranium One has a worldwide presence in uranium exploration, mining and production. Mantra Tanzania Limited, the Tanzania-based subsidiary of the target firm, owned a uranium mining project in Tanzania.

In approving this merger, the Commission once again intimated its international focus, citing the acquiring firm's world-leading uranium production and high quality uranium mines. Form the analytical point of view the Commission determined that the merger would not lead to the creation or strengthening of a dominant position in the relevant market, nor was there a possibility of the merged firm acting unilaterally and harming competition. One possible reason for this conclusion could be the fact that Uranium One did not have an existing presence in Tanzania and the structure of the market would therefore not be altered.

<http://www.competition.or.tz/index.php?option=com_content&view=article&id=48:lorem-ipsum-is-simply-dummy-text-of-the-printing&catid=22:news-and-events&Itemid=144> accessed 26 August 2019 (FCC Newsletter).

858 FCC Newsletter (January-March 2012) 2.

3.2.6.4.3 Hybrid test

3.2.6.4.3.1 Analytical approach

As noted at the beginning of this chapter, Namibia, Botswana, Kenya and Zimbabwe have a statutory hybrid test.[859] Their analytical approaches however are in line with the substantial lessening of competition approach and involve applying a non-exhaustive multi-factor analysis on the basis of the conventional theories of harm i.e. unilateral, coordinated and foreclosure/conglomerate effects. The factors taken into account as well are more or less invariable across the board i.e. market definition, concentration, barriers to entry, countervailing power, the counterfactual, efficiencies etc. with the importance of particular factors depending on the specific case in question. The post-merger market power level is as well highlighted as a crucial factor in determining whether a substantial lessening of competition is likely to occur.[860]

3.2.6.4.3.2 Case Studies

Botswana

Kalend (Pty) Ltd (Kalend) & Bokamoso Private Hospital (BPHT)[861]

The transaction involved an acquisition by Kalend of 100 percent of the shares in BPHT. BPHT was a dominant player in the business of health

---

859 The Competition Act of Kenya no 12/2010 s 46 sub-s 2; The Competition Act of Botswana no 17/2009 s 59 sub-s 2; The Competition Act of Namibia no 2/2003 s 47 sub-s 2; The Competition Act of Zimbabwe ch 14/28 s 32 sub-s 4.

860 Competition Authority of Botswana Merger Assessment Guidelines, chs. 5-6 <http://www.competitionauthority.co.bw/sites/default/files/MERGER_ASSESSMENT_0.pdf> accessed 26 August 2019 (Botswana Merger Guidelines); Competition Authority Of Kenya Consolidated Guidelines on the Substantive Assessment of Mergers under the Competition Act, paras 42-49 <http://www.cak.go.ke/images/docs/Merger%20Guidelines.pdf> accessed 26 August 2019 (Kenya Merger Guidelines); Namibian Competition Commission Merger Guidelines, ch. 8 <http://www.nacc.com.na/cms_documents/820_merger_guidelinesapril16.pdf> accessed 26 August 2019 (Namibia Merger Guidelines) (The Merger Guidelines of Botswana and Namibia are substantially similar).

861 Competition Authority of Botswana Annual Report 2012/2013, 21 <http://www.competitionauthority.co.bw/annual-reports> accessed 26 August 2019 (Botswana Annual Report).

care provision in Botswana. Kalend however, though incorporated in Botswana, was not an active market player. Therefore, though the post-merger market share was expected to be 37 percent, which was 12 percent higher than the dominance threshold of 25 percent, there would still be no change to the market structure. The Authority's analysis in this case was more focused on determining the effect of the transaction on the market structure more so because of the fact that the market was concentrated.

The Authority found that there was no risk of a substantial lessening of competition irrespective of the high concentration levels of the market for provision of health care services. Provision of supplies and services was expected to continue and the existing competitive constraints were deemed to be sufficient to curb any anti-competitive behaviour of the merged firm. The Authority's approval was hinged on the merged firm not abusing its already dominant position.

G4S (Botswana) Limited, Trojan Security Services (Trojan) & Facilities Management Group (Shield Security, PS Cleaning and Facilities Management Business)(FMG)[862]

G4S notified the Competition Authority of its proposed 100 percent takeover of Trojan and FMG. G4S is active in the security industry in Botswana. Trojan was incorporated in Botswana as a security service provider but was not active on the market and acted as a holding company for intellectual property rights and various client contracts for two other security companies. FMG, whose subsidiaries included Shield Security and PS Cleaning, was active in the security industry as well as providing cleaning and facilities management services.

The Competition Authority established that there was a product overlap between G4S, Trojan and FMG (through Shield Security) in the security service industry. In respect of this particular market the Competition Authority found that there would be a change to the market structure which would reduce the number of competitors. The merger would therefore have a negative effect on competition due to the fact that the merged firm's market share in the security services industry would rise to 40 percent, substantially higher than the 25 percent required for a presumption of dominance, raising abuse of dominance concerns.

The Competition Authority thus concluded that in respect of the provision of security services, the merger would likely result in a substantial lessening of competition. The Competition Authority therefore prohibited

862 Botswana Annual Report 2011/2012 18.

the merger of the security service provision part of the transaction i.e. between G4S, Trojan and Shield Security. The merger between G4S and FMG in respect of the cleaning and facilities management business was allowed to proceed.

Cottesloe Consultants (Cottesloe) & Bokomo Botswana (Bokomo)[863]

Bokomo, a joint venture between a Botswana firm and a South Africa firm, proposed to acquire 50 percent shares in Cottesloe, both companies being incorporated in Botswana. Bokomo was engaged in the milling, poultry and the fast-moving consumer goods business in Botswana. Cottesloe was also active in the poultry industry, specifically in the production and distribution of day old chicks in Botswana.

The Competition Authority found that there was no horizontal product overlap as the merger would result in a vertically integrated firm. The post-merger firm was therefore expected to retain the same market share in the respective relevant markets of the pre-merger firms. The merger was therefore not likely to cause a substantial lessening of competition or a restriction of supply or services. In respect of the hatchery business, the Competition Authority regarded the presence of a competitor holding 60 percent of the market share as sufficiently capable of acting as a competitive restraint on the merged firm.

One of the Authority's competition concerns however was the fact that the vertical integration could bolster the merged firm's position in the hatcheries market, which only had two dominant players. The merger was therefore approved but subject to some behavioural conditions; the merged firm was required to notify and seek authorization from the Competition Authority before entering into any upstream or downstream distribution agreements in order to forestall any foreclosure.

Kenya

Buzeki Dairy Limited (Buzeki) & Brookside Dairy Limited[864]

Brookside, a company incorporated in Kenya and engaged in the dairy business in Kenya, Uganda and Tanzania, proposed to acquire the business and assets of Buzeki, also incorporated in Kenya and engaged in dairy business in Kenya. The Authority found that there were overlaps between

863 Botswana Annual Report 2011/2012 21.

864 Competition Authority of Kenya Annual Report 2013/2014, 21 <https://www.cak.go.ke/sites/default/files/annual-reports/FY%202013-2014%20CAK%20Annual%20Report.pdf> accessed 5 September 2019 (Kenya Annual Report).

the two companies in respect of milk purchase from farmers, processing and marketing of fresh milk and the production and marketing of long life (UHT) milk, yoghurt, butter and ghee.

The relevant product market was determined to be that of (processed and unprocessed) marketed milk, both through formal and informal channels. In order to determine substitutability, the Authority utilised a 16 percent value added tax that the government had imposed on processed milk as a proxy for the purposes of conducting a SSNIP test. The decline in sales as a result of the price increase would therefore be an indicator of the substitutability of processed milk with other products. The data indicated that as a result of the tax, sales of processed milk by both Brookside and Buzeki had markedly declined. The Authority considered this decline as an indication that consumers readily substituted to unprocessed milk, hence confirming the substitutability between processed and unprocessed milk.

There was also significant competition from mini-industries, cottage industries, milk bars, milk producers, dairy co-operatives and informal traders. The post-merger market share in respect of the processed and unprocessed milk market would therefore not enable an exercise of market power that would lead to a substantial lessening of competition. The Authority also considered the efficiencies gained that would enable Brookside to compete locally and internationally. The proposed merger was therefore approved.

Real Insurance Company Limited (Real) & British–American Investments Company (Kenya) Limited (Britam)[865]

This merger involved a proposed acquisition of Real by Britam. Britam is incorporated and carries out its business in Kenya as well as in Uganda and South Sudan through subsidiaries. Real is also incorporated in Kenya with subsidiaries in Tanzania, Malawi and Mozambique. Both companies are active in the insurance business, with Britam being active in both life and non-life and Real active in non-life. The relevant market was therefore determined to be that of non-life insurance owing to an overlap between the two companies in the non-life insurance market in Kenya.

The post-merger market share would however not be significant enough to give rise to any substantial lessening of competition concerns. The Authority was however more concerned about the job losses that may result from the merger. This was mainly because of duplication of roles within the company which would occasion a restructuring that would lead to

865 Kenya Annual Report 2013/2014 22.

redundancies. The Authority therefore approved the merger on condition that at least 85% of the employees of Real would be retained.

Toyota Tshusho Corporation (Toyota) & CFAO[866]

Both firms were active in the motor vehicle and spare parts distribution, repairs and maintenance service business in Kenya through their subsidiaries.

The relevant product markets were determined to be the supply of personal saloon cars, passenger commercial vehicles, light, medium, heavy and prime cargo commercial vehicles, motorcycles, spare parts and repair and maintenance of motor vehicles. The relevant market was largely determined based on consumer choices. The product market that raised post-merger dominance concerns was that for personal saloon cars.

In respect of the market for the supply of saloon cars falling within the 1800cc capacity and below, Toyota through its Kenya subsidiary had 44.5 percent market share which would rise to 53.1 percent post-merger. In respect of saloon cars falling within the 1800cc capacity and above, Toyota's pre-merger market share stood at 41.4 percent and would rise to 58.4 percent post-merger. Toyota would therefore be in a position of dominance.

The Authority nonetheless approved the transaction on condition that the post-merger firm does not infringe the Competition Act. The authority also undertook to monitor the market behaviour of the merged firm.

Namibia

Colas South Africa (Pty) Ltd (Colas South Africa) & The Roads Contractor Company Ltd (RCC) and Guinea Fowl Investments Seventeen (Pty) Ltd (Guinea)[867]

This transaction involved an acquisition by Colas and RCC of equal shareholding in Guinea. Colas South Africa is a South Africa registered but wholly owned subsidiary of a company incorporated in France. Colas South Africa conducted business in Namibia through its subsidiaries, i.e. Colas Namibia and Dust-a-Side Namibia. Colas Namibia was engaged in the business of importing, manufacturing and supplying bituminous binders used in road surfacing work in Namibia. RCC, wholly owned by

866 Kenya Annual Report 2012/2013 20.

867 Competition Commission of Namibia: Newsletter vol. 4 no. 1 (2014) 22 <http://www.nacc.com.na/publications/newsletters.php> accessed 5 September 2019 (Namibia Newsletter).

the Namibia government, was in the business of road construction and maintenance as well as rail construction, plant hire and civil engineering.

Colas South Africa and RCC sought to acquire Guinea in order to transfer the road surfacing business to the acquired company. The Commission determined the relevant market to be that of road surfacing in Namibia. However, the Commission was specifically concerned about the effect the joint acquisition will have on the interaction between the upstream market for bituminous products and the downstream market for road surfacing. The acquisition was likely to result in foreclosure, with the supply of bituminous products to Colas main competitor being at risk.

The Commission found that the transaction would likely result in a substantial lessening of competition in both the upstream and downstream markets. A strengthening of dominance and a restriction of trade would also occur in the upstream market. The Commission further considered whether there were any pro-competitive benefits that could outweigh this detriment but found none. On the public interest front, the transaction would also affect the smaller subcontractors, which the Commission determined to be largely in the hands of historically disadvantaged people by preventing their subcontracting to the RCC. This could consequently have led to job losses. The Commission therefore decided to prohibit the transaction.

Guinea Fowl Investments Twenty Five (Pty Ltd (Guinea Fowl) & the Private Label Store Card Portfolio of Edgars Stores Namibia (Pty) Ltd (Edgars)[868]

The merger involved a proposed acquisition of Edgars by Guinea Fowl. Guinea Fowl, which was to be renamed to EFS Namibia (Pty) Limited, was a fully owned special purpose vehicle of the Barclays Africa Group Limited (BAGL) acquired for the purposes of the transaction. It was therefore not engaged in any business in Namibia. BAGL operates in Namibia through its wholly owned subsidiary ABSA Bank Limited (ABSA). ABSA which represents as a licensed representative office provides financial services.

Edgars is a wholly owned subsidiary of Edcon (Pty) Limited (Edcon), a South Africa registered company. Edcon operated a department store division in Namibia through Edgars and other related undertakings and offered customers private label store cards which could be used to buy various items including clothing, mobile phones, cosmetics and books.

868 Namibia Newsletter vol. 4 no. 2 2014 16.

The Commission determined the relevant market to be that of provision of unsecured credit to individuals in Namibia. The transaction would give rise to horizontal overlaps as a result of a similar private label store cards business that was conducted as a joint venture between ABSA and Woolworths Financial Services (Pty) Limited (Woolworths). The Commission was particularly concerned about the possibility of exchange of commercially sensitive information between Edcon and Woolworths as a result of the ABSA link. BAGL however provided an undertaking to retain confidentiality in respect of the relations between Edcon and Woolworths.

On the back of this undertaking the Commission approved the proposed transaction on grounds that there was no likelihood of a substantial lessening of competition or an acquisition or strengthening of a dominant position.

Metcash Trading Namibia (Pty) Ltd (Metcash) & Sefalana Cash & Carry (Namibia) (Pty) Ltd (Sefalana)[869]

The Commission was notified of the proposed acquisition by Stefalana of Metcash. Stefalana, incorporated in Namibia but owned by a Botswana company, was engaged in the business of wholesale and retail merchandise trade including groceries in Namibia. Metcash, also incorporated in Namibia but owned by a South Africa undertaking, similarly engages in wholesale and retail merchandise trade in Namibia including groceries and liquor.

The Commission found that there was no overlap on the liquor market. In respect of the other wholesale and retail business, the Commission determined that Stefalana and Metcash operated in different geographical markets i.e. different towns within Namibia hence there was no overlap. There was no risk of an increased market share that would threaten competition as there were several competitors in this market. There was therefore no risk of a substantial lessening of competition or an acquisition or strengthening of a dominant position.

Zimbabwe

Renaissance Merchant Bank Limited (Renaissance) & National Social Security Authority (NSSA)[870]

The NSSA, the statutory social security insurance authority in Zimbabwe, proposed to acquire a controlling interest in Renaissance, a bank estab-

869 Ibid 17.
870 Competition and Tariff Commission of Zimbabwe: Annual Report (2012) 37.

lished under the banking laws of Zimbabwe. Given the conglomerate nature of this merger, the Commission determined the relevant markets to be the provision of merchant banking services and the provision of social security services in Zimbabwe. NSSA was however the beneficiary of a statutory monopoly in the social security services market. The merchant banking services market was therefore the focus of the Commission's merger analysis as it was here that the effects of the transaction on competition would be felt.

Taking the four merchant banking players in Zimbabwe, the Commission calculated the HHI and determined that the relevant market was highly concentrated. The market share of the four players in the banking industry as a whole was however quite low. The Commission examined the proposed transaction as a conglomerate merger with vertical linkages, taking the following factors into consideration in determining whether there would be a substantial lessening of competition; market entry conditions, concentration, acquisition of market power, removal of efficient competition and failing firm consideration.

The transaction was determined as not likely to lead to a substantial lessening of competition or the creation of a monopoly situation. Rather, given that Renaissance was found to be a failing firm, the merger would result in pro-competitive benefits by preventing a failing firm from exiting the market. From the public interest perspective, the Commission considered that jobs would be protected and the stability of the financial market would be ensured. The proposed merger was approved unconditionally.

Zimbabwe Online (Pvt) Limited (ZOL) & Data Control & Systems (1996) Limited (DCS)[871]

DCS, a licensed internet access provider (IAP) in Zimbabwe, proposed to wholly acquire ZOL, an internet service provider (ISP) in Zimbabwe. Given the supplier (DCS) and customer (ZOL) relationship between the two firms, the Commission determined the transaction to be a vertical merger. The relevant market was defined as provision of IAP and ISP services in Zimbabwe.

The IAP services market, classified on the basis of revenue and bandwidth, was found to be highly concentrated. Whereas the IAP market had high barriers to entry (licensing fees and substantial capital requirements),

<http://www.competition.co.zw/publications/annual-reports> accessed 5 September 2019 (Zimbabwe Annual Report).

871 Zimbabwe Annual Report 2012 39-40.

the ISP market had low barriers to entry (mainly because it was largely unregulated) and hence had many market participants.

Given the vertical nature of the merger the biggest concern was foreclosure. The Commission as well examined the transaction on the basis of market entry conditions, concentration, acquisition of market power, removal of efficient competition and failing firm consideration. The conclusion however was that the merger would not result in a substantial lessening of competition in either of the markets. One of the determining aspects was the fact that there was a regulator on the market that prevented any anti-competitive behaviour from market participants. The approval of the merger was however conditional on the merged firm ensuring access to other IAP and ISP service providers.

Makro Zimbabwe (Makro) & OK Zimbabwe Limited (OK)[872]

This transaction involved a proposed acquisition by OK of the business assets of Makro. Both companies were incorporated in and active in Zimbabwe, with OK being a publicly listed company and Makro a fully owned subsidiary of a South Africa company. OK was engaged in retailing of a broad range of products and Makro in the wholesale of general merchandise. The Commission determined the relevant market in this case to be the distribution of fast moving consumer goods in Zimbabwe.

The Commission's focus in this case was on the level of market concentration, which was calculated using the HHI and concentration ratios. The market was however found not to be concentrated, with the post-merger market share of the merging firms marginally increasing. Other factors, i.e. acquisition of market power, removal of competition, market entry and degree of countervailing power were also analysed but no threat to competition was identified. The Commission also sought the views of competitors and customers regarding the transaction.

The Commission also took into account public interest considerations, requiring the safeguarding of jobs for Makro's employees and the supply chain of local suppliers. The merger was thus approved subject to commitments regarding these employees and suppliers.

872 Zimbabwe Annual Report 2011 44-45.

3.2.6.4.4 Observations from the case studies

Rather than going into the detail of what the competition authorities decided in each of these cases, the case studies serve as brief examples of which factors came into play when the various authorities conducted their substantive analyses.

In the case of Tanzania, it is more or less clear that on the basis of their structured dominance-based substantive analysis, defining the relevant market will play a central role which will be followed by the determination of the market share of the firms in question. On this basis the authority determines whether the merger will lead to the creation or strengthening of a dominant position. This straightforward and structured approach centred on market definition, market shares and concentration levels is evident in the *Helios* and *Uranium One* case studies.

The approach is however not very far removed from that in the jurisdictions which employ the substantial lessening of competition standard. Although these jurisdictions do indeed utilise the multi-factor approach that is typical of the SLC standard, market concentration still plays a prominent role in the substantial analysis. The SLC multi-factor approach does not advocate for a particular analytical structure or for certain factors to take precedence. However, even on a case-by-case analysis we note that most of the cases do indeed follow a structure which begins with defining the relevant markets and determining the shares.

From the macro-perspective, this could be an indication that many markets in the SLC jurisdictions are still concentrated and a structured approach that is focused more on defining the market parameters and determining concentration levels as the main factors will in many cases address most of the competition authorities' concerns.

In Mauritius, the *LC Events*, the *Swan Group* and the *Holcim* case studies all indicate markets that were concentrated or easily susceptible to monopoly situations. The competition authority in these mergers did utilise the multi-factor approach but the ultimate focus was on market shares and concentration levels. The same can be said of the other jurisdictions in many instances. The *Colas* merger in Namibia revealed a highly concentrated road construction market that was also highly susceptible to vertical foreclosure. The focus of the Zimbabwe authority in the *Renaissance Merchant Bank* and the *Makro* merger was as well on determining the level of concentration in each of the markets; though the former was eventually determined on the basis of a failing firm scenario.

In Malawi, the *Toyota* merger revealed a very concentrated market where the merging parties held large market shares. The *Toyota* merger was also determined against a backdrop of a highly concentrated and monopolised market in Zambia and Kenya. The determination in the *Dhunseri* case also fell upon whether or not the market structure in terms of market shares would be altered.

Other cases are decided on the basis of the conclusion that there would be no change to the market structure or concentration levels. The *Kalend* merger in Botswana shows that irrespective of the fact that one of the parties was already dominant in the market for health care provision; the fact that the purchaser was a foreign undertaking with no local presence meant that there was no threat to competition. In the *Bokomo* merger as well the authority in making its determination focused on the fact that the market structure would remain largely the same.

The concentration levels in a number of these markets can be attributed to high barriers to entry; which could be due to the fact that some of the markets require substantial capital investment, substantial regulatory compliance requirements or a host of other factors which make it difficult for small players to enter into the market. The Toyota merger for instance revealed that entry into the market was almost entirely dependent on obtaining a license from the manufacturers to distribute which was not an easy task. The Swan Group merger also revealed that the insurance market in Mauritius tends towards concentration, probably due to stringent regulatory requirements.

Another noteworthy aspect of the concentrated markets is that a number of the largest firms in these markets have foreign ownership, with the foreign owners having operations in various jurisdictions. This again could be a pointer to the capital-intensive nature of some industries, which most probably locks out smaller local investors especially where specific resources in question are not available locally. The Holcim merger in Mauritius shows that the cement market was highly concentrated and tending towards monopoly, with cement supply relying largely on imports. The Mauritian subsidiaries in this case were part of a large international network.

There are however markets where in spite of there being large market players with regional presence, small and medium size enterprises are still able to thrive on account of low barriers to entry, low capital requirements as well as relatively easy to fulfil regulatory requirements. A case in point is the Buzeki merger in Kenya. The fact that there was intense competition from mini-industries and lenient regulation in respect of the sale of unprocessed milk meant that the merging parties still faced intense competition post-merger and would be unable to exercise market power.

From a development economics perspective, a more than half of the mergers in the case studies reveal active foreign and intra-regional investment. From a merger regulation perspective, this reveals that there was indeed the need for a regional regulator. The COMESA Competition Commission has received quite a number of merger notifications and reviewed numerous mergers since commencing operations at the beginning of 2013.[873] From the substantial review perspective, the COMESA Competition Commission also tends to focus on determining the level of concentration in the relevant market but from the Common Market perspective. The *PPC International*, *CFR* and *CNRC* mergers all point to a focus on the market structure within the Common Market and the effect that the transactions would have had on the level of concentration and the probability of abuse of dominance within the relevant market.

The level of post-merger market concentration in terms of market share and the ability to utilise a dominant position to exercise market power does play a central role in the European Union and the United States as well. However, the fact that many of the EU and US markets tend to be highly diversified means that the multi-factor approach may not necessarily be concluded as easily on the basis of the level of post-merger market shares and concentration levels. This diversification also means that more considerations will be taken into account in defining the relevant market, establishing the market share or determining the level of concentration as compared to the Sub-Saharan Africa jurisdictions.

3.2.7 Efficiencies

3.2.7.1 Economic efficiency, consumer welfare and total welfare

There is broad consensus that a main outcome of effective competition in the market is the enhancement of efficiency. In the race to be ahead of their competitors, business rivals ideally seek optimal allocation of resources to ensure efficient production of goods and provision of services as well as minimizing the costs of production. It has also been widely

873 See COMESA Merger Statistics <http://www.comesacompetition.org/wp-content/uploads/2016/06/No-of-Mergers-Handled-by-CCC-2013-June-2016.pdf> accessed 5 September 2019.

proffered that effective competition leads to dynamic efficiencies by encouraging producers to be innovative and to continuously improve their products resulting in technological progress over time.[874]

From the point of view of developing and transition economies, some have contended that there should be a greater focus on dynamic efficiency than on static efficiency.[875] One of the main counter-arguments is that developing countries are still having a hard time achieving static efficiencies and are in most cases lacking the framework needed to benefit from innovation.[876] A correlation is in this regard drawn between the level of development and the relative importance of static and dynamic efficiencies. Progress in development translates into gains in static efficiency, that is, better resource allocation and improved production methods, which in turn results in an increasing importance of dynamic efficiency. In this case, welfare gains become increasingly dependent on dynamic efficiencies of competition. An appropriate competition law framework is therefore considered an important tool to ensure that these (progressive) efficiency gains brought about by effective competition in the market are not lost.[877]

Gains in efficiency should ultimately translate into welfare gains for society. An increase in static and dynamic efficiency results in better prices and in the long run better products. However, whereas the welfare of society is considered as the ultimate goal, consumer welfare is considered to be an intermediate goal of effective competition.[878]

Yet, a prudent approach dictates that the discussion of welfare should be advanced in perspective. From the economics perspective, consumer welfare is maximized where the allocative and productive efficiencies result in

---

874 Whish and Bailey (2012) 3-5.

875 Ajit Singh, 'Competition and competition policy in emerging markets: International and development dimensions' (2002) G-24 Discussion Paper Series, Paper No. 18. United Nations 15-16 <https://unctad.org/en/docs/gdsmdpbg2418_en.pdf> accessed 17 July 2019.

876 Frank Emmert, Franz Kronthaler, Johannes Stephan, 'Analysis of statements made in favour of and against the adoption of competition law in developing and transition economies' (2005) Institut Für Wirtschaftsforschung Halle Report, 9 <https://www.iwh-halle.de/fileadmin/user_upload/publications/iwh_sonderhefte/SH_05-1.pdf> accessed 17 July 2019.

877 Emmert et al (2005) 9. See also Simon J. Evenett, 'Study on Issues Relating to a Possible Multilateral Framework on Competition Policy' (2003) Report prepared for the Secretariat of the World Trade Organization 14.

878 Simon Bishop and Mike Walker, *The Economic of EC Competition Law: Concepts, Application and Measurement* (Sweet & Maxwell, 3rd edn, 2010) paras. 2.16 – 2.20.

consumers paying less than they are normally willing to pay for a product, that is, a consumer surplus.[879] There is however extensive debate regarding the normative foundations of competition law especially in the context of the efficiency-welfare paradigm. One such debate is regarding whether the target of efficiency gains should be the enhancement of consumer welfare or total welfare. The total welfare standard, also known as economic surplus, refers to the sum of both the consumer surplus and producer surplus. The producer surplus arises where the producer sells at a price that is higher than cost or higher than the minimum price he is willing to sell for.[880]

Drexl observes that the dynamic nature of competition as a process should be taken into account in the consideration of an appropriate welfare standard. Particularly, the long-term effects of efficiency claims are difficult to predict. Therefore, whereas in the short-term a merger for instance may result in welfare gains in the form of productive efficiency (a result which would be affirmed under a total welfare standard), in the long term the reduced competitive pressure may result in harm to competition.[881]

Kaplow, while taking the perspective of a distributive objective, considers the advancement in competition law of a consumer welfare standard (which would give more weight to consumer surplus than to producer surplus) as an indirect means to redistribute income is inefficient in comparison to a tax and transfer system, which would be beneficial for both producers and consumers. Kaplow favours competition law pursuing a total welfare standard, with the aim being a maximisation of both consumer and producer welfare.[882]

Kerber considers that the discussion of a total welfare versus consumer welfare standard doesn't appropriately capture the complexity of the normative problems regarding the foundations of competition law. He considers that neither a pure total-welfare standard nor a pure consumer-welfare standard is most appropriate. Without making any normative recommen-

---

879 See for instance Louis Kaplow, 'On the Choice of Welfare Standards in Competition Law' in Daniel Zimmer (ed), *The Goals of Competition Law* (Edward Elgar, 2012) 3.

880 Kaplow (2012) 3-4.

881 Josef Drexl, 'Consumer welfare and consumer harm: adjusting competition law and policies to the needs of developing jurisdictions' 265-295 in Michal Gal, Mor Bakhoum, Josef Drexl, Eleanour Fox and David Gerber (eds), *The Economic Characteristics of Developing Jurisdictions: Their Implications for Competition Law* (Edward Elgar, 2015) 287.

882 Kaplow (2012) 1-5.

dations, one of his suggestions is a 'weighted-surplus standard' where different weights are given to producer or consumer surplus depending on the context of the application of competition policy.[883] Notwithstanding the extensive academic discourse, the consumer welfare standard is the preferred approach in many jurisdictions.

Drexl advocates a dynamic approach to competition policy which considers the context in which the policy is applicable. For developing jurisdictions, a consideration of their particular socio-economic and political circumstances becomes imperative. The need to develop competitive markets would support the adoption by developing jurisdictions of policies that protect the competitive process. This would cater for a proper analysis of the longer-term need to develop competitive markets as opposed to short-term benefits resulting from static efficiency gains which would arise for instance from a merger aimed at achieving economies of scale. Drexl notes that protecting the competitive process as an appropriate concept for developing jurisdiction competition policies is inclusive. It for instance allows a consideration of the role played by small-scale producers and suppliers within the competition ecosystem and the need to protect their interests.[884]

Regarding the appropriate welfare standard for developing jurisdictions, the ESA jurisdictions invariably categorise consumer welfare as one of the core competition policy goals. Yet, certain public interest considerations such as the effect of a merger on a particular industrial sector or region, the ability of national industries to compete internationally or the ability of small or medium sized enterprises to compete on any market arguably point to a total welfare approach where the welfare of local producers are considered very important in the analysis of a merger. This indeed reinforces the need to take a contextual approach in ESA jurisdictions where a consideration of their particular socio-economic and political circumstances becomes imperative.

Economic efficiency in the context of the small market economy

Concomitant to the need for a contextualized approach to competition policy in developing jurisdictions, Gal (2003) identifies three main charac-

---

883 Wolfgang Kerber, 'Should competition law promote efficiency? Some reflections of an economist on the normative foundations of competition law' in Josef Drexl, Laurence Idot and Joel Moneger (eds), *Economic Theory and Competition Law* (Edward Elgar, 2009) 93-120, 114.

884 Drexl (2012) 283-286.

teristics of small economies:[885] high industrial concentration levels, high barriers to entry and below minimum efficient scale (MES) levels of production. MES refers to the production level needed to minimize to the greatest extent the average unit cost of production. The greatest challenge for small economies in this regard is the matching of demand to MES. This is because in most cases the MES is large in comparison to the level of demand.[886]

Where the market is characterized by a large MES in comparison to demand, a prospective market entrant contemplating operating below the MES will face higher production costs and would not be able to realise productive efficiencies. If these costs cannot be offset, then the prospective entrant would opt to stay out of the market. On the other hand, if the prospective market entrant contemplates operating above MES, then the demand would dictate that the selling price of the products be reduced substantially, which on the long run would be unsustainable and may force the entrant to exit if all other market actors maintain their output above MES. A situation therefore arises where high cost-related entry barriers exist. Additionally, such markets can support a relatively small number of firms operating at MES thus resulting in high concentration levels. This challenge is particularly acute in industries that rely heavily on scale economies to sustain production and profitability.[887]

This is therefore largely correlative to the observable trend in small market economies where on the one hand there is relatively high concentration and high cost-related entry barriers in manufacturing and productive industries which rely on scale economies and on the other hand highly competitive retail and service sector which are not as dependent on scale economies.[888] Small economies may further affect the realization of dynamic efficiencies where for instance firms uncertain of the market acceptance of new products arising from more advanced production methods may be reluctant to adopt these methods.[889]

---

885 Michal S. Gal, *Competition Policy for Small Market Economies* (Harvard University Press, 2003), defines a small market economy as 'an independent sovereign economy that can support only a small number of competitors in most of its industries'.

886 Gal (2003) 14-18.

887 Gal (2003) 18-23.

888 Gal (2003) 20.

889 C.D. Edwards, 'Size of Markets, Scale of Firms and the Character of Competition' in Robinson E.A.G. (ed) *Economic Consequences of the Size of Nations*

Gal observes that these economic characteristics of small economies give rise to competition policy concerns related to increased predisposition to concentrate especially under an oligopolistic structure. This naturally raises concerns regarding explicit or implicit collusive behavior. Gal notes that the small economies have certain characteristics that make it harder for countervailing forces to effectively address oligopolistic tendency to collude, notably their highly concentrated markets and the significant barriers to entry. Such collusive behavior may lead firms to adopt inefficient strategies such as limiting output to below-MES levels to maintain the collusively set supra-competitive prices. These small economy market characteristics not only facilitate oligopolistic collusion but also enhance the probability of non-collusive oligopolistic structures.[890]

In the same way that the homogenous nature of small economies simplifies the possibility of coordinating competitive ventures, it also limits the variety of non-coordinated competition options. It therefore would be no surprise that individual oligopolistic pricing decisions may appear highly coordinated where in fact they arise from the market options available to the oligopolist.

Gal considers that horizontal mergers in oligopolistic markets may be an avenue for firms to realize scale economies. A merger in this regard would allow firms to retain their aggregate/collusive level of output while at the same time strengthening their market power or increasing interdependence. Effective merger regulation in this respect is particularly important for small economies.[891]

Such characteristics of small economies play a significant role in curtailing their economic performance. Small economies in this regard face two major handicaps: inability to realize economies of scale without tending towards concentration and lack of competitive conditions in many industries. Properly tailored and well implemented competition policies are in this regard considered necessary to fill the gap that market forces are unable to fill in small economies.[892]

Economic efficiency in this regard is a very important competition policy goal in small economies, even considering other societal goals that such economies may pursue. Protection of the competitive process should

---

(Palgrave Macmillan 1960) 117-130. See also James S. Coleman, *'Foundations of Social Theory'* (Belknap Press, 1990).

890 Gal (2003) 32-35.

891 Gal (2003) 34.

892 Gal (2003) 43-45.

remain a core goal of competition policy to ensure that small economies achieve efficiency. This is however without being overly simplistic regarding the factors facing small economies and the need to contextualize competition policy.[893]

3.2.7.2 Efficiency Defence in Merger Regulation

From the perspective of assessing efficiencies as a defence raised in support of a problematic merger, a core question is whether merger-specific economies of scale, that is, productive efficiencies, outweigh losses in terms of allocative efficiencies (price increase).

In a highly competitive market participating firms would typically seek to set the most competitive price to attract the largest number of customers. To achieve this, the firm would need to increase its productive efficiency, whereby it minimises its production costs in order to maximise on profit. The firm would also seek to improve on the allocative efficiency so as to cut down on the deadweight losses and increase their profit base by making sure more consumers who are willing to pay a price that covers the marginal cost have access to its products.

The ICN merger guidelines workbook provides that as part of an 'integrated' approach, efficiencies may be incorporated into the assessment carried out by competition authorities. This involves taking into account of the net effect of the merger on competition factors such as price and incentives of the merged firm.[894] The information asymmetry however means that the critical information necessary to assess efficiencies is usually in the hands of the merging parties. Efficiencies are therefore mostly considered from the perspective of claims made by the merging parties, principally where the merger would otherwise be prohibited for its anti-competitive effects. Authorities usually face the difficult task of weighing prospective efficiencies against possible anticompetitive effects that may result from a merger. The evidential burden on the merging parties is however high and is difficult to meet.[895]

---

893 Gal (2003) 51-53. See also Roger Zäch, 'Competition law should promote economic and social welfare by ensuring the freedom to compete – a lawyer's view' in Josef Drexl, Laurence Idot and Joel Moneger (eds), *Economic Theory and Competition Law* (Edward Elgar, 2009) 121-125.

894 ICN Merger Guidelines Workbook 63.

895 ICN Merger Guidelines Workbook 61.

The European Commission when taking into consideration a claim of merger-related efficiencies requires the merging parties to prove that the efficiencies are specific to the merger, that they will result in consumer benefit and that they are verifiable by reasonable means.[896] It should also be shown that the efficiencies are unachievable by less anticompetitive means. These conditions are to be achieved cumulatively making it very difficult for merging parties to convince competition authorities.

Where sufficient evidence is available to indicate that the merger will generate efficiencies that will be beneficial to consumers and counteract the anticompetitive effects of the merger, the Commission may decide that the merger need not be prohibited..[897]

In the *Aerospatiale-Alenia* case, the Commission, in response to an argument by the parties that the merger would have availed cost savings, stated that the cost savings were of little effect to the overall operation and could have still been achieved through better management. In effect they were not merger specific.

The US Horizontal Merger Guidelines require similar criteria to be met for efficiency claims to be considered:

> Cognizable efficiencies are merger-specific efficiencies that have been verified and do not arise from anticompetitive reductions in output or service. To make the requisite determination, the Agencies consider whether cognizable efficiencies likely would be sufficient to reverse the merger's potential to harm customers in the relevant market, e.g., by preventing price increases in that market.[898]

The difficulty in quantifying efficiencies in a merger setting as well as the heavy evidential burden placed on the merging parties is further reflected in the US Horizontal Merger Guidelines:

> Efficiencies are difficult to verify and quantify, in part because much of the information relating to efficiencies is uniquely in the possession of the merging firms. Moreover, efficiencies projected reasonably and in good faith by the merging firms may not be realized. Therefore, it is incumbent upon the merging firms to substantiate efficiency claims so that the Agencies can verify by reasonable means the likelihood and magnitude of each asserted efficiency, how and when each would be

896 ICN Workbook 63-64; EU Merger Regulation para 78; US Horizontal Guidelines 30-31; Pioneer (n 775) para 315.

897 EU Horizontal Merger Guidelines paras 76-88.

898 US Horizontal Guidelines para 10.

achieved (and any costs of doing so), how each would enhance the merged firm's ability and incentive to compete, and why each would be merger-specific.[899]

According to the US Horizontal Merger Guidelines 'only those efficiencies likely to be accomplished with the proposed merger and unlikely to be accomplished in the absence of either the proposed merger or another means having comparable anticompetitive effects.'[900]

The Bundeskartellamt has a more restrictive approach regarding the role of efficiencies. Other than having an influence on the balancing clause (as regards the pro or anticompetitive effects of a merger) and on ministerial authorization, efficiency considerations do not play a significant role in the Bundeskartellamt's decision making unless they have a direct bearing on competition in the market.[901] The Bundeskartellamt argues against a broad efficiency consideration on the basis of a cost to added value analysis. The view is the added cost is not proportional to the value added by such recognition of efficiencies, in addition to the difficulty in assessing merger-specific efficiency gains.[902]

Efficiencies are taken into consideration when authorities weigh the pro-competitive benefits of a merger as against its competitive harm. The European Commission for example would allow a merger on the basis of sufficient evidence adduced by the merging parties to show that as a result of the merger the merging parties would be able or incentivised to 'act pro-competitively for the benefit of consumers' in a way that would counteract the negative externalities on competition that the merger would bring about (a consumer welfare approach).[903] A similar position is reflected in the US Horizontal Merger Guidelines where the Agencies would 'consider whether cognizable efficiencies likely would be sufficient to reverse the merger's potential to harm customers in the relevant market'[904]

The Competition Authorities in South Africa have indicated the inclination to adopt the EU and US points of view in respect to the assessment of efficiencies. The scepticism towards projected efficiencies that is reflected in the US has been reiterated by the South Africa Competition Tribunal.[905]

899 US Horizontal Guidelines para 10.
900 Ibid 30.
901 Bundeskartellamt Guidance para 17.
902 Ibid.
903 EU Horizontal Merger Guidelines para 77.
904 US Horizontal Guidelines para 10.
905 Pioneer (n 775) para 294.

The US and EU positions as regards the likelihood, timeliness, sufficiency, ability to be quantified and verifiability by reasonable means of the efficiencies, as well as the direct causal link of the efficiencies to the merger are adopted by the South African authorities. The standard adopted in South Africa for establishing countervailing efficiency gains is high as well.[906]

What sets South Africa apart from the US and the EU, as well as bringing in the developing country perspective, is the integral part that public interest plays in the assessment of countervailing efficiencies. Where a public interest concern is in question, the countervailing efficiencies must as well be justified on public interest grounds.[907] In the *Metropolitan and Momentum* case, the public interest concern in question was substantial job losses. The South Africa Competition Tribunal determined that where the efficiency claims are in connection to private interests and not public interests they would not be accepted.[908] In South Africa therefore, private countervailing efficiencies would be considered at the competition assessment stage whereas at the public interest stage there would need to be a further showing of the public interest benefit.[909] Where for instance the efficiencies gained through job cuts are necessary to keep a factory operational so as to prevent adverse economic effects to a particular region, they would be justifiable on public interest grounds.[910]

The public interest justifications that the South Africa Competition Tribunal has pointed out in the context of employment loss include saving a failing firm and cost savings which will be passed to consumers and which can only be brought about by job cuts. Increased competitiveness of the merged firm through efficiencies achievable again only through the job cuts is also considered as a viable justification.[911] The increased competitiveness of the merged firm achieved through enhanced efficiency may as well be used to argue in favour of improving the international competitiveness of a local firm. However, as seen in the *Tongaat-Hulett*

906 Ibid para 315; US Horizontal Guidelines para 10; *The Tongaat-Hulett Group Limited and Transvaal Suiker Beperk, Middenen Ontwikkeling (Pty) Ltd, Senteeko (Edms) Bpk, New Komati Sugar Miller's Partnership, TSB Bestuursdienste*, Competition Tribunal case no: 83/LM/Jul00, 27 November 2000, 97-100.

907 SA Competition Act s 12 sub-s 1(a) (i) & (ii) and sub-s 3.

908 *Metropolitan Holdings Limited and Momentum Group Limited*, Competition Tribunal case no: 41/LM/Jul10, 9 December 2010, para 71.

909 Ibid para 72.

910 Ibid para 75; SA Competition Act, s 12 sub-s 3.

911 Metropolitan Decision (n 902) para 77

decision, the South Africa Competition Authorities still hold the standard of proof in this respect very high.[912]

On the question of merger specificity, the European Commission makes it clear that over and above the direct causal link between the merger and the efficiencies, there must be an absence of realistically attainable less anticompetitive ways to achieve this efficiency.[913] This position is reflected as well in the United States and South Africa.[914] Verifiability requires a reasonable likelihood of materialisation of the efficiencies. In addition, the efficiencies need to be quantifiable and the verification has to be by reasonable means.[915] The efficiencies need to be substantial or of a magnitude sufficient to counteract any potential harm to consumers or allay concerns on anticompetitive effects. As noted in the US Horizontal Merger Guidelines, the fact that the efficiencies are based on a projection which even where reasonable and in good faith may not be realised, the evidential burden on the parties is justifiably high.[916] The European Commission further provides that this uncertainty means that the efficiencies need to be achievable in a timely manner.[917] In addition to the specificity and verifiability, the benefits accruing from the efficiencies should be passed on to the consumers. As the European Commission puts it, 'the relevant benchmark in assessing efficiency claims is that consumers will not be worse off as a result of the merger.'[918] In perspective, the main trade-off is arguably that the merging parties will be incentivized not to exercise ex-post market power owing to the sufficiency of the efficiencies.[919]

The decisions from the three jurisdictions are testament to the difficulty faced by the merging parties in proving specificity. In *FTC v. H.J. Heinz* for instance, the parties had claimed that the transaction would result in merger-specific savings. The proposed merger would have resulted in the second and third biggest producers of jarred baby food coming together. The FTC expressed the concern that this would reduce competition and result in price increases, in addition to the low probability of a new entrant that would challenge the merged firm. The FTC however found that on a balance of effects the efficiencies would not off-set the anti-competitive

912 Tongaat-Hulett Decision paras 104-111.
913 EU Horizontal Merger Guidelines para 85.
914 US Horizontal Guidelines 30; Pioneer (775) para 315.
915 EU Horizontal Merger Guidelines para 86; US Horizontal Guidelines 30.
916 US Horizontal Guidelines 30.
917 EU Horizontal Merger Guidelines para 83.
918 EU Horizontal Merger Guidelines para 79.
919 Lindsay and Berridge (2009) para 18-011.

effects in addition to the fact that they could have been achieved by other less anti-competitive means. The case went to the Court of Appeals where the court determined that there was insufficient evidence presented by the parties to support their efficiency claim, resulting in the eventual abandonment of the proposed merger.[920]

In the proposed merger between *Ryan Air and Air Lingus*[921] the European Commission was tasked with determining whether the efficiency claims in a case involving the two biggest airlines operating in Ireland were sufficient to offset the post-merger monopoly concerns. The materialization of the efficiencies was found to be uncertain especially when considered that the claimed efficiency gains (such as cutting on staff costs) did not sufficiently address the effect on aspects such as quality of service. Certain cost savings were also found to relate largely to fixed costs, leading the European Commission to question whether they could be passed on to the consumers. On the overall, the case was considered to be one of a merger-to-near-monopoly, hence even the claimed efficiencies would be sufficient to offset potential anticompetitive effects, it would still remain highly unlikely that the merger would be declared compatible with the common market.[922]

In the *Pioneer Hi-Bred* case, the South Africa Competition Tribunal found that certain claimed efficiencies arising from joint work that had been carried out between the parties were independent of the merger hence not specific. In addition, any dynamic efficiency that would flow from the creation of new maize varieties were not timely enough as they would require several years to materialize. In addition, there was insufficient evidence presented by the parties to show that the efficiencies would substantially pass on to the consumers. The South Africa Competition Tribunal in this regard took a consumer welfare approach.[923]

In assessing the merging parties claimed efficiencies, the Competition Tribunal made substantial reference to the United States and European Union position. They reiterated that efficiencies need to be likely, timely and sufficient as well as being quantifiable, verifiable by reasonable means and as a direct result of the merger. In other words, the standard for establishing countervailing efficiency gains is likewise high. The Tribunal for instance specifically made reference to the treatment in the United

920 *FTC v. H.J. Heinz Co. and Milnot Holding Corporation* 246 F.3d 708 (2001).

921 *Ryanair / Aer Lingus*, Case No COMP/M.4439 (2007).

922 Ibid paras 1141 – 1152.

923 Pioneer (n 775) paras 317-334.

States of projected efficiencies with scepticism as well as the EU position in respect of the need for the efficiencies to be realized within a short period of time.

In spite of the high standard of proof that the authorities require in respect of efficiencies, they are still part of the multi-factor approach and will rarely play a deciding role in extreme cases, as evidenced by the European Commission's decision in *Ryanair*. They may be useful in tipping the scale where borderline cases are involved. There is also a general congruence in respect of the main considerations in the assessment of efficiencies. How the different authorities apply these main considerations will depend largely on the cases before them. However, the public interest perspective evidenced by South Africa shows that from an emerging market or developing country perspective, efficiencies that have public interest repercussions will be subject to greater scrutiny and may even play a more concrete decisive role.

3.2.7.3 Efficiencies in the ESA Context

The broad reluctance to accepting efficiencies have as well been expressed in Kenya, Seychelles, Tanzania, Zambia as well as in the COMESA merger guidelines. The main factors taken into account by authorities in the United States, the European Union and South Africa in the assessment of efficiencies i.e. specificity, likelihood, timeliness, sufficiency, ability to be quantified, verifiability, unattainability by any other means, having a direct causal link to the merger and beneficial to consumers are also considered by most of the ESA jurisdictions.[924]

Efficiencies in the ESA jurisdictions, as is the case in the European Union and the United States, are also taken into consideration when authorities consider the pro-competitive benefits of a merger in light of the competitive harm that may arise.[925] This comparison of the pro-competitive benefits to the anti-competitive harm, as we have seen, is

---

924 Kenya Merger Guidelines paras 198-199; Namibia Merger Guidelines para 12.3; Seychelles Merger Guidelines paras 11.8-11.9; Tanzania Merger Guidelines 15; Zambia Merger Guidelines para 97; COMESA Merger Guidelines paras. 8.101 et seq.

925 EU Horizontal Merger Guidelines para 77; US Horizontal Merger Guidelines para 10; Kenya Merger Guidelines para 201; Namibia Merger Guidelines para 12.1; Tanzania Merger Guidelines 15; Zambia Merger Guidelines para 97; COMESA Merger Guidelines paras. 8.101 et seq.

regarded as an overall balancing test in Seychelles, COMESA, Malawi and Mauritius.[926] In Zambia and Botswana the balancing test is specifically categorised as one of the public interest considerations. In Tanzania it is listed among other public interest considerations in determining what public benefits will arise from the merger.[927]

The public interest angle to the consideration of countervailing efficiencies means that in respect of most of the ESA jurisdictions the efficiencies must additionally be justified in light of their effect on public interest. This means that where for instance there are significant internal efficiencies to be gained in terms of cost-cutting measures, they will be deemed as detrimental if these cost-cutting measures include significant job losses.[928]

Apart from the more critical role played by public interest in the consideration of efficiencies in many of the ESA jurisdictions, there is an overall similarity with the United States and the European Union in the assessment of efficiencies.

3.2.8 The Public Interest Assessment

One aspect of the substantive assessment of mergers in South Africa as well as the reviewed ESA jurisdictions (except for Seychelles and Mauritius) that brings out the emerging and developing market point of view and marks a point of substantial divergence from the EU and the US is the inclusion of a public interest analysis in the substantive analysis.

3.2.8.1 South Africa

The preamble to the SA Competition Act reflects some of the broad public interest concerns that it seeks to address. Concerns such as addressing the unjust restriction on economic participation by all South Africans, opening up the economy to greater ownership by a larger number of South

926 Seychelles Competition Act s 23 sub-s 2(a); COMESA Competition Regulations art 26(1); Malawi Competition Act s 38 sub-s 2; Mauritius Competition Act s 50 sub-s 4.

927 Zambia Competition Act s 31(a); Tanzania Competition Act s 13 sub-s 1(b)(vi); Botswana Competition Act s 59 sub-s 2(a).

928 SA Competition Act s 12 sub-s (1)(a) (i) & (ii) and sub-s 3.

Africans, balancing of worker, owner and consumer interests, making the local markets more competitive globally have been expressed.

The SA Competition Act requires the Competition Commission and Competition Tribunal, in their assessment of whether the merger would substantially prevent or lessen competition, to decide on the merger based on whether it can or cannot be justified based on substantial public interest considerations.[929] The public interest consideration plays a central role even in the eventuality that the merger would result in a SLC. An otherwise anti-competitive merger could therefore be approved based on public interest considerations. A merger that does not result in a SLC may also be prohibited based on public interest factors.

The connection between the competition test and the public interest test has been explained by the Tribunal in its determination on a merger between *Harmony Gold Mining Company and Gold Fields.*[930] It explained that the public interest inquiry is not independent of the decision on competition but rather has to be conducted in relation to the finding on competition.

In making the public interest decision, it is imperative that the Competition Commission and Competition Tribunal take into consideration the effect of the merger on 'a particular industrial sector or region; employment; the ability of small businesses, or firms controlled or owned by historically disadvantaged persons, to effectively enter into, participate in or expand within the market; the ability of national industries to compete in inter-national markets; and the promotion of a greater spread of ownership, in particular to increase the levels of ownership by historically disadvantaged persons and workers in firms in the market.'[931] These are the five pillars of public interest assessment in South Africa's merger review.

929 SA Competition Act s12a sub-s 1(b).

930 *Harmony Gold Mining Company and Gold Fields*, case no. 93/LM/Nov04, 18 May 2005.

931 SA Competition Act s12a sub-s 3. Several changes were introduced into the SA Competition Act via the Competition Amendment Act, 2018 (Act No. 18 of 2018). Certain amendments to the public interest provisions came into effect in July 2019. This included substituting in s12a sub-s 3(c) the words 'to become competitive' with the words 'to effectively enter into, participate in or expand within the market'. There was also the addition of s12a sub-s 3(e) in relation to 'the promotion of a greater spread of ownership, in particular to increase the levels of ownership by historically disadvantaged persons and workers in firms in the market'. Neither the Background Note nor the Public Interest Guidelines reflect these changes yet. There is therefore no detailed analysis of the newly added s12a sub-s 3(e).

This setting of limits on the application of public interest considerations is important given the ambiguity and uncertainty that can result from a broad application of public interest factors in merger regulation.

The Commission has issued draft guidelines on the assessment of the public interest provisions (Public Interest Guidelines)[932] as well as a background note on how it developed the guidelines (Background Note)[933]. The Commission notes that the lack of guidelines on the application of the public interest provisions has presented challenges to the Competition Commission, Competition Tribunal and other stakeholders, noting that a rigorous and standardized approach in assessing public interest issues has to be adopted.

The Commission sets out a five-step overall approach taken when assessing public interest concerns under each of the four pillars:[934]

i) a determination of the likely effect of the merger on public interest;
ii) a determination of whether the effect is merger specific;
iii) a determination on the substantiality of the effect;
iv) a consideration of any justifications provided by the parties; and
v) a consideration of possible remedies that mitigate on the likely negative effect.

The Commission clarifies that the five steps are not necessarily to be considered cumulatively.

The Tribunal in a case between *BB Investment Company (Pty) Ltd and Adcock Ingram Holdings (Pty) Ltd*[935] provided some guidance on what merger specificity entails. The public interest concern in this case was the eventual redundancy of 51 employees post-merger. The Tribunal noted inter alia that a merger specific effect is 'an outcome that can be shown, as a matter of probability, to have some nexus associated with the incentives of the new controller.'[936]

---

932 Competition Commission South Africa, Guidelines on the assessment of public interest provisions in merger regulation under the Competition Act No. 89 of 1998 (Public Interest Guidelines).

933 Competition Commission South Africa, Background note to the public interest guideline (Background Note) <http://www.compcom.co.za/wp-content/uploads/2015/01/Final-Background-Note-to-Public-Interest-Guideline-210115.pdf> accessed 5 September 2019.

934 Public Interest Guidelines para. 6.1.

935 *BB Investment Company (Pty) Ltd and Adcock Ingram Holdings (Pty) Ltd*, Competition Tribunal case no: 18713 (19 August 2014).

936 Ibid para 56.

3.2.8.1.1 Employment

The SA Competition Act, recognizing the often-vulnerable position of employees in light of merger transactions, accords trade unions and employees a right to take part in the merger review process including the right to access notification information.[937] The question of confidentiality of information, which is central to any merger analysis, has been addressed by the Tribunal in this regard. The Tribunal in the case of *Unilever and Robertsons*[938] noted inter alia that it could not have been the intention of the legislation that information on employment that bears directly on employee interests should remain confidential.[939]

The legal basis for analyzing the public interest concerns in respect of prospective job losses was explained by the Tribunal in its decision in *Metropolitan and Momentum*.[940] It should basically be established whether there is a prima facie case of substantial job losses and if such a prima facie case exists whether the merging parties can justify these job losses.[941] The evidential justification provided by the merging parties must present a countervailing public interest of equal substantiality to the job losses for example a failing firm.[942]

The assessment of a particular case will naturally follow the five step approach. The likely effect on employment for instance could either be positive, negative or neutral. In the case of *AgriGroupe and AFGRI*[943], the merging parties concluded an agreement with concerned government departments that addressed various public interest concerns that had been raised. In the agreement, the merging parties *inter alia* committed not to undertake any retrenchments, not to relocate the offices outside of South Africa for a given duration, in addition to providing funding to emerging farmers and assistance to the farmers and relevant government

---

937 Background Note para 5.1.1. This includes for instance the right of trade unions and employees to access a copy of the merger notification (SA Competition Act s 13A sub-s 2) as well as the opportunity to participate in the actual proceedings (Competition Commission Rules rule. 37).

938 *Unilever Plc et al. and Robertsons Foods (Pty) Ltd*, Competition Tribunal case no: 55/LM/Sep01 (6 March 2002).

939 Ibid para 40.

940 Metropolitan Decision (n 902).

941 Ibid para 69.

942 Ibid para 70.

943 *AgriGroupe Holdings (Pty) Ltd and AFGRI Ltd*, Competition Tribunal case no. 017939 (15 April 2014) (AgriGroupe Decision).

departments.[944] This agreement in essence meant that as a result of the merger various positive effects would arise. The Tribunal concluded that the agreement did indeed meet the public interest concerns that had been raised.

Negative effects will naturally be linked to job losses. The Tribunal has however noted that its intervention only aims at safeguarding the status quo that is under threat from the merger. It cannot however impose new benefits. In the *Walmart and Massmart*[945] decision for instance, the Tribunal determined that a pre-merger policy adopted by Massmart in respect of collective labour relations was outside its ambit. It expressed the view that protecting existing rights falls within its public interest mandate but creating new rights would be in excess of its competence.[946] The Appeal Court reiterated the Tribunals view that a discourse on employee or union rights would fall within the sphere of the labour courts.[947]

As highlighted above, in the *BB Investment Company case*, merger specificity will fall on whether the effect on employment was caused by the merger or some other factors i.e. the establishment of a direct causal link between the job losses and the merger. The job losses in focus are those that occur just prior, during or just after the merger filing. In *Walmart and Massmart* for instance, the Appeal Court pointed out the fact that job losses that occur just prior to the consummation of a merger can in some cases be sufficiently linked to the merger decision-making process hence requiring the parties to make a justification.[948] The question of specificity becomes relevant where the merging parties present an argument that job losses indicated on the merger filing are not merger specific. The Commission otherwise operates on a presumption that reported job losses are merger specific.[949]

The question of substantiality would necessarily depend on the case in question. In the decision on *Metropolitan and Momentum*[950] for instance, the Tribunal stated that 'if on the facts of a particular case, employment loss is of a considerable magnitude and that short term prospects of re-em-

---

944 Ibid paras 60-64.

945 *Walmart Stores Inc and Massmart Holdings Limited*, Competition Tribunal case no. 73/LM/Dec10 (29 June 2011) (Walmart Tribunal Decision).

946 Ibid paras 67-68.

947 *Walmart and Massmart et al.*, Competition Appeal Court, case nos. 110/CAC/Jul11 and 111/CAC/Jun11, 9 March 2012 (Walmart Appeal Court Decision).

948 Ibid para. 140.

949 Background Note para 5.1.3.

950 Metropolitan Decision (n 902).

ployment for a substantial portion of the affected class are limited, then prima facie this would be presumed to have a substantial adverse effect on the public interest'. In this instance the substantiality fell on the magnitude of the job losses and a limitation on re-employment prospects for a majority of the affected employees. The Tribunal has cautioned against an approach that only focuses on the number of jobs, noting that the general effect of the merger on employment is important.[951]

The Commission highlights that the factors to be considered are the number of employees likely to be affected; the percentage of the affected workforce; the affected employees' skill levels and the likelihood of the employees being able to obtain alternative employment in the short term considering various factors.[952]

Once merger specificity and substantiality have been determined, the burden shifts to the parties to justify the merger. The Tribunal in the *Metropolitan and Momentum case* set out two criteria to be satisfied by the parties both of which have to be met: that a rational process was used in determining the number of jobs to be lost; and that there was an equally significant and countervailing public interest argument which is cognizable under the Act. There is however no fixed criteria put in place for assessing rationality. What is rational varies from case to case. What is generally sought is a well-reasoned and consistent approach, which indicates a clear link between the justification and the job losses.[953]

In the *Metropolitan and Momentum case*, the Tribunal further set out possible countervailing public interest justifications. They include situations where: the merger would save a failing firm; the job losses will help the parties achieve post-merger (cost) efficiency that would enable them to compete with rivals and which they would not be able to achieve without the merger; or reduced costs for the consumer which can only result from or materially depends on the job losses.[954]

The Tribunal also stresses the need for the parties to properly engage with employees or the Commission for the justification to be met.[955]

---

951 In *Nedbank Limited and Imperial Bank Limited*, Competition Tribunal case no. 70/LM/Oct09, 12 January 2010, the Tribunal criticized the Commission's approach in quantifying the scale of the jobs lost as a percentage of the overall workforce, terming it erroneous and not connected to the Act's purpose.

952 Background Note 17-19.

953 Background Note 20.

954 Metropolitan Decision para 77.

955 Background Note 22.

In terms of remedies the Commission indicates that the approach will in most cases follow the trend of requiring a moratorium on merger specific retrenchments from the merging parties.[956] The length of the moratorium would however be determined on a case by case basis.

3.2.8.1.2 Competitiveness of small businesses

The Commission in its Background Note highlights various instances in which the effect of a merger on small businesses was argued. In the *Walmart and Massmart* merger for example, the concern was expressed that the parties would switch from the local suppliers to cheaper foreign suppliers post-merger owing to their extensive global network and global purchasing power.[957] In this case, the merging parties were eventually required to set up a fund that would go towards the development of local suppliers to be spent over a period of five years.[958]

The Commission highlights the requirement that any claims based on public interest effects should be sufficiently supported by evidence.[959] In the *AgriGroupe and AFRI* decision, for instance, concerns raised by the government that the merging parties would increase grain storage costs and export grains to other countries thus affecting food security in South Africa were disregarded for lacking an evidentiary basis.[960]

Overall, looking at the *Walmart* and the *AgriGroupe* decisions, the trend seems to be in favor of an approach that is consultative and that may include setting up a fund that will support the small businesses.[961]

It is important to note that section 12a sub-s 3(c) of the SA Competition Act was amended to substitute the words 'to become competitive' with the words 'to effectively enter into, participate in or expand within the market'. Neither the Background Note nor the Public Interest Guidelines have been amended yet to reflect any change to the Commission's approach under this rubric. This amendment may very well be a further

956 Background Note para 5.1.4.

957 Walmart Tribunal Decision para 73.

958 Ibid paras 119-120; see also Walmart Appeal Court Decision paras 2, 26, 151, 152 & 166. The Appeal Court criticized the Tribunal's failure to review the terms and conditions under which the proposed fund would be put into operation.

959 Background Note 28.

960 AgriGroupe Decision paras 31-37.

961 Background Note 29-30.

elaboration under the SA Competition Act of the Commission's already existing approach.

3.2.8.1.3 Impact on particular industrial sector or region

The assessment of the effect of a merger may begin with a consideration of whether the firm targeted is South African and what business it is involved in within South Africa.[962] Instances given include whether domestic production would be affected by the merger if the target firm was involved in manufacture or whether the merger would lead to more importation rather than use of locally sourced products to the detriment of the local industries.

In the merger between *Thaba Chueu and SamQuarz*[963] the prohibition of the merger fell on the fact that the merging parties may be incentivized to restrict access to raw materials by local producers of steel and glass (input foreclosure), with the cost implication being passed on to downstream industrial customers. This decision was however reversed by the Tribunal which found that a long-term supply agreement between the merging parties and two of the largest local customers sufficiently addressed the public interest concern.[964]

On the issue of substantiality, the Commission is inclined to consider the 'strategic nature of the sector or product' to the economy in the region in question or in South Africa.[965] The Commission is also inclined to factor in the effect of the merger on public policy goals. As regards the proposed merger between *Iscor and Saldanha*[966] for example, the merger was determined to be anticompetitive on account of the competition test as it would have resulted in both horizontal and vertical effects. The pub-

962 Background Note para. 5.3.2.

963 *Thaba Chueu Mining (Pty) Ltd v Samquarz (Pty) Ltd*, Competition Tribunal case no. 10/AM/Jan12, 15 November 2012. The majority shareholding in Thaba Chueu was held by a company that was wholly owned by a Spanish holding company. Both the acquiring firm, Thaba Chueu, and the target firm, Samquarz, were involved in the mining of silica which is a raw material for the production of steel and glass. Whereas Thaba Chueu's sole customer was its majority shareholder, Samquarz was a supplier to a number of South African companies.

964 Ibid paras 86-87.

965 Background Note para 5.3.3.

966 *Iscor Limited and Saldanha Steel (Pty) Ltd*, Competition Tribunal case no. 67/LM/Dec01, 4 April 2002.

lic interest consideration however led to both the Commission and the Tribunal deciding that the merger should be approved. Saldanha, a steel producing company, was otherwise a failing firm and its closure would have had a detrimental impact on the region.[967] Saldanha was additionally involved in a number of Corporate Social Responsibility projects and programs, a fact which served to mitigate the anti-competitive effects of the merger.[968]

3.2.8.1.4 International competitiveness of national industries

The SA Competition Act categorizes the effect of a merger on the international competitiveness of national industries as a matter of public interest. The Commission in this regard seeks to determine whether or not the merger should be allowed to proceed based on whether it would increase or hinder the international competitiveness of the industry in question.[969] The effect, as is the case of the other public interest considerations, needs to be specifically attributable to the merger.

In the proposed merger between *Telkom SA and BCX*[970], the Tribunal found that a determination of the merger to be anti-competitive based on the SLC test was further reinforced by the fact that the merger would have a negative effect on international competitiveness of South African firms.[971] Telkom, which was regarded as the monopoly provider of fixed line infrastructure and services, sought to acquire BCX, a company active in the Information and Communications Technology (ICT) sector. Telekom's intention basically was to maintain its monopoly through tapping into the revenue streams which it was already losing owing to the convergence occurring in the rapidly developing and increasingly competitive ICT sector.[972] The Tribunal stated that although in this particular case there had already been a finding that the merger would result in a

967 Ibid para 156.
968 Ibid para 146.
969 Background Note para 5.4.1.
970 *Telkom SA Limited and Business Connexion Group Limited*, Competition Tribunal case no: 51/LM/Jun06, 20 August 2007.
971 Ibid para 300. The Tribunal as well reiterated the fact that a finding based on the competition test has to be made independently of the public interest consideration. Once the finding on competition is made then the public interest analysis can take place.
972 Ibid paras 307-308.

substantial lessening of competition through horizontal effects and that it would not result in any positive public interest effect, in which case the analysis should have ended, it considered that the negative impact the merger would have on public interest would bolster its prohibition.[973]

The affected markets were determined to be pivotal not only to the development of South Africa's ICT sector but the economy as a whole. The ICT sector is regarded as playing an important part in the competitiveness of South African companies.[974] A public policy of deregulation of the ICT sector had been adopted in order to increase competition. The Tribunal indeed noted that deregulation is the preferred policy measure when seeking to increase competition in a particular sector.[975] The merger was viewed as aiming to take advantage of a policy that sought to make the ICT sector efficient through increased competition by extending its monopoly into this sector. Telkom's entry into the deregulated ICT market through BCX was particularly of concern because BCX was already well positioned in the market and a potential competitor to Telkom.[976]

In the proposed merger between *Tongaat-Hulett and Transvaal Suiker Beperk*[977] the Tribunal has in fact expressed its inclination to the view that robust competition in the domestic market translates to success in the international markets. In this case, Tongaat-Hulet Group (THG) sought to acquire the sugar, molasses and animal feed business of Transvaal Suiler Beperk (TSB) as well as the issued share capital of one of the companies under the TSB group of companies. Both THG and TSB consist of a group of companies that are involved in the sugar industry in South Africa.[978] THG and TSB were also stated to be the second and third largest sugar producers in South Africa respectively, with THG also regarded as being internationally cost competitive.[979] The owners of TSB stated that their decision to sell was informed by a drop in world sugar prices, the deregula-

973 Ibid paras 310-317.

974 Ibid paras 301-302.

975 Ibid para 303.

976 Ibid para 310.

977 *The Tongaat-Hulett Group Limited and Transvaal Suiker Beperk, Middenen Ontwikkeling (Pty) Ltd, Senteeko (Edms) Bpk, New Komati Sugar Miller's Partnership, TSB Bestuursdienste*, Competition Tribunal case no: 83/LM/Jul00, 27 November 2000.

978 Ibid paras 3-5.

979 Ibid paras 15-16.

tion of the sugar industry and their inability to achieve economies of scale. THG on its part sought to expand and lower production costs.[980]

The Commission's analysis of the proposed merger had revealed that it would result in concentration levels beyond the accepted thresholds even by the standards used in other major jurisdictions. This would still be the case even if the relevant market were defined to be not just South Africa but the Southern African Customs Union as the merging parties had proposed it should be.[981] On the basis of the finding that the merger would impede potential competition and that there was insufficient countervailing buyer power, the Tribunal concluded that the merger would confer on the parties great market power, which would serve to substantially lessen competition in the South African market for refined white sugar.[982] The pro-competitive benefits were deemed to be insufficient to offset the proposed merger's negative effect.

The parties had as well asserted that the merger would enhance the international competitiveness of the South African sugar industry especially in terms of cost competitiveness. The Tribunal however noted that South Africa was already a low cost producer. The parties had as well argued that the merger would improve scale economies but the data did not support this argument. The Tribunal concurred with the Commission's perspective that THG and TSB both had a sizable international presence.[983] The Tribunal did not discount the view that in some instances scale economies could support an argument that domestic dominance could facilitate international competitiveness. However, in the absence of specific data in support of such a view, the Tribunal tends towards a presumption that active domestic competition is better for international competitiveness.[984]

One of the reasons the Tribunal did not accept the parties' argument on scale economies was the fact that there was no evidence indicating that the merger would also improve the productive efficiency by increasing productive capacity. The Tribunal has however accepted a public interest defense of international competitiveness where it was shown that the merger would improve cost competitiveness through increased production capacity. This was one of the reasons put forward by the Department of

980 Ibid paras 8-9.
981 Ibid paras 58-59.
982 Ibid paras 85, 95-96.
983 Ibid para 115.
984 Ibid para 116.

Trade and Industry in support of the otherwise anti-competitive *Iscor and Saldana* merger.

3.2.8.1.5 National Security

Although not included in the list of public interest factors in section 12A of the SA Competition Act, there is a requirement for the president to constitute a committee to look into whether a merger involving a foreign acquiring firm is likely to have an adverse effect on the national security interests of the country.[985] A foreign acquiring firm will therefore be required to notify this committee in addition to notifying the Commission.[986]

The president is required to identify and publish a list of national security interests touching on markets, industries, goods or services, sectors or regions in respect of which such a merger involving a foreign acquiring firm is to be notified.[987] There is no definition in the SA Competition Act of what constitutes a national security interest. However, the factors to be considered in determining what constitutes a national security interest include[988]:

i) South Africa's defence capabilities and interests;
ii) the use or transfer of sensitive technology or knowhow outside of South Africa;
iii) the security of infrastructure, including processes, systems, facilities, technologies, networks, assets and services essential to the health, safety, security or economic wellbeing of citizens and the effective functioning of government;
iv) the supply of critical goods or services to citizens, or the supply of goods or services to government;
v) enabling foreign surveillance or espionage, or hinder current or future intelligence or law enforcement operations;
vi) South Africa's international interests, including foreign relationships;

---

985 This is one of the changes that were introduced into the SA Competition Act via the Competition Amendment Act, 2018 (Act No. 18 of 2018).

986 SA Competition Act s 18A ss 6.

987 SA Competition Act s 18A ss 3.

988 SA Competition Act s 18A ss 4.

vii) enabling or facilitating the activities of illicit actors, such as terrorists, terrorist organisations or organised crime; and

viii) the economic and social stability of the Republic.

3.2.8.2 The ESA Jurisdictions

3.2.8.2.1 Public Interest in the Laws

With the exception of Seychelles and Mauritius, all the other jurisdictions in focus, including COMESA, incorporate public interest considerations into their substantial analysis. There are a few differences in the manner in which the public interest is expressed statutorily, but the factors that are taken into account tend to be similar across the board.

In Zimbabwe, for instance, public interest is incorporated very broadly. The statutory formulation is such that even the competition tests are considered from a public interest perspective. Therefore, a merger is considered to be contrary to the public interest, if it will result in a substantial lessening of competition or lead to the creation of a monopoly situation that would be contrary to the public interest. A monopoly situation that would be contrary to the public interest is further analysed on the basis of various factors, a number of which are focused on efficiencies which would be gained for the benefit of the wider public. Public interest factors such as the effect of the monopoly on employment and on exports or trade are also considered.[989]

The balancing of the pro-competitive benefits of a merger in order to determine whether they outweigh anti-competitive harm is a factor that is taken into account in more or less all jurisdictions, including the developed countries. Although theoretically this balancing act, as can be said of merger regulation, constitutes a consideration of the welfare of the public, it is in most instances from the perspective of the substantial analysis not included as a specific public interest factor. It is regarded as an overall balancing test. In respect of the jurisdictions in focus the competition statues of Seychelles, COMESA, Malawi and Mauritius incorporate it as an overall balancing measure.[990] In the Zambia and Botswana statutes,

989 Zimbabwe Competition Act ss 32 sub-s 4 and 32 sub-s 5.

990 Seychelles Competition Act s 23 sub-s 2(a); COMESA Competition Regulations art 26(1); Malawi Competition Act s 38 sub-s 2; Mauritius Competition Act s 50 sub-s 4.

the balancing test is specifically categorised as one of the public interest considerations. In Tanzania it is included, alongside other public interest elements, as a factor to be considered in determining whether the merger will avail benefits to the public.[991]

The Kenya and Namibia statutes do not draw a clear line between the public interest factors and the competition test. They incorporate a general list of factors, comprising both the competition as well as public interest factors, which are taken into consideration by the authority. This list includes the balancing test.[992]

The public interest factors that are common among the jurisdictions include some specific objectives such as the effect of the merger on[993]:

(i) employment;
(ii) a particular industrial sector or region;
(iii) the ability of national industries to compete internationally;
(iv) the ability of small or medium sized enterprises to compete on any market (or the ability of firms owned by historically disadvantaged persons to access or compete in any market) and
(v) export earnings and trade.

These factors are the same as those taken into account in South Africa. Some unique considerations are also included such as Tanzania's consideration of environmental impact.

Given the fact that public interest can be subject to very broad interpretation, one has to consider whether these factors, from a legislative construction perspective, constitute a non-exhaustive list. South Africa for instance makes it clear that its list of factors, i.e. the five pillars of public interest, is a closed list.[994] However, the statutory wording used by a number of the jurisdictions indicates that the list of public interest factors is non-exhaustive and the authority therefore has the discretion to take into consideration any other factors deemed to touch upon the public interest. The wording in the Botswana, Kenya, Namibia and Zambia statutes specifically provides that the authority is permitted to consider any factors it

---

991 Zambia Competition Act s 31(a); Tanzania Competition Act s 13 sub-s 1(b)(vi); Botswana Competition Act s 59 sub-s 2(a).

992 Kenya Competition Act s 46 sub-s 2(c); Namibia Competition Act s 47 sub-s 2(c).

993 Zimbabwe Competition Act s 32 sub-s 5; Malawi Competition Act s 38 sub-s 1; Zambia Competition Act s 31; Tanzania Competition Act s 13sub-s 1(b)(vi); Botswana Competition Act s 59 sub-s 2; Kenya Competition Act s 46 sub-s 2(c); Namibia Competition Act s 47 sub-s 2.

994 See ch 3.2.8.

considers to touch on public interest, over and above those specifically listed in the statute.

The Botswana and Namibia merger guidelines specify that the list of factors is neither exclusive nor prescriptive but rather indicative of what is to be taken into consideration.[995] Namibia further explains in its merger guidelines that although the factors should not be regarded as limitless and the Commission will ordinarily limit itself to the list of factors, it is still hard to categorise them as limited. The same view is expressed in the Botswana merger guidelines.[996] The Zambia merger guidelines specify that although the main public interest focus will be on efficiencies, effect on employment and failing firm scenarios, the Commission will still consider *unspecified general issues.* The unspecified general issues will however not be decisive for the final determination.[997]

The wording in the Zimbabwe, Malawi and Tanzania statues is more conservative and open to interpretation as being restricted to the factors outlined. In addition, Malawi and Tanzania do not list the factors as public interest factors per se but as part of a general list of factors to be taken into consideration in determining whether the merger will be beneficial to the public or advantageous to the country. The factors are not framed from the perspective of whether or not they will determine whether the merger will be approved or not.[998]

A distinguishing factor between the ESA countries and South Africa is that none of the ESA countries currently include national security interests as part of the merger regulation considerations.

COMESA takes a very broad approach to the consideration of public interest factors. The specific public interest factors to be taken into account are not listed. Rather, the Commission is mandated to take account of all matters it considers relevant with due regard to broad factors touching on maintenance of competition, efficiency and safeguarding all the market participants.[999]

995 Botswana Merger Guidelines para 7.3; Namibia Merger Guidelines para 13.4.
996 Namibia Merger Guidelines para 13.4; Botswana Merger Guidelines para 7.3.
997 Zambia Merger Guidelines paras 95-102.
998 Op. Cit. n 983.
999 COMESA Competition Regulations art 26(4).

3.2.8.2.2 Implications of the public interest considerations

The inclusion of public interest considerations into the substantial analysis means that proposed transactions that have already been subjected to the competition tests may still liable to be prohibited or approved on account of the public interest test, irrespective of the outcome of the competition analysis. This is the position adopted not only by South Africa but a number of the other jurisdictions.

The Botswana merger guidelines specify that, 'after considering the SLC and dominance test, the CA may also determine whether a merger can or cannot be justified on public interest grounds... The implication of the consideration of issues that impact on public interest is that a transaction with no anti-competitive consequences may be prohibited or approved subject to certain conditions, where the CA is of the view that it is likely to have an adverse effect on public interest'.[1000]

The Namibia merger guidelines also adopt this approach.[1001]

The Zambia merger guidelines also espouse the view that, 'the Act states that a benefit to the public could "outweigh any detriment attributable to a substantial lessening of competition" and it follows that an otherwise pro-competitive merger could be prohibited - or in both cases approved with appropriate remedies in place.'[1002]

The Kenya merger guidelines as well provide that, 'the Authority will conduct a competitive effects assessment to establish whether or not the merger is likely to prevent or lessen competition in the post-merger market. Then the Authority will assess whether or not the merger will have a substantial negative effect on public interest. The logical outcome of such an assessment can be that a merger that raises no concerns about its competitive effect can be prohibited on public interest grounds and a merger that does raise concerns because it is likely to lead to anticompetitive effects can be allowed on public interest grounds.'[1003]

The COMESA merger guidelines do not elaborate on the public interest approach. However, the wording of article 26 of the COMESA Competition Regulations leaves no doubt that a pro or anti-competitive merger will also be subjected to a public interest assessment which will determine whether it will be approved or prohibited.

1000 Botswana Merger Guidelines paras 7.1-7.2.
1001 Namibia Merger Guidelines paras. 13.1 and 13.3.
1002 Zambia Merger Guidelines para. 92.
1003 Kenya Merger Guidelines para 218.

Zimbabwe has adopted an over-arching public interest consideration. The review of mergers is therefore always with regard to the effect on public interest. Malawi and Tanzania take into consideration public interest only in respect of assessing the benefits of a merger.

Other than the inclusion by some of the jurisdictions of a brief guide in their merger guidelines as to the application of public interest considerations, none have published (in a similar way to South Africa) substantive public interest guidelines. Nonetheless some procedural similarities can be identified between the jurisdictions. The Zambia merger guidelines for instance provide that only public interest factors which are 'merger-specific and have a timely, likely and substantial impact on social welfare and/or economic development' will be given substantial consideration. This is similar to the five-step analytical approach outlined in the South Africa public interest guidelines. The Kenya merger guidelines also underline the need for merger specificity.[1004]

The Kenya merger guidelines also highlight various specific objectives such as fast-tracking mergers involving small and medium enterprises in order to improve their ability to enter into and competitively participate in the market. Also subjecting to greater scrutiny mergers which could affect vulnerable members of society (e.g. those concerning utilities) and those which have an effect on media plurality for the purpose of ensuring there is no control and manipulation of the media.[1005]

3.2.8.2.3 Public Interest in merger cases

A number of the case studies considered in the analysis of the competition tests reveal that public interest considerations often figure into the decision-making. In some instances the public interest determinations are imposed on the parties in the form of conditions subject to which transactions are approved. There are also some cases which raised competition concerns but were approved on the basis of the substantial public interest benefits that they would avail. None of the cases considered were however prohibited purely on the basis of public interest considerations.

1004 Zambia Merger Guidelines para. 93; South Africa Public Interest Guidelines para 6.1; Kenya Merger Guidelines para 217.

1005 Kenya Merger Guidelines paras 211-214.

In the *Helios*[1006] merger in Tanzania we note that the authority took into consideration the public interest benefits set out in the statute. This included the fact that through the merger there would be a reduction in the telecommunications masts put up which would impact the environment positively. Also, the fact that there would be increased efficiency, job creation, technical progress and increased foreign direct investment augured well for the transaction. However none of these factors were conditions for the approval. The authority already determined that the merger was not likely to lead to a creation or strengthening of a dominant position.

In the *Colas*[1007] case, the Namibia authority conducted a public interest analysis to determine whether to approve an anti-competitive merger. It however emerged that the merger would have been detrimental to historically disadvantaged smaller contractors, which would lead to job losses, in addition to not contributing any countervailing pro-competitive benefits. The merger had already been found likely to result in a substantial lessening of competition and was therefore prohibited owing to the absence of public interest benefits.

In the *Renaissance*[1008] merger in Zimbabwe we see that the authority from a public interest perspective took into account the fact that it was a failing firm scenario and the merger would have prevented job losses. In the *Makro* merger the Zimbabwe authority approved the merger on account of public interest commitments by the parties to ensure that employees and local suppliers would be protected.

In a merger involving an acquisition of *Petrologistics*, a Botswana company involved in liquid fuel distribution by *Grindrod Mauritius*, a Mauritian logistics company, the approval was hinged on the implementation by Grindrod of initiatives that would enable the locals or locally-owned companies in Botswana to effectively penetrate the fuel distribution market. This is irrespective of the fact that the merger was found to raise no competition concerns. Similar conditions were imposed by the Botswana authority in respect of helping to develop the local dairy industry in the merger between *Clover SA* and *Clover Botswana*. In the proposed merger between *Vivo Energy Holdings* and *Shell Botswana*, the Botswana authority

---

1006 *Helios Towers Tanzania Infraco Limited (HTT) & Millicom International Cellular (MIC) Tanzania Limited*, cap 3.2.6.

1007 *Colas South Africa (Pty) Ltd (Colas South Africa) & The Roads Contractor Company Ltd (RCC) and Guinea Fowl Investments Seventeen (Pty) Ltd (Guinea)*, cap 3.2.6.

1008 *Renaissance Merchant Bank Limited (Renaissance) & National Social Security Authority (NSSA)*, cap 3.2.6.

took into account the unemployment levels in the country and approved the merger subject to a commitment by the parties that the employment levels would not be affected negatively as well as a commitment to inject capital for aspiring entrepreneurs and downstream traders. In this merger as well there was no threat to competition. There are indeed a number of transactions in Botswana whose approval was conditional on the effect on employment or on the incorporation of local entities and citizens, irrespective of the fact that no serious competition concerns arose.[1009]

The COMESA Competition Commission has also factored public interest into its decisions. In the *PPC International*[1010] decision we note that the Commission took into consideration the effect of the merger on foreign investment, economic development as well as infrastructure and industrial needs within Rwanda and the Common Market as a whole. In this instance however the Commission had already determined that there would be no negative effect on competition within the Common Market. In the *CFR*[1011] merger the Commission also considered the positive impact that technology improvement will have on enhancing the consumer welfare in the Common Market. However, even in this case the merger had already passed the competition analysis. Although public interest considerations are integral to the substantial analysis, so far public interest has not played a decisive role in the COMESA decision making. Looking at the statistics, COMESA indicates that so far there has been no single merger that has been prohibited. The vast majority of mergers have been approved unconditionally and only a handful have been approved subject to conditions.

One may say that there is generally a higher likelihood or tendency of a merger that has negative public interest consequences but which does not affect competition being approved subject to public interest conditions. Given that prohibition of mergers seldom happens, then it would likewise be a rare occurrence for a merger to be prohibited on public interest grounds. The public interest benefits would likewise need to be very significant in order to save an otherwise anti-competitive merger. From this perspective one may say that transacting parties need not worry too much about public interest. This however does not take away from the uncertainty occasioned by very widely crafted public interest provisions, more so when they constitute part of the substantial merger analysis.

1009 Botswana Annual Report 2012/2013 18 et seq.
1010 Op. cit. n 827.
1011 Op. cit. n 832.

3.2.9 Remedies and Enforcement

3.2.9.1 Negotiated Solutions

In cases where a merger raises competition law concerns, competition authorities would seek to achieve an agreement with the merger parties where there is a window open for steps to be taken by the parties to prevent the proposed merger from having a negative effect on competition. This usually entails commitments or undertakings made by the parties and conditions imposed by the competition authorities to remedy potential anticompetitive effects. This is indeed a nod to the fact that mergers may result in benefits being passed on to consumers. Therefore, where there is an opportunity to remedy the anticompetitive aspects of a merger, it should be allowed to proceed.[1012]

The European Commission relies on commitments made by the parties and does not unilaterally impose conditions. The reasoning is that the information necessary to determine the effectiveness of the commitments is with the parties. Therefore, where the European Commission determines that a modification of the proposed transaction by the parties would alleviate the competition concerns, it is upon the parties to propose remedies that will be sufficient to address these concerns.[1013] The European Commission thereafter assesses the proposed modifications and if satisfied that they are indeed sufficient to eliminate the concerns, it will approve the transaction subject to these modifications.[1014]

1012 See FTC, 'Negotiating Merger Remedies: Statement of the Bureau of Competition of the Federal Trade Commission' (2012), 4 <https://www.ftc.gov/system/files/attachments/negotiating-merger-remedies/merger-remediesstmt.pdf> accessed 6 September 2019 (FTC Remedies Statement). See also DOJ, 'Antitrust Division Policy Guide to Merger Remedies' (2011), 1 <https://www.justice.gov/sites/default/files/atr/legacy/2011/06/17/272350.pdf> accessed 6 September 2019 (DOJ Remedies Guide); Merger Remedies: Competition Commission Guidelines (cc8, 2008) (UK Remedies Guidance) para 1.14.; See also UK Enterprise Act s 30 which requires the CMA to have regard to relevant customer benefits such as lower prices, higher quality and greater choice when assessing merger remedies.

1013 See Commission Notice on remedies acceptable under Council Regulation (EC) No 139/2004 and under Commission Regulation (EC) No 802/2004 [2008] OJ C267/01 (EU Remedies Notice) para 6; See also EU Merger Regulation art 6(2) and 8(2).

1014 EU Remedies Notice paras 7-8.

The FTC and the DOJ similarly consider remedy proposals from the parties in those cases where they find that appropriately tailored remedies may sufficiently address competition concerns. The staff of the FTC and the DOJ will engage the parties to the transaction in negotiations in order to come to an appropriate settlement.[1015] The FTC and the DOJ cannot by themselves order the implementation of the negotiated settlement. They are required to initiate a court process whereby the settlement will be part of a court decision or consent decree. The DOJ also employs a 'fix-it-first' policy where the merger parties are given the opportunity to remedy the situation pre-consummation, thus negating the need for the DOJ to file a case.[1016]

Although the Competition Commission and the Competition Tribunal of South Africa do not provide specific guidelines on remedies, their decisions indicate that they do rely on undertakings or remedy offers made by the parties when crafting their conditional approvals.[1017] They may also engage in negotiations in an effort to come up with the most suitable remedy.[1018] Unlike the European Union, however, the South Africa authorities may readily impose conditions or issue orders especially where public interest is concerned.[1019] In such cases the parties are faced with the choice of either accepting the conditions or facing a prohibition.[1020]

1015 FTC Remedies Statement 4. The ultimate decision on whether the terms of a proposed settlement are satisfactory lies in a majority vote by the FTC Commissioners; DOJ Remedies Guide 2.

1016 DOJ Remedies Guide 22-25; For discussion see Broder (n 520) para 6.12(A).

1017 In *AgriGroupe/AFGRI* Competition Tribunal case no. 017939 (2014) for instance, an agreement by the merging parties where they committed not to undertake any retrenchments, not to relocate the offices outside of South Africa for a given duration, in addition to providing funding to emerging farmers and assistance to the farmers and relevant government departments was regarded by the Tribunal as sufficient to address the public interest concerns that had been raised.

1018 Bellis (2014) 745.

1019 See SA Competition Act s 58. The Tribunal may issue an order in respect of divestiture.

1020 In the *Adcock/BB Investment* merger the parties had argued that various retrenchments that would ensue from the merger were not merger-specific. The Commission however recommended to the Tribunal an approval subject to a limit on the number of retrenchments. The Tribunal however imposed a condition prohibiting any retrenchments for a one-year time period. In the *Ferro/Arkema* merger the Tribunal similarly a imposed condition barring retrenchment of employees for a certain time period. (see http://www.comptri

In the United Kingdom, the CMA also engages in negotiations with the parties based on proposals made by the parties to remedy anticompetitive effects.[1021] The CMA however may come up with possible remedies in the course of its investigation where it reaches a provisional finding that a proposed merger may result in a significant lessening of competition.[1022] In such a case the parties' proposals and the CMA's provisional findings would constitute the basis of remedy discussions. Once a final decision has been made by the CMA regarding remedies, the CMA will require an undertaking from the merging parties in respect of the implementation of the remedies.[1023] Where an undertaking from the parties is not forthcoming, the CMA has the power to impose an order in respect of the implementation of remedies.[1024]

The Kenyan authority as well engages the merging parties in consultations in respect of remedies and other conditions in a bid to ensure the benefits of the merger can be realised. The ultimate decision on the conditions and their implementation naturally lies with the authority.[1025] The Competition Commission of Mauritius also seeks to engage parties in remedy design in order to achieve the most appropriate remedies, while still reserving the right to impose remedies.[1026] The Zimbabwe Competition Act also makes provision for negotiations to be undertaken between the Commission and the parties in a bid to *inter alia* 'alter' a merger situation that exists or may come into existence.[1027]

The Zambia merger guidelines also indicate that the parties will be given a chance to make representations before any directions are given by the Commission in respect of remedies. There is no indication whether the Commission will actively engage the parties in consultations in the determination of suitable remedies.[1028]

---

b.co.za/publications/press-releases/tribunal-approves-adcock-bb-investment-merger-with-employment-conditions/ and http://www.comptrib.co.za/publications/press-releases/tribunal-approves-ferro-arkema-merger-with-pricing-and-divestiture-conditions/) accessed 6 November 2018.

1021 UK Enterprise Act s 82; UK Procedural Guidance para 14.

1022 UK Remedies Guidance paras 1.21-1.24.

1023 UK Enterprise Act s 82; UK Remedies Guidance paras 1.26-1.27.

1024 UK Enterprise Act s 83; UK Procedural Guidance para 14.1; UK Remedies Guidance paras 1.26-1.30.

1025 Kenya Merger Guidelines paras 227 et seq.

1026 Mauritius Merger Guidelines paras 3.2 et seq.

1027 Zimbabwe Competition Act s 30.

1028 Zambia Merger Guidelines para 105; Zambia Competition Act s 59.

The Seychelles remedy guidelines point to a largely one-sided affair where the Commission designs and ensures the implementation of the remedies without broadly engaging the parties in consultations.[1029] The Botswana Competition Act also provides for the issuance of directions by the Commission to remedy, mitigate or prevent adverse effects of a merger. There is no provision for consultations with the parties. In the case of abuse of dominance however there is provision for the parties to express their views before any remedies are applied. The Botswana merger guidelines are however silent on remedies, making mere reference to the statute.[1030]

The COMESA Regulations and merger guidelines do not provide any information on the Commission's approach to remedies. This is as well the case with Namibia, Tanzania and Malawi.

Merger remedies are classified into two main categories; structural and behavioural.[1031]

3.2.9.2 Structural Remedies

Structural remedies are aimed at preventing the negative effects of a proposed merger on the structure of the market.[1032] The remedies are therefore directed at the structure of the merging parties. Structural remedies are mostly employed when dealing with horizontal mergers where they are regarded as particularly suited to address the possibility of the merging party obtaining excess market power.[1033] Structural remedies are one-off. They therefore do not require regular compliance monitoring.[1034] The most

---

1029 Fair Trading Commission of Seychelles: Penalties and Remedies 8 et seq (Seychelles Remedy Guidelines); Seychelles Competition Act s 42.

1030 Botswana Competition Act s 46 and s 60; Botswana Merger Guidelines para 2.5.

1031 ICN, Merger Remedies Review Project (Bonn, 2005) <http://www.internationalcompetitionnetwork.org/uploads/library/doc323.pdf > accessed 6 September 2019 (ICN Remedies Report) para 3.6.

1032 ICN Remedies Report para 3.6.

1033 OECD, Remedies in Merger Cases (DAF/COMP(2011)13) <http://www.oecd.org/daf/competition/RemediesinMergerCases2011.pdf> accessed 6 September 2019 (OECD Remedies Study) 12.

1034 See for instance Stephen Davies and Bruce Lyons, *Mergers and Merger Remedies in the EU: Assessing the Consequences for Competition* (Edward Elgar 2007) 41-43; Dorte Hoeg, *European Merger Remedies: Law and Policy* (Hart Publishing 2014). Structural remedies result in lasting on-going effects on the relevant market

commonly adopted structural remedy is divestiture. This entails the sale of assets or other parts of the business to third parties. Such divestitures may consequently lead to the creation of an additional competitive force or the bolstering of an already existing competitor.[1035]

Most experienced competition authorities express a preference for structural remedies particularly divestiture. The European Commission has indeed expressed the opinion that structural remedies are preferable because they have a durable effect and do not require medium or long-term monitoring.[1036] The European Commission further opines that divestitures are the best means to address horizontal overlap concerns, in addition to the fact that they may also deal with vertical and conglomerate issues.[1037]

The FTC and the DOJ have also expressed preference for structural remedies in the form of divestiture. The FTC points out that a proposal by the merging parties to divest a business unit will usually speed up a settlement. The DOJ reiterates the courts view in *United States v. E.I. du Pont de Nemours* that divestiture is 'simple, relatively easy to administer and sure' to preserve competition.[1038]

The position in the United Kingdom is likewise similar with the CMA expressing the view that structural remedies are preferable, terming them as 'likely to deal with an SLC and its resulting adverse effects directly and comprehensively at source by restoring rivalry' in addition to not requiring monitoring and enforcement once they have been implemented.

Proposals by the merging parties that incorporate structural remedies have therefore enjoyed the highest success rates in these three jurisdictions.

The South African authorities also employ structural remedies, chief among them divestiture.[1039] However, unlike the United States, the European Union and the United Kingdom, the South African competition authorities have shown a preference for behavioural remedies even in horizontal merger cases. A statistical analysis of the merger remedies practice

---

structure hence according a clean-break between the merging parties and the purchaser of the disposed of assets or business parts.

1035 ICN Remedies Report para 3.8.

1036 EU Remedies Notice para 15.

1037 EU Remedies Notice paras 17, 22.

1038 FTC Remedies Statement 5; DOJ Remedies Guide 6; See also generally FTC, 'A Study of the Commission's Divestiture Process' (1999) <https://www.ftc.gov/sites/default/files/attachments/merger-review/divestiture.pdf> accessed 6 September 2019.

1039 SA Competition Act s 60; OECD Remedies Study 268.

indicated that even in horizontal mergers, the use of behavioural remedies is still more prevalent than the use of structural remedies.[1040]

3.2.9.3 Behavioural Remedies

Behavioural or conduct remedies are targeted at the future conduct of the merging parties.[1041] A behavioural remedy would therefore require the merged entity to meet certain obligations or refrain from taking a certain course of action. Behavioural remedies are regarded as ideal in vertical and conglomerate mergers, especially in those instances where the risk of market foreclosure is high.[1042] Unlike the one-off nature of structural remedies, behavioural remedies require continuous monitoring to ensure that the merged entity adheres to the commitments.[1043]

A number of jurisdictions express their reluctance to accept behavioural remedies on their own mainly due to the fact that they require ongoing monitoring. They are hence costly and difficult to enforce. The European Commission for instance states that behavioural remedies 'may be acceptable only exceptionally in very specific circumstances'. They will be accepted if they can be implemented and monitored effectively and if they do not distort competition.[1044] The benchmark is that the remedies need to be as efficient and effective as divestitures.[1045] Some of the key remedies employed include access commitments (such as to infrastructure or key technology). The standard for these remedies is that they should lead to actual and sufficient entry of new competitors and the entry should be timely and likely.[1046]

The United Kingdom has also expressed reluctance to rely on behavioural remedies on the basis of the view that they may not sufficiently address the significant lessening of competition and may occasion market outcome distortions, on top of the costly monitoring and enforcement re-

1040 See Avias Ngwenya and Genna Robb, 'Theory and practice in the use of merger remedies: considering South African experience' <http://www.compcom.co.za/wp-content/uploads/2014/09/NgwenyaRobbMerger-Remedies.pdf> accessed 6 September 2019.
1041 ICN Remedies Report para 3.6.
1042 OECD Remedies Study 12.
1043 OECD Remedies Study 11.
1044 EU Remedies Notice para 17.
1045 EU Remedies Notice para 61; OECD Remedies Study 236.
1046 OECD Remedies Study 237.

quirements.[1047] Behavioural remedies are therefore limited to cases where structural remedies are not workable or the negative effects on competition are expected to be of short duration or where they will ensure that the benefits of the merger will be preserved.[1048] The remedies include enabling measures such as access and supply commitments and those aimed at controlling outcomes such as price caps.[1049]

Although the US agencies also express a preference for structural remedies, both the FTC and the DOJ readily employ behavioural remedies. The agencies also note the effectiveness of behavioural remedies in dealing with vertical cases, though they may also be employed in certain horizontal cases.[1050] These behavioural remedies include non-discrimination requirements, mandatory licensing, transparency, anti-retaliation provisions, and prohibitions on certain contracting practices.[1051]

South Africa's preference towards behavioural remedies becomes apparent especially when looking at public interest cases. Undertakings by merging parties not to terminate employees, obligations to train employees or moratoriums on retrenchment are often required in cases where employment is at risk. Other remedies include supply conditions where foreclosure looms large, as well as access and interoperability conditions.[1052]

In reality however some cases are not clear-cut. The authorities in the United States, South Africa and the United Kingdom would in certain instances normally require an optimal mix of both structural and behavioural remedies. Where structural remedies are adopted, they may also require some behavioural remedies to make them fully effective. In such cases therefore, the behavioural remedies play a supportive role.[1053]

3.2.9.4 The ESA Remedies Approach

The Kenya Competition Authority does not express any preference when it comes to the two types of remedies. Its preferred approach is one that involves a mix of structural and behavioural remedies, but ultimately tak-

1047 UK Remedies Guidance para 2.14.
1048 UK Remedies Guidance para 4.1.
1049 UK Remedies Guidance para 4.
1050 FTC Remedies Statement 5; DOJ Remedies Guide 12-13.
1051 DOJ Remedies Guide 13.
1052 OECD Remedies Study 269.
1053 DOJ Remedies Guide 18-19; UK Remedies Guidance paras 2.15-2.21; OECD Remedies Study 207, 270.

ing a case by case approach. The Authority also takes cognisance of the fact that certain remedies, presumably behavioural, are costly in terms of implementation and monitoring. Divestiture is naturally the preferred structural remedy. Public interest as well plays a key role in the choice of remedy. Therefore, depending on the case in question, public interest remedies revolving around factors such as employment and employee training, support of local sectors will take centre stage. This was for instance the concern in the *Buzeki* case where the Kenya Competition Authority approved the merger on condition that 85% of the employees of the acquired firm would be retained.[1054]

The Zambia Commission as well does not clearly express any preference for one type of remedy over the other. However, if the wording of the merger guidelines is to be strictly interpreted, the imperative 'will use' in respect of structural remedies and 'may also use' in respect of behavioural remedies may indicate a preference for structural remedies. There is as well the acknowledgement that a mix may be involved depending on the case in question.[1055]

The Seychelles Commission also prefers to adopt a combination of remedies. In addition to structural and behavioural remedies, the Commission also categorises advocacy as a possible remedy. This is more of a policy approach that is not directed at the parties but rather at government policies. The Commission would in this case recommend the modification or removal of policies which it finds to be contributing to the competition challenges arising out of its investigations. Such a remedy is however likely not targeted at merger regulation. When choosing behavioural remedies, the Commission considers factors such as their relative feasibility over structural remedies, particularly where the anticompetitive effects are expected to be short term or where structural remedies may eliminate benefits that may have been passed to consumers. The Commission recognises the risks and challenges entailed in both structural and behavioural remedies, principally the need for ongoing monitoring for behavioural remedies or the lack of a purchaser, customer or staff losses if a structural remedy such as divestiture is adopted.[1056]

The Mauritius Commission as well does not express any preference for one type of remedy over the other. The Commission merely points out broadly its preference for remedies that promote and protect compe-

1054 Kenya Merger Guidelines 53 et seq.
1055 Zimbabwe Merger Guidelines para 104.
1056 Seychelles Remedy Guidelines 11 et seq.

tition rather than just reducing the effects of insufficient competition. They however similarly recognise the challenges posed by choosing either behavioural or structural remedies. The main structural remedy, short of blocking the transaction, is as well divestiture. This was for instance the case in the *Holcim and Lafarge* case where a divestiture undertaking by the merging firms addressed the Commission's concerns regarding substantial lessening of competition post-merger. Behavioural remedies naturally depend on the case in question. The Commission highlights measures such as price controls or enabling/access measures that help to ease entry for other market participants. Like Seychelles, the Mauritius Commission as well recognises recommendations to government as a type of soft remedy.[1057]

The Zimbabwe Competition Act provides for orders that the Commission may make entailing a mix of both structural and behavioural remedies but leaving the Commission with discretion to determine the most suitable remedy on a case by case basis. Again, no preference for any type of remedy is expressed.[1058] There is however no separate guideline published.

3.2.9.5 Enforcement

The European Commission has the power to carry out various enforcement actions under the EU Merger Regulations. For instance, failure to notify a notifiable merger as well as implementing it prior to notification or implementing a prohibited merger could result in serious consequences for the parties concerned. In the worst-case scenario, the European Commission may require the dissolution of the merger or the disposal of shares or assets acquired. Unlike the United States, the European Commission cannot challenge a consummated merger which was not notifiable under the EU Merger Regulations.[1059]

Where the dissolution is not possible the Commission will seek other restorative measures.[1060] The Commission may also impose a fine of up to

---

1057 Mauritius Remedy Guidelines 14 et seq.

1058 Zimbabwe Competition Act s 31.

1059 OECD, Investigations of Consummated and Non-notifiable Mergers: European Union DAF/COMP/WP3/WD(2014)19, paras 7-13 <http://ec.europa.eu/competition/international/multilateral/2014_feb_mergers_investigations_en.pdf> accessed 6 September 2019.

1060 EU Merger Regulation art 8(4).

10 percent of the aggregate turnover of the undertakings in question where there is a failure to notify a notifiable transaction, an implementation of a prohibited merger or a failure to comply with imposed conditions. Even the provision of wrong or misleading information may attract a fine of up to one percent of the aggregate turnover of the undertakings concerned.[1061]

Unlike the Commission, the DOJ and the FTC themselves do not have the power to carry out enforcement. Where the parties seek to proceed with a transaction that may lead to a substantial lessening of competition or that violates the Clayton Act requirements, then the agencies need to approach the court to obtain an injunction.[1062] The agencies may additionally seek other civil penalties of up to USD 16,000 for reporting violations.[1063] If parties fail to comply substantially with notification requirements or with a request for additional documents or information, the DOJ or the FTC need to apply to the court for compliance orders or any other equitable relief the court deems fit.[1064] Already consummated mergers would still be subject to the same remedies sought for reportable mergers, i.e. divestiture or civil penalties where they were notifiable and raise substantial competition law concerns.[1065]

In most cases, once the court issues an injunction, the parties abandon the merger owing to the long process involved with a full trial. Where the parties abandon the merger, the DOJ usually seeks no further relief. However, the FTC may in some cases institute further administrative proceedings where they would for instance require the parties to notify a future transaction even where it doesn't fall within its jurisdiction under the HSR Act[1066]

In respect of South Africa, the Commission and the Tribunal are empowered to issue decisions, judgments and orders which have the same force as a court order.[1067] The Tribunal may issue orders preventing the

---

1061 EU Merger Regulation art 14.

1062 Clayton Act s 7 sub-s a(f); Broder (n 520) 173.

1063 Clayton Act s 7 sub-s a(g); See also FTC, A Brief Overview of the Federal Trade Commission's Investigative and Law Enforcement Authority (July 2008) <https://www.ftc.gov/about-ftc/what-we-do/enforcement-authority> accessed 6 September 2019.

1064 Clayton Act s 7a sub-s g(2).

1065 OECD, Investigations of Consummated and Non-notifiable Mergers: United States para 18.

1066 Broder (2012) 173-174.

1067 SA Competition Act s 64 sub-s 1.

implementation of a merger contrary to the SA Competition Act.[1068] Where a merger has been implemented in contravention of the SA Competition Act, whether by failure to notify where there is an obligation to notify or contrary to a conditional approval or a prohibition may be met with administrative fines or in the worst case scenario an order for divestiture.[1069] The administrative penalty imposed by the Tribunal however should not be more than 10% of the firm's turnover in and exports from South Africa.[1070] The Tribunal may also impose an administrative penalty where an order of the Commission, the Tribunal itself or the Appeal Court has not been complied with.[1071] If an administrative penalty imposed by the Tribunal has not been complied with, the Commission may institute court proceedings within a three year timeline to recover the administrative penalty.[1072]

Given that notification in the United Kingdom is voluntary there is no penalty for failing to notify. However, where there is a reference to a phase two investigation or the CMA has taken interim action or has made certain orders, failure to comply may be met with various monetary penalties as well as possible civil proceedings. Provision of false or misleading information may be treated as a criminal offence leading to fines or possible imprisonment.[1073]

The enforcement measures in the ESA jurisdictions indicate broad similarity to the approach in the United States, the European Union and South Africa. Where a merger has been implemented in contravention of the Act, the approach of the Botswana Authority is first to issue directions to stop the parties from taking any further steps and requiring the submission of information on the merger. This may in the worst case lead to a termination of the transaction upon investigation. The Authority must however seek a court order requiring the parties to make good a default. Non-compliance may as well constitute an offence attracting penalties such as fines and even imprisonment.[1074]

In Kenya and Malawi, the implementation without notification of a notifiable merger or the general failure to comply with an order or other statutory requirements is also an offence which may lead to fines and

1068 SA Competition Act s 27 sub-s 1(d).
1069 SA Competition Act ss 59-60; SA Commission Rules rule 34.
1070 SA Competition Act s 59 sub-s 2.
1071 SA Competition Act s 59 sub-s 1(c)
1072 SA Competition Act s 64 sub-ss 2 and 3.
1073 UK Procedural Guidance para 7.
1074 Botswana Competition Act ss 63-64 and s 76.

imprisonment. The imposition of the penalties or enforcement of orders is however under the courts' jurisdiction. This is already keeping in mind that the statutes also provide that qualifying mergers implemented without meeting the notification requirement are regarded as having no legal effect.[1075]

It is also an offence in Mauritius to implement a qualifying merger without compliance with the statute. The parties may similarly face financial penalties or imprisonment. The Mauritius Commission may require a divestiture or adoption of behavioural remedies where a problematic merger has already been completed. However, where it comes to the enforcement of orders or undertakings given by the parties, the Commission has to apply to a court judge in chambers for the appropriate order. The courts as well generally have jurisdiction to try offences and impose penalties.[1076]

The picture is the same across the other jurisdictions. Mergers implemented in contravention of the law are also considered void and may as well be subject to various relief measures including divestiture. Namibia, Tanzania, Zambia, Seychelles and Zimbabwe also regard the implementation of mergers contrary to the law as an offence to be met with pecuniary penalties with imprisonment also being a possible punishment in Namibia, Seychelles, Zambia and Zimbabwe. The authorities themselves as well do not have the power to enforce their orders and directions. They must seek a court order where a merger has been implemented in contravention of the statute. In Zambia, however, the Competition Tribunal has the power to enforce orders.[1077]

Implementation of a notifiable merger in contravention of the COMESA Competition Regulations also renders the transaction void and of no legal effect within the Common Market. The COMESA Competition Commission is also empowered to impose penalties for non-compliance. Parties may as well be required to dissolve a merger or take other remedial steps required by the Commission. Penalties imposed by the Commission

---

1075 Kenya Competition Act, s 42, s 89 and ss 91-92; Malawi Competition Act s 35 sub-s 2, s 40 and ss50-51.

1076 Mauritius Competition Act s 59, s 61 sub-s 2, s 65 and s 71.

1077 Namibia Competition Act s 51, s 53, s 62 and ss 63-64; Seychelles Competition Act s 46 and s 53; Tanzania Competition Act ss 57-58 and s 60; Zambia Competition Act s 37, s 64, s 73, ss 82-83 and s 86; Zimbabwe Competition Act s 33, s 34A and s 47.

may be recovered via civil proceedings instituted before the COMESA Court of Justice.[1078]

3.2.10 The optimal merger review process for ESA

3.2.10.1 Introduction

Although international merger regulation will benefit most from the convergence of the different procedural approaches, procedural harmonization is the harder to achieve. One may make a case for the convergence of aspects such as the kind of notification system to use. The majority of jurisdictions do already opt for a (mandatory) pre-merger notification regime. The classification of mergers in terms of whether they arise as a result of the exercise of decisive or material influence or on the basis of the value of the transaction may also be amenable to convergence.

There are indeed aspects such as remedies where there seems to be convergence around structural and behavioural modes of relief. However, when it comes to certain core aspects such as notification thresholds as well as the review process, the various economic or even political factors specific to the different jurisdictions make convergence to a particular procedural standard a challenging notion.

The challenges faced by the divergent procedural approaches are particularly felt in the case of transnational mergers where the transactional costs of compliance with multiple merger regulatory regimes become burdensome.

One common line of congruence among the European Union, the United States, South Africa, the ESA jurisdictions as well as the majority of merger regulation jurisdictions is the fact that most mergers do not raise substantial competition concerns, or where they do they are subjected to conditional approval.[1079] In this regard, though convergence may not

---

1078 COMESA Competition Regulations art 24 and art 26; COMESA Merger Guidelines paras. 5.31 et seq; Treaty Establishing the Common Market for Easter and Southern Africa (COMESA Treaty), art 23 <http://www.comesacompetition.org/wp-content/uploads/2016/03/COMESA_Treaty.pdf> accessed 6 September 2019.

1079 See for instance European Commission, Competition Merger Brief, issue 1/2014 <http://ec.europa.eu/competition/publications/cmb/2014/CMB2014-01.pdf> accessed 6 September 2019; Bowman Gilfillan (n 631); UK procedural Guidance para 3.6; DOJ Remedies Guide 1; ICN, 'Recommended Practices for

be realistically possible, various common principles and practices may be adopted to streamline the procedural aspects in the various jurisdictions. Accordingly, the ICN and OECD have spearheaded these efforts by developing recommended practices on review procedures.

Looking at the procedural approaches of the various ESA countries in comparison to the European Union and the US reveals broad congruence on procedural aspects. For instance, we note that pre-merger notification based on asset and turnover thresholds being met is widely adopted. Even the choice of remedies is primarily centred on structural and behavioural solutions. Where there are differences in approach such as the level of the notification threshold, the review process, notification fees, or the behavioural remedy adopted, these may be acceptably divergent owing to the different economic and political circumstances that tend to be highly jurisdiction specific.

The analysis however reveals certain gaps in the procedural approach of a number of the ESA jurisdictions. Some of these gaps are statutory in origin while others are a result of the absence of published guidelines from the competition authority. The gaps are however hard to rationalise given the fact that competition law (and merger regulation in particular) is an area of law that has benefited from an enormous harmonization effort. The result of this effort is the publication of recommendations, model laws and guidelines, principally from the ICN and the OECD, that have been designed to be adaptable to nascent and developing regimes.

In relation to the substantive assessment of mergers, the discussion of the competition test paints a picture of congruence especially where the multi-factor effects-based analytical approach typical of a SLC type of standard is employed. The authorities in these jurisdictions all adopt an approach that takes advantage of the flexibility allowed by this standard to adapt to the requirements of the case before them. This is evident in the way a vital concept such as market definition may be given a back seat where more probative factors are necessary to address a particular case. This flexibility to adequately address competition law concerns in respect of which the market dominance test is too narrow (particularly unilateral effects arising from non-collusive oligopolies) as well as giving merger-related efficiencies the appropriate weight in the course of analysis are arguably the most beneficial imports of a SLC standard. The OECD

Merger Analysis' <http://www.internationalcompetitionnetwork.org/uploads/library/doc316.pdf> accessed 6 September 2019 (ICN MA Recommendations), 1.

does indeed note that a growing number of jurisdictions are moving away from the dominance test and increasingly embracing the SLC test.[1080]

From a different perspective it may be argued that developing jurisdictions that are new to merger regulation and whose markets are not advanced may benefit from the structured and predictable approach of a narrowly interpreted dominance test to build analytical competence. The experience thus far of the European Union after changing from a (broadly interpreted) dominance test to the SLC type test may in this regard be highly instructive for jurisdictions employing a dominance test or contemplating changing to a SLC type test.

In the context of a suitable substantive standard for Sub-Saharan Africa, public interest also plays a crucial role in determining what the optimal substantive standard should be. The greatest concern surrounding a public interest standard in the substantive analysis is how to ensure predictability and legal certainty in the application of this largely amorphous concept. The approach of the South African regime that seeks to set parameters which delineate and set limits to the application of public interest to its substantive analysis can likewise shed some light on the suitable approach to be adopted by the ESA jurisdictions.

3.2.10.2 Defining Mergers

The importance of clear definitions for essential terms cannot be overstated when it comes to statutory construction and legal drafting. Definitions are indeed an essential aspect in fostering legal certainty. Clear definitions are likewise indispensable when it comes to statutory interpretation. However, some of the ESA jurisdictions reviewed already in some instances fall short on this aspect.

Looking at the definition of mergers for instance, the majority of the reviewed ESA jurisdictions underline the necessity of a change of control or the bringing under common control and establishment of a controlling interest in determining whether a merger has arisen or not. It goes without saying that parties to a transaction will need clarity as to whether a transaction satisfies this requirement.

Most jurisdictions subscribing to the change of control standard for defining mergers already make it clear whether the level of control will be based on material influence or decisive influence. As noted however

1080 See overview of OECD Merger Review Standard.

Malawi, Tanzania and Seychelles do not clarify the level of control required to constitute a controlling interest. Their respective guidelines are also silent on this aspect. Zimbabwe on its part defines controlling interest to arise where any control whatsoever can be exercised over a (legal) person, in effect also leaving wide open the level of control. The COMESA Regulations also use the terms of any control whatsoever in respect of the establishment of a controlling interest. In COMESA's case however, the merger guidelines clarify that the COMESA Commission's focus is on decisive influence. In Zimbabwe's case, the fact that there are no published guidelines means the uncertainty persists.

Although parties will in most cases be able to seek guidance from the relevant competition authority, such a core aspect of determining whether a merger arises should already be captured in the statute. This is more so given the fact that the other reviewed ESA jurisdictions already provide statutory guidance on the aspect.

3.2.10.3 Options for notification

The voluntary and mandatory pre-merger notification systems both have their pros and cons. A mandatory pre-merger notification system facilitates the ex-ante detection of problematic mergers and therefore avails the opportunity on the regulator to impose an appropriate remedy or in the worst-case scenario to prohibit a merger.[1081] Considering the absence of a mandatory notification system, the regulator would have to expend significant resources towards investigations aimed at rooting out already consummated transactions that raise competition law concerns. In such cases even finding an appropriate remedy may prove to be onerous. A mandatory notification system places the burden of providing the information necessary to make the decision on the parties which translates to cost savings on the part of the regulator.[1082] It also makes it possible for the

1081 See for instance FTC and DOJ, 'Hart-Scott-Rodino Annual Report: Fiscal Year 2014', 18 <https://www.ftc.gov/system/files/documents/reports/federal-trade-commission-bureau-competition-department-justice-antitrust-division-hart-scott-rodino.s.c.18a-hart-scott-rodino-antitrust-improvements-act-1976/150813hsr_report.pdf> accessed 6 September 2019.

1082 Chongwoo Choe and Chander Shekhar, 'Compulsory or Voluntary Pre-Merger Notification? Theory and Some Evidence' (2010) 28(1) International Journal of Industrial Organization 9 <https://ssrn.com/abstract=1541703> accessed 6 September 2019.

regulator and the merging parties to negotiate the most effective remedies. A nod from the regulator subsequent to the review of a transaction also means that the parties may enjoy certainty as to the legality of their transaction, having in mind though that some regulators retain the power to review approved transactions in the future.

On the flip side, the merging parties should contend with additional transaction costs that come with compliance, which includes having to hold off the completion of their merger. The regulator also should bear the cost of reviewing transactions that do not raise substantial competition concerns.

A voluntary notification system has the advantage of relieving the regulator of the burden of reviewing numerous non-contentious transactions. These cost savings though should be compared to the cost of carrying out ex-post investigations to determine whether consummated transactions give rise to substantial competition concerns. It should be considered as well that structural remedies such as divestitures may be more challenging to achieve once the merger has been completed. Although, as experienced by the UK, many transacting parties do opt to voluntarily notify their transactions, there still exists the danger of largely anticompetitive mergers being consummated and possibly going undetected. Merging parties may very well be hoping to escape detection where notification is not mandatory.[1083]

An optimal voluntary notification system is therefore one that provides sufficient incentives for parties to problematic mergers to notify their transactions. This would avail the benefits of a mandatory pre-merger notification system as well as cutting the costs the regulator should incur on reviewing non-problematic cases and investigating non-notified problematic cases. One of the ways in which voluntary systems have incentivised the notification of problematic mergers is by imposing high costs for failure to notify.[1084]

Most large economies employ the mandatory pre-merger notification system. Large diversified economies usually entail greater merger activity. This means that they are more difficult to monitor and a regulator would expend significant resources in trying to detect and weed out the

---

1083 Julie N Clarke, 'The International Regulation of Transnational Mergers' (PhD Thesis, Queensland University of Technology 2010), 208.

1084 Chander Shekhar and Philip Williams, 'Should the Pre-Notification of Mergers be Compulsory in Australia?' (2004) 37 The Australian Economic Review 382, 385; Ibid.

problematic cases. The risk that parties to a problematic merger would consummate it with the hope of escaping detection and the probability of successfully doing so is therefore higher.[1085] A voluntary pre-merger notification system that has incentives for the notification of problematic mergers may therefore be more effective in more concentrated economies i.e. developing economies where detection is easier.

What therefore is the optimal notification system for developing economies such as those in Sub Saharan Africa? From the perspective of costs, one should weigh the cost of investigating non-problematic mergers in mandatory notification against that of a market intelligence function in voluntary notification. Some studies posit that on a balance of costs the voluntary system is less costly and avails the same benefits as those of a mandatory system.[1086] Accordingly it has been argued that if coupled with sufficient incentive for the notification of problematic mergers as well as some minimum mandatory information requirements, a voluntary system may present the optimal approach for developing economies. Or better yet, a voluntary notification system with a requirement for mandatory notification in specific sectors of strategic interest to the country.[1087] However, even such a hybrid system would depend greatly on the capacity of the regulator to effectively monitor the market and identify problem cases.

Of the reviewed ESA jurisdictions only Malawi employs a voluntary notification system. However, given the nascent nature of Malawi's merger regulation system and the fact that there is still insufficient publicly accessible data on the effectiveness of its voluntary system, it is quite difficult to assess whether its voluntary system is more effective for a developing jurisdiction than the widely adopted mandatory system.

1085 Clarke (2010), 210.

1086 See for instance Chongwoo Choe and Chander Shekhar, Compulsory or Voluntary Pre-Merger Notification? A Theoretical and Empirical Analysis (June 26, 2006). <https://ssrn.com/abstract=912925> accessed 6 September 2019.

1087 Paas-Mohando (2005) 553.

3.2.10.4 Notification and review

3.2.10.4.1 Nexus with the jurisdiction

One of the core recommendations made by the ICN and the OECD is the need for merger laws to extend jurisdiction only to mergers that have sufficient connection to the reviewing jurisdiction.[1088] The ICN further recommends that this connection should be based on activity (e.g. turnover and assets) within the jurisdiction by the two parties to the transaction, more so the activities of the target business in the jurisdiction. The activities in question should be limited to those directly affected by the transaction. There should therefore be a 'significant, direct and immediate economic effect' within the relevant jurisdiction. Transactions that do not give rise to appreciable competitive effects within the jurisdiction based on this local nexus should therefore be excluded.[1089] Jurisdictions that also consider the worldwide activities of the merging parties should therefore ensure that this sufficient local nexus is first established.

The European Union for instance considers both worldwide turnover as well as turnover arising specifically within the common market in respect of at least two of the involved undertakings.[1090] They as well employ a simplified procedure in respect of those transactions that do not raise substantial concerns within the common market and are hence normally cleared in spite of them falling within the jurisdiction of the EUMR.[1091] The United States does take into consideration the worldwide activities of the merging parties, but only in relation to their effect within the United States. The United States focuses on assets and commercial activity in or into the United States and the actual value of the transaction within the United States.[1092] South Africa as well considers worldwide assets and turnover, only to the extent that they have an effect in, into or from South Africa. In addition, when calculating the value of the transferred firm,

---

1088 OECD, Recommendation of the Council on Merger Review (2005), 2 <https://www.oecd.org/competition/mergers/40537528.pdf> accessed 5 February 2017 (OECD Merger Recommendations); ICN, Recommended Practices for Merger Notification Procedures, 1 <http://www.internationalcompetitionnetwork.org/uploads/library/doc588.pdf> accessed 6 September 2019 (ICN Procedural Recommendations).

1089 ICN Procedural Recommendations para 1B.

1090 EU Merger Regulation art 1.

1091 Simplified Procedure Notice paras 1-2.

1092 Clayton Act s 7a.

only the value of the transferred business is taken into consideration. The transaction therefore has to have a substantial nexus to South Africa.[1093]

Zambia specifically addresses the issue of nexus within its merger guidelines. The Zambia Commission provides that it will assert jurisdiction in respect of mergers concluded outside of their territory where the local nexus is sufficiently material, such as a subsidiary presence or where the enterprise has achieved a certain percentage of sales in Zambia. The focus is specifically on the local target undertaking.[1094] The Kenya merger guidelines also highlight the need for the appropriate nexus of the transaction within Kenya, with factors such as assets and turnover and other revenues in Kenya, direct or indirect control over strategic commercial affairs and decisions which have an effect on trade in or into Kenya playing a crucial role in determining the nexus.[1095] COMESA as well requires a territorial nexus on the basis of an appreciable effect on trade within the common market and deems it to be established where the regional dimension requirement is met and the worldwide turnover and asset thresholds are triggered, the focus as well being on the common market activities of the target undertaking.[1096] In respect of the consideration of worldwide assets and turnover COMESA is similar to the European Union and South Africa.

3.2.10.4.2 Notification threshold

The purpose of notification thresholds is basically to screen out transactions that do not raise significant competition concerns.[1097] The OECD additionally views it from a cost/benefit analysis, where expenditure on mergers that are unlikely to raise competition concerns should be avoided. The focus is thus on those transactions where the marginal benefit of review would exceed the marginal costs.[1098] The ICN and the OECD have made recommendations intended to facilitate the achievement of this

1093 SA Threshold Guidance ss 1-3.

1094 Zambia Merger Guidelines paras 10 et seq.

1095 Kenya Merger Guidelines paras 13-14.

1096 COMESA Merger Guidelines paras 3.1 et seq.

1097 ICN, Setting Notification Thresholds for Merger Review (Kyoto 2008), 4 <http://www.internationalcompetitionnetwork.org/uploads/library/doc326.pdf> accessed 6 September 2019 (ICN thresholds Guidance).

1098 OECD, Local Nexus and Jurisdictional Thresholds in Merger Control, DAF/COMP/WP3(2016)4, 5 (OECD Thresholds Guidance).

purpose as closely as possible. The ICN for instance highlights the need for clarity and simplicity, basing thresholds on objectively quantifiable criteria and on information that is readily available to the merging parties.[1099]

The ICN further points out factors to consider when setting thresholds. In respect of the type of threshold, most jurisdictions look at the asset and turnover of the merging parties. Some jurisdictions use a market share based threshold. The OECD and the ICN point out that those jurisdictions that base their thresholds solely on the local assets or turnover find it easier to determine the local nexus as well as having an easier time applying the criteria.[1100] Most jurisdictions that also consider worldwide turnover also employ additional criteria to ensure that the local nexus is sufficiently established i.e. local turnover and assets.[1101] The EU and the US fall into this category. South Africa as noted in the previous section employs even further criteria to ensure sufficient local nexus.

Although market shares are viewed as better suited to determine the probable effects of a proposed merger, the ICN and the OECD note that the transaction costs and uncertainty resulting from their use reduces the practicality and outweigh the benefits.[1102]

Other recommendations made by the ICN include exempting transactions that do not raise competitive concerns, regular review and benchmarking of thresholds based on historical data, consulting stakeholders during the threshold reform process or even considering a cap on the number of annual reviews. The ICN also notes that the size of the economy corresponds to the threshold level; hence smaller economies will have lower thresholds.[1103]

Most jurisdictions, including most of the ESA jurisdictions reviewed, regard a sufficient nexus to be established when their territory specific asset and turnover based notification thresholds are met.[1104] Once the threshold is met the merger is presumably one that will have a significant effect within the particular territory. Thus, for instance a foreign merger that would result in a local subsidiary or locally situated assets and revenues being significantly affected would also qualify for notification.[1105]

1099 ICN Procedural Recommendations para II.
1100 ICN Thresholds Guidance para IVB; OECD Thresholds Guidance 11.
1101 OECD Thresholds Guidance paras 3.1-3.2.
1102 OECD Thresholds Guidance 14; ICN Thresholds Guidance para II.
1103 ICN Thresholds Guidance paras C-J and V.
1104 See Annex.
1105 Botswana Competition Act s 52 sub-s 2(d); Kenya Competition Act s 41 sub-s 2(d); Namibia Competition Act s 42 sub-s 2(d); Zimbabwe Competition Act s

We have noted however, that Botswana, in addition to an asset and turnover threshold also utilises a share-of-the-market threshold. Seychelles and Mauritius only utilise a share of market threshold. Malawi has not set thresholds because they employ a voluntary notification system.[1106]

Whether or not an asset or turnover based threshold or a market-share-based one is effective should naturally be considered from the perspective of the main purpose of setting the notification thresholds, but a trade-off with legal certainty is needed. The aim is to make sure only transactions that raise substantial competition concerns are notified. The thresholds should also ensure that the notified transaction is sufficiently linked to the jurisdiction. A solution for the ESA jurisdictions in this regard may be to adopt a hybrid model similar to the one in South Africa, providing for different thresholds for voluntary and mandatory notification.

Asset and turnover thresholds are based on information provided by the parties. Market share thresholds require market investigation which result in more costs for the regulator and may yield inaccurate information. A market-share-based threshold would especially be difficult to implement in a large economy with many market participants. It is arguable that it is relatively easier for Mauritius and Seychelles to implement market-share-based thresholds based on the smaller size of their economies, which may translate to comparatively transparent markets. But compared to the other ESA jurisdictions that apply asset and turnover thresholds, Mauritius and Seychelles may have a more onerous task. The challenge here again is the unavailability of published information to assess effectiveness.[1107]

3.2.10.4.3 Review

The OECD and the ICN also recommend the adoption of several broad principles such as timeliness in review, efficiency and effectiveness, transparency and predictability, procedural fairness, expedited review of non-problematic cases, reasonable information requirements, opportunities for the parties to consult the regulator during review, third-party participation

2 sub-s 1; Mauritius Competition Act s 47 sub-s 2; Tanzania Competition Act s 2; Zambia Competition Act s 24 sub-s 3(d); Seychelles Competition Act s 1 sub-s 2.

1106 See Annex.

1107 See also ch 3.2.10.3.

to the extent they have legitimate interest and confidentiality in the handling of business secrets.[1108]

The ability to actively engage the regulator in pre-and post-notification consultations is vital to ensuring that the merger review proceeds smoothly. In this regard, it is highly commendable that the regulators in all the jurisdictions reviewed permit and in some cases even encourage the parties to approach them in order to not only determine whether their merger should be reviewed or not but also to address vital issues that will make the review as trouble-free as possible. The OECD and ICN have indeed recommended that the review process be kept highly consultative where even third-parties with legitimate interest can participate. This also helps with the expedited review of the non-problematic cases.

A look at the statutory review timelines also reveals on average a similarity across the ESA jurisdictions as well as the European Union and the United States, with the United States, Malawi and Botswana having the shortest timelines. Additionally, we note that among the ESA jurisdictions, only COMESA, Zambia and South Africa explicitly categorize their review time into phases. Non-problematic cases are hence subjected to a shorter review time. The phased approach should indeed be adopted by all the ESA jurisdictions.

Overall, parties would naturally seek shorter timelines. However, the timeline of review may be affected by a number of factors and may ultimately depend on the case in question. Problematic cases may for instance lead to requests for more information which may lead to longer timelines. Shorter timelines may for example require capacity increases for the regulator which may be restricted by resource availability.

The failure of many of the ESA jurisdictions to regularly publish information on their decisions and in some cases providing very general information on their review process may in some way also have a bearing on timelines. Where parties are forced to actively engage the regulator on issues that are easily addressed by providing sufficient public information, available capacity that would be better used to review transactions is redirected. Zimbabwe for instance merely provides that determinations are to be made as expeditiously as possible with Mauritius and Seychelles providing no information on review timelines in their guidelines. This in effect gives the regulator a lot of discretion and leaves the parties with a great deal of uncertainty.

1108 OECD Merger Recommendations paras 2-7; ICN Procedural Recommendations.

The dearth of published information for many of the ESA jurisdictions makes it difficult to assess the effectiveness of their review process. This information asymmetry makes it difficult to assess the level of transparency and predictability of decisions. Most of the published decisions as well reveal very little information on the decision-making process of the authorities. This also makes it difficult to assess to what level recommended principles such as efficiency and effectiveness are being achieved by the authorities.

3.2.10.5 The gap in the dominance test

The OECD notes that when one looks at how the tests are practically applied in the various jurisdictions, there is no clear cut line dividing the dominance and the SLC tests.[1109] Therefore, whereas market shares and concentration levels are of greater importance, at least statutorily, when employing a dominance test, the practical implications of the factual economic analysis carry the day in determining how important their role is.[1110] The view that there is convergence in merger analysis across the major jurisdictions employing the two tests was expressed by the European Commission in its Green Paper on the review of the then merger regulations.[1111]

The European Commission as well highlighted the evolution that the dominance standard had undergone in the European Union since its adoption. This evolution created room for adaptation to developments in economic theory as well as facilitating the use of more refined methods in measuring market power, thus permitting the flexibility needed to carry out an effects-based analysis.[1112]

Prior to the European Union and Germany changing from the dominance test to the SIEC test, the Bundeskartellamt published an opinion comparing the two tests in order to show that there was no urgency to

1109 OECD: Substantive Criteria used for Merger Assessment, DAFFE/COMP(2003)5 <http://www.oecd.org/competition/mergers/2500227.pdf> accessed 6 September 2019 (OECD Substantive Criteria).

1110 Ibid 7.

1111 Green Paper on the Review of Council Regulation (EEC) No 4064/89, COM/2001/0745, para 162 (Green Paper).

1112 Ibid para 163.

change from the dominance standard as it was sufficient to address any concerns that may come up.[1113]

The Bundeskartellamt compared the approach taken in various developed jurisdictions and noted that the basic substantive criteria taken into consideration is the same irrespective of which test is employed. They also noted that neither tests (as applied in these jurisdictions) focused on a specific fixed set of criteria. Both tests ultimately sought to keep in check the market power post-merger. The Bundeskartellamt further noted that there was no significant distinction in terms of *rigour*, *flexibility* and *effectiveness* when it comes to the manner in which the various authorities use the two tests to address issues arising from oligopolistic dominance, vertical or conglomerate mergers.[1114] The analytical approach of the Bundeskartellamt does confirm the flexible approach in determining oligopolistic dominance even under the previous dominance test.

The question therefore is how broad an interpretation the dominance test can be given. Would a broad enough definition be sufficient to cover any unanticipated and possibly anticompetitive transaction? An analysis conducted under the SLC test would naturally be flexible enough to cover both unilateral and coordinated effects as well as issues arising out of vertical and conglomerate mergers. This is because the main concern of the SLC test is the effect the transaction would have on the post-merger market, specifically whether the transaction would result in a substantial lessening of competition.[1115] A broad enough definition under the dominance test, similar to the evolved dominance test in the European Union and Germany prior to changing the competition test, would be able to cover issues arising out of collective dominance/ dominance arising out of coordinated or collusive conduct.

However, even with this broad definition there are certain anticompetitive effects which cannot be subsumed under the dominance test. The main concern in this regard is in respect of unilateral effects arising from non-collusive oligopolies.

1113 Bundeskartellamt, 'Prohibition Criteria in Merger Control: Dominant Position versus Substantial Lessening of Competition?' <http://www.bundeskartellamt.de/SharedDocs/Publikation/EN/Fachartikel/Prohibition%20Criteria%20in%20Merger%20Control%20-%20Dominant%20Position%20versus%20Substantial%20Lessening%20of%20Competition.pdf?__blob=publicationFile&v=3> accessed 6 September 2019.

1114 Ibid 34.

1115 OECD Merger Review Standard 16; OECD Substantive Criteria 8.

The concerns over a gap in the then dominance standard in use in the EU with regard to non-collusive oligopolies came to light following the decision of the General Court in *Airtours and First Choice*. Although the post-merger market would be such that the major tour operators in the UK would go down from four to three, the Commission failed to provide a solid case for its argument that there would be collective dominance as there was no evidence to show that there would be coordinated effects. And going by the Commission's own analysis, there was the implication that each of the merging firms post merger would still be able to unilaterally exercise market power, without individually meeting the criteria for single dominance.[1116] In essence, this meant that there was a gap in the dominance standard.

The issue was therefore how to address the perceived gap(s) in the dominance test without necessarily compromising on legal certainty as well as retaining the vital experience that had been gained through the application of an evolved dominance test. The solution would need to ensure that there would be statutory flexibility to deal with any perceived gap cases while at the same time ensuring that the experience gained with the dominance test does not go to waste.[1117]

The solution was the adoption of the SIEC test with a particular focus on the creation and strengthening of a dominant position as the main example of a significant impediment to effective competition.[1118] This particular focus on the creation or strengthening of a dominant position enabled the retention and continued use of the significant merger regulation experience under the dominance test.

The experience in practice indicates that not much change has occurred to the Commission's analytical approach, which is largely indicative of the already evolved practice under the dominance test. Cases that fall within the gap have as well not been prevalent.[1119]

One of the main concerns regarding the change from the dominance to the SLC test is the period of legal uncertainty subsequent to such a

1116 Airtours Decision para 96.

1117 Whish and Bailey (2012) 866.

1118 Ibid. point out that the SIEC test arose from a simple rearranging of terms that were already present in the old Regulation; the previous wording was targeted at mergers that would create or strengthen a dominant position leading to a SIEC.

1119 Lindsay and Berridge (2009) para 2-019. See also Nicholas Levy, 'The EU's SIEC Test Five Years On: Has it Made a Difference?' (2010) 6(1) European Competition Journal 211.

change. As noted by the OECD, Australia is an example of a jurisdiction that experienced a period of increased rejection of reviewed mergers following its switch to a SLC standard.[1120] The EU approach is in this regard certainly instructive for jurisdictions seeking to have a relatively smooth transition from a dominance standard to a SLC standard. The retention of accumulated practice as well as addressing gap cases when they do arise means that legal certainty can to a large extent be preserved.

Subsequent to the *Airtours and First Choice* decision, various policy proposals have been made in the context of the OECD as to amendments that countries employing the dominance test could introduce to cover the shortfall in the dominance test in relation to unilateral effects arising from non-collusive oligopolies. These included:

1. weakening the definitional link between market power and dominance;
2. varying the approach to market definition depending on the type of merger being reviewed;
3. consistently adopting particularly narrow market definitions;
4. adopting different dominance thresholds for single and collective dominance;
5. lowering the market power threshold required to find dominance;
6. extending collective dominance to cover anticompetivtive oligopolistic inter-dependence falling short of "co-ordinated effects.[1121]

As noted by the OECD, such amendments would result in greater flexibility and a broader scope of the dominance test but at the expense of introducing legal uncertainty on its application as well as the reluctance of courts to endorse such proposals.[1122] From the perspective of a nascent developing country regime, such legal uncertainty could be compounded by the relative inexperience of the authorities. Rather than take this route, the OECD notes that a number of jurisdictions simply opted to change to the SLC standard in order to ensure legal certainty.[1123]

1120 OECD Substantive Criteria 10.

1121 OECD Merger Review Standard 19; OECD Substantive Criteria 20-21.

1122 OECD Merger Review Standard 19.

1123 OECD Merger Review Standard 20-22.

3.2.10.6 The ESA Perspective on the Competition Test

The ESA jurisdictions in focus, with the exception of Tanzania, already employ the substantial lessening of competition test. Their guidelines as well reflect an approach focused on exploiting the flexibilities of the effects-based analysis. They detail a multi-factor analytical style that emphasizes on a case-by-case approach, where the most relevant factors will be at the forefront. The case studies however reveal that the actual analysis is highly structured and focused on defining markets and determining market shares and concentration levels. This is evidence of markets that are still very concentrated. However, the fact that they already utilize the substantial lessening of competition test means that they have embraced a system that grants the necessary flexibility to grow and develop in a manner that will address evolving market needs without the need to worry about gaps that cannot be addressed by their choice of standard. Indeed, concerns over non-collusive oligopolies may be acute in the ESA region, both on a national and regional level given their highly concentrated markets.

Tanzania however has a highly concentrated market which currently appears to be satisfactorily addressed by the dominance standard. In this regard there is no urgent need for switching to the substantial lessening of competition standard. If that point does indeed arise in the future it would be prudent to take the EU approach of making a statutory amendment but largely retaining the analytical approach to prevent uncertainty. This approach would allow for the gradual development of a new analytical dispensation but from a case by case perspective.

3.2.10.7 Public interest considerations

Public interest is a difficult concept to capture in precise words. In broad terms public interest encompasses the welfare of society or the public as a whole rather than an individual's or specific group interests.[1124] Protecting the public interest from a legal viewpoint requires putting in place legal measures to safeguard the welfare of society. The well-being of society

1124 Black's Law Dictionary defines public interest as 'The welfare of the public as compared to the welfare of a private individual or company. All of society has a stake in this interest and the government recognises the promotion of and protection of the general public.'

however depends on a multitude of factors which are all dependent on the circumstances in question. Public interest is therefore multifaceted and dynamic and can arise in many fields of law. It could touch on environmental issues, labour aspects, national security, media freedom or a host of other areas affecting the public. The ambiguity of the concept means that its inclusion in a specific law should ideally be accompanied by a clear definition or guidelines as to which specific public interest areas are in focus. It is however not easy to encapsulate public interest as it is largely dynamic and can evolve depending on what is considered to be touching on the interests of the public at a given period in time.

From the perspective of merger regulation, the ambiguity raises concerns, more so given the fact that merger regulation should seek to foster predictability and legal certainty. This is especially because inclusion of public interest in merger regulation introduces largely non-competition based considerations. It is admittedly difficult to capture all the public interest concerns that a merger may affect. What the law should endeavour to do is to at the very least categorise the most important public interest concerns.

Article 21(4) of the EU Merger Regulations for instance allows the Member States to *take appropriate measures to protect legitimate interests* where such measures are not taken into consideration in the EU Merger Regulation. Such measures however need to be in line with the general principles and other provisions of EU law. Some of these general principles are reiterated in the recitals of the EU Merger Regulations and include free movement of capital and maintaining an open market economy with free competition within the internal market.[1125] The EU Merger Regulations categorise *public security, plurality of the media and prudential rules* as legitimate public interest concerns within this context. Any public interest considerations not falling within these three areas need to be approved by the European Commission.

The Enterprise Act in the United Kingdom as well contains provisions that allow for public interest intervention in mergers.[1126] The Secretary of State may intervene in merger cases being reviewed by the Competition and Markets Authority (CMA) on the grounds of a public interest concern. This intervention is in respect of cases that do not fall within the jurisdic-

1125 EU Merger Regulation rec 2.

1126 UK Enterprise Act (2002 c. 40), chapter 2 & 3 *as amended by* UK Enterprise and Regulatory Reform Act (2013 c.24), part 3 and 4 (UK ERR Act).

tion of the EU Merger Regulation.[1127] The public interest considerations are specified as the interests of national security and the need for accurate presentation on news and free expression of opinion. National security here has the same meaning as public security in Article 21(4) of the EU Merger Regulations.[1128] The Secretary of State also intervenes in special public interest cases where the merger does not otherwise meet the threshold. They are in respect of mergers involving firms which may be privy to government information which is confidential or touches on defence or media-related mergers.[1129] The Secretary of State is also empowered by the Enterprise Act to add, remove or amend any public interest consideration in this section, but this is subject to parliamentary approval.[1130] Where the merger falls within the jurisdiction of the European Commission the Secretary of State issues the CMA with a European Intervention Notice.[1131]

The main public interest intervention in the United States is aimed at protecting national security. The Committee on Foreign Investments in the United States (CFIUS), which is established under the Foreign Investment and National Security Act of 2007 (FINS Act), has the power to review transactions which would result in the control of a US business by a foreign person so as to ascertain whether such transactions would have an effect on US national security.[1132] Section 723 of the Defense Production Act[1133] contains a non-exhaustive list of factors that are to be considered in a national security intervention which include: the potential effects of the transaction on deals involving military goods with other countries, the potential effects of the transaction on the international technological leadership of the United States in areas affecting US national security, the potential national security-related effects on US critical infrastructure, such as major energy assets, and the potential national security-related effects on US critical technologies.

1127 UK Enterprise Act s 42 *as read with* UK ERR Act, s 35.

1128 UK Enterprise Act s 58.

1129 UK Enterprise Act c 3.

1130 UK Enterprise Act s 58 sub-s 3; see also Whish (n 78) 956-957.

1131 UK Enterprise Act s 67.

1132 Foreign Investment and National Security Act 2007 (50 USC app 2061).

1133 Defense Production Act 1950 (50 USC app 2170) s 721 of the Defense Production Act was amended by the FINS Act mainly to reform the process used to examine foreign investments where they touch on national security as well as to empower the Committee on Foreign Investment in the United States to intervene in these circumstances.

Taking the European Union, the United States and the United Kingdom as examples we see that public interest intervention is not part of their main merger analysis. It is to be carried out in exceptional circumstances. However, in spite of public interest intervention being an exception to the rule there is growing concern regarding a perceived broadening of the intervening circumstances especially where foreign investment is involved in perceived critical areas of national interest. This again reflects the dynamic nature of public interest.[1134] Keeping in mind that public interest concerns such as public security and national security are not defined, any odd number of national interests could be added into this category.[1135] Therefore, even with the public interest intervention being the exception to the rule coupled with a deliberate effort to narrowly craft the intervention circumstances, public interest considerations could still prove problematic for transacting parties.

Where a transaction which on the basis of a competition analysis would not be prohibited and may very well result in a net pro-competitive benefit passed on to society has to be examined on the basis of a public interest concern, one of the challenges becomes whether it is the competition or the public interest considerations that prevail. The issue is more acute where public interest considerations are part and parcel of the substantial merger analysis, as is the case in South Africa and the ESA jurisdictions. In South Africa, it is the effect of the transaction on the public interest that would take precedence. As discussed earlier in this Chapter, the competition and the public interest analysis are carried out interdependently in South Africa. A transaction that would result in a negative effect on competition could be given the nod on the basis of public interest factors. A merger that does not substantially lessen competition may also be prohibited based on its effect on public interest. Additionally, only a public

---

1134 See for instance Dave Poddar and Gemma Stooke , 'Consideration of Public Interest Factors in Antitrust Merger Control' (2015) Competition Policy International <https://www.competitionpolicyinternational.com/consideration-of-public-interest-factors-in-antitrust-merger-control/> accessed 9 September 2019 for a brief discussion of public interest interventions and Freshfields Bruckhaus Deringer: Antitrust and Public Interest <http://www.freshfields.com/en/global/TKT2015/8__Antitrust_and_the_public_interest/> accessed 9 September 2019 which discusses briefly circumstances where intervention was sought where foreign investment in critical national interest areas.

1135 Neither the EU Merger Regulation nor the FINS Act provides definitions of public or national security.

interest-based defence can be used to counter a negative public interest effect of a proposed transaction.[1136]

Critically, it is interesting to note that the public interest grounds in the European Union and the United States are non-economic. The public interest grounds in South Africa are mainly economic (largely industrial policy-oriented) but have recently been expanded to include national security. One could even argue that, from the European Union and United States perspective, economic reasons other than competition-oriented ones, should not justify a prohibition of a merger. This is different in South Africa and the other ESA jurisdictions.

Another specific concern arising out of the inclusion of a public interest standard within merger regulation, especially where the same is broadly construed, is the risk of regulatory opportunism or capture by which the independence and integrity of the competition authority in decision making may be compromised by agents within and outside of the authority.[1137] Regulatory capture arises more often than not in competition law enforcement. Where the interests of government and large economic players or specific interest groups intertwine the enforcement function of the competition authority may be interfered with.[1138] It may however also arise where a broadly defined public interest standard allows for vested interests that are not strictly in the public interest to be introduced into the analysis of the merger.

This is more likely to occur where another government agency e.g. a ministry is responsible for the public interest intervention, such as is the case in the UK where the Secretary of State intervenes in public interest cases. However, even where the competition authority is tasked with the public interest analysis, regulatory capture concerns may still arise. This may be the case especially where the constitution of the competition authority is largely politically influenced. This can easily prove more problematic within the context of developing countries where political influence in institutional affairs is often high.[1139]

1136 SA Competition Act s 12A. See also Harmony Gold Mining Company (n 933).

1137 See for instance Frédéric Boehm, 'Regulatory Capture Revisited: Lessons from Economics of Corruption' (July 2007) <https://pdfs.semanticscholar.org/0568/264e283cf0c69f97680152c270666649671f.pdf> accessed 9 September 2019.

1138 See Michal S. Gal, 'The Ecology of Antitrust: Preconditions for Competition Law Enforcement in Developing Countries', 10 in Philippe Brusick, Ana Maria Alvarez and Lucian Cernat (eds), *Competition, Competitiveness and Development: Lessons from Developing Countries* (UNCTAD 2004).

1139 Ibid.

From a broad policy perspective public interest cannot be divorced from merger regulation. The maintenance of economically efficient and competitive markets plays an important part in ensuring the economic welfare of society. Reading public interest considerations into merger analysis however requires special care. Merging parties rely on the certainty, predictability and timeliness of merger analysis. Public interest considerations should therefore not adversely affect this certainty, timeliness and predictability. This means that it should ideally be narrowly constructed and preferably comprised of clear guidelines that ensure that factors taken into account are transparent and clearly outlined.

The inclusion of a broadly interpreted public interest standard in the substantive analysis by the majority of the ESA jurisdictions in focus is therefore where the main challenge lies. The fact that South Africa clearly provides that its list of intervening factors is exhaustive in addition to publishing guidelines on the substantial application of the public interest provisions increases the level of certainly regarding the application of public interest. This is however not the case with the other ESA jurisdictions which have not restricted their instances of public interest intervention. The ESA jurisdictions in this regard need not look farther than South Africa in terms of a model for the substantial application of public interest provisions that greatly fosters a level of certainty.

3.2.10.8 Choice of remedies

In respect of remedies the ICN recommends that the remedy chosen by the regulator should be aimed at adequately addressing the harm that the merger may occasion. These remedies should be developed in a transparent and inclusive process where both the regulator and the merging parties are able to discuss and come to an agreement as to which remedies are suitable. The remedies should as well be effective, easily administrable and the regulator should be able to ensure the implementation, monitoring and enforcement of the remedies.[1140]

The United States, the European Union, South Africa and the United Kingdom, as do most jurisdictions, provide the merging parties with an opportunity to engage the regulator in pre-notification discussions. They also maintain regular communication throughout the review process as well as negotiating proposals for remedial action with the merging par-

1140 ICN Procedural Recommendations para XI.

ties.[1141] These jurisdictions also express the need to preserve competition; therefore only the remedies that they deem effective in this regard will be considered.[1142] The US for instance expresses the need for a close connection between the remedy and the prospective competitive harm. In the UK the effectiveness is also linked to cost therefore the least costly remedy that is deemed effective will be considered. The UK also has regard to customer benefits in connection with price, quality and innovation.[1143] The adopted remedies should ensure that the efficiencies that would be achieved by the merger are retained.[1144]

The ICN principles are as well reflected in a number of the ESA merger guidelines. The Mauritius remedies guidelines highlight the need for effectiveness, timeliness and proportionality in terms of a cost of implementation to expected benefits. The Kenya merger guidelines point to the need for comprehensive impact in terms of effectiveness of the remedies with an acceptably low-level risk of certain issues not being addressed. The practicality of implementation, monitoring and enforcement as well as appropriate duration and timing are also highlighted. The Seychelles remedies guidelines also express similar objectives.[1145]

Similar to the European Union, the United States and South Africa, we note that Kenya, Zambia, Zimbabwe and Mauritius reflect in their guidelines an inclusive approach that involves the parties in the remedy determination process. However, the information available on Seychelles and Botswana indicates that the regulator one-sidedly makes the determination. The risk here is that the remedies developed may not be optimally effective, and may even have a punitive effect on the parties.

In terms of the type of remedy, we note that the European Union and the United States express a preference for structural remedies. The ESA jurisdictions however express no such preference. The approach is mostly to appropriately mix both structural and behavioural remedies. Behavioural remedies may in some instances be more appropriate especially for those

---

1141 See generally OECD Remedies Study.

1142 EU Remedies Notice para 9; UK Remedies Guidance para 1.8.

1143 UK Remedies Guidance paras 1.9 -1.20.

1144 OECD Remedies Study 222.

1145 Seychelles Merger Guidelines paras 4.3 et seq; Kenya Merger Guidelines para 231; Competition Commission of Mauritius Guidelines on Remedies and Penalties (2009) , paras 3.3 et seq <http://www.ccm.mu/English/Documents/Legislations/CCM6%20-%20Guidelines%20-%20Remedies%20and%20Penalties_Nov09.pdf> accessed 9 September 2019 (Mauritius Remedies Guidelines).

ESA jurisdictions that actively seek to address public interest concerns such as employment.

Looking at Namibia, Tanzania, Malawi, Botswana, Zimbabwe and COMESA the question of a lack of published guidelines arises again in respect of the approach on remedies.

3.2.10.9 Conclusion

3.2.10.9.1 The procedural approach

A one-size-fits-all approach is indeed not possible in respect of merger regulation procedure. Different jurisdictions have diverse circumstances and needs that call for different approaches. A large and diversified economy like the US for instance has more to benefit from a mandatory pre-merger notification system because the chances of a problematic merger escaping detection in the absence of such a system are higher. A smaller, less diversified economy may be able to adjust well to a voluntary system of pre-merger notification provided they have sufficient capacity to monitor the market and weed out problematic mergers as well as imposing a penalty that would sufficiently incentivize the notification of the most problematic mergers.

This is not to say that there aren't any procedural aspects that can be harmonized. For instance, classifying mergers according to whether they are a result of the exercise of decisive or material influence or based on the value of the transaction is amenable to harmonization. In respect of remedies, we see that the United States, the European Union, South Africa as well as the ESA jurisdictions employ structural and behavioural modes of relief. Most of the core procedural aspects such as notification thresholds and the review process itself however remain a convergence challenge. Economic, geographic and political differences between the jurisdictions make convergence of such factors a daunting task.

Although a harmonized procedural standard is very difficult to achieve, the adoption and approximation of various procedural principles, based on the ICN and OECD recommendations, can bring about a level of predictability in a highly diverse regulatory landscape. These guidelines and recommendations are drafted so that they are easily adaptable to a nascent and developing jurisdiction. The recommendations are in many respects specifically targeted at these jurisdictions, helping them avoid reinventing the wheel.

In the face of globalization and the multi-jurisdiction nature of many transactions the diversity of procedural approaches makes regulatory compliance quite a daunting task. The transactional cost of compliance becomes a big challenge. Even where a particular jurisdiction is not directly involved, the effects of the proposed merger within that jurisdiction may trigger the intervention of the regulator. The ICN and the OECD have recommended greater cooperation and coordination between various regulators in the review and enforcement of such cases.

The general feeling one gets when reading the statutes and guidelines of a number of the ESA jurisdictions is one of incompleteness or superficiality. Some statutes such as the Mauritius, Malawi and Seychelles Acts have very superficial merger regulation provisions which are as well not accompanied by sufficiently defined terms.

Other statutes such as those of Malawi, Zimbabwe and to some extent Tanzania do not address merger regulation distinctly or under a separate chapter in the statute. Rather the merger regulation provisions are bundled in among other provisions. In as much as this is may be a legislative drafting preference one may easily conclude that merger regulation is a rather insignificant aspect of their competition laws. Some guidelines such as those of Tanzania and Malawi are to a large extent cursory, with many vital aspects not clearly addressed. As revealed in the sections of this chapter, a variety of vital items of information and guidance are not covered by some of the statutes and guidelines. It may be argued that this may be purposeful drafting to leave room for the regulator to adapt to diverse circumstances. This however would not auger well for accountability and certainty.

It is however not a blanket criticism. Some of the statues such as the COMESA, Kenya, Zambia, Botswana and Namibia address merger regulation quite comprehensively. Regulatory law is in fact dynamic and should always be regarded as having room for modification and improvement.

However, in as much as it may not be possible to cover all scenarios in the regulations and guidelines especially for a nascent and developing jurisdiction, a lack of focused drafting becomes apparent where there already exist recommendations, model provisions and guidelines. The international development of competition law is by analogy comparable to a well-lit street with numerous guideposts and street signs. Not only do we have the ICN, OECD and UNCTAD guidance, there are also commentaries and well drafted guidelines from developed jurisdictions such as the United States and the European Union that can be useful guides. This is not to mention the various peer reviews by UNCTAD some of which already concretely point out where the gaps in legislation are. It therefore does not make sense for a jurisdiction to take a dirt road or attempt to reinvent the wheel. The argument here does not advocate for a direct implementation or supplanting of these recommendations and guidelines. The focus should be on adapting the recommendations and guidance to the specific circumstances within the jurisdiction.

These shortfalls also need to be considered in light of the insufficiency of publicly accessible detailed decisions. This lack of information gives the sense that the regulator has room to exercise substantial discretion and arbitrariness, contrary to the need for predictability in merger regulation. From the perspective of an investor the uncertainty acts as a big disincentive.

Overall, these shortcomings give the sense that merger regulation is not regarded as an important regulatory field. This should however not be the case given the great impact that merger regulation has on international investment and business.

3.2.10.9.2 The substantive approach

The notion of convergence towards a single substantive standard is without a doubt appealing. It would enhance international cooperation and coordination more so where transnational merger transactions are involved. It would also reduce uncertainty and increase to great extent predictability for the parties to these transactions, making them more likely than not to structure deals. Many jurisdictions are indeed converging towards substantial lessening of competition as the ideal standard in respect of the competitive effects analysis. What is clear however, as noted by the OECD as well as the Bundeskartellamt, is that the analytical approach in the developed jurisdictions irrespective of the competition test employed already indicates a level of substantial convergence. Nonetheless, it is apparent that the SLC test has the flexibility to address transactions that may not be captured under the dominance test.

The analytical approaches in the US, the EU and South Africa attest to this high level of convergence in terms of the competition analysis. South Africa has as well indicated the willingness to make reference to the US and the EU in the course of merger analysis. Merger analysis in South Africa is however comparatively more advanced than in other Sub-Saharan

Africa jurisdictions. For this reason, it may not be prudent to conclude that one size fits all in the Sub-Saharan Africa context.

Although admittedly the SLC standard is superior to the dominance test in terms of flexibility, a change to the SLC standard may not be urgent for those Sub-Saharan Africa jurisdictions such as Tanzania that still employ the dominance test. They may simply be at a stage in which their markets are highly concentrated where structural considerations revolving around market shares and concentration levels are sufficient. This is indeed the case with the reviewed ESA jurisdictions.

The Sub-Saharan Africa jurisdictions may alternatively change the statutory legal standard but retain their current practice to maintain certainty and predictability. They would then still have the flexibility to address any gaps when they arise.

The greater concern however is to what extent public interest considerations should be factored into the substantive merger analysis. Looking at the US, the EU and the UK on the one hand and South Africa and the reviewed ESA jurisdictions on the other, we see that the developed jurisdictions take public interest into consideration in exceptional, primarily non-economic, circumstances whereas developing countries would tend towards incorporating economics-based public interest concerns into the substantial analysis. This is because the socio-economic context in which merger regulation applies in Sub-Saharan Africa may require a more central role to be played by public interest factors. Looking at South Africa for instance, one of the public interest concerns highlighted in the Competition Act is the unjust restriction on economic participation by all South Africans as well as the need to open up the economy to greater ownership by more South Africans. A transaction which would result in the concentration of economic power in the hands of those seen as historically privileged economically or job losses suffered by those regarded as locked out of the economy would most likely be thoroughly scrutinised on public interest grounds even though it may have passed the competition test.

Even where public interest is considered in exceptional circumstances, there is still a concern that a perceived broadening of intervening public interest instances would have an effect on certainty, predictability and timeliness. Incorporating it into the substantive analysis should therefore ideally be accompanied by a clear definition with a narrow set of intervening circumstances as well as guidelines on how the competition authority would apply these circumstances. The continued effort by South Africa in this regard is indeed exemplary for the other ESA jurisdictions.

3.3 *Extraterritoriality*

3.3.1 Introduction

The interaction between states is traditionally governed by a mutual recognition and respect of the sovereignty and territorial integrity existing between them. Based on the territoriality principle, a state may only exercise jurisdiction within the confines of its national borders. However, from the global economic perspective, the increased globalization of the world economy and the rise of international business mean that national borders are increasingly becoming blurred.[1146] Multinational companies have a global footprint and the consequences of their conduct, even if carried out in a single jurisdiction, can have a ripple effect on all the jurisdictions where they do business. The effects of such conduct are thus liable to trigger the exertion of extraterritorial jurisdiction by the affected states, even where the conduct is not directly carried out in those states.

In the competition law context, the absence of an internationally binding instrument means that there are numerous overlapping national competition laws with potential extraterritorial implications to varying levels.[1147] This extraterritorial jurisdiction can be exercised on a prescriptive and an enforcement level.[1148] Prescriptive jurisdiction entails states adopting legislative measures conferring on the appropriate institution the right to enforce the law. The more problematic aspect is the enforcement jurisdiction which entails actual steps being taken to enforce the law that has been prescribed.[1149]

There is no treaty instrument harmonizing the application of extraterritorial jurisdiction.[1150] This means that seeking to exercise domestic laws in

---

1146 *See for instance* IBA, Report of the Task Force on Extraterritorial Jurisdiction 5, 45 (International Bar Association 2009) <http://tinyurl.com/taskforce-etj-pdf> accessed 9 September 2019 (IBA Task Force Report). *See also* ILC, Report on the work of its fifty-eighth session, Supplement No. 10 (A/61/10) Annex E. Extraterritorial Jurisdiction <http://www.tjsl.edu/slomansonb/5.1_UNExtra.pdf> accessed 9 September 2019.

1147 Jennifer A Zerk, 'Extraterritorial Jurisdiction: Lessons for the business and human rights sphere from six regulatory areas', 92 (Corporate Social Responsibility Initiative Working Paper No. 59. 2010) <http://www.hks.harvard.edu/m-rcbg/CSRI/publications/workingpaper_59_zerk.pdf.> accessed 9 September 2019.

1148 IBA Task Force Report 47.

1149 IBA Task Force Report 46.

1150 *See for instance* IBA Task Force Report.

a foreign state *prima facie* goes against the principle of territoriality. One of the accepted principles on which a state may exercise its jurisdiction beyond its territory is the nationality principle. According to this principle, a state may exercise its jurisdiction over the acts of its nationals (including corporations) abroad.[1151]

There is however increasing consensus around the view that extraterritorial jurisdiction in competition law is acceptable where there are economic effects within a particular territory in question arising out of conduct or arrangements occurring outside of that territory.[1152] The effects doctrine basically espouses a state's right to exercise jurisdiction over foreign entities on the basis of (substantial) economic effects produced in its territory as a direct result of the foreign entity's conduct.[1153]

Even though there is broad consensus on the validity of the effects doctrine, extraterritorial jurisdiction cannot be exercised without cooperation between the states. A balance has to be achieved between extraterritorial application of domestic laws and a comity approach of allowing the state with the closest connection to the transaction to handle the case.[1154]

The ability to exercise enforcement jurisdiction also largely depends on the economic clout a particular jurisdiction enjoys. Therefore, whereas the US and the EU may be able to enjoy higher success rates of extraterritorial enforcement, the same cannot be said of the ESA jurisdictions. Economic clout would also easily result in the parties willingly cooperating with the regulator.

With a specific focus on merger regulation, this chapter delves into the extraterritorial application of domestic rules by the United States, the European Union, South Africa as well as the ESA jurisdictions. It additionally discusses the various arrangements and agreements concluded in respect of coordination and cooperation in the exercise of extraterritorial jurisdiction.

1151 See IBA Task Force Report 45; ILC Report on the work of its fifty-eighth session, Supplement No. 10 (A/61/10) Annex E. Extraterritorial Jurisdiction.
1152 IBA Task Force Report 48.
1153 Ibid 12.
1154 IBA Task Force Report 47.

3.3.2 The Merger Regulation Context

Prescriptive jurisdiction in the context of merger regulation is mainly exercised by way of financial thresholds which if reached by the merging parties, the requirement to notify to and obtain clearance from the regulator will be triggered.[1155] Most merger regulation systems contain prescribed thresholds that trigger jurisdiction. An additional factor that influences the extraterritorial nature of the prescriptive jurisdiction is how a merger is defined and classified. Many jurisdictions target both direct and indirect acquisitions of interest. South Africa for instance defines a merger in terms of a direct or *indirect* acquisition or establishment of direct or *indirect* control.[1156] Article 3(1) of the EUMR as well defines an acquisition inter alia in terms of obtaining direct or *indirect* control. The Hart-Scott-Rodino Act also captures both direct and indirect acquisitions of interest.[1157]

Most of the ESA jurisdictions as well define a merger as the direct or indirect acquisition by one undertaking of controlling interest in another *inter alia* through acquiring the controlling interest in a foreign undertaking that has a controlling interest in a subsidiary within the territory. In some jurisdictions, such as Kenya and Tanzania, there is a statutory provision extending jurisdiction to transactions occurring outside of the country that results in the change of control of a business within the country.[1158]

If such a transaction for instance triggers the notification threshold in the ESA jurisdiction in question, because of either the assets or turnover, or, the market share presence of the foreign undertaking(s) local interests then the notification requirement will rise. The presumption is that the triggering of the notification threshold already confirms that the transaction has a sufficient local nexus and would have a significant enough effect within the territory to warrant the regulator considering it.

The most common way in which the definition of a merger to include indirect acquisition of control or interest has an implication on extraterritorial jurisdiction is through a parent-company and subsidiary

---

1155 Zerk (2010) 93.

1156 SA Competition Act s 12 sub-s 1.

1157 Clayton Act s7a.

1158 Botswana Competition Act s 52 sub-s 2(d); Kenya Competition Act s 6 and s 41 sub-s 2(d); Namibia Competition Act s 42 sub-s 2(d); Zimbabwe Competition Act s 2 sub-s 1; Mauritius Competition Act s 47 sub-s 2; Tanzania Competition Act s 2 and s 7; Zambia Competition Act s 24 sub-s 3(d); Seychelles Competition Act s 1 sub-s 2.

relationship.[1159] This is indeed the case of multinational companies which establish subsidiaries in different countries. A merger transaction between two parent companies in jurisdiction A would indirectly affect their subsidiaries in jurisdiction B in a manner that may trigger the notification requirement in jurisdiction B, if the thresholds set in jurisdiction B are met.

A key concern in terms of extraterritoriality is therefore the review of a single transaction in multiple jurisdictions. If the thresholds in several jurisdictions are met then the merging parties would be required to file notifications and obtain consent from these various regulators. Questions such as whether the effect of the merger is substantial enough in a particular jurisdiction to warrant review arise. This is more so when the likelihood of a prohibition in one jurisdiction prevents the transaction from proceeding or where two agencies analysing the same transaction arrive at different conclusions.[1160]

The European Union, the United States and South Africa have set thresholds based on assets and turnover.[1161] In the United States, we have seen that where the size of the parties and the size of the transaction meet the prescribed threshold, then the transaction becomes notifiable, irrespective of whether there is a change of control or not.[1162] The European Union takes into consideration both worldwide turnover as well as turnover arising specifically within the common market in respect of at least two of the involved undertakings.[1163] The thresholds in South Africa are set in respect of only those assets or turnover of the merging parties that would have an effect within the country, the focus being specifically on the value of the transferred business or assets that would come under the control of the acquiring party within the country. The worldwide assets and turnover of the parties are not considered.[1164]

The question therefore arises whether the thresholds lead to a notification requirement for only those transactions with the most substantial impact or closest connection to the jurisdiction. Of the three jurisdictions, the threshold in South Africa requires the closest nexus of a transaction to the jurisdiction. However, even where the drafting of the thresholds

1159 See for instance Sutherland and Kemp (2014) para 8.2.2.5.
1160 IBA Taskforce Report 57-58.
1161 See discussion on Notification Thresholds, cap 3.2.
1162 Clayton Act s7a.
1163 EU Merger Regulation art 1 and 3.
1164 SA Threshold Guidance ss 1-3.

ensures the closest nexus to the transaction, the mere scale of certain transactions may lead to the triggering of the notification requirement in several jurisdictions where they have a presence. The level of the notification thresholds in jurisdictions such as the United States and the European Union in comparison to those in smaller jurisdictions such as South Africa means that multinational firms with a presence in the smaller jurisdictions may still find themselves having to file notifications in the smaller jurisdictions.[1165]

The International Bar Association in its report on extraterritoriality notes that the size of the transaction test in the United States may be met just because the size of the parties, irrespective of the transaction not having a substantial impact within the United States.[1166]

The thresholds set in the European Union also mean that undertakings that carry out a substantial portion of their business outside of the European Union, or transactions concluded outside of the European Union with little effect within the common market would still trigger jurisdiction. One example given is of two undertakings which meet the threshold but which conclude a joint venture outside of the European Union which would have little to no impact within the European Union. Such a transaction would still be notifiable, albeit using the simplified procedure.[1167]

3.3.3 Experience in the EU, the US, South Africa and Eastern and Southern Africa

3.3.3.1 The United States

The United States approach on the scope of its jurisdiction in antitrust cases had traditionally been one of strict territoriality. In *American Banana Co. v. United Fruit Co*[1168] the court stated that it was surprising to hear the argument that acts causing damage that were done outside the jurisdiction of the US could be governed by the act of Congress. The court expressed the view that:

> a statute will, as a general rule, be construed as intended to be confined in its operation and effect to the territorial limits within the

1165 IBA Task Force Report 58.

1166 Ibid.

1167 Whish and Bailey (2012) 499.

1168 *American Banana Co. v. United Fruit Co* 213 U.S. 347 (1909).

> jurisdiction of the lawmaker, and words of universal scope will be construed as meaning only those subject to the legislation.

The notion that the jurisdiction of a state may be extended beyond its territory based on effects produced within its territory was however subsequently lent credence by the US courts in *United States v Aluminium Co of America*[1169] (Alcoa) where Judge Learned Hand stated that:

> it is settled law…that any State may impose liabilities, even upon persons not within its allegiance, for conduct outside its borders which has consequences within its borders which the State reprehends; and these liabilities other States will ordinarily recognise.[1170]

The case did not however address the question of the substantiality of these effects. Substantiality was later statutorily addressed by the Foreign Trade Antitrust Amendment Act of 1982 (FTAIA) which restricted the application of the Sherman Act to conduct involving trade and commerce with foreign states that has a 'direct, substantial, and reasonably foreseeable effect' on trade and commerce with the US.[1171]

The effects doctrine as encapsulated in the FTAIA subsequently received support from the Supreme Court in *Hartford Fire Insurance Co v California*[1172] where the court stated that 'it is well established by now that the Sherman Act applies to foreign conduct that was meant to produce and did in fact produce some substantial effect in the United States.'[1173]

The effects doctrine has also been applied by the FTC to merger cases. For instance, in *Institut Merieux*[1174] the FTC intervened in a proposed merger between Institut Merieux, a French company, and Connaught BioSciences, a Canadian company, both of which had a sizable presence in the US market for rabies and polio vaccines respectively. The merger would put Institut Merieux in a dominant position in the market for rabies and polio vaccines.

The transaction was to be concluded outside the United States but it triggered the notification requirement in the US. Its consummation would therefore have violated section 7 of the Clayton Act and section 5 of the FTC Act. The FTC expressed the view that the effect of the transaction

---

1169 *United States v Aluminium Co of America* 148 F.2d 416 (2d Cir. 1945).
1170 Ibid 444.
1171 15 U.S. Code § 6a.
1172 *Hartford Fire Insurance Co v California* 509 U. S. 764 (1993).
1173 Ibid 796.
1174 Institut Merieux, S.A., No. 891-0098, 55 Fed. Reg. 1614 (Jan. 17, 1990).

would have been to substantially lessen competition in the relevant lines of commerce in the United States.[1175] The merging parties agreed to sign a consent agreement and the FTC issued a consent order thereafter, requiring inter alia the leasing of the rabies vaccine business to a FTC approved lessee for at least 25 years and FTC approval before acquiring interest in a company producing human vaccine for at least 10 years.[1176]

More importantly, this case brought to light some of the challenges faced in exercising extraterritorial enforcement jurisdiction. Chief among them is how to fashion an appropriate and effective remedy where it should be enforced abroad, hence requiring the cooperation of a foreign state. The FTC indeed noted that the assets available within the United States were not sufficient to craft an effective remedy.[1177] The FTC also noted the willingness of parties (to transactions which are extraterritorial) to accommodate the requirements of the regulator where the parties seek to access the market as influential in the exercise of prosecutorial discretion.[1178]

In this case therefore, the willingness of the parties to enter into a consent agreement played a big role. Absent such willingness the choice is either to seek the cooperation of the counterpart state to exercise jurisdiction or simply to defer it in the interests of comity. Without this cooperation, it would not be possible to enforce an order in a foreign territory.[1179] The FTC highlighted the need for it to ensure that its obligations under bilateral (cooperation) agreements are met as well as a consideration of public interest and comity before referring cases to the court.[1180]

3.3.3.2 The European Union

The EU competition rules are also applied extraterritorially. As stated by the Commission, 'application of EU competition rules to a restriction of competition by a foreign undertaking is justified when a sufficient connection between the activity concerned and the EU territory (or part

1175 Ibid 744.
1176 Ibid 745-761.
1177 Deborah K. Owen and John J. Parisi, 'International Mergers and Joint Ventures: A Federal Trade Commission Perspective' (1990) Fordham Corporate Law Institute 1,7-9.
1178 Ibid.
1179 Ibid 10-17.
1180 Ibid.

of the EU territory) affected is established.'[1181] The Commission points out that there are three grounds on which EU competition law can be exerted extraterritorially: the single economic entity doctrine by which a parent company and its subsidiaries are taken as one undertaking; the implementation doctrine by which *inter alia* agreements, concerted practices and decisions concern or are implemented by a foreign undertaking within the EU; and the effects doctrine.[1182]

The Court of Justice has however not specifically relied on the effects doctrine. This is mainly because the other two grounds have largely been sufficient. Therefore, the need for reliance on an effects doctrine has not arisen.[1183] In the *Dyestuffs*[1184] case for instance, the Court of Justice employed the single economic entity doctrine. This case was in respect of illegal price fixing which was carried out by three non-EU undertakings through subsidiary companies within the European Union. The court held inter alia that:

> Where an undertaking established in a third country, in the exercise of its power to control its subsidiaries established within the community, orders them to carry out a decision to raise prices, the uniform implementation of which together with other undertakings constitutes a practice prohibited under article 85 (1) of the EEC treaty, the conduct of the subsidiaries must be imputed to the parent company.
> for the purpose of applying the rules on competition, unity of conduct on the market as between a parent company and its subsidiaries overrides the formal separation between those companies resulting from their separate legal personality.[1185]

Whether an undertaking and its subsidiary can be considered a single economic entity turns upon the exercise of decisive influence by the parent company upon the subsidiary. The court pointed out that decisive influence can be determined for instance from lack of independence and autonomy of the subsidiary in decision making and determining its course of action in the market or a majority shareholding by the parent.[1186]

1181 European Commission, Roundtable on Cartel Jurisdiction Issues, including the Effects Doctrine DAF/COMP/WP3/WD(2008)93, para 5.

1182 Ibid paras 6-8.

1183 Whish and Bailey (2012) 495.

1184 C-48/69 *ICI v Commission* (1972) ECR 619 (Dyestuffs case summary).

1185 Dyestuffs case summary para 11.

1186 Dyestuffs case summary paras 132-137.

In the *Wood Pulp*[1187] case, the Commission was of the view that jurisdiction could be claimed based on the effects doctrine. The Court of Justice however steered clear of adopting the effects doctrine, rather choosing to rely on the implementation doctrine. In this case, several producers established outside of the European Union had entered into a price agreement on the basis of which they would charge their customers within the European Union. The Court of Justice held inter alia that:

> Where producers established outside the Community sell directly to purchasers established in the Community and engage in price competition in order to win orders from those customers, that constitutes competition within the common market.
> It follows that where those producers concert on the prices to be charged to their customers in the Community and put that concertation into effect by selling at prices which are actually coordinated, they are taking part in concertation which has the object and effect of restricting competition within the common market within the meaning of Article 85 of the Treaty.[1188]

In this regard, the Court of Justice was of the view that it was unnecessary to have recourse to the effects doctrine and that the territoriality principle was sufficient to address this case.[1189]

The EU Merger Regulation has likewise been found to be applicable to transactions that occur outside the European Union but which are liable to significantly impede competition within the European Union. In *Gencor/Lonrho*[1190], a merger between two South African undertakings was declared by the Commission to be incompatible with the common market (hence prohibited) on the grounds that it would lead to a collective dominant position (a dominant duopoly) in the world market for platinum and rhodium. This would lead to a significant impediment to effective competition within the common market.[1191] The Commission expressed the view that:

1187 Joined cases C-89/85, C-104/85, C-114/85, C-116/85, C-117/85 and C-125/85 to C-129/85 *Ahlström Osakeyhtiö and others v Commission* (1988) ECR 5193 (Wood Pulp case).

1188 Wood Pulp case para 1 (summary).

1189 For discussion see Whish and Bailey (2012) 497.

1190 Case No IV/M.619 *Gencor/Lonrho*, OJ 1997 L 11, 30.

1191 Ibid paras 219-220.

> the platinum market is a world market and prices for platinum in the European Community are set at the world market level. Therefore, anticompetitive effects of the operation in the platinum market would be felt in the European Community, for example, through higher prices for all the platinum sold in the European Community... For the same reasons as set forth in the discussion on the platinum market, the characteristics of the rhodium market imply that post-merger competition between the remaining players will not be enough to secure effective competition in this market. Therefore, the operation would create a dominant duopoly position in the medium term in the rhodium market as a result of which effective competition would be significantly impeded in the common market.[1192]

Gencor appealed the decision to the General Court. One of the arguments was that the EU Merger Regulation could not be applied in respect of transactions relating to economic activities in a non-member country and which had been approved by the authorities in that country, in this case South Africa.[1193] As regards the territorial scope of the EU Merger Regulation the General Court held inter alia that:

> Article 1 does not require that, in order for a concentration to be regarded as having a Community dimension, the undertakings in question must be established in the Community or that the production activities covered by the concentration must be carried out within Community territory.

The General Court further noted that the transaction was indeed one with a community dimension, having been satisfied that both the worldwide and community-wide turnover thresholds had been exceeded. Additionally, each of the merging undertakings did not achieve more than two thirds of their community-wide turnover in one Member State.[1194]

On the issue of whether the Commission's decision violated public international law the General Court found that:

> Application of the Regulation is justified under public international law when it is foreseeable that a proposed concentration will have an immediate and substantial effect in the Community.

1192 Ibid paras 206-210.
1193 [1999] ECR II-753 *Gencor v Commission..*
1194 Ibid para 80.

The conclusion of the General Court therefore was that the Commission had not overstepped its jurisdictional mandate.

Irrespective of which grounds jurisdiction is based on, the way the final decisions and orders or penalties shall be enforced still needs to be addressed. A decision may be served on the subsidiary of a non-EU undertaking or even upon the undertaking itself.[1195] However, where the decision includes orders or penalties, their enforcement in a foreign State would not be possible without some form of cooperative mechanism, or as was the case with the *Institut Merieux* case in the United States, the willingness of the undertaking.[1196] The General Court highlighted the need to take into consideration the principles of non-interference and proportionality, recognising the important role that comity considerations play in the exercise of extraterritorial jurisdiction. In this case however, the General Court held that none of these principles were violated.[1197]

3.3.3.3 South Africa

When compared to the European Union and the United States, South Africa hardly has any experience in exercising its antitrust jurisdiction extraterritorially. The competition authorities have however expressed willingness to apply the SA Competition Act extraterritorially on the grounds of an effects-based approach in the case of *American Natural Soda Ash Corporation and another v Competition Commission and others*.[1198]

In this case, Botswana Ash (Botash), a soda ash producer based in Botswana filed a complaint with the Competition Commission alleging that American Natural Soda Ash (Anash) was engaging in price fixing, market allocation and predatory pricing. Anash opposed this and filed a counter-alleging that Botash was engaging in predatory pricing against it.[1199] The matter was subsequently referred by the Competition Commission to the Competition Tribunal. One of the questions posed was in respect of the meaning of section 3(1) of the SA Competition Act which

---

1195 For discussion see Whish and Bailey (2012) 498-499.

1196 Ibid. Action could as well be taken in respect of assets that are within the EU.

1197 Gencor Decision para 102.

1198 *American Natural Soda Ash Corporation and another v Competition Commission and others* Case 12/CAC/Dec01, 30 October 2003 (Ansac Appeal Decision).

1199 *American Natural Soda Ash Corporation and another v Competition Commission and others* South Africa Competition Tribunal 49/CR/Apr00 and 87/CR/Sep00, 30 November 2001, 2 (Ansac Tribunal Decision).

provides inter alia: 'This Act applies to all economic activity within, or having an effect within, the Republic.'

At the outset, the Tribunal noted that,

> It appears to be common cause between the various parties that this 'activity', given that it originates in an agreement concluded in the US, has an extraterritorial dimension. All the parties agree that the Act has some measure of extra-territorial reach.

The question remains what the extent of this reach is. The Tribunal went on to further elaborate that section 3(1) provides for two ways to found jurisdiction; this being in respect of activity 'within', on the one hand and activity having an 'effect within', on the other.[1200] The Tribunal expressed the view that section 3(1) is to be interpreted as widely as possible.[1201] Within this context of interpreting section 3(1) as widely as possible, the Tribunal further opined that the word 'effect' bears the ordinary meaning of 'a *result, consequence or outcome*' thus not necessarily denoting a positive or a negative outcome. Hence jurisdiction is not founded only where there is a negative effect. However, prohibition only occurs where the effect is deemed to be negative.[1202]

One of the arguments presented by Botash and the Commission, which was subsequently endorsed by the Tribunal, was that the US Sherman Act, unlike the SA Competition Act, does not have a section 3(1) type of application clause hence the need to develop an 'effects doctrine'.[1203] This in essence means that the Tribunal regards section 3(1) of the SA Competition Act as a statutory prescription of the effects doctrine.[1204]

On appeal, the Competition Appeal Court expressed a similar opinion to that of the Commission and the Tribunal, stating that the word 'effect' as used in section 3(1) should be given its ordinary grammatical meaning, which in this case is neutral in nature.[1205] The Competition Appeal Court similarly noted that it was not in question that the SA Competition Act applies extraterritorially, further expressing the opinion that:

> The question is not whether the consequences of the conduct is criminal or, for that matter, anti-competitive, but whether the conduct com-

1200 Ansac Tribunal Decision 4.
1201 Ansac Tribunal Decision 11.
1202 Ansac Tribunal Decision 9, 28-31.
1203 Ansac Tribunal Decision 11.
1204 Ansac Tribunal Decision 29.
1205 Ansac Appeal Decision para 13.

plained of has 'direct and foreseeable' substantial consequences within the regulating country. In other words, the 'effects' in the present case must be such that they fall within the regulatory framework of the Act, whether they are anti-competitive or not.[1206]

3.3.3.4 Experience in the ESA Jurisdictions

The ESA jurisdictions, including South Africa, practically have no experience with the extraterritorial enforcement of their jurisdiction. The Toyota Tshusho merger is however an appropriate case study of the challenges faced by the ESA jurisdictions in respect of extraterritorial jurisdiction.

The Toyota Tshusho Case Study

This global merger had a significant effect on competition in the automobile market in many countries, with the ESA jurisdictions of Malawi, Kenya, Tanzania, Zambia and Mauritius being significantly affected. It was estimated for instance that post-merger, 70 percent of the market for new cars in Zambia as well as 40 percent of the market for new cars and 60 percent of the market for new saloon cars in Kenya would be in the hands of *Toyota*. The merger was approved with conditions in Malawi and Kenya. It was initially prohibited in Zambia but subsequently approved owing to changes that affected the relevant car market structure.

Of interest is the regard that the parties had for the approval of the merger in the affected ESA jurisdictions. In the response by CFAO to the offer by Toyota, it was expressed by Toyota that the transaction would be notified to the competition authorities in Malawi, Kenya, Tanzania, Zambia and Mauritius to obtain authorization. This was an acknowledgement by Toyota that the transaction had indeed surpassed the notification thresholds in these jurisdictions and that it would significantly affect competition in their relevant markets.

It was also observed that notification in some of the jurisdictions has an effect of suspending the transaction until the authorization of the competition authority is obtained. Toyota had as well offered to make commitments to the competition authorities which, together with conditions and undertakings which the authorizations may be subject to, was noted would have a significant effect on the relevant activities, profits and financial situation of their entities in the ESA jurisdictions.

1206 Ibid. paras 18.

However, although their interests in these jurisdictions would have been significantly affected, the only requirement for the transaction to proceed was the obtaining of approval from the European Commission.[1207]

This leads back to the question of the economic importance of a jurisdiction when it comes to the enforcement of extraterritorial jurisdiction. The assets in the five ESA jurisdictions would have been significantly affected depending on the steps taken by the competition authorities. However, the material significance of these assets and interests to the merging parties does not seem to have been sufficient enough to put the transaction on hold. Zambia had in fact initially prohibited the transaction but it was not clear what steps would have been taken to effectively enforce the prohibition. The effect of a freeze on the assets of the merging parties within Zambia would in most likelihood have resulted in a detrimental effect to the new car market; given the fact that 70 percent of that market was at stake.

Naturally the cooperation of the parties to the transaction would be the most prudent and effective avenue for the affected jurisdictions. The willingness of the merging parties to cooperate is however more important from a foreign investment perspective. This is especially so where the merging parties are in effect forced to choose between the benefits of the transaction to their business vis a vis the economic importance of the ESA jurisdictions in question.

This means that the ESA jurisdictions would in most cases be forced into a compromise, where the consequences of a hard enforcement stance may lead to the loss of a very important investor.

3.4 *Comity and Cooperation*

3.4.1 European Union and United States

Efforts to exercise extraterritorial jurisdiction without some deference or consideration of the affected state(s) would naturally prove to be a challenging endeavour. The United States for instance because of extraterritorial action arising from the principles originating from the *Alcoa* case[1208]

1207 CFAO response to Tender Offer initiated by Toyota Tshusho Corporation, para 1.4 available at: www.cfaogroup.com.

1208 *United States v Aluminium Co of America* 148 F.2d 416 (2d Cir. 1945).

encountered diplomatic notes of concern as well as diplomatic protests.[1209] Some countries even enacted blocking statutes which aim to restrict the effects of laws from other States from hampering commercial activities within their jurisdictions.[1210]

This led to the US courts seeking ways in which this extraterritorial reach could be tempered. In *Timberlane Lumber Co. v. Bank of America National Trust & Savings Association*[1211] the Ninth Circuit Court of Appeal adopted a three-step interest-balancing approach in determining whether to exercise jurisdiction. The court considered whether:

> (1) the alleged restraint affects, or was intended to affect, the foreign commerce of the United States; (2) the deed was of such a type or magnitude so as to be cognizable as a violation of the Sherman Act; and (3) an extension of extraterritorial jurisdiction would violate international comity and fairness.' The court referred to this as a 'jurisdictional rule of reason.[1212]

The *Timberlane* test was however rejected by the District of Columbia Circuit Court of Appeals in *Laker Airways Ltd. v. Sabena, Belgian World Airlines.*[1213] The court rejected the interest-balancing approach to determining the exercise of extraterritorial jurisdiction, noting that,

> the usefulness and wisdom of interest balancing to assess the most "reasonable" exercise of prescriptive jurisdiction has not been affirmatively demonstrated. This approach has not gained more than a temporary foothold in domestic law. Courts are increasingly refusing to adopt the approach. Scholarly criticism has intensified. Additionally, there is no evidence that interest balancing represents a rule of international law. Thus, there is no mandatory rule requiring its adoption here, since Congress cannot be said to have implicitly legislated subject to these international constraints.[1214]

1209 *See for instance* British protests, reprinted in International Law Association, Report of the Fifty-First Conference, 404, 579, 582 (1964).

1210 Joseph P Griffin, 'Foreign Governmental Reactions to U.S. Assertions of Extraterritorial Jurisdiction' (1998) 6 Geo. Mason L. Rev. 505; see also Zerk (2010) 95-96.

1211 *Timberlane Lumber Co. v. Bank of America National Trust & Savings Association* 549 F. 2 d 597 (9th Cir. 1976).

1212 Ibid para 80.

1213 *Laker Airways Ltd. v. Sabena, Belgian World Airlines* 731 F.2d 909 (1984 U.S. App. Decision).

1214 Ibid part II(E), 2b.

It is noteworthy that the court criticised the subjection to an interest-balancing test of an already congressionally granted prescriptive jurisdiction.

The Supreme Court in *Hartford Fire* also considered the question as to which point comity considerations come into play; whether prior to the determination of jurisdiction or after. The Supreme Court expressed the view that comity considerations are applicable subsequent to the determination of jurisdiction, though in this case comity considerations did not counsel against jurisdiction.[1215]

The OECD recognised also this challenge and started to recommend that its Member States exercise 'negative' comity, i.e. exercising deference in taking enforcement actions in consideration of foreign interests and subsequently advocated for 'positive' comity which entails cooperation between states in the pursuit of enforcement action.[1216] The DOJ and the FTC have also incorporated the commitment to comity in their Antitrust Enforcement Guidelines for International Operations.[1217] They have expressed agreement to consider the legitimate interests of other nations in line with OECD recommendations.[1218] More concretely, the DOJ and the FTC have incorporated a non-exhaustive list of factors they take into consideration in determining whether the interests of another state would be affected significantly including:

> the relative significance to the alleged violation of conduct within the United States, as compared to conduct abroad; the nationality of the persons involved in or affected by the conduct; the presence or absence of a purpose to affect U.S. consumers, markets, or exporters; the relative significance and foreseeability of the effects of the conduct on the United States as compared to the effects abroad; the existence of reasonable expectations that would be furthered or defeated by the action; the degree of conflict with foreign law or articulated foreign economic policies; the extent to which the enforcement activities of

---

1215 Hartford fire Decision 797.

1216 See OECD, Recommendation of the OECD Council concerning International Co-operation on Competition Investigations and Proceedings, C(2014)108 <https://www.oecd.org/daf/competition/2014-rec-internat-coop-competition.pdf> accessed 19 September 2019 (OECD Cooperation Recommendation); See also Andrew T. Guzman (ed), *Cooperation, Comity and Competition Policy* (OUP, Oxford 2011) 15.

1217 DOJ and FTC, Antitrust Enforcement Guidelines for International Operations (April 1995) <https://www.justice.gov/atr/antitrust-enforcement-guidelines-international-operations> accessed 9 September 2019.

1218 Ibid para 2.92.

> another country with respect to the same persons, including remedies resulting from those activities, may be affected; and the effectiveness of foreign enforcement as compared to U.S. enforcement action.[1219]

The EU legislation does not provide for the principle of comity. The Commission as well has not published any guidelines on their position regarding comity. An understanding of the EU position regarding comity can however be gained by looking into the various bilateral agreements on competition law cooperation concluded by the European Union where comity principles are incorporated. The EU/US Agreements of 1991 and 1998 for instance incorporate both negative and positive comity principles.[1220] Article VI of the 1991 Agreement provides inter alia that:

> within the framework of its own laws and to the extent compatible with its important interests, each Party will seek, at all stages in its enforcement activities, to take into account the important interests of the other Party. Each Party shall consider important interests of the other Party in decisions as to whether or not to initiate an investigation or proceeding, the scope of an investigation or proceeding, the nature of the remedies or penalties sought, and in other ways, as appropriate.

Article V of the 1991 Agreement provides for positive comity stating inter alia that:

> if a Party believes that anticompetitive activities carried out on the territory of the other Party are adversely affecting its important interests, the first Party may notify the other Party and may request that the other Party's competition authorities initiate appropriate enforcement activities.

Article III of the 1998 Agreement (on positive comity) further provides that:

> The competition authorities of a Requesting Party may request the competition authorities of a Requested Party to investigate and, if warranted, to remedy anti-competitive activities in accordance with the Requested Party's competition laws. Such a request may be made

---

1219 Ibid para 3.2.

1220 1991 EU/US Competition Cooperation Agreement, (1995) O.J. L 95/47; Agreement between the European Communities and the Government of the United States of America on the application of positive comity principles in the enforcement of their competition laws, [1998] O.J. L 173/28.

> regardless of whether the activities also violate the Requesting Party's competition laws, and regardless of whether the competition authorities of the Requesting Party have commenced or contemplate taking enforcement activities under their own competition laws.

The Commission however points out that the positive comity provisions are not used frequently because the firms themselves tend to approach the regulator they feel is best placed to deal with the matter.[1221] The Commission view is reinforced by the fact that these positive comity provisions have rarely been invoked.

The European Union has also concluded an agreement on trade, development and cooperation with South Africa which incorporates various provisions on competition law.[1222] Article 38 of this Agreement is in respect of positive comity and states that, 'whenever the Commission or the South African Competition Authority has reason to believe that anti-competitive practices ... are taking place within the territory of the other authority and are substantially affecting important interests of the Parties, it may request the other Party's competition authority to take appropriate remedial action in terms of that authority's rules governing competition.'[1223]

In cases where real conflict exists, the EU and US authorities will in most likelihood seek a claim based on overriding interests in the enforcement and altogether disregard comity. In the Laker decision for instance, the US Court of Appeals was of the view that;

> If promotion of international comity is measured by the number of times United States jurisdiction has been declined under the "reasonableness" interest balancing approach, then it has been a failure. Implementation of this analysis has not resulted in a significant number of conflict resolutions favoring a foreign jurisdiction. A pragmatic assessment of those decisions adopting an interest balancing approach indicates none where United States jurisdiction was declined when there was more than a de minimis United States interest. Most cases in which use of the process was advocated arose before a direct conflict

---

1221 See 1991 EU/US Competition Cooperation Agreement <http://ec.europa.eu/competition/international/bilateral/usa.html> accessed 9 September 2019.

1222 Agreement on Trade, Development and Cooperation between the European Community and its Member States, of the one part, and the Republic of South Africa, of the other part (OJ L 311, 04/12/1999 P. 0003 – 0415).

1223 Ibid Article 38(1).

> occurred when the balancing could be employed without impairing the court's jurisdiction to determine jurisdiction. When push comes to shove, the domestic forum is rarely unseated.[1224]

The reluctant tone of the US Supreme Court towards the use of comity to defer taking action could as well be felt in its *Hartford Fire* decision. Justice Scalia even makes the point that courts are generally reluctant to refuse the exercise of jurisdiction conferred upon them.[1225] The reasoning of the European Union General Court in the *Gencor* decision where a comity-related argument that advocated for deference was rejected also lends credence to this opinion.[1226]

3.4.2 South Africa

As noted earlier in this Chapter South Africa has practically no experience in exerting its competition law extraterritorially. There are consequently no guidelines from the competition authorities or case law from the courts that outlines the South African position on comity. The Competition Tribunal however touched on the issue of comity in the *Ansac* case. The Competition Tribunal outlined substantially the comity position in the US and the EU, though not clearly stating the position they themselves take.

The Competition Tribunal of South Africa however displayed an inclination towards the pessimistic position taken in the US in respect of comity. The Tribunal makes the point that cases where jurisdiction has been declined on a comity basis are rare, quoting *Laker Airways v. Sabena, Belgian World Airlines* where the US court stated, 'when push comes to shove, the domestic forum is rarely unseated'.[1227]

3.4.3 Eastern and Southern Africa

Some of the ESA jurisdictions also express their intention to pursue a comity approach where the legitimate interests of another state are at

1224 *Laker Airways Ltd. v. Sabena, Belgian World Airlines* 731 F.2d 909 (1984 U.S. App. Decision) part II(E), 2b.

1225 Hartford fire Decision 818.

1226 Gencor v Commission para 103.

1227 *Laker Airways Ltd. v. Sabena, Belgian World Airlines* 731 F.2d 909 (1984 U.S. App. Decision).

stake. The Zambia and Botswana Competition Acts for instance provide for an avenue for a foreign competition authority to request their respective authorities to investigate and decide where that authority has reasonable grounds to believe that certain anticompetitive practices occurring in Zambia and Botswana are detrimental to competition in the requesting authority's country. This is however mainly based on a reciprocity agreement being concluded, where the other country also undertakes to exercise comity.[1228] The other reviewed ESA jurisdictions are to a large extent silent on the question of comity.

Even where formal agreements are not in place, the multi-jurisdictional nature of certain transactions may necessitate cooperation between reviewing jurisdictions as was the case in the *Holcim/Lafarge* merger where the Mauritian authority collaborated with the European Commission in the absence of any formal agreement.[1229]

Such cooperative efforts are in line with the recommendations of the ICN and the OECD, the ICN having pointed out that cooperation ultimately leads to greater convergence between jurisdictions. Cooperation is however a largely voluntary endeavour and relies heavily on the goodwill of the cooperation partners.

It has however been argued that comity and cooperation would ultimately yield to national interests where a genuine conflict exists, a position that has been intimated at in the United States, the European Union and South Africa.[1230]

The OECD in its recommendation on international cooperation defines cooperation as including:

> a broad range of practices, from informal discussions to more formal co-operation activities based on legal instruments at the national or international level, employed by competition authorities of Adherents to ensure efficient and effective reviews of anticompetitive practices and mergers with anticompetitive effects affecting one or more Adherents. It may also include more general discussions relating to competition policy and enforcement practices.[1231]

It recommends: a commitment to cooperation such as taking steps to reduce the negative impact that legislation has on effective cooperation;

1228 Zambia Competition Ac, s 65; Botswana Competition Act s 77.

1229 See chapter 3.2.6.

1230 See chapter 3.4.

1231 OECD Cooperation Recommendation 3.

consultation and comity; notifying investigations and proceedings to countries that would be affected; thereafter coordinating these investigations and proceedings with the concerned authorities as well as exchanging information with due regard to confidentiality.[1232]

These recommendations are indeed reflected in the various competition law cooperation agreements concluded on bilateral and multilateral levels.[1233] The ICN points out that apart from facilitating effective cooperation, these agreements play a big part in fostering the convergence of competition law.[1234] The ICN has also prepared a practical guide to international enforcement cooperation in mergers.[1235] The ICN states that the guide is intended to serve as 'a voluntary and flexible framework for interagency cooperation in merger investigations; (ii) practical guidance for agencies seeking to engage in such cooperation; and (iii) practical guidance for merging parties and third parties seeking to facilitate cooperation'.[1236] The ICN makes the point that cooperation in merger review is voluntary with the agencies having total discretion on whether to cooperate or not.[1237] The cooperation agreements, though advocating for greater cooperation than that achieved through traditional and positive comity, are thus regarded as being more of soft law owing to their non-binding

1232 See generally OECD Cooperation Recommendation.

1233 See for instance 1991 EU/US Competition Cooperation Agreement, (1995) O.J. L 95/47 and the Agreement between the European Communities and the Government of the United States of America on the application of positive comity principles in the enforcement of their competition laws, (1998) O.J. L 173/28; Cooperation Arrangement Between the Commissioner of Competition (Canada), the Australian Competition and Consumer Commission and the New Zealand Commerce Commission Regarding the Application of their Competition and Consumer Laws <http://www.competitionbureau.gc.ca/eic/site/cb-bc.nsf/eng/01595.html> accessed 9 September 2019; Best Practices on Cooperation between EU National Competition Authorities in Merger Review <http://ec.europa.eu/competition/ecn/nca_best_practices_merger_review_en.pdf> accessed 9 September 2019.

1234 ICN, International Enforcement Cooperation Project <http://www.internationalcompetitionnetwork.org/uploads/library/doc794.pdf> accessed 9 September 2019.

1235 ICN, Practical Guide to International Enforcement Cooperation in Mergers <http://www.internationalcompetitionnetwork.org/uploads/library/doc1031.pdf> accessed 9 September 2019 (OECD Enforcement Cooperation Guide).

1236 ICN Enforcement Cooperation Guide para 3.

1237 ICN Enforcement Cooperation Guide para 5.

nature.[1238] They are thus largely dependent on the goodwill of the cooperation partners for them to be effective.

3.4.4 Conclusion

Extraterritoriality has indeed become a part and parcel of competition law. It was an inevitable eventuality once businesses went global and more jurisdictions adopted competition laws. Extraterritorial jurisdiction is claimed based on legal theories such as the effects doctrine, the implementation doctrine or the economic entity doctrine. The ability to effectively exercise extraterritorial jurisdiction however depends on several factors.

One of the main factors is how important the jurisdiction is economically. Jurisdictions such as the United States and the European Union are therefore going to have a higher success rate because their markets are very important for business. The willingness of the parties to cooperate with the US regulator in *Institut Merieux* is a good example of how the importance of the United States to the merging parties helped to avoid an impasse. The economic influence required to exert extraterritorial enforcement jurisdiction is indeed lacking in the ESA jurisdictions. One effective way may be to leverage on the COMESA Commission as a regional regulator whose jurisdiction may constitute a sufficiently influential economic area.

From the perspective of a developing country the need to attract Foreign Direct Investment may caution against an aggressive extraterritorial enforcement strategy. Where for instance the importance of a merger transaction is, in the view of the investor, greater than their business interests in the developing country, the investor may decide to pull out of the jurisdiction or even ignore the challenge. Any of these consequences would jeopardise the investment in the country and at the same time bring to question the effectiveness of the competition law. On the other hand there is the need for developing countries to protect their markets from harmful effects that may be occasioned by transactions concluded beyond their borders. A balance therefore needs to be achieved. However, as evidenced by South Africa, even though the competition laws of developing countries do sanction extraterritoriality, there is rarely if ever an attempt to exert it, which in most cases may be due to a lack of capacity to do so.

1238 American Bar Association, *International Antitrust Cooperation Handbook* (ABA Book Publishing 2004), 5-6.

In the absence of any internationally binding instrument on competition law or on the exercise of extraterritorial jurisdiction comity and cooperation play very important roles. The exercise or enforcement of extraterritorial jurisdiction would lead to friction between the affected countries in the absence of comity and cooperation. From the perspective of merger regulation, comity and cooperation are very important in facilitating the quick progress of a transaction where multiple regulators are involved as well as averting the risk of divergent outcomes. Comity and cooperation measures are however not legally binding and therefore rely largely on the goodwill of the various actors to succeed.

Effective comity and cooperation coupled with a legislative effort to ensure that there is a sufficient nexus between transactions and the country where extraterritorial jurisdiction has been triggered would therefore go a long way in alleviating the challenges posed by multi-jurisdiction review and extraterritoriality.

3.5 Institutional design

3.5.1 Introduction

Competition law can only be effective if it is properly implemented. At the heart of this implementation are the institutions which are in most cases established by the competition statutes as the autonomous custodians of competition law. A properly designed and well-functioning institution will therefore determine how effective the competition law is. At the same time, as highlighted by UNCTAD, the different environments in which competition policy operates (more so as regards the respect that government and business actors accord competition policy and its institutions) necessitates differences in the way in which the competition regime is designed.[1239]

1239 UNCTAD, Foundations of an effective competition agency TD/B/C.I/CLP/8 <http://unctad.org/en/docs/ciclpd8_en.pdf> accessed 10 September 2019. In para 1 it is pointed out that 'in some countries or territories, business persons and government appreciate the goals of competition and respect the institutions, and other objectives of society take competition into account. In others, business persons and government officials are learning to adapt to a competition regime and to appreciate its objectives, even if the law remains not quite adapted to the legal, economic and institutional establishment. In

There are many factors that go into determining the optimal design for an effective antitrust institution.[1240] One of the more important elements of institutional design for competition authorities is autonomy. The ability to reach determinations without interference from outside forces as well as without internal constraints is important in ensuring the integrity of decision-making. Some of the factors that come into play in determining the extent of this autonomy include the sources of funding, the appointing authorities and the transparency of the appointment process.

The structure of the institutions is also crucial in ensuring the efficient fulfilment of their mandate. In this regard, the level of integration of competition functions is central to maintaining efficiency. Where multiple institutions are involved in the implementation of competition law there is always the risk of overlapping jurisdiction. Additionally, where the competition regulation functions constitute part of a broader government agency or ministry then the mandate may be constrained to a broader ministerial or political function which may not necessarily conform to the objectives of competition regulation.

With a comparative review the US, the EU, South Africa and ESA this chapter will focus on two important aspects of institutional design; the structuring of the institutions and the level of institutional independence. The intention is to establish some parameters necessary for an effective institutional dispensation in a Sub-Saharan African context.

3.5.2 Institutional Structure

Most competition institutions can be categorised into three structural models: an integrated model consisting of a specialised agency mandated with investigation, enforcement and adjudication; a bifurcated tribunal model consisting of a specialised agency responsible for investigation and

yet others, the "barefoot competition office" struggles for recognition and respect, marooned after a high tide of a structural adjustment programme.'

1240 Id at para 2 '…independence; transparency; accountability; assuring due process; being well funded in proportion to the mandate; being staffed by well-educated, well-trained and non-corrupt persons; and having an appellate process that itself is well structured and non-corrupt. More recent discussion about competition agencies indicates that evaluation is necessary too. Among the internal processes, defining objectives and priorities, appropriately allocating resources, and taking effective decisions are necessary to an effective competition agency.

enforcement, and a separate specialised tribunal that undertakes adjudication; and a bifurcated judicial model consisting of a specialised agency which undertakes investigation and enforcement with the adjudication being undertaken by the courts. In all cases however the right of access to courts and appeal persists. Hence the elements of a judicial model can be said to be present in most if not all cases.[1241]

Although the United States has several state enforcement agencies as well as the possibility for private enforcement, the two main antitrust enforcement agencies are the FTC and the antitrust division of the DOJ.[1242] As regards antitrust enforcement the US system has aspects of both an integrated model and a bifurcated judicial model. The antitrust division of the DOJ being an arm of the executive takes enforcement action in the federal district courts with the availability of a right of appeal to a court of appeals and discretionary review by the Supreme Court.[1243]

The FTC operates both an integrated agency model and a bifurcated judicial model. The FTC therefore internally investigates antitrust violations and, apart from mergers, adjudicates on them. Both the FTC and the DOJ are involved in the investigation of mergers. Owing to this overlapping jurisdiction they operate a system whereby they notify each other and decide which agency is best suited to handle a merger.[1244] In order to bar a merger transaction from proceeding, the FTC is required to seek injunctive relief from a federal district court.[1245]

In terms of expertise both the FTC and the DOJ are noted to employ a significant number of PhD level economists in addition to attorneys, paralegals and other administrative staff. The economists are well integrated into the agency functions, participating in key strategy meetings alongside the attorneys, making recommendations and being able to influence directly the key decision makers.[1246]

One of the main challenges with the US system is hence the overlap between the DOJ and the FTC. Although arguments have been present-

---

1241 Eleanor M. Fox and Michael J. Trebilcock (eds), *The Design of Competition Law Institutions* (1st edn, OUP 2013) 5.

1242 For overview see First H, Fox M. Eleanor & Hemli E. Daniel, 'The United States: The Competition Law System and the Country's Norms' in Eleanor M. Fox and Michael J. Trebilcock (eds), *The Design of Competition Law Institutions* (OUP 2013).

1243 15 U.S.C § 29.

1244 FTC Premerger Notification Overview 11; Clayton Act, 15 U.S.C. § 18a.

1245 Clayton Act, s 7a(f); See also FTC Premerger Notification Overview 13-14.

1246 Fox and Trebilcock (2013) 364-365.

ed for and against a single regulator based on consistency of decisions, efficiency and the support the two agencies render to each other[1247], the Antitrust Modernisation Commission found that the costs and disruption that would ensue from attempting to move to a single regulator would outstrip the benefits.[1248]

The European Union operates an integrated agency model with the European Commission being responsible for antitrust enforcement.[1249] Within the European Commission, the specific organ responsible for the enforcement of competition law is the Directorate General for Competition headed by a Director General, with two of the Deputy Directors General being specifically in charge of the administration of antitrust and mergers.[1250] The Directorate General for Competition also has a Chief Competition Economist office manned by specialized economists, with the chief economist appointed by the European Commission.[1251]

The decisions of the European Commission are subject to review by the Court of Justice.[1252]

South Africa has a tribunal model with the three institutions responsible for the enforcement of competition law being the Competition Commission, the Competition Tribunal and the Competition Appeal Court.[1253]

In respect of mergers, the Competition Commission can approve or prohibit small and intermediate mergers. Large mergers are within the Competition Tribunal's jurisdiction on reference from the Competition Commission.[1254] The Commissioners as well as members of the Tribunal are required to be experienced in economics, law, commerce, industry or

---

1247 See for instance Gelhorn E. et al., 'Has Antitrust Outgrown Dual Enforcement? A proposal for Rationalization' (1990) 35 Antitrust Bull. 695 (which supports a single regulator) versus ABA, Study on the Role of the Federal Trade Commission, 58 Antitrust L.J. 53 (1989) (against a single regulator).

1248 Antitrust Modernization Commission: Report and Recommendations (2007), 129-130 <http://govinfo.library.unt.edu/amc/report_recommendation/amc_final_report.pdf> accessed 10 September 2019.

1249 TFEU art 103; See generally EU Merger Regulation.

1250 TFEU art 244-250; *See also* About the European Commission <http://ec.europa.eu/about/index_en.htm#president> accessed 10 September 2019.

1251 See Directorate-General for Competition <http://ec.europa.eu/dgs/competition/index_en.htm> accessed 10 September 2019.

1252 EU Merger Regulation art 21.

1253 SA Competition Act ch 4.

1254 SA Competition Act ss 13-16.

public affairs.[1255] The Competition Appeal Court is a specialized arm of the High Court and hears appeals from the Tribunal's decisions.[1256] South Africa and the European Union therefore do not have the challenge of overlapping jurisdiction that is faced by the United States.

The table below outlines the institutions responsible for competition law enforcement within the reviewed ESA jurisdictions:

Table 10: Institutional Structure of the ESA Jurisdictions

Jurisdiction[1257]	*Enforcement Authorities*		
COMESA	COMESA Competition Commission	Board of Commissioners	COMESA Court of Justice
Botswana	Competition Authority	Competition Commission	High Court & Court of Appeal
Kenya	Competition Authority	Competition Tribunal	High Court
Namibia	Competition Commission	Minister	High Court
Zimbabwe	Competition and Tariff Commission	Administrative Court	-
Zambia	Competition and Consumer Protection Commission	Competition and Consumer Protection Tribunal	High Court
Mauritius	Competition Commission	Supreme Court	-
Seychelles	Fair Trading Commission	Appeal Tribunal	Supreme Court
Tanzania	Fair Competition Commission	Fair Competition Tribunal	-

1255 SA Competition Act s 22 sub-s 1 and s 28 sub-s 2. Judges however cannot be members of the Tribunal.

1256 SA Competition Act s 17, Within the court structure it is noted that there still persists the possibility of appeal to the Supreme Court of Appeal and the Constitutional Court; see Dennis Davis and Lara Granville, 'South Africa: The Competition Law System and the Country's Norms' in Eleanor M. Fox and Michael J. Trebilcock (eds), *The Design Of Competition Law Institutions* (1st edn, OUP 2013).

1257 COMESA Competition Regulations part 2; Botswana Competition Act parts II, III, X and XI; Kenya Competition Act parts II, IV and VII; Namibia Competition Act chs 2, 4 and 5; Zimbabwe Competition Act parts II, IV and VI; Zambia Competition Act parts II, IV, VIII and IX; Mauritius Competition Act parts II, III, VI and VIII; Seychelles Competition Act parts II, III, VI and VII; Tanzania Competition Act parts XI, XII and XIII; Malawi Competition Act parts II and VI.

Malawi	Competition and Fair Trading Commission	Judge in Chambers	-

In all jurisdictions, we note that the right of access to courts is maintained. In Tanzania appeals to the Fair Competition Tribunal are final. This tribunal is however headed by a judge of the High Court. Its orders and decisions are granted equal status to that of the High Court.

The structures in Kenya, Zambia, Seychelles and COMESA are in line with a bifurcated tribunal model. The COMESA Board of Commissioners has the power to review the decisions of the COMESA Commission. The Board of Commissioners therefore plays a tribunal role in this respect. Namibia has a peculiar model where the relevant Minister plays the role of reviewing the Commission's decision, a role that would normally be played by a specially constituted tribunal.[1258]

Zimbabwe, Mauritius, Tanzania and Malawi have integrated models. The Fair Competition Tribunal in Tanzania is in fact a judicial authority whose responsibility is to hear appeals from the decisions of the Fair Competition Commission.[1259]

Botswana has elements of both an integrated model and a bifurcated tribunal model. The Competition Authority is empowered to make determinations in certain cases, such as in merger regulation. However, several anticompetitive practices should only be investigated and referred to the Commission for determination.[1260]

In terms of composition all the reviewed ESA jurisdictions require candidates with expertise in the relevant fields, mainly competition, economics, law, commerce and industry.[1261]

The ideal structure is indeed one that has fewer decision-making bodies. This increases efficiency and prevents overlaps as well as ensuring the consistency of decisions. From this perspective, the ESA jurisdictions have adopted structures that avoid overlaps in so far as specific sector regulation is not considered.

1258 Namibia Competition Act s 49.

1259 Op. cit. note 1247.

1260 Botswana Competition Act s 5.

1261 Namibia Competition Act s 5 sub-s 2; COMESA Competition Regulations arts 9 and 13; Kenya Competition Act s 10; Malawi Competition Act s 5; Tanzania Competition Act s 63 sub-s 5; Seychelles Fair Trading Commission Act s 5 sub-s 2; Mauritius Competition Act s 7 sub-s 2; Zimbabwe Competition Act s 6 sub-s 2; Botswana Competition Act s10 sub-s 2.

3.5.3 Institutional Independence

Antitrust institutions need to autonomously carry out their mandate to maintain trust and confidence in their findings and increase the transparency of their processes. To this end, appointment of officials, funding and the ability to make decisions without undue involvement of external actors is crucial.

3.5.3.1 Appointments

The FTC commissioners as well as the head of the DOJ's antitrust division are appointed by the President with the advice and consent of the Senate.[1262] In respect of the European Union, each Member State of the European Union nominates a Commissioner to the European Commission who is then approved by the European Parliament and appointed by the Council of the European Union. The European Commission in turn undertakes the appointment of the Directors General and the Deputy Directors General.[1263]

The appointment of Commissioners and members of the Tribunal in South Africa is however not subject to the same checks and balances as the United States and the European Union. In the European Union and the United States, we note that the appointment is subject to a vetting process whereby the Senate and the European Parliament are involved in the approval of candidates. In South Africa, the appointment of the Commissioners is wholly carried out by the Minister of Trade and Industry.[1264] The chairperson and members of the Tribunal are appointed by the President on recommendation by the Minister or in response to a public call for nominations.[1265]

The Minister is therefore the main determinant of the composition of the Commission and the Tribunal. Although the SA Competition Act sets out the qualifications required for the officials there is no ruling out the possibility of bias (for instance political bias) and non-transparency in appointments where one person is responsible. A proper appointment

1262 15 U.S.C § 41; 28 U.S.C §§ 503, 506.

1263 TFEU arts 244-250; *See also* About the European Commission <http://ec.europa.eu/about/index_en.htm#president> accessed 10 September 2019.

1264 SA Competition Act s 22.

1265 SA Competition Act s 26 sub-s 2.

process should not only involve the executive but also the legislature to ensure appointments are free of bias.[1266]

This same challenge is seen in the broader ESA context. As is the case with South Africa, appointments are carried out either by the relevant Minister or by the President with the recommendation of the relevant Minister.[1267] Mauritius seeks greater inclusivity in the appointment of commissioners by involving the opposition, presumably the political opposition party, in the appointment consultations.[1268] COMESA being a regional body naturally follows a more balanced appointment system that seeks to ensure regional balance, with appointments being carried out by a Council of the various Ministers from the Member States.[1269]

In some of the ESA jurisdictions, even the remuneration of the Commissioners is dependent on the relevant Minister(s).[1270]

Where a single appointing authority has leverage in terms of appointment and in some cases remuneration, more so where the appointing authority is a single individual, there is always the risk that the appointees may be greatly influenced by the appointing authority in carrying out their functions.

3.5.3.2 Funding

Competition institutions require sufficient finances to effectively achieve their mandate. Financial independence is also acknowledged as being key to ensuring independence of objectives and functions.[1271] Resource constraints is more so an issue of the new competition institutions especially those in developing countries. Apart from sufficiency there also should be accountability for all sources of such income.

The sources of finance for the South African Competition Commission are listed in the Act as: 'money that is appropriated by Parliament for the Commission; fees payable to the Commission in terms of this Act; income

1266 UNCTAD (n 1229) para 18.

1267 Botswana Competition Act s 10; Malawi Competition Act s 5; Kenya Competition Act s 10; Seychelles Fair Trading Commission Act s 5; Tanzania Competition Act s 63; Namibia Competition Act s 5; Zimbabwe Competition Act s 6.

1268 Mauritius Competition Act s 7.

1269 COMESA Competition Regulations arts 9 and 13.

1270 See for instance Malawi Competition Act s 7; Namibia Competition Act s 9; Kenya Competition Act s 11.

1271 Ibid para 20.

derived by the Commission from its investment and deposit of surplus money...; and money received from any other source'.[1272]

The deposit is specified to be an on-call or short-term fixed deposit with a bank registered in South Africa. The investment is via an investment account held at a statutorily established Corporation for Public Deposits.[1273] In respect of money received from any other source, mechanisms should be in place to ensure that it is not from sources that are liable to compromise the integrity of the institution and its decisions. The Act however further requires that audited accounts be maintained detailing any income and expenditure as well as a statement of income and expenditure which will be used to estimate the following financial year's budget.[1274]

Being too reliant on budgetary allocations can compromise the financial independence of a competition authority, especially where such allocations are uncertain or subject to wider budget austerity measures. In this regard, means of self-funding such as through charging fees for instance could be bolstered especially in developing countries where budgetary allocations may in some cases be uncertain.[1275]

Some developing country competition institutions may be run as a department of a larger ministry and their budget may be constrained to an allocation from the ministry's budget. In such cases not only would the financing for operations probably constrained, but also the decision-making capacity and the performance of the agency.

Many of the ESA jurisdictions rely on budgetary allocations as well as various statutory fees, including merger notification fees. Statutory measures requiring the keeping of accounts, carrying out of audits and preparing annual reports are also put in place to maintain accountability. Some authorities may also invest funds that are not immediately required.[1276]

Malawi for instance additionally relies on grants and donations as well as taking out loans from any source within or outside the country. The authorities in Kenya and Tanzania also accepts grants, donations and bequests without qualifications as to which sources may or may not be

---

1272 SA Competition Act s 40.

1273 Ibid s 40 sub-s 6.

1274 SA Competition Act s 40 sub-ss 2-5.

1275 UNCTAD (n 1229) para 20.

1276 Botswana Competition Act ss 21 and 23; Malawi Competition Act ss 26, 29 and 30; Kenya Competition Act ss 78, 81, 82 and 83; Mauritius Competition Act ss 33-35; Seychelles Competition Act ss 27-29; Tanzania Competition Act ss 78-82; Namibia Competition Act ss 17-21; Zimbabwe Competition Act ss 23-26.

appropriate. The Namibia Competition Act as well lists *money vesting in or accruing to the Commission from any other source*. The COMESA Commission relies on subventions from the Member States, fees and other charges as well as grants and donations from what are termed as co-operating partners.

It goes without saying that grants and donations as well as loans from some sources may compromise an authority's integrity. This is more so the case where such funds are accepted from 'any' source or from unspecified sources, which may even include a party being investigated or a party to a transaction being reviewed.[1277] The aim should naturally be to ensure that an account is taken of all sources of income, including the exclusion of sources which may serve to compromise the authority.

3.5.3.3 Autonomy

Turning again to institutional structure, some developing country competition authorities may be run as a department within a larger ministry hence being bound to the policy objectives of the ministry and the government in place. The probability that politics could play a role in administrative functions as well as decision making and enforcement is very high in such cases.[1278] This may be a challenge for Namibia for instance, where the relevant Minister has the power to review the decisions of the Commission.[1279]

Even where the institution may be structurally independent, the extent to which statutorily based intervention by other government agencies and agents are sanctioned may affect the independence of the competition institution. In South Africa for instance there are certain special interest industries such as banking where merger transactions cannot be approved or prohibited by the competition authority without input from the relevant government agency in charge of the industry.[1280] In these cases we note that the intervention is very specific and is geared towards specific objectives.

1277 Malawi Competition Act s 26; Kenya Competition Act s 78; Tanzania Competition Act s 78; Namibia Competition Act s 17; COMESA Competition Rules rule 16.

1278 UNCTAD, Model Law on Competition, paras 4-6 <http://unctad.org/en/Docs/ciclpL2_en.pdf> accessed 10 September 2019.

1279 Namibia Competition Act s 49; See also ch 10.3.

1280 SA Competition Act s 18, in respect of mergers in the banking industry.

Indeed, where external intervention is sanctioned it should be in respect of very clearly laid out instances and with the aim of achieving specific objectives. In the case of Sub-Saharan African jurisdictions, the biggest challenge in this respect is public interest. Some competition laws allow for ministerial intervention where public interest is at stake.[1281] The problem however is that a number of Sub-Saharan African jurisdictions do not clearly specify what constitutes public interest and where the limits lie in interventions in such cases. The risk of prioritization of non-competition goals which are geared towards achieving political objectives rather than the protection of competition is therefore high. It has been noted that the adoption of non-competition goals, 'opens the door to discretionary decisions, political intervention and more generally the capture of enforcement decisions by particular interests'.[1282]

Another question is whether public interest is dealt with within the authority or externally. The integration of public interest analysis within the competition institution would not only increase efficiency but also reduce the probability of political interference and of irrelevant factors being considered. However, a lack of clearly outlined objectives in public interest analysis may also lead to bureaucratic capture; in respect of which officials pursue their own interests or can be easily influenced in decision making.[1283]

3.5.4 Other factors

There are many other factors that go into determining a suitable institutional design. Competition authorities should for instance ensure that they regularly publish information with due regard to commercially sensitive and confidential information to ensure accountability and transparency. This includes statutes and guidelines, decisions, annual reports. Many Sub-Saharan Africa competition institutions do not regularly publish information making it difficult to establish the reasoning behind their decisions and bringing to question the transparency of their procedures.

1281 For discussion see ch 3.

1282 Mario Mariniello, Damien Neven and Jorge Padilla, 'Antitrust, Regulatory Capture, and Economic Integration' (2015) E15Initiative. Geneva: International Centre for Trade and Sustainable Development (ICTSD) and World Economic Forum, 1<www.e15initiative.org/> accessed 10 September 2019.

1283 Ibid 2.

Additionally, they should be able to effectively enforce their decisions, should be adequately staffed with skilled professionals as well as cooperate and coordinate with other affected government agencies.[1284]

3.5.5 Conclusion

There is no template when it comes to designing competition institutions. There are different social, political and economic conditions in which a competition policy is required to operate which necessitates different approaches to institutional design.

Looking for instance at what constitutes an optimal structural model, it has been noted that jurisdictions with strong courts would be able to rely on a judicial model.[1285] This is more so the case where there is a specialised court where the judges are knowledgeable in antitrust matters. Developing countries with weak court systems would therefore benefit more from having integrated models or a model with a specialised tribunal. The competition institutions also need to be run by individuals with relevant expertise to properly execute the mandate. In this regard the United States, the European Union and South Africa have prioritised staffing of the agencies with qualified professionals.

For the ESA jurisdictions where presumably the competition law enforcement is new and may not be effectively addressed judicially, one may argue that the tribunal and integrated models are ideal. This is indeed the case with most of the reviewed ESA jurisdictions having adopted the tribunal and integrated models, again on a presumption that the institutions have been staffed by appropriately qualified individuals. The integration of functions into specialised institutions also ensures that there are no overlaps, which affects efficiency and consistency of decisions.

There are however other factors that cut across the board and can be regarded as foundational when it comes to optimal institutional design. The independence of the institution is one such aspect. Competition authorities should be able to carry out their mandate autonomously, without external interference and with sufficient resources both financial and in terms of skilled human capital.

Their procedures and decisions should be transparent, and there should be measures put in place to ensure that there is accountability. Transparen-

1284 UNCTAD (n 1229) 11.
1285 Fox and Trebilcock (2013) 5.

cy should also extend to the way in which appointments are made to ensure that there is sufficient vetting of candidates.

In terms of institutional independence, the ESA jurisdictions need to address issues such as appointment of officials and sources of funding. Appointments should be subject to a system of checks and balances, such as parliamentary approval, where candidates are properly vetted to ensure that appointees are not easily influenced by the appointing authority. Most of the reviewed ESA jurisdictions also need to put restrictions on some of the acceptable sources of funding to ensure that the integrity of their decisions is not questioned.

Another challenge already addressed in different contexts is the insufficiency of publicly accessible information in respect of many of the ESA jurisdictions. This results information asymmetry which in turn affects the transparency of their procedures and decisions.

Many of the challenges that are identified as facing emerging competition authorities can be linked to a weak competition culture. A supportive attitude especially from government and business actors towards competition policy and respect for competition institutions would go a long way in ensuring that the institutions are progressively enabled to effectively achieve their mandate. There may certainly be more institutional challenges facing the ESA jurisdictions. However, dealing with those that are apparent and relatively straight forward to address would go a long way in inspiring confidence in their ability to effectively meet their mandate.

4 Conclusions and Recommendations

4.1 Procedural Merger Regulation

The focus of transacting parties will invariably be on the compliance steps they need to take and the duration of time before they can proceed with their transaction. From an international business context, the parties may be required to notify their transaction in several jurisdictions where notification thresholds are triggered. One of the most vital requirements in this regard is information. Competition authorities need to ensure that they make publicly available their up-to-date statutes, guidelines as well as publishing detailed decisions. Having all this information available makes navigating the regulatory landscape easier for transacting parties. It also ensures that there is transparency and that decisions of the competition authority are predictable. Having easily accessible and comprehensive information as well curbs discretionary decision making on the part of the regulator and ensures that arbitrary decisions are not taken.

Many of the ESA jurisdictions unfortunately fail to adequately publish information. This is more so in respect of decisions. Most published decisions do not provide information on the analytical approach of the authority. The authorities should therefore make a concerted effort to ensure that up-to-date and detailed information is made publicly available, having regard to the confidentiality of the parties involved where publication of decisions is involved.

Some of the statutes and guidelines also give a feeling of incompleteness in drafting, which should not be the case given the fact that the ICN and OECD have provided recommendations and guidelines on practically every important aspect of merger regulation which can be suitably adapted to fit the ESA context. The ICN and OECD as well continue to regularly review and update their recommendations and guidelines, most of which are drafted with the intention of making them easily adapted to the developing jurisdiction context. The recommendations provided in the UNCTAD peer reviews of competition laws similarly serve as useful guides in fixing gaps in legislation. There are as well extensive publications and commentaries on merger regulations for the developed jurisdictions such as the US and the EU from which some guidance can be drawn. South Africa has already shown willingness to rely on the US and the EU in its own decision making. There are in addition avenues for consultation within the ICN, OECD as well as the recently constituted African Competition Network.[1286]

Based on the review of the procedural approach of the ESA jurisdictions, some concrete recommendations (in the form of filling statutory or information gaps) as well as proposals can be made.

4.1.1 Classification of mergers

The review revealed that Malawi, Tanzania and Seychelles do not clarify what level of control constitutes a controlling interest. Zimbabwe on its part opted for a very wide approach by defining controlling interest to include any control. The ability to exercise material influence, which is the standard adopted in Botswana, Kenya, Mauritius and Zambia, or better yet the ability to exercise decisive influence may in this case be appropriate options in determining a change of control threshold to filter out non-probative transactions.

4.1.2 Notification thresholds

Of the ESA jurisdictions, Malawi is the only one that lacks a notification threshold. A notification threshold would be important even though Malawi operates a voluntary notification system. The notification threshold may be used to determine relevant merger situations as is the case in the UK, thus preventing unnecessary voluntary notifications. Having in mind that anti-competitive mergers are still subject to sanctions in Malawi, parties would still seek the authority's clearance before proceeding with their transactions. Not having a notification threshold simply means that parties unsure of the status of their transactions, even those who would fall below a would-be threshold, would still voluntarily file a notification. This would lead to more unnecessary work for the authority.

The notification threshold could also be used to trigger a mandatory requirement for the provision of certain important information by the merging parties which may then prompt the authority to investigate further or clear the transaction.

1286 See Africa Competition Forum <http://www.africancompetitionforum.org/> accessed 10 September 2019.

4.1.3 Notification system

For the ESA context, a suitable notification system should be simple, effective, implementable and enforceable. It should take into account the fact that a vast majority of mergers are non-problematic. Therefore, the already restrained resources of the authority should not be spent assessing such cases. The simplicity of the system would also mean that it can easily be implemented. It should also be predictable, hence contributing to legal certainty and make compliance by merging parties straightforward, thus enhancing the ease of doing business.

In this regard, a hybrid notification system consisting of voluntary notification but with certain mandatory information requirements would be optimal at the national level. Given the concentrated nature of the markets the investigative function of the authority, which is a core function in a voluntary system, may not be too expensive. The central role played by public interest factors in most of the ESA jurisdictions means that the investigative function may in some cases require the expenditure of resources to investigate transactions which from a competition perspective may not be problematic, but which nonetheless raise public interest concerns. Financial penalties for failure to notify problematic cases should also be set at a level that provides sufficient incentive to notify such cases.

However, given the regulatory certainty that merging parties seek before completing a transaction, the most probable result is that most transacting parties would at the very least seek negative clearance. In this regard, an asset and turnover based threshold may be set which triggers mandatory pre-merger consultation with the authority rather than pre-merger notification. The information provided in the pre-merger consultation would then lead to either a negative clearance or to a full assessment.

For transactions that do not meet this threshold, the option for pre-merger consultation as well as negative clearance would still be available without the need for the authority to expend resources on a detailed investigation. This system should also cater for those exceptional circumstances where transactions that do not meet the consultation threshold would still be investigated. This is especially the case where for instance public interest factors such as the risk of job losses come into play.

At the regional level, mandatory pre-merger notification for transactions meeting the notification threshold should be retained. The size of the regional market means would make it challenging for the regional regulator to investigate transactions.

4.1.4 Review

The notification threshold in such a hybrid system would serve not only to trigger the mandatory information requirement and pre-merger consultation but also to ensure that there is a sufficient nexus of a transaction to the ESA jurisdiction in question. The threshold should also be focused towards assets and turnover arising within the jurisdiction rather than worldwide turnover. This is to ensure that only transactions that have a significant, direct and immediate economic effect within the jurisdiction are reviewed.

The fact that the hybrid system would result in fewer transactions being reviewed means that more resources can be focused on the problematic cases. This may lead to a lower review timeline.

4.2 Substantive Merger Regulation

The recommended standard when it comes to substantive competition law assessment in merger regulation is the SLC test. The ICN and the OECD note the flexibility with which the SLC test can be used to address competition law issues, easily responding to a case-by-case approach where the most relevant factors to a reviewed transaction take centre stage. The dominance test is widely viewed as being focused on structural issues, where market shares and concentration levels are the most relevant to the analysis of any transaction. It is in this regard viewed as being rigid and unable to be easily adapted to cases requiring a consideration of factors that are not structural. However, as seen in the EU and Germany, the dominance standard can still evolve to adapt to the evolving needs of merger review. This adaptation however was identified as having its limits. The dominance standard has been criticised for being unable to address what is regarded as the dominance gap, i.e. cases that would give rise to non-collusive oligopolies.

The reviewed ESA jurisdictions, except for Tanzania, already subscribe to the SLC test. They are therefore already part of the global convergence towards the SLC standard, which, as noted by the OECD is already widely adopted and preferred among jurisdictions. The question therefore is whether the SLC test is suitable for the ESA jurisdictions. The ESA markets are still concentrated. The reviewed decisions reveal that structural considerations such as market share and concentration still play a central role in merger assessment. From this perspective, the more structured dominance test would aptly cater for their merger regulatory needs. This however does not mean that the jurisdictions need to revert to a dominance test. The flexibility and adaptability of the SLC test means that it is still able to address a structural merger analysis. The SLC test is in fact flexible enough to subsume the dominance test.

In the same vein, there is no urgent need for Tanzania to change to the SLC standard given its concentrated market. Tanzania in this regard appears to already fulfil its regulatory mandate using the dominance test. Looking at the EU and Germany, Tanzania may also opt to evolve and expand within the dominance standard. The EU and Germany have indeed acknowledged that their procedures did not change with the adoption of the SIEC standard. If Tanzania does opt to change its standard, a statutory change to the SLC test would as well not prove to be a challenge.

The main challenge for most of the ESA jurisdictions is the inclusion of public interest in the substantive merger review. Public interest is arguably an acceptable divergence when it comes to the ESA jurisdictions. The socio-economic context in which some of the competition laws are adapted may require the kind of intervening public interest circumstances espoused in the majority of the ESA statutes. Taking South Africa for instance the need to protect historically disadvantaged members of society and to ensure that they have equal opportunity to actively participate in the economy is vital in ensuring inclusivity. Public interest factors such as protection of employment, ensuring equal participation of small businesses, ensuring the global competitiveness of local industries which are the main public interest factors espoused may therefore be highly justifiable from developing jurisdictions point of view.

The challenge lies in ensuring that the inclusion of public interest does not compromise legal certainty. South Africa recognised this challenge and limited its public interest intervention to a fixed number of factors. This is however not the case for the other ESA jurisdictions. Their public interest analysis in most cases incorporates an open-ended list of factors. The regulatory uncertainty is amplified by the fact that a lot of discretion is left in the hands of the regulator to determine what factors to take into consideration.

The public interest intervening circumstances should be well defined and limited to ensure that there is regulatory certainty and to take away the substantial amount of discretionary power granted to the regulator, which may easily be abused. In addition to the closed list of public interest factors, the competition authorities should publish guidelines where transacting parties and the public at large are clearly informed of the analytical approach when it comes to considering the specific public interest factors. The South Africa public interest guidelines are highly instructive in this regard.

4.3 Extraterritoriality and Comity

Effective exertion of extraterritorial jurisdiction in merger regulation depends largely on economic influence. This is especially the case where such economic influence can get the merging parties to willingly cooperate with the enforcing jurisdiction, as evidenced by the willing cooperation of the parties to the *Institut Merieux* merger with the US regulators. The business interests of the parties within the enforcing jurisdiction should be significant enough to incentivize the willingness of the merging parties to cooperate. The ESA jurisdictions, at least individually, do not have the necessary economic influence to exert extraterritorial pressure especially where large multinationals are involved, as evidenced by the *Toyota Tshusho* merger.

An effective solution in this regard would be to leverage on the regional regulator, in this case the COMESA Competition Commission. The Common Market for Eastern and Southern Africa is without a doubt a relatively significant economic area, which continues to attract substantial FDI and M&A activity. Whereas the loss of one country's market within COMESA may be relatively inconsequential to the broader commercial interests of a multinational, the probability of being locked out of the whole Common Market may be sufficient incentive for cooperation with the regional regulator. This is keeping in mind that most multinationals will have a regional strategy rather than focusing on a specific country. A focused effort by the Member States to empower the regional regulator would in this regard enable the regional regulator to effectively protect the economic interests of the Member States.

Where the parties to a transaction that is settled abroad do not willingly cooperate with the competition authority, cooperation with the jurisdiction where the transaction is being effected becomes indispensable. A strict enforcement strategy would not be effective in a foreign jurisdiction without deference by or cooperation with the foreign regulator in the interests of comity. Therefore cooperation, either informally or formally through the conclusion of cooperation agreements, becomes very important and should no doubt become an important part of the regulatory strategy of the ESA jurisdictions. This is especially important given the increasingly international focus of merger regulation.

4.4 Institutional Design

Proper implementation of merger regulation laws hinges on an effective institutional design. Two important factors in the optimal designing of an institution are the structure, in terms of the decision-making bodies, and how independently the institution can carry out its mandate.

An optimal structure is one that is as integrated as possible, avoiding overlapping functions and ensuring that the decision-making rests to the greatest extent within the specifically constituted decision-making bodies. Integrated decision-making also eliminates the possibility of contradictory decisions and minimises the extent to which external influence can compromise the integrity of the institution.

Except for Namibia, the reviewed ESA jurisdictions have in this regard adopted highly integrated institutional structures, with functions either wholly carried out by a single authority or commission, or with a tribunal that serves a review function or a decision-making role in certain cases, with access to courts of law being available in practically all cases. Integrated structures have indeed been recommended for developing jurisdictions, where the courts may not necessarily be specialised in dealing with competition law issues. The recommendation for Namibia in this case would be to remove the review function from the Minister and have it given to either a specially constituted tribunal or a specialised section of the courts of law.

The only question is whether the ESA jurisdictions have sufficient capacity and expertise to properly implement the law. Notwithstanding the absence of specific data to verify this, the challenge of capacity constraints always arises for developing jurisdictions. Continued capacity building is therefore a ubiquitous recommendation when it comes to developing country institutions.

One of the forums in which such cooperation as well as capacity building can be carried out is within the African Competition Forum. Its mission is:

> to promote the adoption of competition principles in the implementation of national and regional economic policies of African countries, in order to alleviate poverty and enhance inclusive economic growth, development and consumer welfare by fostering competition in mar-

kets, and thereby increasing investment, productivity, innovation and entrepreneurship.[1287]

It has a membership of 33 out of the 54 African states. COMESA is also a member of the ACF. The fact that even countries that have not implemented competition laws are members indicates the goodwill that the ACF has generated. One of the key areas ACF is looking to focus on is technical assistance in drafting and revising competition policy.[1288]

In respect of institutional independence, sources of funding and the appointment of officials stand out as points of concern for the ESA jurisdictions. Many the reviewed ESA jurisdictions need to make restrictions on sources of funding that are likely to compromise the integrity of the competition authority. Donations and grants from parties that would prospectively be under review is one such restriction. In terms of appointment, a system such as parliamentary vetting which ensures checks and balances should be adopted, rather than having a Minister holding such appointment powers. This would ensure that there are no biased appointments or appointment of officials who can easily be influenced.

4.5 Conclusion

At the beginning of the study various specific questions were raised regarding merger regulation in ESA: Where do the merger regulation regimes in ESA fall within the global convergence in merger regulation? How do the substantive as well as the procedural merger regulation standards fit the context of ESA? Is there a need for redefined merger regulation systems for ESA? If so is the appropriate merger regulation regime?

From the development economics point of view, the questions raised were: Can a nexus be made between the adoption of competition law by the ESA jurisdictions and an increase in economic development? Can an increase in FDI and M&A activity be attributed to the merger regulations? Do the merger regulations enhance or facilitate the ease of doing business?

Merger regulation in ESA is in many aspects, both substantively and procedurally, already converged or increasingly converging to the developing global standards. From a substantive perspective, the majority of

1287 Info available on the Africa Competition Forum website <http://www.africancompetitionforum.org/about-us/who-we-are> accessed 25 September 2019.

1288 Ibid.

the ESA jurisdictions already apply the SLC test which is already flexible enough to meet the needs of a nascent regime, even those having highly concentrated markets like the ESA countries. This high level of concentration means that even countries like Tanzania that employ the dominance test are still able to meet their regulatory needs. Certain core divergences in the substantive approach, such as substantive public interest assessment, are arguably acceptable provided they are well defined with clearly set boundaries that ensure there is certainty in their application. Currently therefore, there is no pressing need for redefining or substantially altering the substantive approach, more so regarding the competition test applied. What is needed is to work on setting the limits of application of the public interest standard.

One aspect that is clear, especially from the procedural point of view, is a need for effective implementation. The question of redefining the merger regulatory landscape or finding a suitable regime cannot be properly addressed before the current systems are effectively implemented so that specific shortcomings can be identified. This implementation should as well include filling in or providing sufficient guidance on those aspects not properly addressed within the existing statutory framework. There is also an urgent need to ensure sufficient publication of information in respect of the statutory approach as well as the decisions made by the authorities. From the perspective of extraterritorial enforcement, a regional (rather than a national) approach which leverages on the economic importance of the regional market will be a more effective and plausible solution for the ESA countries. In this sense, ensuring that the COMESA framework is properly supported and facilitated will enable the COMESA competition commission to in turn address those extraterritorial transactions that have an adverse effect within the regional market.

Effective implementation ultimately hinges on the development of a proper competition culture as well as the goodwill to address the various challenges or shortfalls existing within the various regulatory regimes in ESA.

Implementation notwithstanding, one may still theorize on whether the procedural approach to merger regulation can be optimized. This is in respect of what can be considered an appropriate regime. A plausible approach may entail the adoption of a hybrid notification system, that is largely voluntary but with certain mandatory information requirements. This would effectively reduce the sizeable workload and expenditure of resources on non-probative merger assessments. It may also result in more streamlined and faster review of the problematic cases. This system may however prove challenging for many competition authorities that rely financially on the filing fees. They may however contemplate introducing a 'service charge' for any substantive pre-merger consultations as well as for the granting of negative clearances.

Although available data does not enable a direct connection to be made between merger regulation on its own and economic development, one can place the role of merger regulation within a wider policy framework that should contribute to the ease of doing business, especially by ensuring that there is no regulatory uncertainty. Merger regulation should indeed strive to make it easier for investors, especially foreign direct investors, to set up or carry out their businesses. To this end, the ESA jurisdictions need to concretely address the challenges arising from their broad public interest assessment as well as the information asymmetry caused by the insufficiency of publicly accessible or available information. From a legislative drafting perspective, there should be more focused drafting of laws and provision of guidelines which will ensure there is less arbitrariness on the part of the regulator, thus improving investor certainty.

This should however be with due regard to an overarching objective of inclusive economic development where the weaker segments of society have been empowered to participate efficiently and effectively in the market.

Annex

Jurisdiction/Notification Thresholds

	Asset and/or Turnover requirements	Notification requirement
COMESA (COMESA Competition Regulations, Art 23(3)-(5); Rules on the Determination of Merger Notification Thresholds And Method Of Calculation, Rule 4)	(a) the combined worldwide aggregate annual turnover or combined worldwide aggregate value of assets, whichever is higher, in the Common Market of all parties to a merger equals or exceeds USD$ 50 million; and (b) the annual turnover or value of assets, whichever is higher, in the Common Market of each of at least two of the parties to a merger equals or exceeds USD$ 10 million, unless each of the parties to a merger achieves at least two-thirds of its aggregate turnover or assets in the Common Market within one and the same Member State.	Mandatory pre-notification (both the acquiring firm and the target firm, or either the acquiring firm or the target firm, operate in two or more Member States)
Botswana (Botswana Competition Act s 47), Regulation 22 of the Competition Regulations of 2018	The assets or turnover in Botswana of the enterprise or enterprises being taken over exceeds P10, 000, 000; or the enterprises concerned would, following implementation of the merger, supply or acquire at least 20 percent of a particular description of goods or services in Botswana.	Mandatory pre-notification
Kenya (Kenya Competition Act, s 42 & 43; Threshold Guidelines, sections 4 - 6)	1. A merger which meets the following threshold shall be notified: a) where the undertakings have a minimum combined turnover or assets (whichever is higher) of one billion shillings and the turnover or assets (whichever is higher) of the target undertaking is above five hundred million shillings; b) where the turnover or assets (whichever is higher) of the acquiring undertaking is above ten billion shillings and the merging parties are in the same market or can be vertically integrated, unless the transaction meets the COMESA Competition Commission Merger Notification Thresholds; c) in the carbon-based mineral sector, if the value of the reserves, the rights and the associated assets to be held as a result of the merger exceeds ten billion shillings; d) where the undertakings operate in the COMESA, have a combined turnover or assets (whichever is higher) not exceeding five hundred million shillings and two-thirds or more	Mandatory pre-notification

	of their turnover or assets (whichever is higher) is generated or located in Kenya. 2. Mergers liable for exclusion i.e. that may be exempt from notification subject to approval of application for exclusion: a) Mergers where the combined turnover or assets of the merging parties is between five hundred million shillings and one billion shillings; b) if the firms are engaged in prospecting in the carbon-based mineral sector, irrespective of asset value. 3. Excluded transactions not requiring approval of the Authority: a) the combined turnover or assets (whichever is higher) of the merging parties does not exceed five hundred million shillings; or b) the merger meets the COMESA Competition Commission Merger Notification threshold and at least two-thirds of the turnover or assets (whichever is higher) is not generated or located in Kenya.	
Zambia (Competition and Consumer Protection Act, s 26 & 27; Zambia Merger Guidelines, annex paras. 13 – 16; See also Getting the Deal Through: Zambia, Merger Control, https://gettingthedealthrough.com/area/20/jurisdiction/50/merger-control-zambia/)	A merger transaction requires authorisation by the Commission where the combined turnover or assets, whichever is higher, in Zambia of the merging parties is at least 50 million fee units in the merging parties' most recent financial year in which these figures are available. Fifty million fee units is equivalent to 15 million kwacha.	Mandatory pre-notification
Zimbabwe (Zimbabwe Competition Act, s 34;ICLG, Zimbabwe: Merger Control Laws and Regulations 2021)	A threshold of combined annual turnover or assets in Zimbabwe, either in general or in relation to specific industries (currently ZWL$10 000 000 of the combined annual turnover or assets in Zimbabwe of the merging parties).	Mandatory pre-notification
Namibia (Namibia Competition Act, ch. 4, s 43 & 44; Determination of class mergers to be excluded from Chapter 4 of Competition Act, 2003, reg 2)	The combined annual turnover or assets in, into or from Namibia of the acquiring undertaking and transferred undertaking is equal to or exceed N$30 million; and The annual turnover and assets in, into or from Namibia of the transferred undertaking are equal to or exceed N$15 million	Mandatory pre-notification
Seychelles (Fair Competition Act, s. 21 & 22; UNCTAD (2014), Voluntary Peer Review of Competition Law and Policy, Seychelles, p. 21)	"all mergers involving an enterprise that: (a) by itself controls; or (b) together with any other enterprise with which it intends to effect the merger is likely to control, 40 per cent of a market"	Mandatory pre-notification

Tanzania (Fair Competition Act, s 11 & 13; Tanzania Merger Guidelines, para 4.1; Fair Competition (threshold for Notification of a Merger) (Amendment) Order, 2017)	A merger is notifiable if it involves turnover or assets above threshold amounts the Commission shall specify from time to time (The current threshold is 3,500,000,000 Tanzanian shillings.	Mandatory pre-notification
Mauritius (Mauritius Competition Act, s 48; Mauritius Merger Guidelines, para. 2.26)	All the parties to the merger, supply or acquire goods or services of any description, and will following the merger, together supply or acquire 30 per cent or more of all those goods or services on the market; or (b) one of the parties to the merger alone supplies or acquires prior to the merger, 30 per cent or more of goods or services of any description on the market; and (c) the Commission has reasonable grounds to believe that the creation of the merger situation has resulted in, or is likely to result in, a substantial lessening of competition within any market for goods or services.	Voluntary pre-notification
Malawi (Competition and Fair Trading Act, s 35 & 36, Malawi Merger Guidelines, paras. 5.1.1 et seq.)	No thresholds provided in the Act. Therefore, any merger that results in a change of controlling interest is notifiable.	Voluntary pre-notification (However, if a merger has not been voluntarily notified to the Commission by the parties and the Commission suspects that the merger may likely result in substantial lessening of competition, the Commission may invoke the powers vested in it by Section 8(2)(c) of the Act and require parties to notify the merger.

Bibliography

References

ABA Study on the Role of the Federal Trade Commission (1989) 58 Antitrust L.J. 53.

Acemoglu, Daron, Johnson, Simon and Robinson, James A., 'Botswana: An African Success Story' In Dani Rodrik (Ed.), In Search of Prosperity: Analytical Narrative on Economic Growth (Princeton University Press 2003).

Ackah, Charles and Morrissey, Oliver, 'Trade Policy and Performance in Sub-Saharan Africa since the 1980s' (Centre for Research in Economic Development and International Trade, University of Nottingham 2005) <https://www.nottingham.ac.uk/credit/documents/papers/05-13.pdf> accessed 23 August 2019.

Adelman, Morris A., 'Economic Aspects of the Bethlehem Opinion' (1959) 45 Va. L. Rev. 684, 688.

Almunia Joaquin, 'Policy Objectives of Merger Control' speech made on September 8, 2011 <http://europa.eu/rapid/press-release_SPEECH-11-561_en.htm?locale=en> accessed 26 August 2019.

American Bar Association, *International Antitrust Cooperation Handbook* (ABA Book Publishing 2004).

Antitrust Modernization Commission: Report and Recommendations (2007) <http://govinfo.library.unt.edu/amc/report_recommendation/amc_final_report.pdf> accessed 10 September 2019.

Anyanzwa, James, 'East Africa competition watchdog begins operations, market studies ongoing' (The East African, 28 March 2018) <https://www.theeastafrican.co.ke/business/East-Africa-competition-watchdog-operations-market-studies/2560-4361580-1rqaquz/index.html> accessed 16 July 2019.

AfDB, 'African Development Report 2014: Regional Integration for Inclusive Growth' (2014) <http://www.afdb.org/fileadmin/uploads/afdb/Documents/Publications/ADR14_ENGLISH_web.pdf> accessed 16 July 2019.

AfDB et al, 'Africa Economic Outlook 2015: Regional Development and Spatial Inclusion' (2015) <http://www.africaneconomicoutlook.org/fileadmin/uploads/aeo/2015/PDF_Chapters/Overview_AEO2015_EN-web.pdf> accessed 16 July 2019.

AFDB, 'Tracking Africa's Progress in Figures' (2014) <http://www.afdb.org/en/knowledge/publications/tracking-africa%E2%80%99s-progress-in-figures/> accessed 16 July 2019.

AFDB, 'African Economic Outlook: Sustainable Cities and Structural Transformation' (2016) <https://www.afdb.org/fileadmin/uploads/afdb/Documents/Publications/AEO_2016_Report_Full_English.pdf> accessed 15 September 2019.

COMESA News, 'New Deadline set for Ratification of Tripartite Free Trade Area' (2021) <https://www.comesa.int/new-deadline-set-for-ratification-of-tripartite-free-trade-area/> accessed 4 May 2021.

Africa Union, 'The African Union Assembly launches the Continental Free Trade Area (CFTA) negotiations' (17 June 2015) <https://au.int/sw/node/29332> accessed 16 July 2019.

Anderson, Robert D. and Holmes, Peter, 'Competition Policy and the Future of the Multilateral Trading System' (2002) 5 Journal of International Economic Law 2.

Anderson, Robert D. and Müller, Anna Caroline, 'Competition Law/Policy and the Multilateral Trading System: A Possible Agenda for the Future' (2015) E15 initiative on Strengthening the Global Trade and Investment System for Sustainable Development <http://e15initiative.org/publications/competition-lawpolicy-and-the-multilateral-trading-system-apossible-agenda-for-the-future/> accessed 17 July 2019.

Arezzo, Emanuela, 'Is there a Role for Market Definition and Dominance in an effects-based Approach?' In: Mackenrodt MO., Gallego B.C., Enchelmaier S. (eds) *Abuse of Dominant Position: New Interpretation, New Enforcement Mechanisms?* MPI Studies on Intellectual Property, Competition and Tax Law, vol 5. (Springer 2008)

Bakhoum, Mor, 'The informal economy and its interface with competition law and policy' in Michal Gal et. al (eds), *The Economic Characteristics of Developing Jurisdictions: Their Implications for Competition Law* (Edward Elgar 2015).

Barry, Frank, Honohan, Patrick and McIndoe-Calder, Tara, 'Postcolonial Ireland and Zimbabwe: Stagnation before Convergence' (2009) IIIS Discussion Paper No. 291, Institute for International Integration Studies <https://papers.ssrn.com/sol3/papers.cfm?abstract_id=1610301> accessed 15 July 2019.

Bayliss, Kate and McKinley, Terry, 'Privatising Basic Utilities in Sub-Saharan Africa: The MDG Impact' (UNDP 2007) <http://www.ipc-undp.org/pub/IPCPolicyResearchBrief3.pdf> accessed 15 September 2019.

Bellis, Jean-François and Elliott, Porter (eds), *Merger Control: Jurisdictional Comparisons* (2nd edn, Thomson Reuters 2014).

Berthelemy, Jean-Claude, Kauffmann, Celine, Valfort, Marie-Anne and Wegner, Lucia, 'Privatisation in Sub-Saharan Africa: Where do we stand?' (OECD 2004) <http://www.oecd.org/dev/emea/privatisationinsub-saharanafricawheredowestand.htm> accessed 23 August 2019.

Bhagavan, M R, 'Zambia: Impact of Industrial Strategy on Regional Imbalance and Social Inequality' (1978) Scandinavian Institute of African Studies 14 <https://www.files.ethz.ch/isn/97149/44.pdf> accessed 15 July 2019.

Bhattacharjea, Aditya, 'Who Needs Antitrust? Or, Is Developing-Country Antitrust Different? A Historical-Comparative Analysis', in Daniel Sokol, Thomas K. Cheng & Ioannis Lianos (eds), *Competition Law and Development* (OUP 2013).

Bishop, Simon and Walker, Mike, *The Economic of EC Competition Law: Concepts, Application and Measurement* (Sweet & Maxwell, 3rd edn, 2010).

Blas, Javier and England, Andrew, 'M&A activity hots up in Africa as investors bet on growth' *Financial Times* (Johannesburg, 2 December 2014) <http://www.ft.com/cms/s/0/47dee88a-795c-11e4-a57d-00144feabdc0.html#axzz3OhsEWIfR.> accessed 15 July 2019.

Bode, Mariana and Budzinski, Oliver, 'Competing Ways Towards International Antitrust: The WTO versus the ICN' (2005) New Developments in Antitrust (Nova No 3).

Bok, Derek, 'Section 7 of the Clayton Act and the Merging of Law and Economics' (1960) 74 Harv. L. Rev 228.

Boehm, Frédéric, 'Regulatory Capture Revisited: Lessons from Economics of Corruption' (July 2007) <https://pdfs.semanticscholar.org/0568/264e283cf0c69f97680152c270666649671f.pdf> accessed 9 September 2019.

Booth, David et. al., 'Drivers of Change and Development in Malawi' (2006) Overseas Development Institute Working Paper 261 <https://www.odi.org/publications/1318-drivers-change-and-development-malawi> accessed 15 July 2019.

Botta, Marco, 'Does the EU Competition Law Model Satisfy the Needs of the Emerging Economies? Lessons from the Countries Without a "Carrot"' in Karolina Podstawa and Laura Puccio (eds), 'Framework for Economic Development in EU External Relations' (2012) European University Institute Working Paper.

Botswana Ministry of Trade and Industry, National Competition Policy of Botswana (2005) <https://www.competitionauthority.co.bw/sites/default/files/National%20Competition%20Policy%20Botswana%202005.pdf> accessed 15 July 2019.

Bowman Gilfillan, 'Merger Control 2016: South Africa Law & Practice' (contribution to Chambers and Partners Global Practice Guides) <http://www.chambersandpartners.com/guide/practice-guides/location/272/8560/2429-200> accessed 23 August 2019.

Bradford, Anu, 'International Antitrust Negotiations and the False Hope of the WTO' (2007) 48 Harvard International Law Journal 2.

Bridges Africa, 'Launch of African Tripartite FTA now set for June' (2015) <http://www.ictsd.org/bridges-news/bridges-africa/news/launch-of-african-tripartite-fta-now-set-for-june> accessed 16 July 2019.

Broder, David, *US Antitrust Law and Enforcement* (2nd edn, OUP 2012).

Bundeskartellamt, 'Prohibition Criteria in Merger Control: Dominant Position versus Substantial Lessening of Competition?' <http://www.bundeskartellamt.de/SharedDocs/Publikation/EN/Fachartikel/Prohibition%20Criteria%20in%20Merger%20Control%20-%20Dominant%20Position%20versus%20Substantial%20Lessening%20of%20Competition.pdf?__blob=publicationFile&v=3> accessed 6 September 2019.

Busuulwa, Bernard, 'Intra-African trade rises as market access between blocs improves' (The East African, 29 August 2015) <http://www.theeastafrican.co.ke/business/Intra-African-trade-up-as-market-access-between-blocs-improves-/-/2560/2850908/-/14qd2iy/-/index.html> accessed 16 July 2019.

Büthe, Tim and Swank, Gabriel T., 'The Politics of Antitrust and Merger Review in the European Union: Institutional Change and Decisions from Messina to 2004' (2006) Harv. Ctr. for Eur. Stud.,Working Paper No. 142.

Choe, Chongwoo and Shekhar, Chander, Compulsory or Voluntary Pre-Merger Notification? A Theoretical and Empirical Analysis (June 26, 2006) <https://ssrn.com/abstract=912925> accessed 6 September 2019.

Choe, Chongwoo and Shekhar, Chander, 'Compulsory or Voluntary Pre-Merger Notification? Theory and Some Evidence' (2010) 28(1) International Journal of Industrial Organization <https://ssrn.com/abstract=1541703> accessed 6 September 2019.

Clarke, Julie, 'The International Regulation of Transnational Mergers' (PhD Thesis, Queensland University of Technology 2010).

Cohn, Carolyn and Fenton, Susan, 'Sub-Saharan Africa M&A deals, debt issuance surge in 2013' *Reuters* (London, 16 January 2014) <http://in.reuters.com/article/2014/01/16/africa-deals-idINL5N0KQ1FF20140116.> accessed 15 July 2019.

Coleman, James S., '*Foundations of Social Theory*' (Belknap Press, 1990).

COMESA, 'COMESA Region Key Economic Infrastructure Projects' (2013) <https://europa.eu/capacity4dev/file/16076/download?token=46F3PgO7> accessed 16 July 2019.

COMESA, 'E-COMESA Newsletter' (12 November 2014) <http://www.comesa.int/attachments/article/1379/e-comesa_newsletter_435.pdf> accessed 12 October 2018.

COMESA, 'Report of the 8th Annual General Meeting of Regulators of Information and Communication for Eastern and Southern Africa (ARICEA)' (2012) < https://ariceaweb.org/attachments/article/18/8th%20ARICEA%20AGM%20final%20report%20with%20annexes%20(2).pdf> accessed 16 July 2019.

COMESA, EAC and SADC, 'First COMESA-EAC-SADC Tripartite Summit Report' (2008), para 9 <http://repository.eac.int/handle/11671/1633> accessed 16 July 2019.

COMESA, EAC and SADC, 'Communiqué of the Second COMESA-EAC-SADC Tripartite Summit' (2011) <http://repository.eac.int:8080/handle/11671/550> accessed 16 July 2019.

COMESA, EAC and SADC, 'Communiqué of the Third COMESA-EAC-SADC Tripartite Summit' (2015) <http://www.sadc.int/files/5914/3401/0196/Communiqu_of_the_3rd_COMESA_EAC_SADC_Tripartite_Summit.pdf> accessed 23 April 2018.

COMESA, EAC and SADC, 'Report of 3rd TTC-MBP, Tripartite Agreement on Movement of Business Persons' (2014) <https://tis.sadc.int/files/8614/1640/5306/Draft_Tripartite_Agreement_on_Business_Persons.pdf> accessed 18 November 2018.

COMESA Merger Statistics <http://www.comesacompetition.org/wp-content/uploads/2016/06/No-of-Mergers-Handled-by-CCC-2013-June-2016.pdf> accessed 5 September 2019.

COMESA, 'Final Communique' of The Eighteenth Summit of the COMESA Authority Of Heads of State and Government' (COMESA 18th Summit 2015) <http://dhanaanmedia.com/wp-content/uploads/2015/03/150331_Final-communique_March-2015_new.pdf.pdf> accessed 5 March 2017.

Competition and Fair Trading Commission of Malawi Annual Reports <http://www.cftc.mw/index.php/2013-12-16-13-35-12/reports/annual-reports/30-20122013-annual-report.html> accessed 26 August 2019.

Competition and Tariff Commission of Zimbabwe Annual Reports <http://www.competition.co.zw/publications/annual-reports> accessed 5 September 2019.

Competition Authority of Botswana Annual Reports <http://www.competitionauthority.co.bw/annual-reports> accessed 22 February 2017.

Competition Authority of Kenya Annual Reports < http://www.cak.go.ke/images/docs/> accessed 22 February 2017.

Competition Commission and Competition Tribunal of South Africa, 'Ten years of enforcement by the South African Competition Authorities: Unleashing Rivalry' (2009) <http://www.compcom.co.za/wp-content/uploads/2014/09/10year.pdf > accessed 16 September 2019.

Competition Commission of Namibia Newsletters <http://www.nacc.com.na/publications/newsletters.php> accessed 5 September 2019.

Competition Commission of South Africa Annual Report 2006/2007, <http://www.compcom.co.za/annual-reports/> accessed 26 August 2019.

Competition Commission South Africa, Background note to the public interest guideline (Background Note) <http://www.compcom.co.za/wp-content/uploads/2015/01/Final-Background-Note-to-Public-Interest-Guideline-210115.pdf> accessed 5 September 2019.

Crettez, Bertrand, Deffains, Bruno and Musy Olivier, 'On Legal Cooperation and the Dynamics of Legal Convergence' (2010) (Economix Working Paper 17), <http://ideas.repec.org/p/drm/wpaper/2010-17.html> accessed 16 September 2019.

CUTS International, 'Competition Regimes of the World: A Civil Society Report: Kenya' (2006) CUTS Civil Society Report <https://competitionregimes.com/pdf/Africa/46-Kenya.pdf> accessed 15 July 2019.

CUTS International, 'Competition Regimes of the World: A Civil Society Report: Mauritius' (2006) CUTS Civil Society Report, 254-259 <https://competitionregimes.com/pdf/Africa/48-Mauritius.pdf> accessed 15 July 2019.

CUTS International, 'Competition Regimes of the World: A Civil Society Report: Malawi' (2006) CUTS Civil Society Report <https://competitionregimes.com/pdf/Africa/47-Malawi.pdf> accessed 15 July 2019.

CUTS International, 'Competition Regimes of the World: A Civil Society Report: Namibia' (2006) CUTS Civil Society Report <https://competitionregimes.com/pdf/Africa/50-Namibia.pdf> accessed 16 July 2019.

CUTS International, 'Competition Regimes of the World: A Civil Society Report: Tanzania' (2006) CUTS Civil Society Report <https://competitionregimes.com/pdf/Africa/56-Tanzania.pdf> accessed 15 July 2019.

CUTS International, 'Competition Regimes of the World: A Civil Society Report: Zambia' (2006) CUTS Civil Society Report <https://competitionregimes.com/pdf/Africa/59-Zambia.pdf> accessed 15 July 2019.

CUTS International, 'Competition Regimes of the World: A Civil Society Report: Zimbabwe' (2006) CUTS Civil Society Report <https://competitionregimes.com/pdf/Africa/60-Zimbabwe.pdf> accessed 15 July 2019.

Davies, Stephen and Lyons, Bruce, *Mergers and Merger Remedies in the EU: Assessing the Consequences for Competition* (Edward Elgar 2007).

Debevoise & Plimpton LLP, 'Merger control in the UK (England and Wales): overview' (Practical Law Global Guide 2015/16) <global.practicallaw.com/0-500-7317> accessed 18 September 2019.

Department of State, 'Proposal for Expansion of World Trade and Employment' (1945, Commercial Policy Series 79) <http://www.worldtradelaw.net/misc/ProposalsForExpansionOfWorldTradeAndEmployment.pdf.download#page=4> accessed 21 December 2018.

DOJ, 'Antitrust Division Policy Guide to Merger Remedies' (2011), <https://www.justice.gov/sites/default/files/atr/legacy/2011/06/17/272350.pdf> accessed 6 September 2019.

Drexl, Josef, 'Consumer Welfare and consumer harm: adjusting competition law and policies to the needs of developing jurisdictions' in Michal Gal et. al (eds), *The Economic Characteristics of Developing Jurisdictions: Their Implications for Competition Law* (Edward Elgar 2015).

Drexl, Josef, 'International Competition Policy after Cancún: Placing a Singapore Issue on the WTO Development Agenda' (2004) 27 World Competition Law and Economics Review 3.

Drexl, Josef, Bakhoum, Mor, Fox, Eleanor, Gal, Michal & Gerber, David (eds), *Competition Policy and Regional Integration in Developing Countries* (Edward Elgar 2012).

Drexl J, 'Economic Integration and Competition Law in Developing Countries' in Josef Drexl, Mor Bakhoum, Eleanor M. Fox, Michal S. Gal & David J. Gerber (eds), *Competition Policy and Regional Integration in Developing Countries* (Edward Elgar 2012).

Duisenberg, Willem F., 'The Past and Future of European Integration: A Central Banker's Perspective' (1999) Per Jacobsson Lecture <http://www.imf.org/external/am/1999/lecture.htm.> accessed 23 August 2019.

Du Plessis, Louise, Judd, Lurie and van Buuren, Amy, 'Competition law in the developing world: A fish out of water?' (Competition Law, Economics and Policy Conference, October 2011) <http://www.compcom.co.za/wp-content/uploads/2014/09/FINAL-PAPER-2011.pdf> accessed 15 July 2019.

EAC, 'East African Community Trade Report' (2013) <http://www.eac.int/sites/default/files/docs/report_eac_trade_2013.pdf> accessed 16 July 2019.

EAC, 'East African Community Trade Report' (2014) <http://www.eac.int/sites/default/files/docs/eac_trade_report_2014.pdf> accessed 16 July 2019.

EAC Secretariat, 'Annual Progress Report of the Council to the Summit of EAC Heads of State for the period December 2013 to November 2014' (2015) <http://www.eac.int/index.php?option=com_content&view=article&id=1807:annual-progress-report-of-the-council-to-the-16th-ordinary-heads-of-state-summit-for-the-period-december-2013-november-2014-&catid=146:press-releases&Itemid=194> accessed 14 September 2015.

EAC Secretariat, 'East African Community Trade Report' (2013) <https://www.eac.int/documents/category/trade-investment-reports> accessed 16 July 2019.

EAC Secretariat, 'Report of the Committee on Fast Tracking East African Federation' (2004) <http://repository.eac.int/handle/11671/1966> accessed 16 July 2019.

EAC Secretariat, 'Status of Elimination of Non-Tariff Barriers in the East African Community' (2014) <http://repository.eac.int/bitstream/handle/11671/416/NTBs%20Vol%207%20-%20compressed.pdf?sequence=1&isAllowed=y> accessed 16 July 2019.

EALA, 'Report of On-Spot Assessment on the EAC Single Customs Territory' (2014) <http://www.eala.org/documents/view/on-spot-assessment-of-the-eac-single-customs-territory-sct> accessed 16 July 2019.

Edwards, C.D., 'Size of Markets, Scale of Firms and the Character of Competition' in Robinson E.A.G. (ed) *Economic Consequences of the Size of Nations* (Palgrave Macmillan 1960).

Egge, Michel D and Cruise, Jason D, 'Practical guide to the U.S. merger review process' (2014) Concurrences N° 1 <https://www.lw.com/thoughtLeadership/practical-guide-us-merger-review-process-012014> accessed 23 August 2019.

Emmert, Frank, Kronthaler, Franz, Stephan, Johannes, 'Analysis of statements made in favour of and against the adoption of competition law in developing and transition economies' (2005) Institut Für Wirtschaftsforschung Halle Report, 9 < https://www.iwh-halle.de/fileadmin/user_upload/publications/iwh_sonderhefte/SH_05-1.pdf> accessed 17 July 2019.

Erasmus, Gerhard, 'The Agreement preceding the Agreement: how the negotiating principles decided the Tripartite FTA game plan' in Hartzenberg T et al (eds) *Cape to Cairo: Exploring the Tripartite FTA agenda* (tralac 2013) <http://www.tralac.org/publications/article/5548-cape-to-cairo-exploring-the-tripartite-fta-agenda.html> accessed 16 July 2019.

Erasmus, Gerhard, 'The Tripartite Free Trade Agreement: Results of Phase One of the Negotiations' (2015) <http://www.tralac.org/publications/article/7803-the-tripartite-free-trade-agreement-results-of-phase-one-of-the-negotiations.html> accessed 16 July 2019.

Ernst and Young, 'The East African Community amends customs duties and common external tariffs' (2018) <https://www.ey.com/Publication/vwLUAssets/The_East_African_Community_amends_customs_duties_and_common_external_tariffs/$FILE/2018G_010349-18Gbl_Indirect_East%20African%20Community%20amends%20customs%20duties%20and%20external%20tariffs.pdf> accessed 16 July 2019.

Ernst and Young, 'East Africa Budget 2015/2016; Economic and Tax Focus' (2015) <http://www.ey.com/Publication/vwLUAssets/EY-east-africa-budget-2015-2016-economic-and-tax-focus/$FILE/EY-east-africa-budget-2015-2016-economic-and-tax-focus.pdf> accessed 5 March 2017.

Ernst and Young, 'Navigating Africa's Current Uncertainties' (2016) <https://www.tralac.org/images/docs/9673/ey-attractiveness-program-africa-2016.pdf> accessed 18 July 2019.

English, Philip, 'Mauritius: Reigniting the Engines of Growth A Teaching Case Study' (2002) Teaching Notes <http://documents.worldbank.org/curated/en/936011468757482849/Teaching-notes> accessed 15 July 2019.

European Commission, Competition Merger Brief, issue 1/2014 <http://ec.europa.eu/competition/publications/cmb/2014/CMB2014-01.pdf> accessed 6 September 2019.

European Commission, Competition: Merger Control Procedures (2013) <http://ec.europa.eu/competition/publications/factsheets/merger_control_procedures_en.pdf> accessed 18 September 2019.

European Commission, Roundtable on Cartel Jurisdiction Issues, including the Effects Doctrine DAF/COMP/WP3/WD(2008)93.

Evenett, Simon J., 'Would Enforcing Competition Law Compromise Industrial Policy Objectives?' in Douglas H. Brooks & Simon J. Evenett (eds), Competition Policy and Development in Asia (Palgrave Macmillan, 2005).

Evenett, Simon J., 'Study on Issues Relating to a Possible Multilateral Framework on Competition Policy' (2003) Report prepared for the Secretariat of the World Trade Organization.

Fair Competition Commission of Tanzania Newsletter (April-June 2011) <http://www.competition.or.tz/index.php?option=com_content&view=article&id=48:lorem-ipsum-is-simply-dummy-text-of-the-printing&catid=22:news-and-events&Itemid=144> accessed 26 August 2019.

Fels, Allan and Ng, Wendy, 'Rethinking Competition Advocacy in Developing Countries' Daniel Sokol, Thomas K. Cheng & Ioannis Lianos (eds), *Competition Law and Development* (OUP 2013).

Fiebig, Andre, 'A Role for the WTO in International Merger Control' (1999-2000) 20 Nw. J. Int'l L. & Bus. 233.

Fine, Ben and Rustomjee, Zavareh, *The Political Economy of South Africa – From Minerals-Energy Complex to Industrialisation* (Hurst and Company 1996).

Fox, Eleanor, 'The Kaleidoscope of Antitrust and its significance in the World Economy: Respecting Differences' in Barry E. Hawk (ed.), *Annual Proceeding of the Fordham Corporate Law Institute Conference on International Antitrust Law & Policy* (Juris 2001), 597-603.

Fox, Eleanor and Healey, Deborah, 'When the State Harms Competition: The Role for Competition Law' (2014) 79 Antitrust. L. J. 769.

Fox, Eleanor and Trebilcock, Michael (eds), *The Design Of Competition Law Institutions* (1st edn, OUP 2013).

Fox, Eleanor, 'US and EU Competition Law: A Comparison' in J. David Richardson and Edward M. Graham (eds), *Global Competition Policy* (Peterson Institute for International Economics 1997).

Fox, Eleanor and Pitofsky, Robert, 'Goals of US Competition Policy' in J. David Richardson and Edward M. Graham (eds), *Global Competition Policy* (Peterson Institute for International Economics 1997).

Fox, Eleanor, 'Competition Law and the Agenda for the WTO: Forging the links of Competition and Trade' (1995) 4(1) Pac. Rim Law & Pol.y. 1.

Fox, Eleanor, 'Antitrust and Regulatory Federalism: Race up, Down and Sideways' (2000) 75 N.Y.U. L. Rev. 1781.

Fox, Eleanor, 'Toward World Antitrust and Market Access' (1997) 91 Am. J. Int'l L. 1.

FTC, 'A Study of the Commission's Divestiture Process' (1999) <https://www.ftc.gov/sites/default/files/attachments/merger-review/divestiture.pdf> accessed 6 September 2019.

FTC and DOJ, 'Hart-Scott-Rodino Annual Report: Fiscal Year 2014' <https://www.ftc.gov/system/files/documents/reports/federal-trade-commission-bureau-competition-department-justice-antitrust-division-hart-scott-rodino.s.c.18a-hart-scott-rodino-antitrust-improvements-act-1976/150813hsr_report.pdf> accessed 6 September 2019.

FTC, 'Negotiating Merger Remedies: Statement of the Bureau of Competition of the Federal Trade Commission' (2012) <https://www.ftc.gov/system/files/attachments/negotiating-merger-remedies/merger-remediesstmt.pdf> accessed 6 September 2019.

Gal, Michal S., Competition Policy for Small Market Economies (Harvard University Press, 2003).

Gal, Michal S., 'When the Going Gets Tight: Institutional Solutions When Antitrust Enforcement Resources Are Scarce' (2010) 41 Loy. U. Chi. L.J. 417, 423–425.

Gal, Michal S. and Fox, Eleanor M., 'Drafting competition law for developing jurisdictions: learning from experience' in Michal Gal et. al (eds), *The Economic Characteristics of Developing Jurisdictions: Their Implications for Competition Law* (Edward Elgar 2015).

Gal, Michal, 'The Ecology of Antitrust: Preconditions for Competition Law Enforcement in Developing Countries' in Philippe Brusick, Ana Maria Alvarez and Lucian Cernat (eds), *Competition, Competitiveness and Development: Lessons from Developing Countries* (UNCTAD 2004).

Gann, Lewis H. and Duignan, Peter, Burden of Empire: *An Appraisal of Western Colonialism in Africa South of the Sahara* (Hoover Institution Press 1967).

Gao, Shangquan, 'Economic Globalization: Trends, Risks and Risk Prevention' ST/ESA/2000/CDP/1 <http://www.un.org/en/development/desa/policy/cdp/cdp_background_papers/bp2000_1.pdf> accessed 22 August 2019.

Gaomab, Mihe, 'Competition Policy and Competitiveness in Namibia' <http://www.nacc.com.na/cms_documents/703_competition_policy_and_competitiveness.pdf> accessed 16 July 2019.

Gardner, Richard N., *Sterling-dollar diplomacy in current perspective: the origins and the prospects of our international economic order* (Columbia University Press 1980).

Gelhorn, Ernest et al., 'Has Antitrust Outgrown Dual Enforcement? A proposal for Rationalization' (1990) 35 Antitrust Bull. 695.

Geroski, Paul, 'Thinking creatively about markets' (1998) 16 International Journal of Industrial Organization 6.

Gertz, Geoffrey, 'Kenya's Trade Liberalization of the 1980s and 1990s: Policies, Impacts, and Implications' (2008) Background paper commissioned by the Carnegie Endowment. <http://carnegieendowment.org/files/kenya_background.pdf> accessed 15 July 2019.

Gerber, David J., *Global Competition: Law, Markets and Globalization* (Oxford University Press 2010).

Gerber, David J., 'Adapting the Role of Economics in Competition Law: A Developing Country Dilemma' in Michal S. Gal et al. (eds), *The Economic Characteristics of Developing Jurisdictions: Their Implications for Competition Law* (Edward Elgar 2015).

Godana, Tekaligne and Odada, John E., 'Sources of Growth in Africa: A Case Study of Namibia' (2002) <http://citeseerx.ist.psu.edu/viewdoc/download?doi=10.1.1.590.3047&rep=rep1&type=pdf> accessed 15 July 2019.

Government of Kenya, Sessional Paper No. 10 of 1965: African Socialism and its application to planning in Kenya (Sessional Paper 1965) <https://www.knls.ac.ke/images/AFRICAN-SOCIALISM-AND-ITS-APPLICATION-TO-PLANNING-IN-KENYA.pdf> accessed 15 July 2019.

Grant, Jeremy and Neven, Damien, 'The attempted merger between General Electric and Honeywell; A case of transatlantic conflict' (March 2005) <http://ec.europa.eu/dgs/competition/economist/honeywell.pdf> accessed 22 August 2019.

Graz, Jean-Christophe, 'The Havana Charter: when state and market shake hands' in Rainer Kattel, Jayati Ghosh & Erik Reinert (Eds), *Handbook of Alternative Theories of Economic Development* (E. Elgar, 2016).

Green Paper on the Review of Council Regulation (EEC) No 4064/89, COM/2001/0745.

Greif, Avner, Institutions and the Path to the Modern Economy: Lessons from Medieval Trade (Cambridge University Press 2006).

Griffin, Joseph, 'Foreign Governmental Reactions to U.S. Assertions of Extraterritorial Jurisdiction' (1998) 6 Geo. Mason L. Rev. 505.

Guzman, Andrew (ed), *Cooperation, Comity and Competition Policy* (OUP 2011).

Hill, Mathew, 'Zambia Blocks Local Merger of Toyota-CFAO on Competition Grounds' (29 January 2013) <http://www.bloomberg.com/news/articles/2013-01-29/zambia-blocks-local-merger-of-toyota-cfao-on-competition-grounds accessed 22 February 2017> accessed 26 August 2019.

Hoeg, Dorte, *European Merger Remedies: Law and Policy* (Hart Publishing 2014).

IBA, Report of the Task Force on Extraterritorial Jurisdiction (International Bar Association 2009) <http://tinyurl.com/taskforce-etj-pdf> accessed 9 September 2019.

ICN, International Enforcement Cooperation Project <http://www.internationalcompetitionnetwork.org/uploads/library/doc794.pdf> accessed 9 September 2019.

ICN: Merger Guidelines Workbook (April 2006) <https://www.internationalcompetitionnetwork.org/portfolio/merger-guidelines-workbook/> accessed 18 September 2019.

ICN, 'Merger Remedies Review Project' (Bonn, 2005) <http://www.internationalcompetitionnetwork.org/uploads/library/doc323.pdf> accessed 6 September 2019.

ICN, Practical Guide to International Enforcement Cooperation in Mergers <http://www.internationalcompetitionnetwork.org/uploads/library/doc1031.pdf> accessed 9 September 2019.

ICN, 'Project on Merger Guidelines' <https://www.internationalcompetitionnetwork.org/portfolio/merger-guidelines-report/> accessed 18 September 2019.

ICN, Recommended Practices for Merger Notification Procedures <http://www.internationalcompetitionnetwork.org/uploads/library/doc588.pdf> accessed 6 September 2019.

ICN, Recommended Practices for Merger Analysis <http://www.internationalcompetitionnetwork.org/uploads/library/doc316.pdf> accessed 6 September 2019.

ICN, Setting Notification Thresholds for Merger Review (Kyoto 2008) <http://www.internationalcompetitionnetwork.org/uploads/library/doc326.pdf> accessed 6 September 2019.

Ihucha, Adam, 'EAC Competition Authority to Start Operations in July' (The East African Standard 18 June 2016) <https://www.theeastafrican.co.ke/business/EAC-competition-authority-to-start-operations-in-July-/2560-3255818-pwwagnz/index.html> accessed 16 July 2019.

ILC, Report on the work of its fifty-eighth session, Supplement No. 10 (A/61/10) Annex E. Extraterritorial Jurisdiction <http://www.tjsl.edu/slomansonb/5.1_UNExtra.pdf> accessed 9 September 2019.

Illy, Ousseni, 'Trade remedies in Africa: experiences, challenges and prospects' (2015) <http://www.ictsd.org/bridges-news/bridges-africa/news/trade-remedies-in-africa-experiences-challenges-and-prospects> accessed 16 July 2019.

Imam, Patrick, 'Effect of IMF Structural Adjustment Programs on Expectations: The Case of Transition Economies' (2007) IMF Working Paper <https://www.imf.org/en/Publications/WP/Issues/2016/12/31/Effect-of-IMF-Structural-Adjustment-Programs-on-Expectations-The-Case-of-Transition-Economies-21449> accessed 15 July 2019.

IMF, 'Malawi: Economic Development Document' (2017) IMF Country Report No. 17/184 <https://www.imf.org/en/Publications/CR/Issues/2017/07/05/Malawi-Economic-Development-Document-45037> accessed 15 July 2019.

Inter-American Development Bank and OECD, 'Merger Control Laws and Procedures in Latin America and the Caribbean' (discussion paper 2005), 7 <http://www.oecd.org/dataoecd/41/57/38835612.pdf> accessed 23 August 2019.

IPAN, 'COMESA Infrastructure kitty hits $22 million' (2015) <http://www.ipan.co.za/?p=314> accessed 16 July 2019.

Jacobs, P.A.M. and van Norden, Simon, 'Why Are Initial Estimates of Productivity Growth So Unreliable?' (2016) 47 J. MACROECONOMICS 200.

Luebking, Johannes, 'T-Mobile Austria/tele.ring: Remedying the loss of a maverick' (Competition Policy Newsletter, 2006) <http://ec.europa.eu/competition/publications/cpn/2006_2_46.pdf> accessed 26 August 2019.

Jones, Clifford A., 'Toward Global Competition Policy?: The Expanding Dialogue on Multilateralism' (2000) 23 World Competition, Issue 2, 95–100. Jones C, 'Toward Global Competition Policy?: The Expanding Dialogue on Multilateralism' (2000) 23 World Competition, Issue 2, 95–100.

Kaonga, Kondwani and Muteto, Parret, 'Understanding Competition and Regulation across Borders: A Toyota Tshusho Case Study' (Competition and Consumer Protection Commission of Zambia, 2015) <https://static1.squarespace.com/static/52246331e4b0a46e5f1b8ce5/t/55349f5ee4b047c173df89f9/1429512030611/Parret+Muteto+et+al_Understanding+Competition+and+Regulation+across+borders.pdf> accessed 26 August 2019.

Kaplow, Louis, 'On the Choice of Welfare Standards in Competition Law' in Daniel Zimmer (ed), *The Goals of Competition Law* (Edward Elgar, 2012).

Kayuni, Happy M., 'Malawi's Economic and Development Policy Choices from 1964 to 1980: An Epitome of 'Pragmatic Unilateral Capitalism' (2011) 20 Nordic Journal of African Studies 2 <http://www.njas.helsinki.fi/pdf-files/vol20num2/kayuni.pdf> accessed 15 July 2019.

Kovacic, William E., 'Getting Started: Creating New Competition Policy Institutions in Transition Economies' (1997) 23 Brook. J. Int'l L. 403.

Kovacic, William and Lopez-Galdos, Marianela, 'Lifecycles of Competition Systems: Explaining Variation in the Implementation of New Regimes' (2016) 79 Law and Contemporary Problems 4.

Krattenmaker T, Lande R and Salop S, 'Monopoly power and Market Power in Antitrust Law' (1987) 76(2) Georgetown Law Journal 241.

Lewin, Michael, 'Botswana's Success: Good Governance, Good Policies, and Good Luck' (2019), <https://www.researchgate.net/publication/265285982> accessed 15 July 2019.

Lewis, David, 'Embedding a Competition Culture: Holy Grail or Attainable Objective?' in Developing Countries' Daniel Sokol, Thomas K. Cheng & Ioannis Lianos (eds), *Competition Law and Development* (OUP 2013).

Levy, Nicholas, 'The EU's SIEC Test Five Years On: Has it Made a Difference?' (2010) 6(1) European Competition Journal 211.

Ligami, Christabel, 'Uganda Ratifies the Monetary Union' (The East African, 7 February 2015) <http://www.theeastafrican.co.ke/news/Uganda-ratifies-the-monetary-union/-/2558/2616360/-/g05itfz/-/index.html> accessed 16 July 2019.

Lindsay, Alistair and Berridge, Alison, *The EU Merger Regulation: Substantive Issues* (4th edn, Sweet and Maxwell, 2009).

Makina, Daniel, 'Historical Perspective on Zimbabwe's Economic Performance: A Tale of Five Lost Decades. Journal of Developing Societies' (2010) 26 Journal of Developing Societies 1 <https://doi.org/10.1177/0169796X1002600105> accessed 15 July 2019.

Mallya, Aileen, 'COMESA-EAC-SADC Tripartite Framework: State of Play' (2011) <https://www.researchgate.net/publication/271524706_COMESA-EAC-SADC_Tripartite_framework_state_of_play> accessed 16 July 2019.

Mandalu, Martin, Thakhathi, DR, and Costa, Hofisi, 'Investigation on Tanzania's Economic History since Independence: The Search for a Development Model' (2018) 4 World Journal of Social Sciences and Humanities 1 <http://pubs.sciepub.com/wjssh/4/1/4> accessed 15 July 2019.

Mario Mariniello, Neven, Damien and Padilla, Jorge, 'Antitrust, Regulatory Capture, and Economic Integration' (2015) E15Initiative. Geneva: International Centre for Trade and Sustainable Development (ICTSD) and World Economic Forum, 1 <www.e15initiative.org/> accessed 10 September 2019.

McDonald, Stephen et al, 'Why Economic Partnership Agreements undermine Africa's Regional Integration' (2013), 4 <https://www.wilsoncenter.org/publication/why-economic-partnership-agreements-undermine-africas-regional-integration> accessed 16 July 2019.

Mehta, Pradeep, Mitra, Siddharta and Dube, Cornelius, 'Competition Policy and Consumer Policy: Complementarities and Conflicts in the Promotion of Consumer Welfare' in Hassan Qaqaya and George Limpile (eds), *The Effects of Anti-Competitive Business Practices on Developing Countries and their Development Prospects* (United Nations Publication 2008).

Mo Ibrahim Foundation, 'Regional Integration: Uniting to Compete' (2014) <http://static.moibrahimfoundation.org/downloads/publications/2014/2014-facts-&-figures-regional-integration-uniting-to-compete.pdf> accessed 16 July 2019.

Monti, Mario, 'Market definition as a cornerstone of EU Competition Policy' speech made on 5 October, 2001, <http://europa.eu/rapid/press-release_SPEECH-01-439_en.htm?locale=en> accessed 26 August 2019.

Mugisa, Evarist et al, 'An Evaluation of the Implementation and Impact of the East African Community Customs Union' (2009) <https://www.academia.edu/27637527/An_Evaluation_of_the_Implementation_and_Impact_of_the_East_African_Community_Customs_Union> accessed 16 July 2019.

Mushakavanhu, Tinashe, 'Kenya is building Africa's biggest wind energy farm to generate a fifth of its power, Quartz Africa' (2015) <http://qz.com/444936/kenya-is-building-africas-biggest-wind-energy-farm-to-generate-a-fifth-of-its-power/> accessed 16 July 2019.

Nelson, Ralph L., *Merger Movements in American Industry* (Princeton University Press 1959).

Ncube, Mthuli, 'Mergers and Acquisitions in Africa' (AFDB 2012) <http://www.afdb.org/en/blogs/afdb-championing-inclusive-growth-across-africa/post/mergers-and-acquisitions-in-africa-10163/.> accessed 15 July 2019.

Ngwenya, Avias and Robb, Genna, 'Theory and practice in the use of merger remedies: considering South African experience' <http://www.compcom.co.za/wp-content/uploads/2014/09/NgwenyaRobbMerger-Remedies.pdf> accessed 6 September 2019.

Ngowi, Honest Prosper, 'Economic development and change in Tanzania since independence: The political leadership factor' (2009) 3 African Journal of Political Science and International Relations 4 <http://www.academicjournals.org/app/webroot/article/article1379789169_Ngowi.pdf> accessed 15 July 2019.

Ngwenya, Sindiso et al, 'Key Issues in Regional Integration' (2013) 2, 131 <https://www.comesa.int/wp-content/uploads/2019/03/key-issues-on-intergration-ii_final_final_cutout_print.pdf> accessed 16 July 2019.

OECD, 'South Africa: Peer Review of Competition Law and Policy' (2003), 9-11 <http://www.oecd.org/southafrica/34823812.pdf> accessed 16 July 2019.

OECD, Investigations of Consummated and Non-notifiable Mergers: European Union DAF/COMP/WP3/WD(2014)19 <http://ec.europa.eu/competition/international/multilateral/2014_feb_mergers_investigations_en.pdf> accessed 6 September 2019.

OECD, Investigations of Consummated and Non-notifiable Mergers: United States DAF/COMP/WP3/WD(2014)23 <https://www.ftc.gov/system/files/attachments/us-submissions-oecd-other-international-competition-fora/consummated_mergers_us_oecd.pdf> accessed 23 August 2019.

OECD, Local Nexus and Jurisdictional Thresholds in Merger Control, DAF/COMP/WP3(2016)4.

OECD, Recommendation of the OECD Council concerning International Co-operation on Competition Investigations and Proceedings, C(2014)108 <https://www.oecd.org/daf/competition/2014-rec-internat-coop-competition.pdf> accessed 19 September 2019.

OECD, Recommendation of the Council on Merger Review (2005) <https://www.oecd.org/competition/mergers/40537528.pdf > accessed 19 September 2019.

OECD, Remedies in Merger Cases (DAF/COMP(2011)13) <http://www.oecd.org/daf/competition/RemediesinMergerCases2011.pdf> accessed 6 September 2019.

OECD, Standard for Merger Review (OECD Policy Roundtables 2009) DAF/COMP(2009)21 <https://www.oecd.org/competition/mergers/45247537.pdf> accessed 17 July 2019.

OECD, Substantive Criteria used for Merger Assessment, DAFFE/COMP(2003)5 <http://www.oecd.org/competition/mergers/2500227.pdf> accessed 6 September 2019.

OECD, Competition Law and Policy in South Africa: OECD Peer Review (2003) <http://www.oecd.org/southafrica/34823812.pdf> accessed 26 August 2019.

OECD, Market Definition, DAF/COMP(2012)19 <http://www.oecd.org/daf/competition/Marketdefinition2012.pdf> accessed 26 August 2018.

OECD, 'The Objectives of Competition Law and Policy' CCNM/GF/COMP(2003)3 <http://www.oecd.org/daf/competition/2486329.pdf> accessed 15 July 2019.

OECD, 'The Role of Efficiency Claims in Antitrust Proceedings' <http://www.oecd.org/competition/EfficiencyClaims2012.pdf > accessed 19 September 2019.

Owen, Deborah K. and Parisi, John J., 'International Mergers and Joint Ventures: A Federal Trade Commission Perspective' (1990) Fordham Corporate Law Institute 1.

Paas-Mohando, Katri, 'Choice of merger notification system for small economies' (2013) 34(10) E.C.L.R., 548.

Peerun-Fatehmamode, Reshma, Bundoo, Sunil and Jankee, Kheswam, 'Competition Scenario in Mauritius' (2006) CUTS International < http://www.cuts-ccier.org/7up3/pdf/CRR-Mauritius.pdf> accessed 15 July 2019.

Poddar, Dave and Stooke, Gemma, 'Consideration of Public Interest Factors in Antitrust Merger Control' (2015) Competition Policy International <https://www.competitionpolicyinternational.com/consideration-of-public-interest-factors-in-antitrust-merger-control/> accessed 9 September 2019.

Press Release nº 21/99, Judgment of the Court of First Instance in Case T-102/96.

Richman, Barak D., 'Contracts and Cartels: Reconciling Competition and Development Policy' in Daniel Sokol, Thomas K. Cheng & Ioannis Lianos (eds), *Competition Law and Development* (OUP 2013).

Robinson, John Alan, and Parsons, Neil, 'State Formation and Governance in Botswana' (2006) 15 Journal of African Economies 1 <https://scholar.harvard.edu/jrobinson/publications/state-formation-and-governance-botswana> accessed 15 July 2019.

Rodriguez, Armando E. and Coate, Malcolm B., 'Competition Policy in Transition Economies: The Role of Competition Advocacy' (1997) 23 Brook. J. Int'l L. 365.

Rodrik, Dani, 'Globalization and growth - looking in the wrong places' (2004) 26(4) Journal of Policy Modelling, 513-517.

Rojid, Sawkut, Afif, Ahmed, and Sacerdoti, Emilio, 'Seychelles: How Classic Policies Restored Sustainability' (2013) World Bank <https://www.worldbank.org/content/dam/Worldbank/document/Africa/Seychelles/sc-how-classic-policies-restored-sustainability.pdf> accessed 15 July 2019.

Rungien, Siven Pillay, 'Competition in Paradise: A look at the competition law and enforcement activities of Mauritius' (2011) Queen Mary University Global Antitrust Review 4 <http://www.icc.qmul.ac.uk/media/icc/gar/gar2011/GAR-journal-2011_10_rungien.pdf> accessed 15 July 2019.

SADC, 'Regional Indicative Strategic Development Plan (RISDP)' (2001) <http://www.sadc.int/files/5713/5292/8372/Regional_Indicative_Strategic_Development_Plan.pdf> accessed 14 October 2018.

SADC Secretariat, '35th Summit of SADC Heads of State and Government' (2015) <http://www.sadc.int/news-events/news/35th-sadc-summit-brochure/> accessed 22 August 2019.

Sagers C (ed), *Handbook on the Scope of Antitrust* (American Bar Association 2015).

Seidler, Valentin, 'Why did Botswana end up with Good Institutions: The Role of Culture and Colonial Rule' (2010) Vienna University for Economics and Business: Institute for Economic and Social History < https://ssrn.com/abstract=3051011> accessed 15 July 2019.

Shekhar, Chander and Williams, Philip, 'Should the Pre-Notification of Mergers be Compulsory in Australia?' (2004) 37 The Australian Economic Review 382.

Sherwood, Marika, 'Pan-African Conferences, 1900-1953: What did 'Pan-Africanism' Mean?' (2012) 4 The Journal of Pan African Studies 10 <http://www.jpanafrican.com/docs/vol4no10/4.10Pan-African.pdf> accessed 16 July 2019.

Simpson, Howard, *Zambia: A Country Study* (Scandinavian Institute of African Studies 1985), pp 11-13 <http://www.diva-portal.org/smash/get/diva2:277702/FULLTEXT01.pdf> accessed 15 July 2019.

Singh, Ajit, 'Competition and competition policy in emerging markets: International and development dimensions' (2002) G-24 Discussion Paper Series, Paper No. 18. United Nations <https://unctad.org/en/docs/gdsmdpbg2418_en.pdf> accessed 17 July 2019.

Skadden, Arps, Slate, Meagher & Flom LLP, 'Merger Control 2016 – USA Law & Practice' (contribution to Chambers and Partners Global Practice Guides) <http://www.chambersandpartners.com/guide/practice-guides/location/272/8096/2500-200> accessed 23 August 2019.

Soludo, Charles C. et. al. (eds), *The Politics of Trade and Industrial Policy in Africa: Forced Consensus*? (The International Development Research Centre 2004) <https://www.idrc.ca/sites/default/files/openebooks/125-6/index.html> accessed 15 July 2019.

Stewart, Taimoon, 'The Fate of Competition Policy in Cancun: Politics or Substance?' (2004) 31 Legal Issues of Econ. Integration 7.

Stocking, George and Mueller, Willard, *The Cellophane Case and the New Competition* (1955) 45 American Economic Review 29.

Suliman, Osman and Ghebreysus, Ghirmay, 'Determinants of Privatisation in Selected Sub-Saharan African Countries: Is Privatisation Politically Induced?' (2001) 26(2) Journal of Economic Development 45.

Sullivan, Lawrence A., Handbook of the Law of Antitrust (West Publishing Company, 1977).

Sutherland, Philip and Kemp, Katharine, *Competition Law of South Africa* (Service Issue 18, LexisNexis 2014).

Svetlicinii, Alexandr, 'EU-US Merger Control Cooperation: A Model for the International Antitrust?' (2006) 11(3) Journal for Legal Theory and Practice of the Jurists Association of Serbia, 113-126 <http://ssrn.com/abstract=1325695> accessed 15 July 2019.

Thorelli, Hans B., *The Federal Antitrust Policy* (Johns Hopkins Press, Baltimore 1955).

The ICPAC Final Report (2000) <http://www.justice.gov/atr/icpac/finalreport.html.> accessed 22 August 2019.

Toye, Richard, 'Developing Multilateralism: The Havana Charter and the Fight for the International Trade Organization, 1947–1948' (2003) 25 International History Review.

Trofimov, Ivan D., 'The Failure of the International Trade Organization (ITO): A Policy Entrepreneurship Perspective' (2012) 5 Journal of Politics and Law 56.

UNCTAD, 'Competition Policy, Trade and Development in the Common Market for Eastern and Southern Africa' (1999) UNCTAD Series on Issues in Competition Law and Policy, Geneva.

UNCTAD, 'Economic Development in Africa Report 2009: Strengthening Regional Economic Integration for Africa's Development' (2009) <http://unctad.org/en/Docs/aldcafrica2009_en.pdf> accessed 16 July 2019.

UNCTAD, Foundations of an effective competition agency TD/B/C.I/CLP/8 <http://unctad.org/en/docs/ciclpd8_en.pdf> accessed 10 September 2019.

UNCTAD: Model Law on Competition (United Nations 2010).

UNCTAD, Model Law on Competition (2010): Revised chapter IX <http://unctad.org/en/Docs/ciclpL2_en.pdf> accessed 10 September 2019.

UNCTAD, 'World Investment Report: Investor Nationality: Policy Challenges' (2016) <http://unctad.org/en/PublicationsLibrary/wir2016_en.pdf> accessed 23 August 2019.

UNECA, 'Towards a Common Currency in the East African Community (EAC) Issues, Challenges and Prospects' (2012) <https://www.uneca.org/sites/default/files/PublicationFiles/towards_a_common_currency_in_the_eac-2012.pdf> accessed 16 July 2019.

UNECA, 'Economic Report on Africa 2008: Africa and the Monterrey Consensus: Tracking Performance and Progress' (2008) <http://www.uneca.org/publications/economic-report-africa-2008> accessed 16 July 2019.

United Nations Industrial Development Organization, 'Foreign Direct Investment in Africa: Determinants and Location Decisions' (2009) <https://open.unido.org/api/documents/4818201/download/Foreign%20Direct%20Investment%20in%20Sub-Saharan%20Africa%20-%20Determinants%20and%20Location%20Decisions> accessed 23 August 2019.

Vandemoortele, Milo and Bird, Kate, 'Progress in economic conditions: Sustained success against the odds in Mauritius' (2011) Overseas Development Institute <https://www.odi.org/sites/odi.org.uk/files/resource-documents/11579.pdf> accessed 15 July 2019.

Werner, Wolfgang, 'A Brief History of Land Disposession in Namibia' (1993) 19 Journal of Southern African Studies 1 <https://www.tandfonline.com/doi/abs/10.1080/03057079308708351> accessed 15 July 2019.

Weymouth, Stephen, 'Competition Politics: Interest Groups, Democracy, and Antitrust Reform in Developing Countries' (2016) 61 Antitrust Bull. 296.

Whish, Richard and Bailey, David, *Competition Law* (7th edn, OUP 2012).

White, Lawrence J., 'The Role of Competition Policy in the Promotion of Economic Growth' (Essay presented at the Competition Policy Research Center of the Fair Trade Commission of Japan's International Symposium, March 30, 2008) <http://web-docs.stern.nyu.edu/old_web/emplibrary/competition%20policy%20and%20growth.ljw%20draft%203-30-08.pdf> accessed 16 July 2019.

Wilcox, Clair, 'The London Draft of a Charter for an International Trade Organization' (1947) 37 Am. Econ. Rev. 529.

Wood, Diane P., 'Antitrust: A Remedy for Trade Barriers?' (1995) Asian Law Program, Japan Information Access Project, Washington, D.C. <http://www.justice.gov/atr/public/speeches/0170.pdf> accessed 16 July 2019.

World Bank, 'World Bank Annual Report' (2007) <http://siteresources.worldbank.org/EXTANNREP2K7/Resources/English.pdf> accessed 16 July 2019.

World Bank Group, 'Structural Adjustment and Zimbabwe's Poor' (2012) <http://lnweb90.worldbank.org/oed/oeddoclib.nsf/DocUNIDViewForJavaSearch/15A937F6B215A053852567F5005D8B06> accessed 15 July 2019.

World Bank Group, 'Global Indicators of Regulatory Governance' <http://rulemaking.worldbank.org/~/media/WBG/CER/Documents/Global-Indicators-of-Regulatory-Governance-Project-Summary.pdf?la=en> accessed 19 September 2019.

World Bank and EAC Secretariat, 'East African Common Market Scorecard 2014: Tracking EAC compliance in the movement of Capital, Services and Goods' (2014) < http://documents.worldbank.org/curated/en/799871468194049251/Main-report> accessed 16 July 2019.

YeungLamKo, Louis, 'The Economic Development of Mauritius Since Independence' (1998) School of Economics, University of New South Wales <http://wwwdocs.fce.unsw.edu.au/economics/Research/WorkingPapers/1998_6.pdf> accessed 15 July 2019.

Zäch, Roger, 'Competition law should promote economic and social welfare by ensuring the freedom to compete – a lawyer's view' in Joseph Drexl, Laurence Idot and Joel Moneger (eds), *Economic Theory and Competition Law* (Edward Elgar, 2009).

Zambia and IMF, 'Enhanced Structural Adjustment Facility: Policy Framework Paper, 1999-2001' (1999) <https://www.imf.org/external/np/pfp/1999/zambia/> accessed 15 July 2019.

Zamfir, Ionel, 'The Tripartite Free Trade Area project Integration in southern and eastern Africa' (2015) <http://www.europarl.europa.eu/RegData/etudes/BRIE/2015/551308/EPRS_BRI(2015)551308_EN.pdf> accessed 16 July 2019.

Zerk Jennifer A., 'Extraterritorial Jurisdiction: Lessons for the business and human rights sphere from six regulatory areas' (Corporate Social Responsibility Initiative Working Paper No. 59. 2010) <http://www.hks.harvard.edu/mrcbg/CSRI/publications/workingpaper_59_zerk.pdf> accessed 9 September 2019.

Agreements, Legislation, Guidelines and Policies

Agreement Establishing a Tripartite Free Trade Area among The Common Market For Eastern And Southern Africa, The East African Community And The Southern African Development Community < https://www.tralac.org/news/article/7646-signed-agreement-establishing-a-tripartite-free-trade-area-among-comesa-the-eac-and-sadc.html> accessed 16 July 2019.

Agreement Establishing the African Continental Free Trade Area (CFTA Agreement) <https://au.int/en/treaties/agreement-establishing-african-continental-free-trade-area> accessed 16 July 2019.

Agreement between the European Communities and the Government of the United States of America on the application of positive comity principles in the enforcement of their competition laws, (1998) O.J. L 173/28.

Agreement on Trade, Development and Cooperation between the European Community and its Member States, of the one part, and the Republic of South Africa, of the other part (OJ L 311 , 04/12/1999 P. 0003 – 0415).

Antitrust Enforcement Guidelines for International Operations (April 1995) <https://www.justice.gov/atr/antitrust-enforcement-guidelines-international-operations> accessed 9 September 2019.

Bekanntmachung der Neufassung des Gesetzes gegen Wettbewerbsbeschränkungen (26 Juni 2013 BGBl. I S. 1750, 3245).

Best Practices on Cooperation between EU National Competition Authorities in Merger Review <http://ec.europa.eu/competition/ecn/nca_best_practices_merger_review_en.pdf> accessed 9 September 2019.

Best Practices on the Conduct of EC Merger Proceedings (20/01/04) <http://ec.europa.eu/competition/mergers/legislation/proceedings.pdf > accessed 23 September 2019.

Cancún WTO Ministerial 2003: Draft Cancún Ministerial Text JOB(03)/150/Rev.2.

Charter of the Organization of African Unity (OAU Charter) 479 U.N.T.S. 39 <https://www.sahistory.org.za/archive/charter-organization-african-unity-479-unts-39-entered-force-sept-13-1963> accessed 16 July 2019.

Charter of the International Competitiveness Advisory Committee (1997) <https://www.justice.gov/atr/charter-international-competitiveness-advisory-committee> accessed 17 July 2019.

Clayton Act, 15 U.S.C. § 18.

COMESA Competition Regulations, gazette vol 17 no 12.

COMESA Market Definition Guidelines (2019) <https://www.comesacompetition.org/wp-content/uploads/2019/08/Final-Guidlines-on-Market-Definition.pdf> accessed 23 September 2019.

COMESA Merger Assessment Guidelines <http://www.comesacompetition.org/wp-content/uploads/2014/10/141121_COMESA-Merger-Assessment-Guideline-October-31st-2014.pdf> accessed 23 September 2019.

Commission Notice on the concept of full-function joint ventures under Council Regulation (EEC) No 4064/89 on the control of concentrations between undertakings (98/C 66/01).

Commission Consolidated Jurisdictional Notice under Council Regulation (EC) No 139/2004 on the control of concentrations between undertakings (2008/C 95/01).

Commission Notice on Case Referral in respect of Concentrations (2005/C 56/02).

Commission Notice on a simplified procedure for treatment of certain concentrations under Council Regulation (EC) No 139/2004 (2013/C 366/04).

Commission Notice on remedies acceptable under Council Regulation (EC) No 139/2004 and under Commission Regulation (EC) No 802/2004 (2008/C 267/01).

Commission Regulation implementing Council Regulation (EC) No 139/2004 (EC) No 802/2004 OJ L 133) amended by Commission Regulation (EC) No 1033/2008 OJ L 279.

Competition Commission of South Africa, Practitioner Update: The application of merger provisions of the Competition Act 89 of 1998, as amended, to joint ventures, <http://www.compcom.co.za/wp-content/uploads/2014/09/Practitoner-Update-Joint-Ventures-Published-version.doc> accessed 17 July 2019.

Competition Authority of Botswana Market Definition Guidelines (2014) <http://www.competitionauthority.co.bw/sites/default/files/MARKET%20DEFINITION%20GUIDELINES.pdf> accessed 26 August 2019.

Competition Authority of Botswana Merger Assessment Guidelines <http://www.competitionauthority.co.bw/sites/default/files/MERGER_ASSESSMENT_0.pdf> accessed 26 August 2019.

Competition Act of Botswana no 17/2009.

Competition Authority of Kenya Consolidated Guidelines on the Substantive Assessment of Mergers under the Competition Act <http://www.cak.go.ke/images/docs/Merger%20Guidelines.pdf> accessed 26 August 2019.

Competition Authority of Kenya, Guidelines on Relevant Market Definition, para. 3 <http://www.cak.go.ke/images/docs/guidelines_for__market_definition1.pdf> accessed 26 August 2019.

Competition Act of Kenya no 12/2010.

Competition Act of Namibia no 2/2003.

Competition Act of Zimbabwe cap 14/28.

Competition and Fair Trading Act of Malawi no 43/1998.

Competition and Fair Trading Commission: Merger Assessment Guidelines <http://www.cftc.mw/index.php/2013-12-16-13-35-12/guidelines/28-mergers-and-acqusitions-guidelines/file.html> accessed 23 September 2019.

Competition Act of Mauritius no 25/2007.

Competition Commission of Mauritius Guidelines: Mergers <http://www.ccm.mu/English/Documents/Legislations/CCM5%20-%20Guidelines%20-%20Mergers_Nov09.pdf> accessed 26 August 2019.

Competition Commission of Mauritius Guidelines on Remedies and Penalties (2009) <http://www.ccm.mu/English/Documents/Legislations/CCM6%20-%20Guidelines%20-%20Remedies%20and%20Penalties_Nov09.pdf> accessed 9 September 2019.

Competition Commission of Mauritius Market Definition and the Calculation of Market Shares (2009) <http://www.ccm.mu/English/Documents/Legislations/CCM2%20-%20Guidelines%20-%20Market%20definition_Nov09.pdf> accessed 26 August 2019.

Competition Act no. 89 of 1998 <http://www.compcom.co.za/the-competition-act/> accessed 26 August 2019.

Competition Commission South Africa, Guidelines on the assessment of public interest provisions in merger regulation under the Competition Act No. 89 of 1998.

Competition Commission of South Africa, M&A Service Standards (2015) <http://www.compcom.co.za/wp-content/uploads/2014/09/Service-Standards_2015_Final.pdf> accessed 23 August 2019.

Competition Commission of South Africa, Determination of Merger Thresholds and Method of Calculation, GN 216 (6 March 2009).

Competition Commission of South Africa, Rules for the Conduct of Proceedings in the Competition Commission, Proclamation No. 12, GG 22025, 01/02/2001.

Competition Tribunal of South Africa, Rules for the Conduct of Proceedings in the Competition Tribunal, GN 22025 vol. 428, 01/02/2001.

Competition and Consumer Protection Act of Zambia no 24/2010.

Competition and Consumer Protection Commission: Guidelines for Merger Regulation <http://www.ccpc.org.zm/wp-content/uploads/2016/04/CCPC-Mergers-Guideline.pdf> accessed 26 August 2019.

Competition and Markets Authority, Mergers: Guidance on the CMA's Jurisdiction and Procedure (2014).

Competition and Markets Authority, Merger Remedies: Competition Commission Guidelines (cc8, 2008).

Cooperation Arrangement Between the Commissioner of Competition (Canada), the Australian Competition and Consumer Commission and the New Zealand Commerce Commission Regarding the Application of their Competition and Consumer Laws <http://www.competitionbureau.gc.ca/eic/site/cb-bc.nsf/eng/01595.html> accessed 9 September 2019.

Council Regulation on the Control of Concentrations between Undertakings (EC) No 139/2004 OJ L 24/1.

Defense Production Act 1950 (50 USC app 2170).

Draft agreement establishing the COMESA, EAC and SADC Tripartite Free Trade Area (2010) <http://www.tralac.org/wp-content/blogs.dir/12/files/2011/uploads/Draft_Tripartite_FTA_Agreement_Revised_Dec_2010.pdf> accessed 20 July 2018.

Doha WTO Ministerial 2001: Ministerial Declaration WT/MIN(01)/DEC/1.

EAC Gazette Notice No. 8 of 2018 <https://www.eac.int/documents/category/gazette> accessed 16 July 2019.

EAC Gazette Notice No. 2 of 2007 <https://www.eac.int/documents/category/gazette> accessed 16 July 2019.

Fair Competition Act of Seychelles no 18/2009.

Fair Trading Commission of Seychelles Act no 17/2009 and no 6/2015.

Fair Trading Commission of Seychelles Guidelines on the Definition of Relevant Market.

Fair Trading Commission of Seychelles: Penalties and Remedies.

Fair Competition Commission of Tanzania Merger Guidelines <http://www.competition.or.tz/attachments/article/59/fcc_merger_guidelines_tanzania.pdf> accessed 26 August 2019.

Fair Competition Act of Tanzania no 8/2003.

Federal Trade Commission Act, 15 U.S.C. § 45.

Foreign Investment and National Security Act 2007 (50 USC app 2061).

FTC, To File or not to File: When you must file a Premerger Notification Report Form (September 2008) <ftc.gov/bc/hsr> accessed 23 September 2019.

FTC, 'What is the Premerger Notification Program?: An Overview' (March 2009) <https://www.ftc.gov/sites/default/files/attachments/premerger-introductory-guides/guide1.pdf> accessed 23 September 2019.

Gesetz gegen Wettbewerbsbeschränkungen (Act against Restraints of Competition) in the version published on 15 July 2005 (Bundesgesetzblatt (Federal Law Gazette) I, page 2114; 2009 I page 3850).

Guidance on Substantive Merger Control (Bundeskartellamt 2012) <http://www.bundeskartellamt.de/SharedDocs/Publikation/EN/Leitlinien/Guidance%20-%20Substantive%20Merger%20Control.pdf?__blob=publicationFile&v=6.> accessed 26 August 2019.

Guidelines for Negotiating the Tripartite Free Trade Area among the Member/Partner States of COMESA, EAC and SADC (2011), para 2 <http://www.tralac.org/images/docs/5284/tfta-negotiating-principles-12062011.pdf> accessed 16 July 2019.

Guidelines on the assessment of horizontal merger under the Council Regulation on the control of concentrations between undertakings, OJ C 31, 5 February 2004.

Guidelines on the assessment of non-horizontal mergers under the Council Regulation on the control of concentrations between undertakings, OJ C 265, 18 October 2008.

Hart-Scott-Rodino Antitrust Improvements Act, 15 U.S. Code § 18a.

Havana Charter for an International Trade Organization (U.N. E/Conf. 2/78 (1948) reprinted in UN. Doc. ICITO/1/4 (1948).

Implementing Council Regulation (EC) No 139/2004 on the control of concentrations between undertakings, (EC) No 802/2004.

Mauritius Fair Trading Commission Act, No 17 of 2009.

Mauritius Competition Commission Rules of Procedure GN 161/2009 <http://www.ccm.mu/English/Documents/Legislations/Rules-of-Procedure-2009-051112.pdf> accessed 23 August 2019.

Namibian Competition Commission Merger Guidelines <http://www.nacc.com.na/cms_documents/820_merger_guidelinesapril16.pdf> accessed 26 August 2019.

Notice on the definition of relevant market for the purposes of Community competition law, OJ (1997) C 372/5.

Organization of African Unity: Declaration on African Cooperation, Development, and Economic Independence, I.L.M 12(4): 996-1013.

Protocol on Trade in the SADC Region (1996), art 2 <http://www.sadc.int/files/4613/5292/8370/Protocol_on_Trade1996.pdf> accessed 22 August 2019.

Republic of South Africa, 'Board of Trade and Industries Act', No 28 of 1923 and No 19 of 1944.

Republic of South Africa, 'Maintenance and Promotion of Competition Amendment Act, No 5 of 1986.

Republic of South Africa, 'Regulation of Monopolistic Conditions Act' No 24 of 1955.

Restrictive Business Practices: Arrangements for Consultations, Decision of 18 November 1960, BISD 9S/28, <http://www.worldtradelaw.net/misc/rbp1.pdf.download> accessed 16 July 2019.

Revised Jurisdictional Thresholds for Section 7A of the Clayton Act, Federal Register / April 2019.

Roadmap for Establishing the Tripartite FTA <http://www.trademarksa.org/sites/default/files/publications/Roadmap%20for%20TFTA%20Negotiation%20-%2012.06.2011.pdf> accessed 16 July 2019.

SADC Declaration on Regional Cooperation in Competition and Consumer Policies (2009) <http://www.sadc.int/documents-publications/show/SADC_Declaration_on_Competition_and_Consumer_Policies.pdf.> accessed 16 July 2019.

Sherman Act, 15 U.S.C. §§ 1, 2.

Singapore WTO Ministerial 1996: Ministerial Declaration WT/MIN(96)/DEC.

The Restrictive Trade Practices, Monopolies and Price Control Act, Laws of Kenya Chapter 504. (RTPM Act).

The United Nations Set of Principles and Rules on Competition TD/RBP/CONF/10/Rev.2 (1980).

Treaty establishing the African Economic Community (AEC Treaty), 30 I.L.M. 1241 (1991)

Treaty Establishing the Preferential Trade Area for Eastern and Southern African States (PTA Treaty), 21 ILM 479 (1981).

Treaty Establishing the Common Market for Easter and Southern Africa <http://www.comesacompetition.org/wp-content/uploads/2016/03/COMESA_Treaty.pdf> accessed 6 September 2019.

Treaty for the Establishment of the East African Community <http://eacj.eac.int/?page_id=33> accessed 17 July 2019.

Treaty of the Southern African Development Community <http://www.sadc.int/files/9113/5292/9434/SADC_Treaty.pdf.> accessed 23 August 2019.

Treaty on the Functioning of the European Union 2012/C 326/01.

UK Enterprise Act (2002 c. 40).

UK Enterprise and Regulatory Reform Act (2013 c.24).

US Non-Horizontal Merger Guidelines <http://www.justice.gov/sites/default/files/atr/legacy/2006/05/18/2614.pdf> accessed 26 August 2019.

WTO, Decision Adopted by the General Council on 1 August 2004 WT/L/579.

1991 EU/US Competition Cooperation Agreement, (1995) O.J. L 95/47.

Cases

Eastern and Southern Africa

Botswana

Cottesloe Consultants (Cottesloe) & Bokomo Botswana (Bokomo)

G4S (Botswana) Limited, Trojan Security Services (Trojan) & Facilities Management Group (Shield Security, PS Cleaning and Facilities Management Business)(FMG)

Kalend (Pty) Ltd (Kalend) & Bokamoso Private Hospital (BPHT)

COMESA

Decision of the Committee of Initial Determination on the Application for Authorisation of the Merger between PPC International Holdings Proprietary Limited ("PPC International") and CIMERWA Limited ("CIMERWA"), Case File No. CCC/MER/8002/2013.

Decision of the Committee of Initial Determination Regarding the Merger between CFR Inversiones SPA and Adcock Ingram Holdings Limited, CASE FILE No. CCC/MER/1223/2013.

Decision of the nineteenth Committee responsible for Initial Determination Meeting Regarding the proposed Merger between China National Tire and rubber Co. Ltd and Pirelli and C.S.p.A, Staff paper No. 2016/03/07/04/JB

PPC International Holdings Proprietary Limited (PPC International) & CIMERWA Limited (CIMERWA)

Kenya

Buzeki Dairy Limited (Buzeki) & Brookside Dairy Limited

Real Insurance Company Limited (Real) & British–American Investments Company (Kenya) Limited (Britam)

Toyota Tshusho Corporation (Toyota) & CFAO

Malawi

Dhunseri Petrochem and Tea Pte Limited & Global Tea and Commodities Limited

First Merchant Bank Limited & International Commercial Bank Limited

Toyota Tsusho Corporation & CFAO Malawi Ltd/Cica Motors Ltd

Mauritius

Event Strategy Ltd & LC Events Co. Ltd CCM/DS/002.

Investigation on the proposed merger of the insurance businesses of Swan Group and Rogers Group: Report of the Executive Director <http://www.ccm.mu/English/Documents/News_2012/29.02.12_2.pdf> accessed 26 August 2019.

Investigation on the proposed merger of the insurance businesses of Swan Group and Rogers Group: Commission Decision CCM/DS/0013.

Proposed Merger between Holcim Ltd & Lafarge S.A: Decision of the Competition Commission (CCM/DS/0016).

Review of Completed Merger of Event Strategy Ltd & LC Events Co Ltd: Final Report <http://www.ccm.mu/English/Documents/Investigations/INV008%20-%20Final%20Report%20Public%20Version.pdf> accessed 25 September 2019.

Namibia

Colas South Africa (Pty) Ltd (Colas South Africa) & The Roads Contractor Company Ltd (RCC) and Guinea Fowl Investments Seventeen (Pty) Ltd (Guinea)

Guinea Fowl Investments Twenty Five (Pty Ltd (Guinea Fowl) & the Private Label Store Card Portfolio of Edgars Stores Namibia (Pty) Ltd (Edgars)

Metcash Trading Namibia (Pty) Ltd (Metcash) & Sefalana Cash & Carry (Namibia) (Pty) Ltd (Sefalana)

South Africa

AgriGroupe Holdings (Pty) Ltd and AFGRI Ltd, Competition Tribunal case no. 017939 ((15 April 2014).

American Natural Soda Ash Corporation and another v Competition Commission and others Case 12/CAC/DEC01 (30 October 2003).

American Natural Soda Ash Corporation and another v Competition Commission and others South Africa Competition Tribunal 49/CR/Apr00 and 87/CR/Sep00 (30 November 2001).

A P Moller-Maersk and Royal P & O Nedlloyd N.V., Competition Tribunal case no 48/LM/May05 (12 May 2006).

BB Investment Company (Pty) Ltd and Adcock Ingram Holdings (Pty) Ltd, Competition Tribunal case no: 18713 ((19 August 2014).

Distillers Corporation (SA) Limited & Stellenbosch Farmers Winery Group Ltd Competition Tribunal case no 08/LM/Feb02 (19 March 2003).

Distillers Corporation (SA) Ltd / SFW Group Ltd and Bulmer (SA) (Pty) Ltd / Seagram Africa (Pty) Ltd, 08/CAC/May01 (27 November 2001).

Ethos Private Equity Fund IV/Tsebo Outsourcing Group (pty) Ltd 30/LM/Jun03 (3 October 2003).

Iscor Limited and Saldanha Steel (Pty) Ltd, Competition Tribunal case no. 67/LM/Dec01 (4 April 2002.

Harmony Gold Mining Company and Gold Fields, case no. 41/LM/Jul10) (19 May 2005).

Massmart Holdings Ltd and Jumbo Cash and Carry (Pty) Limited Competition Tribunal case no 39/LM/Jul01 (10 October 2001).

Medicross Healthcare Group (Pty) Ltd v Competition Commission 55/CAC/Sep05.

Metropolitan Holdings Limited and Momentum Group Limited, Competition Tribunal case no 41/LM/Jul10 (9 December 2010).

Mondi Ltd & Kohler Cores and Tubes a division of Kohler Packaging Limited Competition Tribunal case no 06/LM/Jan02 (20 June 2002).

Nedbank Limited and Imperial Bank Limited, Competition Tribunal case no. 70/LM/Oct09 (12 January 2010).

Nestle (SA) (Pty) Limited & Pets Products (Pty) Limited Competition Tribunal case no 21/LM/Apr01 (18 June 2001).

Pioneer Hi-Bred International Inc and Pannar Seed (Pty) Ltd v Competition Commission case no 81/AM/Dec10 (9 December 2011).

Primedia Ltd v Competition Commission 39/AM/May06 (9 May 2008).

Sasol Limited et al., Competition Tribunal case no 101/LM/Dec04 (23 February 2006).

Telkom SA Limited and Business Connexion Group Limited, Competition Tribunal case no: 51/LM/Jun06 (20 August 2007).

Thaba Chueu Mining (Pty) Ltd v Samquarz (Pty) Ltd, Competition Tribunal case no. 10/AM/Jan12 (15 November 2012).

The Tongaat-Hulett Group Limited and Transvaal Suiker Beperk, Middenen Ontwikkeling (Pty) Ltd, Senteeko (Edms) Bpk, New Komati Sugar Miller's Partnership, TSB Bestuursdienste, Competition Tribunal case no: 83/LM/Jul00 (27 November 2000).

Unilever Plc et al. and Robertsons Foods (Pty) Ltd, Competition Tribunal case no: 55/LM/Sep01 (6 March 2002).

Walmart and Massmart et al., Competition Appeal Court, case nos. 110/CAC/Jul11 and 111/CAC/Jun11 (9 March 2012).

Walmart Stores Inc and Massmart Holdings Limited, Competition Tribunal case no. 73/LM/Dec10 (2010) (29 June 2011).

Tanzania

Helios Towers Tanzania Infraco Limited (HTT) & Millicom International Cellular (MIC) Tanzania Limited.

Uranium One Inc. and Mantra Australia

Zambia

Toyota Tshusho Corporation (TTC) & CFAO

Zimbabwe

Makro Zimbabwe (Makro) & OK Zimbabwe Limited (OK)

Renaissance Merchant Bank Limited (Renaissance) & National Social Security Authority (NSSA)

Zimbabwe Online (Pvt) Limited (ZOL) & Data Control & Systems (1996) Limited (DCS)

European Union

Aerospatiale-Alenia/De Havilland Commission decision 91/619/EEC [1991] OJ 334/42.

Ahlström Osakeyhtiö and others v Commission (1988) ECR 5193.

Airtours/First Choice commission decision 2000/276/EC [1999] OJ 93/1.

EDP v Commission Case T-87/05 [2005] E.C.R. II-3745.

Case 85/76 *Hoffmann-La Roche* [1979] E.C.R. 461.

Case 322/81 *Michelin v Commission* [1983] E.C.R. 3461.

Case No IV/M.619 *Gencor/Lonrho*, OJ 1997 L 11.

Gencor v Commission, judgement of the General Court, case T-102/96.

General Electric v Commission Case T-210/01 [2005] E.C.R. II-5575.

ICI v Commission (1972) ECR 619.

T-Mobile Austria/tele.ring case COMP/M.3916.

United Brands Company and United Brands Continental Bv v Commission (Case 27/76), [1978] ECR 207; [1978] 1 Common Market Law Review (CMLR) 429.

Volvo/Scania [2001] OJ L 143/74.

Germany

Total Deutschland GmbH and OMV Deutschland GmbH, B8 – 175/08.

United States

American Banana Co. v. United Fruit Co 213 U.S. 347 (1909).

Brown Shoe Co., Inc. v. United States 370 U.S. 294 (1962).

FTC v. H.J. Heinz Co. and Milnot Holding Corporation 246 F.3d 708 (2001).

Hartford Fire Insurance Co v California 509 U. S. 764 (1993).

Institut Merieux, S.A., No. 891-0098, 55 Fed. Reg. 1614 (Jan. 17, 1990).

Lafarge S.A.; Blue Circle Industries PLC; Blue Circle North America, Inc.; and Blue Circle, Inc. (2001), 66 Fed. Reg. 34,682.

Laker Airways Ltd. v. Sabena, Belgian World Airlines 731 F.2d 909 (1984 U.S. App. Decision).

Ryanair / Aer Lingus, Case No COMP/M.4439 (2007).

Timberlane Lumber Co. v. Bank of America National Trust & Savings Association 549 F. 2 d 597 (9th Cir. 1976).

Tenet Health Care Systems and Slidell Memorial Hospital (2003) <http://www.ftc.gov/opa/2003/04/lahospmerger.htm> accessed 26 August 2019.

United States v Aluminium Co of America 148 F.2d 416 (2d Cir. 1945).

United States v. E.I. du Pont de Nemours & Co., 351 U.S. 377 (1956).

United States v. Franklin Electric Co., United Dominion Industries, Ltd., and United Dominion Industries, Inc., 130 F. Supp. 2d 1025 (W.D. Wis. 2000).

United States v. Interstate Bakeries Corp. and Continental Baking Co., 60 Fed. Reg. 40,195 (Aug. 7, 1995).

Webpages

About the European Commission <http://ec.europa.eu/about/index_en.htm#president> accessed 10 September 2019.

Africa Competition Forum <http://www.africancompetitionforum.org/> accessed 10 September 2019.

African Union, CFTA: Continental Free Trade Area, <https://au.int/en/ti/cfta/about > accessed 16 July 2019.

ARICEA Constitution. <https://ariceaweb.org/index.php?option=com_content&view=article&id=4&Itemid=13> accessed 16 July 2019.

AU in a Nutshell <https://au.int/en/au-nutshell> accessed 16 July 2019.

Bundeskartellamt: Legislation <http://www.bundeskartellamt.de/EN/AboutUs/Bundeskartellamt/legislation/legislation_node.html> accessed 26 August 2019.

COMESA's Regional Payment and Settlement System (REPSS) Goes Live <https://www.bou.or.ug/bou/media/statements/COMESA_REPSS.html> accessed 16 July 2019.

COMESA-EAC-SADC Tripartite <https://www.eac.int/tripartite> accessed 16 July 2019.

COMESA Competition Commission MOUs <http://www.comesacompetition.org/?cat=14.> accessed 25 September 2019.

Deal Drivers Africa (2016) <http://dealdriversafrica.mergermarket.com/overview-ma-activity-in-africa> accessed 25 September 2019.

Directorate-General for Competition <http://ec.europa.eu/dgs/competition/index_en.htm> accessed 10 September 2019.

EAC Common Market: Overview <https://www.eac.int/common-market> accessed 16 July 2019.

EAC, Customs <https://www.eac.int/security/index.php?option=com_content&id=29:eac-portal> accessed 16 July 2019.

EAC, Five Commissioners of the EAC Competition Authority sworn in at the EAC <https://www.eac.int/press-releases/605-1048-346-five-commissioners-of-the-eac-competition-authority-sworn-in-at-the-eac> accessed 16 July 2019.

Freshfields Bruckhaus Deringer: Antitrust and Public Interest <http://www.freshfields.com/en/global/TKT2015/8__Antitrust_and_the_public_interest> accessed 9 September 2019.

FTC, A Brief Overview of the Federal Trade Commission's Investigative and Law Enforcement Authority (July 2008) <https://www.ftc.gov/about-ftc/what-we-do/enforcement-authority> accessed 6 September 2019.

History of the EAC <https://www.eac.int/eac-history> accessed 16 July 2019.

ICN: About <http://www.internationalcompetitionnetwork.org/about.aspx.> accessed 22 August 2019.

ICN: History <http://www.internationalcompetitionnetwork.org/about/history.aspx.> accessed 22 August 2019.

International Trade Centre (ITC) <http://www.trademap.org/Country_SelProduct_TS.aspx> accessed 16 July 2019.

Japan International Cooperation Agency, The Data Collection Survey for Djibouti Corridor: Final Report <http://open_jicareport.jica.go.jp/pdf/12302642_01.pdf> accessed 22 August 2019.

Mauritius: Economic Outline <http://www.mauritiustrade.mu/en/trading-with-mauritius/mauritius-economics-outline> accessed 15 July 2019.

Non-Tariff Barriers: Reporting, Monitoring and Eliminating Mechanism <http://www.tradebarriers.org/about> accessed 16 July 2019.

OECD: Competition <http://www.oecd.org/daf/competition/.> accessed 22 August 2019.

OECD: Competition Global Relations <http://www.oecd.org/daf/competition/competitionglobalrelations.htm.> accessed 22 August 2019.

SADC Integration Milestones <http://www.sadc.int/about-sadc/integration-milestones/> accessed 22 August 2019.

SA Competition Commission: File a merger <http://www.compcom.co.za/file-a-merger/> accessed 25 September 2019.

SADC Facts and Figures <http://www.sadc.int/about-sadc/overview/sadc-facts-figures/> accessed 25 September 2019.

The GATT years: From Havana to Marrakesh <http://www.wto.org/english/thewto_e/whatis_e/tif_e/fact4_e.htm#rounds.> accessed 23 August 2019.

The Schuman Declaration – 9th May 1950 <http://europa.eu/about-eu/basic-information/symbols/europe-day/schuman-declaration/index_en.htm.> accessed 23 August 2019.

UNCTAD: Intergovernmental Deliberations <http://unctad.org/en/Pages/DITC/CompetitionLaw/Intergovernmental-Deliberations.aspx.> accessed 22 August 2019.

UNCTAD: Mandate and Key Functions <http://unctad.org/en/Pages/DITC/CompetitionLaw/ccpb-Mandate.aspx.> accessed 22 September 2019.

Unilateral Declaration of Independence of Rhodesia <https://www.nationsencyclopedia.com/knowledge/Unilateral_Declaration_of_Independence.html> accessed 15 July 2019.

WTO: Built-in Agenda: Work set out in existing agreements <https://www.wto.org/english/thewto_e/minist_e/min99_e/english/about_e/04agen_e.htm> accessed 16 July 2019.

WTO, Day 5: Conference ends without Consensus <http://www.wto.org/english/thewto_e/minist_e/min03_e/min03_14sept_e.htm> accessed 17 July 2019.

WTO: How the negotiations are organised <https://www.wto.org/english/tratop_e/dda_e/work_organi_e.htm> accessed 16 July 2019.

WTO, Members and Observers <http://www.wto.org/english/thewto_e/whatis_e/tif_e/org6_e.htm.> accessed 25 September 2019.

WTO, Press Brief on Competition Policies <http://www.wto.org/english/thewto_e/minist_e/min96_e/comppol.htm.> accessed 23 August 2019.

WTO, The 128 countries that had signed GATT by 1994 <http://www.wto.org/english/thewto_e/gattmem_e.htm.> accessed 23 August 2019.

WTO, The First WTO Ministerial Conference <http://www.wto.org/english/thewto_e/minist_e/min96_e/min96_e.htm.> accessed 23 August 2019.